David R. Winnington-Ingram

Glasshampton Monastery

Candlemas   2015

AUGUSTINE AND THE TRINITY

Augustine of Hippo (354–430), whose accounts of the Trinity have heavily influenced much subsequent Western theology, has often been accused of over-emphasizing the unity of God and thus been maligned as a source of persistent problems in contemporary religious thought. In *Augustine and the Trinity*, Lewis Ayres offers a new treatment of this important figure, demonstrating how Augustine's writings offer one of the most sophisticated early theologies of the Trinity developed after the Council of Nicaea (325). Building on recent research, Ayres argues that Augustine was influenced by a wide variety of earlier Latin Christian traditions which stressed the irreducibility of the Father, Son and Spirit. Augustine combines these traditions with material from non-Christian Neoplatonists in a very personal synthesis. Ayres also argues that Augustine shaped a powerful account of Christian ascent towards understanding of, as well as participation in, the divine life, one that begins in faith and models itself on Christ's humility.

LEWIS AYRES is Bede Professor of Catholic Theology at the University of Durham. He is co-editor with Frances Young and Andrew Louth of *The Cambridge History of Early Christian Literature* (2004).

AUGUSTINE AND THE TRINITY

LEWIS AYRES
Bede Professor of Catholic Theology
University of Durham
Associate Professor of Historical Theology
Emory University

CAMBRIDGE UNIVERSITY PRESS
Cambridge, New York, Melbourne, Madrid, Cape Town,
Singapore, São Paulo, Delhi, Tokyo, Mexico City

Cambridge University Press
The Edinburgh Building, Cambridge CB2 8RU, UK

Published in the United States of America by
Cambridge University Press, New York

www.cambridge.org
Information on this title: www.cambridge.org/9780521838863

© Lewis Ayres 2010

This publication is in copyright. Subject to statutory exception
and to the provisions of relevant collective licensing agreements,
no reproduction of any part may take place without the written
permission of Cambridge University Press.

First published 2010
4th printing 2012

A catalogue record for this publication is available from the British Library

Library of Congress Cataloguing in Publication data
Ayres, Lewis.
Augustine and the Trinity / Lewis Ayres.
p.   cm.
Includes bibliographical references and indexes.
ISBN 978-0-521-83886-3
1. Augustine, Saint, Bishop of Hippo.   2. Trinity.   I. Title.
BR65.A9A98 2010
231′.044–dc22
2010034947

ISBN 978-0-521-83886-3 Hardback

Cambridge University Press has no responsibility for the persistence or
accuracy of URLs for external or third-party internet websites referred to in
this publication, and does not guarantee that any content on such websites is,
or will remain, accurate or appropriate. Information regarding prices, travel
timetables, and other factual information given in this work is correct at
the time of first printing but Cambridge University Press does not guarantee
the accuracy of such information thereafter.

... cui trinitati pie sobrieque intellegendae omnis excubat vigilantia christiana et omnis eius provectus intenditur

The goal of all Christian watchfulness and all Christian progress is a pious and sober understanding of the Trinity

De libero arbitrio 3. 21.60

Contents

Acknowledgements	*page* x
List of abbreviations	xiii
Introduction	1

PART I ORIGINS — 11

1 Giving wings to Nicaea — 13
- On being and not being a 'Platonist' — 13
- Olivier Du Roy's thesis — 20
- A bridge too far: Du Roy's method — 22
- The tripotent Father, Son and Spirit — 26
- *De beata vita* — 30
- Augustine's engagements — 37

2 From Him, through Him and in Him — 42
- Latin pro-Nicene theology — 43
- An anti-Manichaean Trinitarianism I: *De moribus ecclesiae catholicae* — 52
- An anti-Manichaean Trinitarianism II: *Epistula* 11 — 59

3 Faith of our fathers: *De fide et symbolo* — 72
- Augustine and Latin anti-Monarchianism — 73
- *Persona, natura, substantia* — 79
- 'Most fittingly called his Word' — 82
- *Spiritus, deitas, communio* — 86
- Taking stock — 92

PART II ASCENT — 93

4 The unadorned Trinity — 95
- *Trinitas quae Deus est* — 95
- The unadorned Trinity — 104

	Towards understanding	116
	Excursus 1: The dating of the *De trinitate*	118
5	*Per corporalia ... ad incorporalia*	121
	Ascent and the liberal arts	121
	Changing attitudes to the *artes*	128
	Analogy in the *Confessiones*	133
6	A Christological epistemology	142
	Augustine finds his Panzer	144
	Faith and contemplation	147
	Faith, desire and Christ	152
	Interlude: Augustine's Panzer and the Latin tradition	155
	Correspondence and mystery: the example of Moses	159
	Faith and grace	166
	Excursus 2: Polemical targets in the *De trinitate*	171

PART III INTO THE MYSTERY — 175

7	Recommending the source	177
	A second rule	178
	The meaning of sending	181
	Revealing and saving	183
	Augustine's novelty?	187
	Creator, creation and the angels	189
	'You have made all things in Wisdom' (Ps. 103.24)	193
8	Essence from essence	199
	The self-same, the identical	200
	The simplicity of God	208
	Predicating relation (*trin.* 5. 3.4–8.9)	211
	Person and nature (*trin.* 5. 8.9–9.10 and 7. 4.7–6.11)	217
	Wisdom from Wisdom (*trin.* 6. 1.1–7. 2.3)	221
	Appropriation (*trin.* 7. 3.4)	227
9	Showing and seeing	230
	subsistentia personarum ('the existence of the persons')	231
	Father and Son: showing and seeing	233
10	Loving and being	251
	The Spirit as agent of unity	251
	Acts 4.32	256
	The Spirit and the life of the Divine Three	258
	And 'from' the Son?	263
	Subsisting relations?	268

Contents ix

PART IV MEMORY, INTELLECT AND WILL 273

11 'But it's not fur eatin' ...' 275
    Introduction 275
    De civitate Dei 11 277
    De trinitate 8: the *exordium* 281
    De trinitate 9. 1.1–5.8: the paradox of self-knowing 285
    De trinitate 9. 6.9–12.18: *verbum interior* 290
    Conclusion: the ghost at the banquet? 293

12 '... It's just fur lookin' through' 297
    Setting up *De trinitate* 10: *se nosse* – *se cogitare* 297
    De trinitate 10. 10.13–12.19: *memoria, intellegentia* and *voluntas* 303
    Reprise: *De trinitate* 14 305
    A Ciceronian triad 308
    Conclusion 315

Epilogue: catching all three 319

Bibliography 327
Scripture index 352
General index 355

Acknowledgements

This book has been written many times. I do not mean simply that I have revised what is here many times, but that I have produced at least three versions of the argument and a number of chapters have long since been consigned to 'the round file'. The realizations that I did not want to write a book that would focus almost entirely on the *De trinitate* – and that I wanted to cover, as far as I could, ground not covered in already published material – were pivotal in my final decisions about the shape of the book. However, the time it has taken to get here means that there are far too many people to acknowledge: I have accordingly tried to mention those who were most instrumental in helping *this* text see the light of day.

I would like to begin with a group that usually appears only at the end of acknowledgement lists. I have been extremely lucky to have had a community of graduate students over the past eight years at Emory who have acted not so much as students or research assistants but as colleagues with whom the ideas explored here could be discussed. I think especially of Mark DelCogliano, Thomas Humphries, Andrew Radde-Gallwitz, Kate Wilkinson and (even though he was seduced into New Testament studies) James B. Wallace. Without these colleagues this book would be considerably worse.

Over the fifteen years since I completed a doctoral dissertation on Augustine's Trinitarian theology, a number of mentors and friends have encouraged, pulled and pushed me towards publication. This book now bears little relation to that first attempt, but that my initial goal of a monograph on Augustine's Trinitarian theology has been met is in part due to the constant pressure of those figures. I think especially of Roberta Bondi, Patout Burns, Brian Daley, Ian Kidd, Robert Markus, Tom Martin and Rowan Williams.

As with any product of this nature, a whole host of friends and colleagues has provided encouragement, responses, suggestions and just basic bibliographical help along the way. Chief among these, of course, is that

Acknowledgements xi

great French American Michel Barnes, a reminder to us all not of Pétain, but of Maréchal Leclerc. After I had finished my doctoral dissertation it was in conversation with Michel that I really learned to do Augustine and it is in conversation with him that this book has been written. We differ over a whole variety of questions, but the modelling in our conversation of a new set of arguments and questions about Augustine's Trinitarian theology – not simply a unified view on all things – is a vital stimulus. Chad Gerber's influence on my treatment of Augustine's earliest work has been extremely important. These others (for the most part) each know how helpful they have been to this enterprise: John Behr, Jonathan Beswick, Alan Brooke, Catherine Chin, Elizabeth Clark, Hubertus Drobner, Mark Elliott, Allan Fitzgerald, Luigi Gioia, Bill Harmless, Carol Harrison, Stanley Hauerwas, Brooks Holifield, Stephen Holmes, Luke Timothy Johnson, Gareth Jones, Roland Kany, Steve Kraftchick, Christopher Lee, Andrew Louth, Matthew Levering, Ian Markham, Endeavour Morse, Gail O'Day, Jack Regan, Dale Smith, Steve Strange, Brent Strawn, Basil Studer, Vincent Twomey, Jim Wetzel, Robert Wilken, Daniel Williams and Robert Wozniak. Kate Brett, my editor (until the final stages) at Cambridge, has been as much friend as editor (despite my endless delays). Few authors are so lucky.

The research for this book has also received support from a number of generous institutions and individuals. Philip Rousseau generously made me a Visiting Fellow of the Center for Early Christian Studies at the Catholic University of America in 2005. The Association of Theological Schools in co-operation with the Lilly Foundation provided a Theological Scholars Grant during 2006–7 and, in co-operation with the Luce Foundation, appointed me to a Henry Luce III Fellowship for 2007–8. Two Deans of the Candler School of Theology, Russ Richey and then Jan Love, have been constantly supportive. Without such wonderful people and institutions who knows if this would ever have appeared?

Anna Catherine Edith, Thomas Francis Augustine and Iain Harry George Gabriel have not been much concerned with Daddy's book: it is not in rhyming couplets, it does not concern Jedi knights and does not come with pictures. But they have been delighted that I have been willing to provide so much paper, with one side oddly used, for colouring and drawing. Their productions on this paper – from treasure maps to 'scary things' – have frequently been wonderfully diverting. Their mother, my wife and closest friend, Medi, has made the sort of sacrifices that academics can understand and should respect more than any other: she has taken time out from her own writing and research to support mine. Augustine knew well that only in lives of mutual service and love is the foundation laid for any individual ascent towards understanding: I may or may not have achieved any of the latter, but I have no doubt about the meaning of the former.

The book is dedicated to the Augustinians of the Chicago province, and of the province of St Thomas of Villanova. Over the past twenty years I have come to know some as friends; others have crossed my paths during many happy visits to Villanova. It is a particular sadness that, among these, Fr. Thomas Martin OSA did not live to receive the copy of this book that was destined for him. He was a good friend over many years. On every occasion the Augustinians I have known have been an embodiment of the *caritas* that Augustine saw as the heart of the body of Christ. He would be humbled that they carry his name.

Abbreviations

ACW	Ancient Christian Writers
AÉPHÉ	*Annuaire de l'École Pratique des Hautes Études, Ve section (des sciences religieuses).*
AL	*Aristoteles Latinus* (Brepols)
ANRW	*Aufstieg und Niedergang der römischen Welt*
Aug(L)	*Augustiniana*
Auglex	C. P. Mayer, *Augustinus – Lexicon* (Basel : Schwabe & Co. AG, 1986–)
AugMag	*Augustinus Magister: Congrès International Augustinien Paris, 21–24 septembre* 1954, 2 vols. (Paris: Études Augustiniennes, 1954)
Aug(R)	*Augustinianum*
AugStud	*Augustinian Studies*
BA	Bibliothèque Augustiniennes
BTL	Bibliotheca Teubneriana Latina (De Gruyter)
CAG	*Commentaria in Aristotelem Graeca*
CCSG	Corpus Christianorum, Series Graeca
CCSL	Corpus Christianorum, Series Latina
CHHP	*Cambridge History of Hellenistic Philosophy*
CPG	*Clavis Patrum Graecorum*
CPL	*Clavis Patrum Latinorum*
CSEL	Corpus Scriptorum Ecclesiasticorum Latinorum
EOMIA	*Ecclesiae Occidentalis Monumenta Iuris Antiquissima*
FoC	Fathers of the Church
GCS	Die griechischen christlichen Schriftsteller
GNO	*Gregorii Nysseni Opera*
HTR	*Harvard Theological Review*
JThS	*Journal of Theological Studies*
LLT	Library of Latin Texts (Brepols)

NPNF	Nicene and Post Nicene Fathers
OCT	Oxford Classical Texts
OLD	*Oxford Latin Dictionary*
PG	Patrologia Graeca
PL	Patrologia Latina
REAug	*Revue des Études Augustiniennes*
RecAug	*Recherches Augustiniennes*
RevBen	*Revue Bénédictine*
RThAM	*Recherches de théologie ancienne et médiévale*
RThL	*Revue Théologique de Louvain*
SC	Sources Chrétiennes
SJT	*Scottish Journal of Theology*
SP	*Studia Patristica*
TS	*Theological Studies*
TU	Texte und Untersuchungen
U	Urkunde
WSA	Works of Saint Augustine
ZNTW	*Zeitschrift für die neutestamentliche Wissenschaft*
ZAC	*Zeitschrift für Antikes Christentum*

Introduction

I

Even as summary accounts continue to repeat the established caricatures of the past century, new readings of Augustine's Trinitarian theology grow in scholarly detail and density. These new readings, which have largely emerged over the past three decades, argue for new accounts of the fundamental dynamics of Augustine's Trinitarianism; they suggest new questions that we should ask if we are to study him well; they suggest new texts from his corpus as paradigmatic. Many of the older readings of Augustine's Trinitarian theology that have been displaced by this body of scholarship – and which, it must be noted, have not been extensively defended in the scholarly literature for many years – tended to view Augustine in highly negative fashion as the initiator of disastrous trends in Western Christian thought. Augustine was presented as marking a shift in the history of early Christian Trinitarianism, his own overly strong commitment to the divine unity partially being the result of his Neoplatonic engagements and strongly influencing those who came after him. This commitment led him away from the heritage of earlier Greek Nicene theology (and, in some readings, from earlier Latin theology). Even many of those who viewed Augustine positively – and saw his differences from his predecessors as merely delineating sets of complementary theological trajectories – operated with similar assumptions about his work. At the same time, his Trinitarian theology was engaged through an almost exclusive focus on the *De trinitate*.[1]

---

[1] The significance of Theodore De Régnon's *Études de théologie positive sur la Sainte Trinité* (Paris: Retaux, 1898) in setting the agenda even for those who reversed or adapted his categories has been frequently noted since the publication of Michel Barnes's 'De Régnon Reconsidered', *AugStud* 26 (1995), 51–79. The two most influential twentieth-century treatments of Augustine, both of which offer the now standard critique, are Michael Schmaus, *Die psychologische Trinitätslehre des hl. Augustinus* (Münster: Aschendorff, 1967) and Olivier Du Roy, *L'Intelligence de la Foi en la Trinité selon Saint Augustin. Genèse de sa Théologie Trinitaire jusqu'en 391* (Paris: etudes Augustiniennes, 1966). In many ways it was reaction to Du Roy's volume that began the shifts

This book is both parasitic on and a contribution to these new readings and it may thus be helpful to note in general terms some of their common themes and emergent trajectories. I say 'emergent trajectories' because, since the mid-1960s, most scholars of Augustine's Trinitarian theology have held to some of the positions I describe here: only in the past fifteen or twenty years has it begun to be possible to point to those who hold to all. It is important to note that these common themes concern not only questions of doctrinal 'content', but also questions of method. Thus, the past few decades have seen a growing emphasis on studying Augustine against the background of his immediate peers and predecessors, both theological and philosophical. In the specific field with which I am concerned, once the unlikelihood of Augustine's Trinitarian theology being best understood as primarily an adaptation of earlier Greek pro-Nicene theology was established by Berthold Altaner, scholars have come to put increasing weight on Augustine's interaction not only with major Latin theologians such as Ambrose and Hilary, but also with the less-well-known figures of late fourth-century Latin theology and on attempting to identify what might have been available to Augustine in translation. At the same time, rather than assuming that Augustine as major thinker must naturally have been in primary dialogue with the major figures of classical philosophy, scholars have come to see his philosophical knowledge as far more piecemeal, far more dependent on his readings in figures such as Cicero and Apuleius who summarized the opinions of those we moderns count as the 'major' figures of the ancient philosophical tradition. Students of Augustine have also become far more attentive to the extent to which his philosophical and theological knowledge grew over his extensive literary career: the Platonic engagements of the *De civitate Dei* tell us little about his knowledge during the 380s.

These methodological emphases have resulted in a greater readiness to note significant development in Augustine's thought and even the experimental quality of some of his mature texts. A text such as the *De trinitate* is thus increasingly viewed not as a non-polemical summative statement, but as the product of many years of development – and of a development that did not end with the final words of that text. Increasing awareness of the peculiar concerns and nature of this work is also leading scholars to become aware of discontinuities as well as continuities between Augustine's statements here and elsewhere in his corpus. Against

---

in reading of Augustine that I sketch here. For further discussion of modern readings specifically of the *De trinitate*, see Roland Kany's excellent *Augustins Trinitätsdenken. Bilanz, Kritik und Weiterführung der modernen Forschung zu 'De trinitate'* (Tübingen: Mohr Siebeck, 2007).

this background Augustine certainly appears as a distinctive figure, but he does so in part because of his highly personal engagement with those predecessors.

In terms of content, the new scholarship that I am delineating here has directly rebutted some of the most common charges against Augustine made in the last century or so. This recent literature has paid much attention to the ways in which Augustine's Trinitarian theology is deeply shaped by Christological themes. Our faith in the Trinity begins in attention to the scriptural rule of faith. Our growth in understanding is shaped by the transformation of intellect and affection from an obsession with the material to a love for the eternal that occurs in Christ (and through the Spirit) that, in turn, is a following in reverse of the route by which Christ's humanity reveals the divine.

Increasing attention to this Christological focus has been closely related to a growing interest in the exegetical foundations of his Trinitarian theology. Rather than viewing Augustine's Trinitarianism as the product of primarily philosophical concerns, recent scholarship has seen Augustine's theology as deeply rooted in the exegetical dimensions of the Trinitarian controversies that were so central a part of late fourth-century theological development. We will see a number of significant examples of this engagement throughout the book.

The same scholarship has argued against the idea that Augustine's Trinitarian theology inappropriately asserts the unity of God over the diversity of the persons. One of my own central arguments in this book will be that while recent scholarship has rightly emphasized Augustine's insistence on the irreducibility of the persons, we can push further and see him as moving, in the decade between 410 and 420, towards a sophisticated account of the divine communion as resulting from the eternal intra-divine acts of the divine three. While this account is stated very tentatively, Augustine is consistently clear that the Trinitarian life is founded in the Father's activity as the one from whom the Son is eternally born and the Spirit proceeds. In this emphasis Augustine is, I will suggest, revealed as one of the most interesting and important interpreters of Nicaea's 'God from God and Light from Light'. Building on the recent work of Richard Cross, I will also argue that Augustine's idiosyncrasy and theological fruitfulness stem in part from the manner in which he rejects the usefulness of genus and species terminologies for describing the relations between the divine three.

It is important to note that the scholarly trends I have summarized here have resulted not only in the development of a sophisticated response to the extensive critique made of Augustine's Trinitarianism over the past century, but also in a reappraisal of the positive reading of Augustine common within the Thomist tradition. In a way parallel to the best of the *ressourcement* movement during the twentieth century, this new reading suggests that while Augustine is at times a precursor of medieval concerns, at many points he is pursuing a different agenda in a different theological and philosophical context. The emergence of this new Augustine, then, need not be tied to an attempt to supplant Thomas, but to present others alongside Thomas as sources for the Catholic theologian.

I intend that this book contribute to these revisionist readings by focusing on two themes: Augustine's struggles to articulate the Trinitarian communion or life of the three irreducible 'persons'; his developing understanding of how we grow in understanding of the Trinity, how we progress towards the contemplation of God that is a participation in the Trinitarian life. Given these foci, it is important to note three things that this book is not. In the first place, it is not a detailed study of the development of Augustine's Trinitarian theology through to the end of his career. I have discussed the development of particular aspects when it was important to do so, but I have made no systematic attempt to describe the history of every theme that I discuss. In particular, although I have made some use of material from Augustine's *Contra sermonem Arrianorum* (418) and from his late polemical engagement with the Homoian bishop Maximinus (427), I offer no extended treatment of these works. Eventually, I hope, Michel Barnes will produce a book on the development of Augustine's Trinitarian theology complementary to this that will fill significant gaps in our knowledge. In the second place, this book is not a commentary on the *De trinitate*. Although I spend considerable time with the *De trinitate*, I frequently use exposition of that text as a way into other key texts of Augustine's corpus that help to illustrate its concerns. In other places I discuss the *De trinitate* in order to highlight its peculiar and at times unique status. This is especially true of the extended discussions of Chapters 10 and 11.[2]

In the third place, this book does not offer a detailed study of how Augustine sees the saving action of God as a Trinitarian event, nor how

---

[2] A full-scale commentary on the work is much to be desired. Basil Studer, *Augustins De Trinitate. eine Einführung* (Paderborn: Schöningh, 2005) is a welcome addition to the literature. But while Studer's work is of great significance for the revisionary scholar of Augustine's Trinitarian theology, in many ways it represents only a bridge between older and newer ways of reading him. For example, it is interesting that he continues (pp. 186–8) to see in Augustine a 'unitarian' tendency in part based on his supposed reliance on a 'psychological' analogy.

he consequently sees Christian life as shaped by the Trinity. Some central themes are developed, others adumbrated. Most importantly, at a number of points through the book I discuss ways in which Augustine understands Christian life as a growth towards a contemplation that is also a participation in the divine life. Augustine sees this growth as occurring through the reformation of the soul by Christ and Spirit. The exploration of faith is an activity both philosophical and, for those so gifted, an integral part of the reformation effected through grace. Chapter 6 hints at a number of ways in which Augustine sees the Spirit as active within the Body of Christ, demonstrating that for all his insistence on the interior leading of the individual Christian, Augustine sees the work of sanctification as a corporate and ecclesial work. The Epilogue to the book in part draws together some of these themes, but there is room here for a host of further studies.

II

Like most authors I would be delighted if readers begin with the Introduction and make their way through the whole of this book. Nevertheless, without offering a hostage to fortune (or reviewers) it may be helpful to note that there are a number of points at which one could begin reading. Chapters 1–3 form a distinct unit, discussing the origins of Augustine's Trinitarian theology. I argue that Augustine's texts, even those written before his baptism in the spring of 387, reveal a twofold engagement with non-Christian Platonism and with Latin pro-Nicene theology. Over the years that follow, these initial engagements are sustained, Augustine's developing Trinitarianism being formed significantly by his anti-Manichaean concerns. These concerns set an agenda and push Augustine in directions that will mark his Trinitarian theology throughout his career. In 393 we see Augustine's pro-Nicene debts emerge with far greater clarity in the *De fide et symbolo*, a text whose importance has been consistently underrated. These chapters revolve around very detailed readings of a few early texts in Augustine's corpus and will be hard going for those readers unfamiliar with this material. Nevertheless, for a persuasive case to be developed, this work is necessary.

Chapters 4–6 also form a unit. Chapter 4 initially considers a summary text from *De trinitate* 1 whose date is uncertain but which likely contains some early material, and ends with a wider consideration of Augustine's attitude to the text of Scripture as a foundation for doctrinal argument. Chapter 5 considers the background to Augustine's account of our possible growth in understanding of Trinitarian faith, looking at his early engagement with the Liberal Arts tradition. It is this engagement, despite a number of significant shifts, that will shape his career-long meditation on the character of understanding and analogical reasoning. Chapter 6 discusses Augustine's 'Christological epistemology' which emerges in and which lies at the heart of *De trinitate* 1–4. Only as we come to understand how Christ teaches about the immaterial and simple divine life through speaking in temporal and material terms can our intellects ascend towards understanding of that divine life.

In Chapters 7–10 I approach Augustine's mature Trinitarian ontology, his account of the divine three as irreducible even as the Trinity is necessarily the one simple source of all. Chapter 7 considers Augustine's treatment of Son and Spirit as revealers of the Father's 'hidden eternity'. It is the revelation by Son and Spirit of the Father that provides the dogmatic foundation for Augustine's account of our ascent towards contemplation. At the same time, this discussion begins to suggest an account of the role of the Father and the nature of the divine communion very different from that one might expect from summary accounts of Augustine's Trinitarian theology. After an initial outline of Augustine's understanding of the divine being and substance, Chapter 8 explores Augustine's rejection of genus and species terminologies for explaining the divine unity and diversity and looks at the alternative language he suggests. Chapters 9 and 10 argue that hints about the relational existence of the divine three found in *De trinitate* 5–7 only come to fruition outside that work, and particularly in exegesis of John 5.19 and Acts 4.32. In his mature reading of these texts Augustine develops an account of the Spirit as the one who – as the Father's eternal gift – eternally brings into unity Father, Son and Spirit. In this account we find one of the most striking and fruitful, if also most idiosyncratic, of pro-Nicene Trinitarian theologies.

Finally, Chapters 11 and 12 also form a unit, focusing on aspects of *De trinitate* 8–10 and 14. My goal here is to draw out the experimental nature of the arguments offered and the problematic status of describing the argument as analogical. The practice of reflection Augustine recommends and models is one in which the terms of Trinitarian faith guide investigation of the *mens*, and investigation of the *mens* promotes understanding of the terms of faith: the entire process occurs within the grace-led life. In these discussions we see the mature product of Augustine's early engagement with the Liberal Arts.

Throughout this text readers expecting detailed engagement with the numerous modern abuses and (more recently) celebrations of Augustine's

Trinitarian theology will be disappointed. I have also restricted my overt discussions of the great body of scholarly writing on Augustine's Trinitarian thought; I have purposely focused on exposition of his texts. Similarly, extensive discussion of Augustine's understanding of what has come to be termed 'selfhood' is also absent. Some of these discussions have been very useful, but I have wanted to resist diverting attention from Augustine's discussions of the Trinity itself. In the interests of retaining readers who may not be familiar with Augustine's texts – and those of the others considered through the book – I have also quoted a little more extensively than strictly necessary.

III

In the preface to *Nicaea and its Legacy* I suggested that this treatment of Augustine would constitute a companion volume. While this is still the case, it is so in ways that may not be immediately clear. Most directly, I intend this book to offer an account of one of the most significant, idiosyncratic and compelling examples of pro-Nicene Trinitarian theology. In *Nicaea*, I argued for the importance of particular shared themes among pro-Nicene theologians and suggested the importance of further work on the relationship between different pro-Nicene traditions. This book offers both an example of how those themes are refracted by one particular author's work and thus something of how that author relates to his own tradition. Rather than assuming that Augustine is representative of 'Western' tradition, I suggest ways in which Augustine demonstrates common themes found in virtually all pro-Nicenes, ways in which Augustine shares themes with other Latin pro-Nicenes, and ways in which Augustine's developing theology separates him from those other groups. Of course, my own thinking about many of the questions in *Nicaea* has itself changed considerably over the past few years. It is my hope to produce a much larger and more comprehensive version of *Nicaea* at some point in the future.

In the second place, my intention is that this book model aspects of the theological practices I commended in the last chapter of *Nicaea* (and which are for the most part a selection of those used by many other historical theologians). Frequently it has been the more polemical aspects of that discussion that have caught the attention of readers.[3] Without much

---

[3] For further discussion of *Nicaea*, see the papers contained in a special edition of *HTR* 100/2 (2007).

overt discussion my hope is that the patterns of attention to Augustine's texts I show here give further indications of how I think some of the positive aspects of that earlier discussion might be borne out.

One aspect of that earlier discussion hidden, I suspect, by the broad nature of my argument about the structure of modern 'systematic' theology, was my statement that I did not think I was offering a dense vision of what theology should 'look like'. While I think I can isolate some of the factors that have made modern systematic theology engage the legacy of Nicaea so thinly, I do not think that we can pretend that we can practise theology simply as Christians did in the late fourth and early fifth centuries. In part, this is so because of some significant differences in the social contexts and structures within which we practise. In part, it is so because Christians (at least those who accept the Spirit's guidance of the Church in the ways at which I hinted there) find themselves at the end of much further definition and discussion of the structure of our basic dogmas and mysteries. In part, it is so because our adaptation of Nicene theological practices should, I suggest, sit alongside our adaptation of some forms of modern historical consciousness. We need to learn a different plurality of reading practices than that which the ancients assumed.

In the context of such uncertainty about the practice of theology – and here it is important to remember that my fundamental concern is with our theological thinking about the most basic questions of dogmatic theology – what then should we do? One aspect of the answer to this question must be that we will not all do the same thing. Just as an author or teacher is most self-deluded when she imagines her book to be the only one on a putative reader's shelf, so we must think of multiple ways beyond modern theological practices. The ways in which I choose to practise as theologian and historian will not be the only game in town. It is against this background that I strongly suggest the importance of learning modes of close attention to those held up before us in the Church's memory. Eventually I will have to produce a longer study of how 'newness' enters theology, but for the moment it is necessary only to restate the principle suggested towards the end of *Nicaea*'s last chapter, that I see little need, in our attempts to understand the most basic articles of faith, for separate moments of 'historical' and 'systematic' theology. My own contribution to conversation about the future of dogmatic theology is to suggest that exploration of the Trinitarian theology of a figure such as Augustine necessarily combines fidelity to those the Church holds up before us in its memory with the arrival of newness into the world.

It may also be worth saying that in any such longer study I would argue that the modes of attention and accountability to the past that a theologian ought to show should be understood not only as displays of appropriate scholarly commitment, but also as modes of prayer. Reverence for those held up in the Church's memory need not be an alternative to critical study, but a mode of testimony to the action of God in human lives that were always only on the path of sanctification: we may combine attention to the failings of those the Church holds up before us with confidence that their thought provides an ever-trustworthy point of reference in our own search to understand the faith. In other terms, attention to the surviving texts of an author is perfectly compatible with imagining those authors not to be dead, but as now living in and through the light of Christ. We imagine them now perhaps not as ever-present defenders of their works, but as aware of the failings of those very same texts, aware that all our searching is completed in final contemplation. Thus our historical investigations may be rigorous and searching even as we are guided towards these authors as constant foci for the attention. That attention rewarded is also of course the work of grace. If our historical work is of value in the struggle to understand what we believe then it is so as both our work and that of the Spirit:

When people see [your works] with the help of your Spirit, it is you who are seeing in them. When, therefore, they see that things are good, you are seeing that they are good. Whatever pleases them for your sake is pleasing you in them. The things which by the help of your Spirit delight us are delighting you in us. 'For what man knows the being of man except the spirit of man which is in him? So also no one knows the things of God except the Spirit of God.'[4]

---

[4] *conf.* 13. 31.46 (CCSL 27. 269).

PART I
Origins

CHAPTER I

Giving wings to Nicaea

'the perception of incorporeal things quite overwhelmed me and the Platonic theory of ideas added wings to my soul …'[1]

ON BEING AND NOT BEING A 'PLATONIST'

There is a long-standing charge that Augustine's Trinitarian theology differed from that of his predecessors and was not a truly Trinitarian theology because it began as an adaptation of Plotinus's or Porphyry's accounts of the three primary realities or *hypostases*.[2] In this chapter and the next I will refute this charge and consider how we can better envisage the multiple influences on Augustine's earliest Trinitarian writing. The last clause of the previous sentence intentionally limits the scope of my investigation. We should not assume that Platonism had an influence of the same character on all aspects of Augustine's theology.[3] The influence that non-Christian

---

[1] Justin, *Tryph.* 2. 6.
[2] The language of three *hypostases* is not, of course, Plotinus's own. At *Enn.* 5. 1.7, for example, Plotinus speaks of the three poetically only as τὰ θεῖα ('divinities'); it is probably Porphyry who is responsible for introducing the terminology in the titles of the *Enneads* (e.g. with reference to *Enn.* 5. 1, *vit. Plot.* 25): Περὶ τῶν τριῶν ἀρχικῶν ὑποστάσεων; and in his own summaries, for example frg 221F (ed. Andrew Smith, *Porphyrii philosophi fragmenta* (Stuttgart: Teubner, 1993)): ἄχρι γὰρ τριῶν ὑποστάσεων ἔφη Πλάτων τὴν τοῦ θείου προελθεῖν οὐσίαν. For a particularly clear discussion of the relationship between Plotinus and Porphyry, see Steven K. Strange, 'Porphyry and Plotinus' Metaphysics', in George Karamanolis and Anne Sheppard (eds.), *Studies on Porphyry*, Bulletin of the Institute of Classical Studies, Supplement 98 (London, 2007), 17–34.
[3] I am consciously using the wider term 'Platonism' rather than 'Neoplatonism' here. Throughout the chapter I will use the term 'Neoplatonism' to refer to texts by the non-Christian authors modern scholars commonly identify as such. I will also use the term to designate ideas that Augustine took from those texts in forms that are distinctively the possession of Neoplatonists as opposed to earlier members of the Platonic tradition. In all other contexts I use the simpler 'Platonism' to designate ideas that are found in a range of Christian and non-Christian authors beyond the bounds of Neoplatonism as such. Many of these ideas were cherished by Neoplatonists, but designating them as such too easily leads students of Augustine to forget that they are not distinctively Neoplatonic.

Platonist texts had on his understanding of dialectic as a philosophical tool will not necessarily have been the same as the influence of those texts on his earliest understanding of the Trinity. Thus my concern is not with 'the influence of Platonism on Augustine', but with the specific influence of Platonism on Augustine's early Trinitarian theology.

It is important, however, to begin by locating the specific arguments of this chapter within the broader context of modern scholarly debate about Augustine's 'Platonism'. While that scholarship has been divided over the possible identification of his early Neoplatonic readings as Plotinian or Porphyrian (and over the role of Christians already influenced by such texts), it has been virtually unanimous in rejecting the idea, popularized by Prosper Alfaric in the first half of the twentieth century, that Augustine converted to Platonism before he converted to Christianity.[4] Rejecting such theories, modern scholarship has focused on identifying the particular texts and doctrines that were of most importance to Augustine and, to a much lesser extent, on understanding how Augustine adapted these doctrines. This last question is, however, of great importance; many significant debates have at their core decisions about the extent to which Augustine's use of a particular Plotinian or Porphyrian terminology implies his acceptance of all that the terminology implied in its original context.[5] These questions have been rendered yet more difficult by the gradual recognition that we must take account of Augustine's *on-going* engagement with Platonic sources. Most importantly, the engagements that are evident in the *Confessiones* or the *De Civitate Dei* cannot be taken as a secure guide to Augustine's readings many years previously.[6]

---

[4] Prosper Alfaric, *L'évolution intellectuelle de saint Augustin. i. Du manichéisme au néoplatonisme* (Paris: Émile Nourry, 1918). No one piece of secondary literature provides a sufficient overview of the vast body of scholarship on Augustine's early knowledge of Neoplatonism. Nevertheless, Robert Crouse, '*Paucis mutatis verbis*: St. Augustine's Platonism', in George Lawless and Robert Dodaro (eds.), *Augustine and his Critics* (London: Routledge, 2000), 37–50, offers a particularly incisive account of the state of play (and his notes refer to just about every significant author in this field). Crouse and I differ over what it means to talk of the 'Neoplatonic tradition', as will become clear later in the chapter. Carol Harrison's recent *Rethinking Augustine's Early Theology: An Argument for Continuity* (Oxford: Oxford University Press, 2006) argues strongly for a fundamental continuity in Augustine's theology.

[5] One of the best examples here is Robert O'Connell's long insistence that Augustine believed in the 'fall' of each soul into the material creation from a prior state of blessedness. The thesis is argued with particular clarity through his *St Augustine's Early Theory of Man, A.D. 386–391* (Cambridge, MA: Harvard University Press, 1968) and *The Origin of the Soul in St. Augustine's Later Works* (New York: Fordham University Press, 1987). On the reaction to O'Connell, see Ronnie Rombs, *St. Augustine and the Fall of the Soul: Beyond O'Connell and his Critics* (Washington DC: Catholic University of America, 2006).

[6] Ignoring this principle seems to me to be particularly endemic among some who argue strongly for the maximal influence of Porphyry on the early Augustine. John J. O'Meara, *Porphyry's*

Focusing on the character of Augustine's *adaptation* of material from Platonic texts is, at the very least, important because Augustine did not participate in some of the most fundamental traditions that linked together late antique Platonists. Platonism was not only a tradition of doctrines, it was also a tradition within which particular texts were valued because of their explanatory and even revelatory power, and it was a tradition within which particular questions had come to be valued as focal points of thought. David Sedley has convincingly argued that late antique Platonists were held together not so much by a set of doctrines, as by a commitment to the authority of Plato and to the traditions of interpretation and commentary of both Aristotle and Plato by which consideration of Plato himself was structured.[7]

While Augustine valued a number of Platonist authors, his knowledge of the texts that formed what we might term the 'imaginative library' of thinkers such as Plotinus and Porphyry was weak. For example, he appears to have known only a little of the commentary traditions noted in the previous paragraph.[8] At the same time a text such as the *Chaldean Oracles*, treated by many late antique Platonists as having the very revelatory power mentioned in the previous paragraph, was probably regarded

---

Philosophy from Oracles in Augustine (Paris: Études Augustiniennes, 1959) offers a particularly clear example of the tendency to use evidence from the post-400 period to interpret Augustine's earliest work. A recent ingenious example is provided by Pier Franco Beatrice, 'Quosdam Platonicorum Libros: The Platonic Readings of Augustine in Milan', *Vigil de Christianae* 43 (1989), 248–81. Beatrice argue that Augustine read fragments of Plotinus in a translation of Porphyry's *Philosophy from Oracles* made by Victorinus (and that the person *immanissimo typho turgidum* at conf. 7. 9.13 is Porphyry). The argument, however, relies on an unwarranted assumption that the presence of anti-Porphyrian themes in the *conf.* 7 account (and in *civ.*) means that the same knowledge of Porphyry must have been present in 386–7. Rejection of this account does not take away from the difficulty of any attempt at solving this question: Beatrice, rightly, draws attention to the difficulty of finding clearly Plotinian allusions in Victorinus – as opposed to extensive engagement with Porphyry – even though he is named by Augustine as the translator of the *platonicorum libros* at *conf.* 8. 2.3.

[7] See David N. Sedley, 'Plato's *Auctoritas* and the Rebirth of the Commentary Tradition', in Jonathan Barnes and Miriam Griffin (eds.), *Philosophia Togata II: Plato and Aristotle at Rome* (Oxford: Clarendon Press, 1997), 110–29. In the background to Sedley's argument lie two other pieces: Pierre Hadot, 'Théologie, exégèse, révélation, écriture dans la philosophie grecque', in Michel Tardieu (ed.), *Les Règles de l'interprétation* (Paris: Cerf, 1987), 13–34; and Pierluigi Donini, 'Testi e commenti, manuali e insegnamento: la forma sistematica e i metodi della filosofica in età potellenistica', *ANRW* II. 36.7 (1994), 5027–100. See also most recently G. R. Boys-Stones, *Post-Hellenistic Philosophy: A Study of its Development from the Stoics to Origen* (Oxford: Oxford University Press, 2001). An excellent introduction to the developed commentary tradition of late antiquity is provided by Richard Sorabji (ed.), *Aristotle Transformed* (London: Duckworth, 1990). See also his excellent collection of source extracts, *The Philosophy of the Commentators 200–600 AD*, 3 vols. (London: Duckworth, 2005).

[8] See Chapter 8, pp. 212ff.

with abhorrence by Augustine, if he knew it.[9] Marius Victorinus and Synesius of Cyrene offer useful points of comparison here as both seem to have engaged this text even as Christians and struggled to find ways in which its mysteries might turn out to be those of the Christian faith.[10] We should also note that Augustine's accounts of philosophical history, found in such different works as the *Contra Academicos* and the *De Civitate Dei*, are frequently dependent on Cicero, on Varro and on Augustine's second-century North African compatriot Apuleius of Madaura.[11]

At the same time, Augustine shows little interest in many of the questions that late antique Platonists treated as nodal points of the arguments and discussions constituting their tradition. The most important examples concern the relationships of participation and dependence between the highest levels of reality: Augustine predicates of God attributes that Plotinus not only attributes only to *either* the One or *Nous*, but which also seem to him mutually exclusive. Augustine predicates of his 'first principle' the activity of thinking without even bothering to refute Plotinus's understanding of why the simple One could not be involved in the divisions of self-thinking.[12] Indeed, one might even say that there is a significant continuity between the way that Augustine and a much earlier thinker such as Irenaeus (engaged with what modern scholars term 'middle' rather than 'neo' Platonism) primarily use qualities predicated of *Nous* to describe the nature of God.[13]

Augustine is then a Platonist in ways that need careful definition. He is a Platonist, first, in the sense that he adopts and adapts a number of *doctrines* that he appears to have encountered in non-Christian Platonist texts. Some of these are peculiarly Plotinian or Porphyrian, others he seems to have met in those authors but are not distinctively theirs. Although there is no space (or need) here to offer an extended

---

[9] Even if from no other source, it seems highly probable that he knew some through Porphyry's use in his *Philosophy from Oracles* (see *civ.* 19. 23).

[10] For a brief introduction to the Chaldean oracles and their interpretation by late antique Platonists, see Polymnia Athanassiadi, 'The Chaldean Oracles: Theology and Theurgy', in Polymnia Athanassiadi and Michael Frede (eds.), *Pagan Monotheism in Late Antiquity* (Oxford: Clarendon Press, 1999), 149–83.

[11] For an initial sense of the significance of Cicero in Augustine's early account of the history of philosophy, see the passages in *acad.* referenced by Maurice Testard in his *Saint Augustin et Cicéron*, 2 vols. (Paris: Etudes Augustiniennes, 1958), 2. 1–7. For Augustine's knowledge of Apuleius, see Harald Hagendahl, *Augustine and the Latin Classics* (Stockholm: Almqvist & Wiksell, 1967), 1. 17–28 and 1. 29–33; James J. O'Donnell, 'Augustine's Classical Readings', *RecAug* 15 (1980), 144–75, for Apuleius, see 149–51.

[12] For example, Plotinus, *Enn.* 5. 3.10–13. Augustine's mature discussion of the ways in which the soul's self-thinking mirrors the divine is examined in Chapters 10 and 11.

[13] See, for example, Irenaeus, *adv. Haer.* 2. 28.4–5 (SC 294. 280).

discussion of exactly what Augustine read in his initial encounters with non-Christian Neoplatonism, it seems most likely that Augustine's earliest readings were from Plotinus.[14] We are, however, unable to say whether he read whole treatises, or only a compilation of extracts translated by Marius Victorinus.[15] Through the first two decades of the fifth century one can trace an increasing engagement with Platonic texts and a deeper knowledge of Porphyry.[16] Thus questions about the content of Augustine's Platonic readings must always be accompanied by temporal specification.

Second, we should not forget that Augustine adopted doctrines from Neoplatonic texts in the context of a struggle to overcome, in the first place, the challenge of Manichaean dualism and materialism and, in the second place, his turn to Ciceronian Scepticism that we can trace during 385–6.[17] It is, then, no accident that Augustine's early accounts of Platonism emphasize the secure epistemological foundation for knowledge of God that he takes Platonism to offer. Similarly, Augustine highlights an anti-Manichaean privative view of evil as one of the key gifts of his Platonic engagements, even though such a theory is hardly a prominent

---

[14] For our purposes it will only matter what Augustine can be shown to have read in his earliest treatments of the Trinity. The literature on this question is vast. For two good summary discussions, see James J. O'Donnell, *Augustine: Confessions* (Oxford: Clarendon Press, 1992), 2. 421–4; Eugene TeSelle, *Augustine the Theologian* (New York: Herder and Herder, 1970), 43–55. In the couple of years following his first discovery in 386 we can trace with a high degree of probability echoes of passages from around nine Plotinian treatises (1. 6, 3. 2–3, 4. 3–4, 5. 1, 5. 5, 6. 4–5). Other scholarship has variously suggested around ten more with varying degrees of plausibility (see TeSelle, *Augustine*, 44–5). For comparative lists that have been suggested, see Du Roy, *L'Intelligence*, 68–71, esp. 70. Lest one's tendency to see possible parallels becomes too strong, all scholars of the question should bear in mind Goulven Madec's strong riposte to Robert O'Connell: 'Une lecture de *Confessions* VII,IX,13–XXI,27. Notes critiques à propos d'une thèse de R.-J. O'Connell', *REAug* 16 (1970), 79–137.

[15] This is a discussion in which there are few certainties. Attempts to argue that Porphyry's *Sententiae* was the source fail both for lack of clear evidence and because of the presence of Plotinian material absent from *sent.* (e.g. the discussion of 'measure' in *Enn.* 1. 8.2, see below, pp. 31f.). Some scholars have suggested Porphyry's lost *Philosophy from Oracles* as the source of the Plotinian passages known to Augustine (see note 16, below). Without any real textual evidence about the contents of the work, Ockham surely encourages us to great caution about this suggestion? Despite the 75 years of scholarship published since his book, Paul Henry, *Plotin et L'Occident. Firmicus Maternus, Marius Victorinus, Saint Augustin et Macrobe* (Louvain: Spicilegium Sacrum Lovaniense, 1934) still offers a model of sanity in its methodological reflections, see esp. 63–103.

[16] The case for knowledge of Porphyry in the Cassiciacum period is much less certain. Du Roy's suggestion that there is no need to suspect the presence of Porphyry at least until Augustine returned to Milan in 387 (*L'Intelligence*, 186–95) has much to recommend it. Extensive knowledge of Porphyry only becomes reasonably easy to demonstrate from c.400.

[17] See *conf.* 5. 18–19, 25, *util. cred.* 20. Du Roy, *L'Intelligence*, 39–52, offers a very useful summary of the ways in which a revival of scepticism was intertwined with Augustine's increasing distrust of Manichaean answers in the months before his conversion. See also Testard, *Saint Augustin et Cicéron*, 1. 81–129.

feature of Plotinus himself and finds itself (obviously enough) in conflict with Plotinus's discussion of (undifferentiated) matter as the most probable source of evil.[18] In this regard Augustine's emphasis upon the structured numerical harmony of all things under their creator is best viewed as an amalgam of some themes from his Neoplatonic readings and material from earlier Latin sources that we place, perhaps too easily, under the heading of 'Pythagorean'.[19] Augustine thus adapts themes from his early Neoplatonic readings for very particular purposes. His enthusiastic self-description as a member of the Platonic 'school' at the end of the *Contra Academicos* is akin to Augustus claiming to be re-establishing the Roman Republic, but preserving those institutions by gradually accumulating and assimilating sufficient avenues of authority that the 'republic' could be sustained within a very different system of governance!

Lastly, we must not forget that Augustine was also a Platonist in the sense that he belonged to a tradition of Christians who had undertaken very similar adoptions and adaptations since at least the mid-second century.[20] Through this chapter and the next I will argue that Augustine's discovery of this tradition in the persons of Victorinus and Ambrose, and then in a host of other Latin theological texts of the fourth century, was probably simultaneous with his discovery of non-Christian Neoplatonism. When we consider developments in his theology that appear to be inspired by his Neoplatonic engagements, we will need to ask how far those developments stem from those engagements, and how far and in what ways they stem from on-going reading of his Christian peers and predecessors.

---

[18] See *Enn.* 2. 4.14–16. I assume here the priority of Plotinus for which I have been arguing and will continue to argue; one could make a stronger case that this theme reflects Porphyry, but it seems to me more likely that we are simply seeing Augustine adapting Plotinian themes for his own anti-Manichaean purposes.

[19] On the phenomenon of 'Neo-Pythagoreanism' in late antiquity and as a feature of Neoplatonic texts, see Dominic J. O'Meara, *Pythagoras Revived: Mathematics and Philosophy in Late Antiquity* (Oxford: Clarendon Press, 1989). Ilsetraut Hadot, *Arts libéraux et philosophie dans la pensée antique* (Paris: Études Augustiniennes, 1984), 101–36, argues that the strong interest in number apparent in *ord.* stems from Augustine's dependence on Porphyry and his Pythagorean tendencies (for the name Pythagoras, see *ord.* 2. 20.54). Her account is, however, at the least controversial. Even if one accepts the convincing arguments of Aimé Solignac, 'Doxographies et manuels dans la formation philosophique de saint Augustin', *RecAug* 1 (1958), 113–48, esp. 124–37, that much of Augustine's preoccupation with number owes to Nichomachus of Gerasa, he himself seems to have been what O'Meara (*Pythagoras*, 22) describes as a 'pythagoreanizing Platonist'. The question of 'Neo-Pythagoreanism' recurs in Chapter 8.

[20] One of the best examples being Ambrose himself, whose debts to Neoplatonism may have been mediated to a remarkably large extent by other Christian authors. See Goulven Madec, *Ambroise et La Philosophie* (Paris: Études Augustiniennes, 1974), ch. 1.

Do I, then, think it helpful to use 'Platonism' or 'Neoplatonism' as a generic heading and then speak of Christian and non-Christian species?[21] No, not as simply put as this. I understand 'Platonism' and 'Neoplatonism' in the first instance as non-Christian traditions, many of whose doctrines were drawn on by Christians in the imperial period. Christian Platonists are in many ways constantly parasitic on this non-Christian tradition, sometimes revealing themselves to be considerably out of step with developments in contemporary Platonism.[22] Some Christians were, of course, exceptions and able to participate in contemporary Platonist debates even while holding to Christian commitments. And yet 'parasitic' in isolation also gives the wrong impression: over time Christian 'Platonists' developed their own traditions of how (and which) Platonist doctrines might be adapted to Christian ends within the bounds of developing Christian discourse. There was thus also an emerging Christian Platonist tradition in late antiquity, even if this tradition did not name itself as such (in distinction from other versions of Christian belief). As will become clear, I am also convinced that the complexity of the links between Christian and non-Christian Platonist is better conceived the more we move away from assuming the fundamental incompatibility between Christianity and the non-Christian Platonism and towards a more piecemeal examination of the use made by Christians of Platonic doctrines.

In the remainder of this chapter I focus first on the most substantive attempt in the last half-century to argue that Augustine's understanding of the Trinity is dependent on Neoplatonism. The bulk of Olivier Du Roy's *L'Intelligence de la Foi en la Trinité selon Saint Augustin* concerns the early Augustine, but his intention is to show that Augustine's early philosophical debts governed his mature *De trinitate* and thus were deeply

---

[21] One of the most articulate advocates for this position is Wayne Hankey. Crouse, in 'Paucis mutatis verbis', quotes his 'Denys and Aquinas: Antimodern Cold and Postmodern Hot', in Lewis Ayres and Gareth Jones (eds.), *Christian Origins: Theology, Rhetoric and Community* (London: Routledge, 1998), 139–84. Of Hankey's recent writing one might also mention his 'Judaism, Islam, and Christianity in Medieval Europe, Difference and Unity: The "Religions of the Book" and their Assimilation of Hellenistic Philosophical Theology', in Susan Harris (ed.), *Multiculturalism and Religious Freedom* (Charlottetown: St Peter Publications, 2005), 81–127. One significant reason for the difference between our accounts is that Hankey uses the term 'Neoplatonism' in ways that enable him to speak of one continuous tradition (even if one that undergoes radical shifts) from Origen and Plotinus through to the Reformation (and beyond). My own concern is with a usage that better captures the dynamics of interaction in late antiquity. We do, however, share a sense that Neoplatonism (partially as a conduit for Platonism more broadly) had a significant *and positive* effect on developing Christianity.

[22] This is not to say that Christians, and Christian Platonists, did not contribute to changes in Platonic traditions, but tracing influence in this direction is a far more complex matter than tracing the influence of non-Christians on Christian writers.

influential on later Western Trinitarian theology as a whole.[23] English-speaking theologians – and some scholars of Augustine – have tended to assume Augustine's Trinitarian theology is dependent on Neoplatonism without offering detailed discussion of that influence. We should no longer let such assumptions pass untested. Consideration of the most detailed argument for wholesale Neoplatonic influence should make clear the importance of exercising more care in our accounts of Augustine's development.

OLIVIER DU ROY'S THESIS

Du Roy's thesis may be summarized in three steps.

(a) In his writings from Cassiciacum, Augustine sees the Incarnate Christ as providing ancillary assistance to those too weak for the true life of reason.[24] The anagogic turn within and ascent towards God that constitutes the life of reason is a participation in the Trinitarian structure of reality. What to the casual reader might seem to be merely faculties or functions of the soul are actually the three divine realities themselves: for example, intellect in human beings is that reality as such.[25] In order to show that the entirety of our return to God is governed by this Trinitarian structure, Du Roy expends considerable effort arguing that *ratio* in these works stands in for the Spirit and is dependent on Plotinus's account of the *logos* that flows from *Psuche*.[26] In this first phase, Du Roy argues, Augustine has some understanding of 'the rule of faith', but his

---

[23] I am very grateful to Kate Wilkinson for her extensive help articulating the flow of Du Roy's argument. In what follows I have also learnt much from Chad Gerber's *The Spirit of Augustine's Early Theology: Contextualizing His Pneumatology* (Aldershot: Ashgate, forthcoming 2011), a work which should be consulted for further treatment of all the texts I have discussed in Chapters 1 and 2.

[24] See, for example, Du Roy, *L'Intelligence*, 170: [commenting on *sol.* 1] 'Mais quelle sera cette voie progressive vers la Lumière? Augustin n'en connaît pas encore d'autre que la recherché philosophique.'

[25] For example, Du Roy, *L'Intelligence*, 143–7, discussing correspondences between texts from *sol.* 1 and *Enn.* 5. 3. Du Roy's reading of *ord.* 2. 11.30–1 discussed below offers another example.

[26] The influence of Plotinus's three *hypostases* is extensively argued first with reference to *ord.* 2. 9.26: see Du Roy, *L'Intelligence*, 127–30. Pages 130–43 then supplement this argument with an extensive treatment of the end of *ord.* 2, esp. 2. 11.30–1, a text I discuss below. The extent to which this scheme also enables an anagogical ascent of the soul becomes clear in his ch. 6, esp. pp. 183–96. I am grateful to Chad Gerber for pointing out to me that it is rarely noticed that Robert O'Connell in his *St. Augustine's Early Theory of Man*, 121–31, esp. 123–4, argues much less tentatively than Du Roy for the equation of *ratio* and Spirit at *ord.* 2. 9.26. I have not dealt with his case in this chapter as it is less developed than that of Du Roy.

interpretation of it is dependent on his grasp of the relations between the Plotinian *hypostases* and is economic in character, entirely focused on explaining how God makes possible our ascent.

(b) Du Roy sees this initial understanding of the Trinity as changing during Augustine's year in Rome (387–8) and during his years in Thagaste prior to ordination (388–91). Slowly Augustine moves away from a model of the anagogic ascent of the soul to one in which the soul ascends towards a vision of the Trinity reflected in the threefold structures of the created order (an order in which multiplicity is always drawn towards unity), and thence to a vision of the Trinity itself. He has advanced beyond his earliest understanding of the Trinity, but is increasingly reliant on an *exitus–reditus* scheme for understanding reality. Father, Son and Spirit share in the creative action, and that which they create is structured to enable our return to contemplation of the Trinity. This understanding of the Trinity is still fundamentally economic. As all the Trinitarian persons have a role in causing, ordering and sustaining the created order, so the persons in reverse order draw human beings back towards God.[27] This picture becomes clear in Augustine's anti-Manichaean commentaries on Genesis begun at Thagaste and in *De musica* 6,[28] and culminates in what Du Roy sees as the latest sections of the *De vera religione*.[29] Here Augustine attempts to meld his new model of the Trinitarian structure of reality with his earlier insight into the soul's interior ascent. The Incarnation – despite Augustine's increasing insistence upon its importance – is still understood as providing a way of knowledge for those unable to ascend by philosophy.[30]

It is also in *De vera religione* and in *Epistula* 11 that we begin to see the effects of this theology. For example, if one assumes that the persons work inseparably and that our most basic knowledge of the Trinity comes

---

[27] The emergence of this theme in *sol.* 2 is discussed in Du Roy, *L'Intelligence*, chs. 6–7. Du Roy contrasts the earlier style of anagogy found at *lib. arb.* 2. 3.7ff. with that found towards the end of this discussion at *lib. arb.* 2. 13.35–16.41. The former section of text relies on a retreat from the senses towards that which enables one's judgement. The latter section (which Du Roy takes to be the result of a later redaction) speaks of ascent culminating in vision of the creative Trinity that has left its mark (through the imprint of wisdom and number) on the creation as a whole. It is this mark in creation that stimulates and enables the return inward. The place of these Trinitarian structures in creation reveals Augustine's increasing reliance on an *exitus–reditus* scheme. For this whole discussion, see *L'Intelligence*, 242–56.

[28] Du Roy's understanding of this theme comes out particularly clearly in his reading of *mus.* 6, see *L'Intelligence*, 282–97.

[29] The argument is pursued through Du Roy, *L'Intelligence*, chs. 9 and 10, but is most clear in discussion of *vera rel.* 55. 110–13: *L'Intelligence*, 369–79.

[30] See Du Roy, *L'Intelligence*, 381, 398–401.

from observation of the creation, then we are led to ask why only the Son becomes incarnate. Our response will eventually be some form of appropriation theory (which Du Roy takes to undermine the distinctiveness of the persons).[31] In this period Augustine also begins to identify the Spirit as both the Charity and the Gift that conforms us to the Son. Lastly, we should note that Du Roy reads the works of this period as demonstrating a wide range of source material, including increasing knowledge of the *regula fidei* and adaptation of Varronian and Ciceronian themes to sketch his emerging account of creation. Nevertheless, a Neoplatonic understanding of anagogy still governs Augustine's patterns of adaptation.[32]

(c) The last stage in Du Roy's thesis concerns the later effects of the early works on Augustine's mature Trinitarian theology. Through developing his 'psychological' analogies Augustine attempts to deepen his account of the soul's anagogy by explaining how the soul discovers itself to be illuminated by the work of the creative Trinity.[33] At the same time, while Augustine certainly spends more time talking about the role of the Incarnate Word, it remains impossible for him to integrate incarnational theology into his account of the Trinity in creation and our ascent towards it.[34] The use of psychological analogies pushes Augustine increasingly clearly towards a monistic account of God in which the distinctions between the persons – and their specific roles in the drama of salvation – are downplayed. Du Roy sees the problems of Augustine's mature theology both as resulting from the experiments of his earliest writings and then as responsible for wider failure in later Western theology.[35]

A BRIDGE TOO FAR: DU ROY'S METHOD

There are some aspects of Du Roy's discussion that I will ignore *in toto* through this chapter. I will save, until Chapters 5 and 6, Du Roy's argument that the Incarnation is persistently extrinsic to Augustine's account of

---

[31] For example, Du Roy, *L'Intelligence*, 397.
[32] For example, Du Roy, *L'Intelligence*, 419: 'J'entends par là cette relative independance de l'intelligence par rapport à la foi, non pas tant dans son contenu, qui reste soumis à la regula fidei, que dans sa démarche et son élan. Cette demarche reste fondamentalement une reprise de l'anagogie plotinienne, personnalisée toutefois en une rencontre et une soumission de l'âme à la Verité.'
[33] Du Roy, *L'Intelligence*, 438.
[34] For both these two sentences, see Du Roy, *L'Intelligence*, 441–50, see also 456–8, esp. 457: 'La profonde expérience de l'amour Chrétien et surtout de l'unité ecclésiale [found in the mature pastoral writing of Augustine] ... n'a pas eu le poids suffisant pour counterbalancer la pente de son intellectualité néo-platonicienne.'
[35] Du Roy, *L'Intelligence*, 458. For his brief sketch of the later legacy of Augustine see 458–66.

Giving wings to Nicaea

how one grows in knowledge of the Trinity.[36] I will also leave aside – until Chapters 10 and 11 – his understanding of the latter half of the *De trinitate* and its legacy for later Western theology. I will focus instead on Du Roy's account of Augustine's earliest Trinitarian theology's 'dependence' on Plotinus's three *hypostases*. One small example of Du Roy's method, his treatment of *De ordine* 2. 11.30–1, will be our point of departure.

The second book of the *De ordine* probably dates from the first months of 387 and is a text to which we will return at a number of points in this chapter and the next.[37] The passage with which we are concerned is the beginning of a section devoted to the meaning of *ratio*:

> Reason is a mental operation [*mentis motio*] capable of distinguishing and connecting the things that are learned. But only a rare class of people is capable of using it as a guide to the knowledge of God or of the soul; either of the soul within us or that which is everywhere [*quae aut in nobis aut usque quaque est animam*]. This is due to nothing else than the fact that, for anyone who has advanced towards objects of sense, it is difficult to return to himself [*redire in semetipsum ... difficile est*] ... My incompetence would be equalled by my arrogance if I should profess that I myself have grasped it already. Nevertheless, insofar as reason has deigned to reveal itself in the things that appear familiar to us, let us now examine it to the best of our ability ... Reason, then, proceeds from a/the rational soul into reasonable things which are done or spoken [*ergo procedit ratio ab anima rationali, scilicet in ea quae vel fiunt rationabilia vel dicuntur*].[38]

Du Roy's interpretation of this passage revolves around a series of parallels he draws with Plotinus's late treatise *Ennead* 3. 2. Plotinus devotes this latter text to an account of the links between our cosmos and *Nous* in order to demonstrate that the world is rationally governed and that we are capable of moving towards its source:

> (3. 2.2) So Intellect [Νοῦς], by giving something of itself to matter, made all things in unperturbed quietness; this something of itself is the rational principle [λόγος] flowing from Intellect. For that which flows from Intellect is the rational principle, and it flows out always, as long as Intellect is present among realities

---

[36] One of the most trenchant critics of Du Roy in this regard has been Goulven Madec. For a taste of Madec's reading of the role of Christ in the earlier works of Augustine, see his *La Patrie et la Voie. Le Christ dans la vie et la pensée de saint Augustin* (Paris: Desclée, 1989), 51–82. See also the brief survey of recent scholarship and bibliography from Basil Studer, *The Grace of Christ and the Grace of God in Augustine of Hippo: Christocentrism or Theocentrism?* trans. Matthew J. O'Connell (Collegeville, MN: Liturgical Press, 1997), 10–13.

[37] The works with which we will be concerned in this chapter are as follows: *Contra academicos* (Book 1 probably dates from late 386, Books 2 and 3 from early 387), *De ordine* (Book 1 probably dates from late 386, Book 2 from early 387), *Soliloquia* (again Book 1 probably dates from late 386, Book 2 from early 387), *De beata vita* (winter 386–7, written between the two books of *c. Acad.*).

[38] *ord.* 2. 11.30–1 (CCSL 29. 124–5).

... This All of ours is not Intellect and rational principle, like the All there, but participates in intellect and rational principle ...

(3. 2.16) The rational principle ... is not pure Intellect or absolute Intellect [οὐκ ἄκρατος νοῦς οὐδ'αὐτονοῦς]; it is not even of the kind of pure soul but depends on soul, and is a sort of outshining of both [ἔκλαμψις ἐξ ἀμφοῖν]; intellect and soul (that is, soul disposed according to intellect) generated this rational principle as a life which containing in silence a certain rationality [γεννησάντων τὸν λόγον τοῦτον ζωὴν λόγον τινὰ ἡσυχῇ ἔχουσαν]. All life, even worthless life, is activity [ἐνέργεια] ... So the activity of life is an artistic [τεχνική] activity ... in the universe the battle of conflicting elements springs from a single rational principle; so that it would be better for one to compare it to the melody which results from conflicting sounds.

To draw these passages from Augustine and Plotinus together, Du Roy makes a series of links. First, he parallels Augustine's talk of reason 'proceeding' with the same language used in a more clearly threefold passage at *De ordine* 2. 5.16. In this passage, which we will consider below, Augustine speaks of *principium* and *intellectus*, and seems to speak of a third reality 'flowing' from the second which is then possibly equated with the Spirit.[39] At the same time Du Roy draws attention to yet another threefold passage at *De ordine* 2. 9.26 which appears to link together *principium*, *intellectus* and *ratio*.[40] On the basis of these links, Du Roy argues that *ratio* at *De ordine* 2. 11.30–1 *must* be more than human reason and, agreeing with earlier source work by Aimé Solignac, he suggests that *ratio* is equivalent to the *logos* of *Ennead* 3. 2, flowing from the world-soul (which Du Roy sees hiding under Augustine's *anima rationalis*) and ordering the cosmos.[41] Having drawn these conclusions, Du Roy reads Augustine's extensive discussions of reason's functions in the remainder of the *De ordine* as an outline of the Spirit's functions. Du Roy is not simply arguing that the Plotinian third *hypostasis* is equivalent to Augustine's Holy Spirit. It is the *logos* of the late *Ennead* 3. 2 that he argues is the source of Augustine's earliest pneumatology.[42]

---

[39] See below, pp. 26f.   [40] See *ord.* 2. 9.26 (CCSL 29. 122).

[41] Du Roy, *L'Intelligence*, 130–42, esp. 134–5, See Aimé Solignac, 'Réminiscences plotiniennes et porphyriennes dans le début du "De ordine" de saint Augustin', *Archives de Philosophie* 19 (1936), 148–56.

[42] This *logos* is probably to be understood as the lowest level of soul; see John Rist, *Plotinus: The Road to Reality* (Cambridge: Cambridge University Press, 1967), 84–102. As Gerber, *The Spirit of Augustine's Early Theology*, ch. 2, points out, Robert O'Connell is one of the few who make the direct equation between Plotinian *Psuche* and Augustine's early account of Spirit. Gerber offers a full discussion of O'Connell's argument which shows it to be even more problematic than that of Du Roy. It should be noted that I have here been convinced by Gerber's argument and the

Du Roy's argument is a detective exercise worthy of the most famous inhabitant of 221B Baker Street, but it rests on weakly founded assumptions and contains serious contradictions. First, he assumes that Augustine makes a clear separation between *intellectus* and *ratio* which follows one Plotinus makes between *Nous* and *Logos* in *Ennead* 3. 2. One might fairly easily, however, read Augustine as seeing significant overlap between the two. In such a reading, both of the passages with which Du Roy parallels *De ordine* 2. 11.30ff. might be read as primarily binitarian, speaking of *principium* and *intellectus* but being simply vague about the relationship between *intellectus* and the *ratio* that is personified as coming from the *principium* and being present in us. Du Roy expends no real effort arguing against such a reading other than offering his chain of links. Second, Du Roy assumes that a few statements of uncertain meaning concerning the soul's divinity override Augustine's clear statements that soul – our souls or the world-soul – stands on our side of a basic Creator/created distinction.[43] Indeed, given the compelling evidence that Augustine did for some time accept Plotinus's account of the world-soul,[44] it seems far more likely that Augustine interpreted Plotinus as possessing a binitarian account of the highest reality. The ease with which modern writing has presented Neoplatonic triadic accounts of the highest realities as an 'obvious' source for Christian Trinitarianism obscures from us the variety of ways in which Christians may have read Neoplatonic texts.[45] Third,

---

account in my 'Giving Wings to Nicaea: Reading Augustine's Earliest Trinitarian Theology', *AugStud* 38 (2007), 23–6, is superseded.

[43] See, for example, *ord.* 2. 5.17 (CCSL 29. 116): 'Anima vero unde originem ducat quidve hic agat, quantum distet a Deo, quid habeat proprium quod alternat in utramque naturam …?' The two *naturae* referred to here are the natures of God and the mortal creation. For the essential mortality of the human soul, see *ord.* 2. 11.31 (CCSL 29. 125): 'homo est animal rationale mortale … Nam ut progressus animae usque ad mortalia lapsus est, regressus esse in rationam debit; uno verbo a bestiis, quod rationale, alio a diviniis separator, quod mortale dicitur.' Cf. *ord.* 2. 18.47. The definition of *homo* probably comes from Cicero, *acad.* 2. 7.21. The account of the soul's status can be helpfully compared to Cicero, *Tusc.* 1. 26.65–27.66: Cicero's account of the soul's divinity is both somewhat imprecise and yet far more direct in its assertion than anything we find in Augustine's *ord*. For the possibility of the soul's reformation see, for example, *ord.* 1. 2.4 and 6.10. It seems to me far more plausible that Augustine's uncertainty about describing the nature and role of the soul stems from his still trying to hold to the idea of the individual soul's fall from a pre-lapsarian state, than from his holding to but never stating clearly a belief in the individual soul's participation in the third of Plotinus's three primary realities.

[44] See *imm. an.* 15. 24, *an. quant.* 32. 68, *mus.* 6. 5.13. For discussion, see Roland Teske, 'The World Soul and Time in Augustine', in *To Know God and the Soul: Essays on the Thought of Saint Augustine* (Washington DC: Catholic University of America Press, 2008), 219–23; Gerard O'Daly, 'anima, animus', *AugLex*. The world-soul appears very clearly as the third *hypostasis* in Porphyry; see, for example, *Sent.* 30.

[45] See John Dillon, 'Logos and Trinity: Patterns of Platonist Influence on Early Christianity', in G. Vesey (ed.), *The Philosophy in Christianity* (Cambridge: Cambridge University Press, 1989),

and along similar lines, Du Roy's argument ignores the fact that we lack any text in which Augustine equates the world-soul and the Spirit. It is implausible that Augustine understood and appropriated something of the Plotinian world-soul *and* saw the *Logos* emanating from that world-soul as the Spirit. Thus, while Augustine seems to have appropriated Plotinian language to describe Father and Son with ease (whether or not those parallels also show the influence of his Latin Christian peers), we have no clear evidence that he did the same with regard to the third Plotinian *hypostasis* and the Spirit. Du Roy's hermeneutic of suspicion pushes the texts towards a bridge too far.

I focus on Du Roy's treatment of the Spirit not only because it reveals methodological questions we must ask of his readings *in toto*, but because of its necessity for his argument. For Du Roy's account of Augustine's failure there *must* be a relationship between Augustine's Holy Spirit and some facet of what Du Roy takes to be Plotinus's system. Only thus can Du Roy show that Augustine's earliest Trinitarian theology should be read as in essence a cosmological system enabling our return to the divine. Releasing ourselves from this account of Augustine will enable us to think again not only about his accounts of the Trinity, but also about his accounts of our ascent towards understanding, our progress in knowledge.

THE TRIPOTENT FATHER, SON AND SPIRIT

The foregoing argument should not, however, be taken as a rejection of Du Roy's book *in toto*. Du Roy offers an excellent description of the anti-sceptical and anti-Manichaean context within which Augustine undertook his initial Platonic readings, and at many points he offers penetrating analyses of the sources Augustine engages in these early works. In what follows I suggest an alternate reading of Augustine's earliest Trinitarian debts drawing on (and at times further criticizing) the work of Du Roy, but also drawing heavily on the work of Nello Cipriani.

At *De ordine* 2. 5.16, Augustine identifies God as Father, Son and Spirit:

> that philosophy which is true and – if I may speak thus – genuine, has no other business than to teach what is the Principle without Principle [*principium sine principio*] of all things, and how great an Intellect rests in it [*quantus que in eo maneat intellectus*], and what has flowed from it for our salvation, but without any

---

1–13, for some helpful remarks. Augustine's possible use of Neoplatonic noetic triads – such as being/life/mind – is discussed in Chapters 5 and 10.

Giving wings to Nicaea 27

degeneration [*quidve inde in nostrum salutem sine ulla degeneratione manaverit*]. The venerated mysteries – which liberate people by a sincere and unshaken faith (not confusedly [*confuse*], as some, or abusively [*contumeliose*], as many, charge) – teach that this Principle is one omnipotent God, and that he is the tripotent [*tripotentem*] Father and Son and Holy Spirit.[46]

Du Roy treats this passage as revealing an unsuccessful attempt by Augustine to unite his Plotinian speculation with the 'rule of faith'.[47] In fact, Du Roy's vague reference to the 'rule of faith', while not strictly inaccurate, misses the extent to which Augustine interweaves themes from his non-Christian Neoplatonist readings with expressions of Trinitarian faith found in the key Latin theologians of the 355–80 period. It misses, in other words, Augustine's engagement with the very Latin Nicene theology that one would expect a Christian of his education and location to read.[48]

The term *tripotens* is extremely rare in Christian Latin, and may have been coined by Marius Victorinus, in whose works it appears twice as a synonym for the Greek τριδύναμις.[49] The term was not used by any other Latin Christian author and appears only this once in Augustine's corpus. Nello Cipriani argues that this parallel is the most obvious of a series of links to Victorinus in the passage.[50] For Cipriani, Augustine's description of the Father as *principium sine principio* does not find clear parallels in Plotinus,[51] but such parallels are to be found in the letter of Candidus the

---

[46] *ord.* 2. 5.16 (CCSL 29. 116).
[47] Du Roy, *L'Intelligence*, 113: 'Ces formules, qui attestent une foi déjà très ferme, voisinent avec des très audacieuses spéculations. Aussi faut-il étudier d'abord comment Augustin conçoit le rapport de cette spéculation avec la régle de foi qu'il entend ne jamais transgresser.'
[48] Augustine himself uses the notion of 'rule of faith' in particularly interesting ways, see my 'Augustine on the Rule of Faith: Rhetoric, Christology, and the Foundation of Christian Thinking', *AugStud* 36 (2005), 33–49.
[49] Victorinus, *adv. Ar.* 1. 50 (CSEL 83/1. 144–5): 'hic est deus ... tripotens in unalitate spiritus ... tres potentias ...'; 1. 56 (CSEL 83/1. 153): 'Facta enim a tripotenti spiritu'. The Greek term is to be found at 4. 21 (CSEL 83/1. 257): 'τριδύναμις est deus, id est tres potentias habens'.
[50] Nello Cipriani, 'Le fonti cristiana della dottrina trinitaria nei primi Dialoghi di S. Agostino', *Aug(R)* 34 (1994), 253–312, here 264–5. Cipriani is one of only a few contemporary scholars who are prepared to countenance Augustine knowing Victorinus's anti-'Arian' works: though he maintains this opinion not in the face of scholarly opposition, but in the face of a scholarly assumption that has received virtually no attempt at validation in recent decades. In Chapter 10 I consider Augustine's possible use of Victorinus in *trin*. See also Cipriani, 'Le opere di Sant'Ambrogio negli scritti di Sant'Agostino anteriori all'episcopato', *La Scuola Cattolica* 125 (1997), 763–800. Two other pieces of particular significance for the interpretation of the texts with which I will be concerned in this chapter are F. Cavallera, 'Les premières formules trinitaires de s. Augustin', *Bulletin de Littérature Ecclésiastique* 31 (1930), 97–123, and J. Verhees, 'Augustins Trinitätsverständnis in den Schriften aus Cassiciacum', *RecAug* 10 (1975), 45–75.
[51] At *Enn.* 1.8.2 – a text Augustine probably read in 386 – the One is described as the *arche* of all. The possibility of influence from Plotinus here is increased when we note that there are strong parallels between the same Plotinian text and *b. vita* 4. 34, discussed in the next section of this chapter.

'Arian' possibly composed by Victorinus as a foil for his own refutation, and the phrase is again used (with approval) in Victorinus's reply.⁵² When we come to Augustine's equation of the Son and *intellectus* we could, of course, fairly easily read this as Augustine's adaptation of Plotinian *Nous*.⁵³ But, if we are secure in noting the other two parallels in Victorinus, then we can at least say that Augustine must have known Victorinus's own description of the Son as *intellectus* and *Nous*.⁵⁴ Moreover, Augustine's description of this *intellectus* as *in [principio] maneat* parallels Victorinus's description of the *Logos* as *in patre manens*.⁵⁵ Cipriani's preference here is for Victorinus as Augustine's source, but I think it more important to note the complexity Cipriani reveals. The evidence does not permit us to make a clear decision between these two possible sources in every case; but overall it does render highly plausible the judgement that Augustine is engaged with both.

It is impossible to discern with certainty the Trinitarian reference of, or sources for, the brief mention in Augustine's text of that which flows from the Son *sine ulla degeneratione manaverit*. Cipriani argues that the verb *mano* is not used in Augustine's early works in a sense that demands we translate as 'emanate', which might be taken to indicate a relationship between Augustine's earliest pneumatology and Plotinus's third *hypostasis*.⁵⁶ Then Cipriani suggests that the text might be taken to be a reference to the Incarnate Christ's descent. But there does seem to be a parallel here to Victorinus's account of the generation of Son and Spirit occurring *nulla ... mutatione*.⁵⁷ While we are now in the realm of speculation, Cipriani has convincingly shown the problematic status of Du Roy's reading.

---

⁵² See *ad. Cand.* 1. 3 (CCSL 83/1. 4): 'Principium autem sine principio. Praecedit enim nullum principium ante se habens'; cf. Victorinus, *ad Cand.* 16 (CSEL 83/1. 33–4). See Cipriani, 'Fonti Christiane', 264–8.

⁵³ The equivalence of *Nous* and *intellectus* is clear enough: the depth of the connection may be seen, for example, in the parallel between Augustine's description of *intellectus* at *ord*. 2. 9.26 as 'in qui universa sunt, vel ipse potius universa' and Plotinus's language at *Enn*. 1. 8.2 and 5. 3.5.

⁵⁴ For example Victorinus, *adv. Ar.* 1. 60.

⁵⁵ Victorinus, *adv. Ar.* 1. 44 (CSEL 83/1. 134). Cf. Ambrose *fid*. 4. 11.143ff.

⁵⁶ Cipriani, 'Fonti Christiane', 266–7. Nevertheless, one cannot rule out a reference to the Spirit. Note, for example, the uses of the same verb to describe God's providential bestowing of goods at *sol*. 1. 1.4, and its use at *b. vita*. 2. 10 to describe what seems to be an allusion to the Spirit's *inflammatio* of Monica (CCSL 29. 71): 'quantum, poteram, intellegente, ex quo illa et quam divino fonte manarent'. In discussing Du Roy's account of *ord*. 2. 11.30, I emphasized the range of assumptions he makes about both Augustine and Plotinus: in the assumption that language of 'emanation' indicates an identity marker of Neoplatonism, I suggest we see a further dimension of the common but erroneous assumptions about Neoplatonism made by scholars of Augustine.

⁵⁷ Victorinus, *adv. Ar.* 4. 21 (CSEL 83/1. 257).

My interest here, however, is not simply in this series of parallels to Victorinus, but also in what Augustine does *not* take from Victorinus. Most importantly, Augustine fails to copy Victorinus's description of the Trinity as *tres potentiae*, a phrase used in the very same texts in which we find *tripotens*. In fact, other than Victorinus, no Latin Nicene Christian author of the fourth century describes God as *tres potentiae*: in the context of late fourth-century pro-Nicene theology, description of God as *una potentia* had become a standard and central formulation.[58] Although Augustine does not yet seem to grasp the extent to which the unity of the divine power was a standard statement of late fourth-century pro-Nicene orthodoxy, in his use of *tripotens* but avoidance of *tres potentiae* we may detect a rudimentary awareness of where Victorinus's theology was idiosyncratic and unacceptable within Augustine's immediate context.

While the prayer with which the *Soliloquia* opens makes no use of power terminology, it does provide a contemporary indication that Augustine already understood Latin Nicene insistence on the divine unity.[59] The prayer begins by addressing the Father as *Deus*, the same term is then used in subsequent phrases which seem to address both Son and Spirit, and the whole passage concludes with the statement that God is 'one God ... one true eternal substance, where is no discord, no confusion ... where Begetter and Begotten are one'.[60] For Augustine to understand the problem with Victorinus's *tres potentiae*, and to be able to replicate statements of the divine unity, he did not need a very detailed knowledge of contemporary Latin Nicene theology, but some knowledge of basic principles is evident — and while Augustine could well have gained this knowledge in conversation with someone such as Simplicianus, we have strong evidence for an initial literary engagement with Latin Nicenes towards the end of 386.[61]

---

[58] See Michel René Barnes, '"One Nature, One Power": Consensus Doctrine in Pro-Nicene Polemic', *SP* 29 (1997), 205–23. At the beginning of the next chapter I discuss the characteristics of Latin pro-Nicene theology.

[59] It must also be remarked that 'power' is rarely an important technical term in Trinitarian theology for Augustine. It is not until late in his career (c.418) that the unity of the divine power appears in summary statements of the divine unity. See, for example, *symb. cat.* 5 and 9; *trin.* 15.3.5, *serm.* 215. 8. This absence tells us little about when Augustine encountered the terminology: it is clear enough that he had, for example, read Ambrose's *De fide* long before 418. In his attack on Faustus (c.398–400) he is also able to articulate a basic definition of power: *c. Faust.* 20. 2 (CSEL 25/1. 542): 'ad uirtutem pertinere uideatur operari et efficere'.

[60] *sol.* 1. 4. (CSEL 89. 7): 'unus deus ... una aeterna et vera substantia, ubi nulla discrepantia, nulla confusion ... ubi qui gignit et quem gignit, unum est'.

[61] Cipriani also suggests a variety of other parallels that seem less compelling. A few, however, deserve note. With reference to this passage, Goulven Madec had suggested that Augustine's description of the mysteries as liberating not 'confusedly' (*confuse*) or 'abusively' (*contumeliose*)

30   *Origins*

In this light it is unlikely either that Augustine's Trinitarianism took form primarily as the filling out of the 'rule of faith' with Plotinian content, or that the full force of Augustine's Trinitarianism is economic. His concern in his earliest texts is most certainly to articulate a notion of God that opposes both Manichaeanism and Scepticism, and to that end Augustine emphasizes God's establishment of a unified and intelligible created order that enables human return to contemplation of God (as we shall discuss further in the following chapters). But, at the same time, Augustine is already struggling to integrate material from non-Christian Platonism with an account of God *in se* found in contemporary Latin theology, most likely learned from Victorinus and Ambrose.

DE BEATA VITA

To take our argument forward we must look back. The short dialogue *De beata vita* was completed in the winter of 386/7 during the writing of the *Contra Academicos* (and probably only a few months before *De ordine* 2), and thus is Augustine's first completed writing as a Christian.[62] At its end we find:

> Thus, whoever is happy possesses his measure, that is, wisdom [*habet ergo modum suum, id est sapientiam*]. (34) But what wisdom should be so called, if not the wisdom of God? We have also heard through divine authority that the Son of God is nothing but the Wisdom of God, and the Son of God is truly God … But do you believe that Wisdom is different from truth? For it has also been said: 'I am the Truth'. The Truth, however, receives its being through a supreme measure, from which it proceeds and towards whom it turns itself when perfected [*Veritas autem ut sit, fit per aliquem summum modum, a quo procedit et in quem se perfecta convertit*] … Who is the Son of God? It has been said The Truth. Who is it that has no father? Who other than the supreme measure? … (35) A certain admonition [*admonitio*], flowing from the very fountain of truth urges

---

was perhaps a reference to the two alternatives of Sabellianism (which confused the persons) and Arianism (which Augustine saw as offering an account that outrageously insulted the Son). Cipriani builds on this suggestion by noting that the terms used in *ord.* parallel *discrepentia* and *confusio* at *sol.* 1. 1.4 (for both Madec and Cipriani, see Cipriani, 'Le opere di Sant'Ambrogio', 768–9). He then notes that on a number of occasions Ambrose describes Sabellius as confusing the persons and the 'Arians' as introducing a separation (*discretio*) of power between Father and Son and as insulting the Son when they claim that 1Cor. 15.42–28 implies the Son's ontological subordination. See Ambrose, *fid.* 1. 1.6, 1. 1.8, 2. 3.33, 5. 12.149 (Ambrose's phrasing may owe something to the letter sent west by the Council of Constantinople in 382). Cipriani similarly parallels Augustine's description of God as *una aeterna vera substantia, ubi nulla discrepentia* with Ambrose's *una sola substantia divinitatis* and his comment on Father and Son, *quibus non discrepare inter se*.

[62] *retr.* 1. 2.

us to remember God, to seek Him, and thirst after Him tirelessly. This hidden sun pours into our innermost eyes that beaming light ... Our mother, recalling here those words that still deeply adhered in her memory, awoke to her faith, as it were, and, inflamed with joy, uttered this verse of our priest: 'nurture those that pray, O Trinity'.[63]

Du Roy acknowledges that in Augustine's description of the Son as Wisdom and Truth we probably see reference to 1 Corinthians 1.24 and John 14.6, but he suggests that we may also see Plotinus's portrayal in *Ennead* 5. 5.8 of Intellect as Wisdom itself and Wisdom as true substance.[64] The heart of Du Roy's treatment, however, concerns Augustine's description of the Father as *summum modum* and of the Son as perfected in generation by turning towards that measure. Augustine is the first Latin theologian to speak of the Father as *summum modum*, and the title is confined to his earliest and Manichaean works.[65] Du Roy (again following Solignac) sees a variety of Plotinian sources behind this language.[66] At *Ennead* 5. 5.4, Plotinus states that the One is the measure of all subsequent to it, and yet not measured. The One cannot be understood as the unity of the duality that is subsequent to it, as if the first in a numerical series.[67] In *Ennead*. 1. 8.2 the One is the measure and limit (μέτρον πάντων καὶ πέρας) of all else, and on this basis Plotinus asserts the non-existence of evil. In this language we probably see one source for the links Augustine draws between the nature of God and the non-existence of evil.[68] At the same time, Augustine's understanding of the Son as turning to the supreme measure 'when perfected' possibly represents a garbled version of

---

[63] *b. vita* 33–5 (CCSL 29. 84–5). The final quotation is from Ambrose, *Hymn* 2 ('Deus Creator Omnium'). If we can suppose that Augustine knew the full text of the final verse from which Monica quotes, then he had already to hand at least one concise statement of the unity of the divine power: 'Christum rogamus et Patrem, Christi Patrisque Spiritum; unum potens per omnia, fove precantes, Trinitas'.

[64] Du Roy, *L'Intelligence*, 155. See Plotinus, *Enn*. 5. 5.8: εἰ ὁ νοῦς ἐγέννησε τὴν σοφίαν· καὶ εἰ φήσουσι, πόθεν; Εἰ δὲ ἐξ αὐτοῦ, ἀδύνατον ἄλλως ἢ αὐτὸν ὄντα σοφίαν. Ἦ ἄρα ἀληθινὴ σοφία οὐσία, καὶ ἡ ἀληθινὴ οὐσία σοφία. The use of *sapientia* in this text does not necessarily reflect 1Cor. 1.24, but the contemporary reference at *c. Acad*. 2. 1.1 is certain and demonstrates that Augustine already knows something of the text's utility.

[65] The term occurs at *c. Acad*. 2. 2, *b. vita* 4. 34, *div. qu*. 6, *nat. b*. 22, 41, and almost at *c. Sec*. 9. Augustine's fullest and clearest usage is at *nat. b*. 22.

[66] Du Roy, *L'Intelligence*, 156–61.

[67] *Enn*. 5. 5.4: '[the One] is a measure and not measured [μέτρον γὰρ αὐτὸ καὶ οὐ μετρούμενον]'.

[68] We should, however, be careful at this point. Plotinus is not simply content (as is Augustine) with asserting evil's non-existence: while he is clear that the soul's evil consists in a declension from goodness and beauty, he also assumes that absolute/primal/essential evil may well be some sort of form of formlessness and stand in relation to the existence of matter as such (*Enn*. 1. 8.3ff.). As ever, Augustine's Platonism is very much his own.

Plotinus's account of the manner in which Intellect is constituted by its gaze upon the one in *Ennead* 5. 1:

> [Soul] is a reflection of intellect – and for this reason it has to look to Intellect; but Intellect in the same way has to look to that God, in order to be Intellect … by its return to it it sees: and this seeing is Intellect.[69]

Du Roy will be on far thinner ice when he turns to the pneumatological material in the passage and to its overall import, but we will come to this separately.

When Cipriani treats this passage he cannot resist pointing out that Du Roy's analysis shows 'un certo imbarrazzo' precisely because Du Roy has been forced to acknowledge Augustine's complex *adaptation* of Plotinian language to his Christian context.[70] Cipriani then suggests that Augustine's patterns of adaptation are themselves echoed in Victorinus. Even if there is no one sentence which directly parallels Augustine's formulations, statements that Christ is the Truth, that the Father is the cause of the Son and the Son 'proceeds' from the Father may be found together on a single page of Victorinus's *Adversus Arium* 1.[71] Cipriani argues that we also find in Victorinus the same combination of technical language linking the Son's procession with the idea of the Son's conversion to the Father.[72] Augustine's insistence that there would be no Truth without

---

[69] *Enn.* 5. 1.6–7: ἀλλὰ ψυχῆς μὲν ἀμυδρὸς ὁ λόγος–ὡς γὰρ εἴδωλον νοῦ– ταύτῃ καὶ εἰς νοῦν βλέπειν δεῖ· νοῦς δὲ ὡσαύτως πρὸς ἐκεῖνον, ἵνα ᾖ νοῦς … ἢ ὅτι τῇ ἐπιστροφῇ πρὸς αὐτὸ ἑώρα· ἡ δὲ ὅρασις αὕτη νοῦς. See also *Enn.* 5. 1.5, 5. 3.11, 5. 4.2ff., 6. 7. I quote from 5 . 1 because of our near certainty that Augustine knew a translation of this text, despite the fact that in the last sentence the subject of ἑώρα is unclear. It could be either the One or Intellect: we have no idea how the translation that Augustine encountered read. In asserting that the Truth turns towards the supreme measure 'when perfected' Augustine seems not to grasp Plotinus's point. There is, as we shall see in Chapter 9, some question as to whether Augustine made use of this Plotinian theme in his mature account of the Son's 'seeing' of the Father.

[70] Cipriani, 'Fonti cristiane', 269.

[71] Cipriani, 'Fonti cristiane', 270. See Victorinus, *adv. Ar.* 1. 13–14 (CSEL 83/1. 72–3): 'Sed maior Pater, quod ipse dedit ipsi omnia et causa est ipsi filio … Christus enim veritas … Quod Christus et a patre processit'.

[72] Cipriani, 'Fonti cristiane', 270–1. Here Cipriani combines two passages from Victorinus. First, *adv. Ar.* 1. 13 (CSEL 83/1. 72): 'Filius autem, ut esset, accepit et in id quod est agere ab actione procedens in perfectionem veniens, motu efficitur plenitude'. With this Cipriani links the account of the Son's conversion towards the Father in *adv. Ar.* 1. 51 (CSEL 83/1. 147): 'rursus in semet ipsam conversa, venit in suam patricam existentiam … et perfecta in omnipotentem virtutem'. Cipriani is drawn to this text because of its use of *conversa*, but in context the text may well be concerned with the Incarnation as much as the eternal generation. Nevertheless, the idea Cipriani needs is expressed even more clearly a few lines above without any ambiguity (CSEL 83/1. 147): 'Sed quoniam … ista motio, una cum sit, et vita est et sapientia, vita conversa in sapientiam et magis in existentiam patricam, magis autem retor motae motionis, in patricam potentiam'. It should, however, be noted that Augustine's 'in quem se perfecta convertit' is odd in seeming to locate the moment of perfecting prior to the turn to the Father. Victorinus is closer

Measure, or vice versa, is paralleled by both Victorinus's and Ambrose's sense that Father and Son are mutually entailing.[73] Finally – and here he stretches the parallel – Cipriani suggests that Augustine's language of the Father as *summum modum* finds a precedent in Victorinus's description of the Father as *inmensus* but the Son as *mensus atque inmensus*.[74]

Cipriani, however, treats this text differently from *De ordine* 2. 5.16. There he attempted to replace Plotinus as the most significant source with Victorinus; here he argues that Augustine's very probable engagement with Plotinus is shaped by his reading of Victorinus and Ambrose.[75] Although I think Du Roy and others before him are correct in their identification of the sources for Augustine's description of the Father as *summum modum*, Cipriani shows here that we need to envisage Augustine undertaking these adaptations in the context of reading other Latin pro-Nicene theologians who read non-Christian Platonists in similar ways. His adaptation of this theme, for example, follows well-established Nicene precedent in presenting the *summum modum* as a Son who is also truly God: the dynamic of unity and distinction between the *summum modum* and God is expressed in Nicene Trinitarian language, not that of any potential non-Christian source. Thus, we need not only to consider the most plausible sources for particular terminologies, we need also to consider the ways in which multiple sources may be reflected, and the ways in which Augustine's Christian readings may be guiding his readings in non-Christian Platonism.

Augustine's description of the 'hidden sun' pouring its 'beaming light' is, Du Roy plausibly suggests, founded in the language of Ambrose's hymns, specifically *Splendor Paternae Gloriae*. Ambrose speaks of the Sun as the 'true Sun' sending its radiance, the Spirit, to illuminate the sensible world.[76] Du Roy, however, also asserts that Augustine interprets this language by means of the notion of *ratio* as it appears in the *Soliloquia* and the *De ordine*.[77] For Du Roy, Augustine uses *admonitio*

---

to Plotinus, as is the mature Augustine (see the discussion of Augustine's interpretation of John 5.19 in Chapter 9).
[73] Cipriani, 'Fonti cristiane', 271. As examples, Cipriani gives Victorinus, *adv. Ar.* 3. 17.20, 1. 42.18; Ambrose, *fid.* 1. 8.55, 4. 9.108.
[74] Victorinus, *Hymn* 1. 11 (CSEL 83/1. 286).
[75] Cipriani, 'Fonti cristiane', 270: 'È opportuno però osservare che alcuni di questi terni potrbebbero essere giunti ad Agostino non solo dalla lettura diretta delle *Enneadi*, ma anche attraverso il filtro delle fonti cristiane'.
[76] Ambrose, *hymn* 2. 5–8 (Fontaine, *Ambroise*, 185): 'Verusque sol, illabere / micans nitore perpeti, / iubarque Sancti Spiritus / infunde nostris sensibus.' For commentary, see Fontaine, *Ambroise*, 188–92.
[77] Du Roy, *L'Intelligence*, 164.

in two discrete senses: the external *admonitio* consists of the teaching of Christ or another teacher whose role is to direct us inwards; the internal *admonitio* is the *ratio* which leads us to contemplate God and is the Spirit.[78]

Cipriani and others have attacked this account, first, by undermining the clear distinction between senses of *admonitio* that Du Roy describes.[79] The term has a foundation in Latin rhetorical tradition where it describes advice or a mild form of *obiurgatio* or pithy rebuke intended to recall someone to awareness of appropriate ends, often by suggesting an appropriate model for imitation.[80] The term is also often distinguished from teaching as such, thus undermining the certainty with which Du Roy locates a certain type of *admonitio* as teaching administered by Christ. Augustine has likely chosen this term because of its traditional connotations in a discussion of the moral life. Furthermore, while Augustine does speak of external and internal *admonitiones*, a number of texts from Augustine's early (if not earliest) works state directly that the two *admonitiones* both form hope and love in the Christian.[81]

Moreover, Augustine's attribution of these functions to the Spirit is best understood, Cipriani argues, within the general thrust of other Latin pro-Nicene theology. Both Ambrose and Victorinus describe one of the Spirit's roles as providing confidence in the faith and knowledge that shapes hope and love, even if the technical rhetorical term *admonitio* is not used directly of the Spirit. Ambrose presents Gratian as handing back the Basilica that had been appropriated for Homoian worship because the Spirit internally instructed Gratian so strongly in the true faith that no external *admonitio* was needed.[82] In a more directly theological vein, Cipriani points to Victorinus's description of the Spirit as complementing the work of Christ by providing knowledge and assurance.[83] These

---

[78] Du Roy, *L'intelligence*, 163–5.
[79] Cipriani, 'Fonti cristiane', 272–81; Jean Doignon, 'La "praxis" de l'admonitio dans les dialogues de Cassiciacum de Saint Augustin', *Vetera Christianorum* 23 (1986), 21–37; for a general treatment of the term in Augustine, see Goulven Madec, '*admonitio*' in *AugLex*.
[80] See, for example, Cicero, *orat*. 2. 83.339. The fullest ancient discussion is to be found in Seneca, *ep*. 94. 25. Quintilian *inst*. 4. 1 offers another nice example of the function of *admonitio* as a device focused on the goal of moving the emotions: 'cuius animus [that is, the mind of the *iudex*] spe metu admonitione precibus, vanitate denique, si id profuturum credemus, agitandus est. Sunt et illa excitandis ad audiendum non inutilia'.
[81] Cipriani cites *div. qu*. 83. 68.5 (c.390?) and *lib. arb*. 3. 20.57 (396?), both of which speak of internal and external drawing by God, but neither of which uses the language of *admonitio*, and *Simpl*. 1. 2.2 (c.396), which does (CCSL 44. 25): 'incipit autem homo percipere gratiam, ex quo incipit deo credere uel interna uel externa admonitione motus ad fidem'.
[82] Ambrose, *spir*. 1. 1.19.   [83] Victorinus, *adv. Ar*. 4. 17.

parallels help to some extent, but they become more convincing when we place our text from *De beata vita* in the wider context of Augustine's other very earliest pneumatological discussion.

The prayer with which the *Soliloquia* commence includes the following section, a section more dense with scriptural citation than any other in the earliest work:

> God, through whom we conquer the enemy [cf. 1John 4.4], it is you whom I beseech; God through whom it has been granted us that we should not perish utterly; God by whom we are reminded so that we might remain on guard; God through whom we separate good from evil; God through whom we flee evil and pursue good … God through whom 'death is swallowed up in victory' [1Cor. 15.54]; God who converts us; God who strips us of that which is not and clothes us with that which is [cf. 1Cor. 15.53–4]; God who makes it possible for us to be heard; God who fortifies us; God who leads us into all truth [John 16.13] … God, who sees to it that 'to those who knock it will be opened' [Matt. 7.8]; God who gives us the 'bread of life' [John 6.38, 45]; God through whom we thirst to drink, and after that drink we will thirst no more [see John 6.35]; God who brings to the world the knowledge of sin, and of justice, and of judgement [John 16.8]; God through whom we condemn the error of those who think that there is no merit in souls before your eyes; God, through whom we are not enslaved to 'weak and needy elements' [Gal. 4.9]; God, who cleanses us and prepares us and for our heavenly reward: come to me in your kindness.[84]

Only Jean Doignon in recent years has argued that the passage as a whole is not structured as a threefold appeal to each of the persons of the Trinity. Doignon prefers to read the text as following established philosophical forms and as a sequential treatment of various aspects of God's role in the soul's ascent.[85] Few scholars have been convinced that Doignon's analysis entirely undermines the plausibility of a Trinitarian reading; it seems more likely that Doignon has opened the way towards seeing this passage as another in which a wide variety of Christian and non-Christian sources are combined. In the prayer as a whole – beyond the passage quoted above – Neoplatonic influence is most clear in Augustine's presentation of the Father as the source of an intelligible and harmonic cosmic order, and of the Son as Truth, Wisdom, Life and the intelligible Light in whom existence itself occurs. It is to this existence in the Truth that we must be recalled through purification. The first two Trinitarian

---

[84] *sol.* 1. 3 (CSEL 89. 6–7; text modified).
[85] Jean Doignon, 'La Prière liminaire des *Soliloquia* dans la ligne philosophique des Dialogues de Cassiciacum', in J. den Boeft and J. van Oort (eds.), *Augustiniana Traiectana* (Paris: Études Augustiniennes, 1987), 85–105, here 87–9. On the prayer, see also Du Roy, *L'intelligence*, 201–3; Cipriani, 'Fonti cristiane', 290–4.

persons are thus entreated within a prayer structured by a vision of ascent and the cosmos typical of the early works.[86]

Doignon reads the section of text quoted above as following the same fundamental lines, the scriptural material merely filling out fundamentally Stoic and Neoplatonic philosophical themes.[87] While Doignon may be correct in his identification of Augustine's philosophical sources, he offers no explanation of why Augustine chooses in this one section to use scriptural texts so densely. Without simply arguing for exclusively theological sources, in opposition to Doignon's classical set, I suggest we can read this discussion as reflecting a very early attempt by Augustine to articulate a pneumatology within a pro-Nicene context, but one that demonstrates Augustine has yet to seize upon any clear focus. Some of the texts Augustine cites are clearly pneumatological. John 16.8 and 16.13 are the most obvious, but they give us little idea of his immediate theological context. Some of the texts are much less obviously pneumatological, Matthew 7.8 and Galatians 4.9. As Cipriani observes, while neither of these texts is used in pneumatological contexts by Victorinus or Ambrose, Victorinus's *Hymn* 2 directly attributes to the Spirit the function of opening the gates of heaven as the witness to Christ.[88] There is, however, more to be said.

Echoes of pro-Nicene pneumatology appear clearly when we consider the *functions* attributed to the Spirit in this passage. The understanding of the Spirit as sustaining in existence is found in both Victorinus and Ambrose.[89] Ambrose also frequently refers to the role of the Spirit in raising the dead (and using 1Cor. 15.52), in part because of a concern to show that the one who works in Christians is the one who has the power of raising the dead.[90] Thus, against a reading of this passage as focused entirely on the Spirit's role in the moral life, Augustine may well be following pro-Nicene precedent in identifying the Spirit's work as that of one who operates with the power of God. The use of John 6.35 and 6.38 or 45 is distinctively Augustine's.

The passage also locates the use of *admonitio* within a wider theological context. *De beata vita* 4. 4–5 and *Soliloquia* 1. 1.3 indicate that Augustine's earliest pneumatology is not best interpreted as the adaptation of Plotinus's *Logos*, but as an attempt to accommodate his initial grasp of pro-Nicene pneumatology within a notion of ascent deeply shaped by his

---

[86] Doignon, 'La Prière liminaire', 89–93.   [87] Doignon, 'La Prière liminaire', 93–6.
[88] Victorinus, *hymn*. 2. 111.   [89] Victorinus, *hymn*. 3. 11; Ambrose *spir*. 2. 5.33 and 35.
[90] Ambrose, *spir*. 3. 20.153–21.159; *exc. Sat*. 2. 75–6.

initial readings in Neoplatonism. Once again we are negotiating a field of uncertainty bounded by Augustine's earliest Christian literary engagements. It is not at all clear how the Spirit's eternal role is envisaged, but we have already seen enough hints to know that Augustine has begun to devote attention to the eternal relationship of Father and Son, and Augustine presents the Spirit here, at a minimum, as a third who operates with divine power.

AUGUSTINE'S ENGAGEMENTS

We must, then, move away from envisaging the independent genius of Augustine using selections of the *Enneads* to reinterpret Latin philosophical tradition and fill out the bare bones of a traditional 'rule of faith'. When we build on the best of Cipriani's arguments to correct Du Roy it is most plausible that Augustine's earliest Trinitarian theology resulted from a reading of both non-Christian and Christian Platonists, the latter sources (most probably Victorinus and Ambrose in the winter of 386–7) being deeply imbued with both adapted Platonic doctrines and some key themes of late fourth-century Latin pro-Nicene theology. Our task, then, is to find a way of describing the relationship between two streams of literary engagement that probably began during the latter half of 386, months before Augustine's baptism. I suggest three conclusions follow from the investigations of this chapter that help towards this end:

(1) Augustine adopted and adapted themes from non-Christian Platonic texts in three areas: his account of the character of divine existence as immaterial, omnipresent and simple; his account of the Father's role as *principium* in the Trinity; his account of the Son as *intellectus*. The first we have not discussed in any detail in this chapter, even though it is presupposed in all of the texts we have considered. This theme is fundamental in Augustine's anti-Manichaean and anti-Sceptical arguments for the cosmos as an intelligible order stemming from the creative activity of the Father (in the Son and through the Spirit).[91] When we see how Augustine also insists on the informing and illuminating presence of the second person throughout the cosmos as continually equal to and 'in' the first, then it is clear that his understanding of the divine nature already provides Augustine with the context in which to assert that the irreducibility of Father, Son and Spirit does not imply belief in three deities or a

---

[91] Chapter 2 offers more extensive references to this theme in the earliest works.

hierarchy of divinity. His arguments to this effect are still hesitant: they will change and mature considerably.

The second and third themes – Augustine's account of the Father's role as *principium* in the Trinity, and his account of the Son as *intellectus* – are apparent in both the *De ordine* and *De beata vita* texts, as we have seen at some length. These two themes not only helped Augustine develop his understanding of the Father's and the Son's individual characteristics, but also of their mutual relations. Augustine understands the Son's equality and inseparability from the Father through an account of the Son as the *intellectus* resting in the Father, and as the Wisdom and Son born from the Father. That the Father is *principium* of Son and Spirit is already clear, although we can say little as yet about the character of that *principium*.

(2) This last example draws our attention to one of the central features of Augustine's early engagement with Neoplatonism in the area of Trinitarian theology: his adaptation is shaped by his understanding of some basic pro-Nicene principles about the relations between the persons. While Augustine draws on some features of Plotinus's account of *Nous* and its relationship to the One, many features that Plotinus would think of as necessary are ignored because of the demands of pro-Nicene theology.

Thus, Augustine's initial readings in Latin Nicene theology seem to have both encouraged and bounded his adaptations of non-Christian Neoplatonism. Latin Nicene theologians – especially Victorinus and Ambrose – *encouraged* Augustine in the sense that they modelled for him ways of using the non-Christian Platonist texts he simultaneously encountered, and areas where such adaptation might be fruitful. At the same time our evidence seems to suggest that his readings in Latin Nicene theology also *bounded* Augustine's adaptation. This 'bounding' does not imply that Augustine's adaptation of non-Christian Platonism was not highly personal, it only indicates that the boundaries within which that adaptation occurred were established by the adaptations of his predecessors and peers, and by the dynamics of their existing theologies. In some cases Augustine directly copies aspects of earlier adaptation, in others he develops his own adaptation but follows clear parallels in his Christian sources. But, as I have noted, he already seems to be aware of how a theology such as that of Ambrose offers a standard of orthodoxy in his context in ways that Victorinus's cannot.

In this analysis, it is also the case that Augustine's earliest Trinitarian theology cannot be understood as functionally economic. While in these earliest works we observe Augustine attempting to articulate an account of God and world that will enable our return to God, it is clear that he was simultaneously beginning to articulate an understanding of how the three irreducible and co-equal persons might be understood to constitute the one God.

(3) We can identify some points at which Augustine did *not* draw to any great extent on the doctrines he found in his early Neoplatonic readings. It is difficult to show that Augustine took from non-Christian Platonism significant material that guided his earliest pneumatology.[92] In broader terms, there is no convincing evidence that Augustine took from Plotinus a conception of *three* 'primary realities' that shaped his overall account of the relations between Father, Son and Spirit. Indeed, one can fairly ask whether there is proof that Augustine at this stage understood Plotinus to have an account of three primary *hypostases*, all of whom Augustine would have recognized as divine. Our evidence allows no certain answer, but it is at least plausible that Augustine saw the three *hypostases* as One, *Nous* and the world-soul (this last being understood as more a created than a divine reality).[93] There may, then, be far more accuracy than scholars customarily assume in Augustine's comment in *Confessiones* 7 that he was encouraged in his initial readings in non-Christian Platonism by finding there echoes of Christian belief in the Father and Son, God and Word.[94] The comment may well be true *both* in the sense that Augustine read those non-Christian texts at the same time and to some extent in the light of his developing understanding of Christian belief *and* in the sense that in those non-Christian texts what he found was indeed echoes of belief in Father and Son, not Spirit.[95]

I suspect that if overheard by many modern theologians my account of Augustine's earliest theology would seem only a little less problematic than Du Roy's. I share with Du Roy the assumption that some Platonic

---

[92] In addition to the directly textual arguments offered in this chapter, it is strange that while Augustine's use of Plotinian material to describe Father and Son is fairly obvious, Du Roy himself has to admit the difficulty of showing the Plotinian sources for Augustine's earliest pneumatology. Why is Augustine's appropriation so hard to trace in the case of this one *hypostasis*?

[93] One might ask whether Augustine engages in any detail with Neoplatonic noetic triads such as that of being/life/mind. I discuss this question in Chapters 5 and 10. There is no presence of such triads in Trinitarian discussions in Augustine's earliest works.

[94] *conf.* 7. 9.13.

[95] I think the first time Augustine directly attributes to a Neoplatonist author belief in *three* divine realities is in his discussion of Porphyry at *civ.* 10. 23 (CCSL 47. 296–7). The passage is an interesting one in the light of this chapter's discussion both because Augustine is clearly puzzled at Porphyry's account (and note that he does not see it as parallel to his own account of the Spirit as *vinculum*) and because Augustine appears to attribute to Plotinus precisely a view of the *principales substantiae* as One, *Nous* and World-Soul.

doctrines were fundamental to Augustine's Trinitarian theology. I also assume that this is so for virtually all significant fourth- and fifth-century Trinitarian writers. Du Roy and I, of course, differ markedly about how Augustine's particular engagement with Platonic doctrines shaped his theology. One of the ways in which we differ is that Du Roy assumes – in a manner that unites him with the greater number of modern systematic theologians – that the degree of influence 'Platonism' has on a theology is virtually an index by which we may judge its corruption. The account I have offered in this chapter not only questions Du Roy's hermeneutic of suspicion as a bad method of reading intellectual development, but it also (if implicitly) questions his assumption that Platonism necessarily corrupts.

Developments in post-critical exegesis have opened the way for very different attitudes to the relationship between Platonic and Christian doctrines. Theologians and historians of theology are now more likely to view the history of exegesis as revealing a plurality of methods rather than a progress from less to more scientific interpretation. In this more pluralistic climate students of early Christianity have become much more attentive to the particular reading practices that shaped pre-modern theologians as they explored the text of Scripture in doctrinal reflection. Elsewhere I have argued for our recognizing the importance of 'grammatical' exegesis within the doctrinal debates of the fourth and early fifth centuries. By the term 'grammatical' I refer to the sorts of reading practices that were learnt at the hands of the *grammaticus* and the *rhetor*. Three such techniques deserve note here. First, one technique already deeply embedded within Christian exegetical practice by Augustine's time was the consideration of particular pieces of scriptural vocabulary by means of the persuasive philosophical and scientific resources of late antiquity. Thus, scriptural use of such terms as *dunamis, hypostasis, ousia* was understood as appropriately parsed by using contemporary arguments about the meaning of such terms. Second, ancient readers learnt to interpret particular scriptural terms and statements in the light of parallels from elsewhere in the text. Third, the same ancient readers learnt to interpret particular sections of text within an overall construction of a text's argument and structure. Once we see how such reading practices constituted a particular style of doctrinal exegesis, and not simply a bad anticipation of modern scholarly practice, then we find ourselves as scholars facing new and hard questions about how we judge the effects of Platonic doctrines on any given author.

One cannot simply assume that the presence of doctrines that originate with non-Christian Platonic authors entails a given author being inevitably subject to the intellectual positions that are supposed to be the necessary corollaries of *any* 'Platonism'. We must make a variety of philosophical, theological and aesthetic judgements about the manner in which and the skill with which Platonic doctrines are integrated with texts taken to be authoritative. We will need, of course, to do so in different ways or to different ends depending on whether we see ourselves as theologians or intellectual historians. Just as Du Roy's generation of scholars developed a new sophistication in their attempts to trace source allusions and borrowings in Patristic authors, changes in our understanding of Patristic exegesis force upon this generation of scholars a need to focus attention on how we interpret the adaptation and often cannibalization of philosophical resources by a given author. We need to be more sophisticated in considering how Christian authors use the ideas they find persuasive and we need to develop more overt criteria by which we assess the character of a synthesis attempted.

Alluding to Plato's *Phaedrus*, Justin Martyr famously writes of his first encounter with Platonism: 'the perception of incorporeal things quite overwhelmed me and the Platonic theory of ideas added wings to my soul'. Something of the sort might well have been said by Augustine himself, but I suspect it is better to put into Augustine's mouth a modified version: 'for me', he might well have said 'Platonism added wings to Nicaea'. Of course the close reader of Justin will note that he immediately continues, 'So that in a short time I imagined myself a wise man. So great was my folly that I fully expected immediately to gaze upon God'. However, the assumption that Augustine's earliest theology followed the same order – Platonism providing its content until Augustine came (but failingly) to his Christian senses – is far more tenuously founded than it seemed either to Du Roy or to those theologians who have argued in his wake.

CHAPTER 2

From Him, through Him and in Him

> In summary: Everything A. wrote from his conversion in 386 down to but not including *vera rel.* on the threshold of ordination can be interpreted either as anti-Manichaean or pro-*disciplina*.[1]

In this chapter, I explore Augustine's increasing knowledge of Latin pro-Nicene theology in the years between 388 and 391. Once again, my aim is not to offer a detailed history of Augustine's development, but to highlight the extent to which the fundamental principles and questions of his Trinitarian theology evolved through an idiosyncratic engagement with the Latin Nicene theologies of the 360–90 period. Augustine continues to bring together Nicene Trinitarian theology and themes from his readings in non-Christian Platonism, but he increasingly does so in the context of an anti-Manichaean polemic. In the 388–91 period Augustine's anti-Manichaean focus shapes fundamental aspects of the manner in which he describes the unified working of Father, Son and Spirit, and is the stimulus behind his discussion of how we may grow in understanding of God through the intelligible order of creation. This period of explicit anti-Manichaean Trinitarianism is thus of vital importance because it is in this context that we see Augustine developing themes central to his mature Trinitarian theology. I will begin, however, not with Augustine, but with his Latin predecessors. It is time to offer a more precise description of the Latin Nicene theology with which Augustine was familiar and in particular of the ways in which those theologians understood the inseparable operation of Father, Son and Spirit.

---

[1] O'Donnell, *Confessions*, 2: 278. To this comment I would add that for Augustine to be anti-Manichaean and 'pro-*disciplina*' is for him also to be anti-Sceptical. Note also that what O'Donnell refers to here as *disciplina* is discussed in Chapter. 4.

From Him, through Him and in Him 43

LATIN PRO-NICENE THEOLOGY

The Latin Nicene texts discussed in Chapter 1 are more appropriately labelled pro-Nicene. By this term I refer to that *interpretation* of Nicaea and of earlier Nicene theologies which formed the context for the establishment of Catholic orthodoxy under the emperors Theodosius and Gratian through the actions of the councils of Constantinople and Aquileia, through imperial decree, and through the slow mutual recognition of a number of different pro-Nicene parties.[2] This theology is not sufficiently defined by reference to Nicaea alone, but only by reference also to a number of the key principles within which Nicaea was interpreted as teaching a faith in three co-ordinate divine realities who constitute one nature, power, will and substance. These principles provided the context for interpreting the traditional Trinitarian *taxis* of Father–Son–Spirit. The Father's status as source of Son and Spirit thus remained central even as pro-Nicenes offered further resources for envisaging the Father's status in new ways. Only a very few of Nicaea's technical terms and phrases play an important role in pro-Nicene self-definition. Latin pro-Nicene theology itself developed considerably in the decades between the late 350s and the early years of Augustine's literary career, and Augustine seems to have understood himself as inheriting a developing tradition.[3]

A number of factors stimulated and shaped the emergence of Latin pro-Nicene theology. Western reaction to the strongly subordinationist 'Blasphemy of Sirmium' of 357, to the series of councils sponsored by the Emperor Constantius in the West during the late 350s, and to the twin councils of Ariminium and Seleucia in 359 contributed to a growing sense that Nicaea's creed and a fuller explication of its judgements could and should form the basis for anti-'Arian' faith.[4] As they came to see that offering such an explication would involve the development of robust pneumatologies in which the Spirit was given clear definition as a third irreducible agent operating with the full power of the Godhead, Latin

---

[2] My description here is brief. For a more extensive discussion of the term, see my *Nicaea and its Legacy: An Approach to Fourth-Century Trinitarian Theology* (Oxford: Clarendon Press, 2004), 236–40. Some further reflection is offered in my '*Nicaea and its Legacy*: An Introduction' and 'A Response to the Critics of *Nicaea and its Legacy*', *HTR* 100 (2007), 141–4, 159–71.

[3] The *locus classicus* for conscious observation of the need for such improvement is *trin.* 6. 1.1.

[4] For discussions of this story, see Daniel H. Williams, *Ambrose of Milan and the End of the Arian–Nicene Conflicts* (Oxford: Clarendon Press, 1995); R. P. C. Hanson, *The Search for the Christian Doctrine of God: The Arian Controversy 318–381 AD* (Edinburgh: T & T Clark, 1988). At a number of places through the book I have discussed particular aspects of Latin Homoian theology. For a general introduction, that of Roger Gryson in SC 267, esp. 101–200, is the best point of departure.

theologians were pushed into a period of intense development. The return to the West of some prominent exiles who had spent time immersed in the Greek theological environment – Hilary of Poitiers, Eusebius of Vercelli, Lucifer of Cagliari – also stimulated the emergence of these new theologies. The extent to which these developments followed the dynamics and possibilities of previous Latin theology and the extent to which they were partly prompted by engagement with contemporary Greek theology is unclear. Some writers – for example, Hilary of Poitiers (c.315–367/8), Ambrose of Milan (333/4–397), Rufinus of Aquileia (c.345–411/12), Niceta of Remesiana (*fl. c.*380–410) – were deeply influenced by Greek theology, in many others – for example, Phoebadius of Agen (bishop 356/7–392), Gregory of Elvira (c.320–c.400) – traces of such influence are absent. The influences on a number of other Latin pro-Nicenes – such as Faustinus (*fl.* 350–85), Damasus (c.305–84), Ambrosiaster (*fl. c.*360–c.380) and some of the minor figures mentioned in Chapters 3 and 4 – are not certain.

In passing we should note that the document which the 'Western' bishops produced at the Council of Serdica in 343 has often constituted a significant crux of interpretation for those seeking to understand Western theology in the 340–60 period. This text – whose original language is uncertain – equates *hypostasis* and *ousia* and asserts that there is only one – the Father's – that is shared with the Son. At the same time, the text presents the Spirit in a somewhat confused manner, asserting that the Spirit was sent by Christ and also speaking of the Spirit as not suffering because it was the man assumed by the Spirit who suffered.[5] There are, however, significant problems with assuming that this text reveals a Latin quasi-Sabellian baseline before the appearance in Latin form of later Greek theologies. First, the same text makes use at a number of points of what we will come to recognize in the next chapter as anti-Monarchian and anti-Sabellian language to insist on the difference between Father and Son. However clumsily the text speaks of the Spirit and uses technical philosophical language, we should judge it in the light of all the traditions on which it draws. Second, it is very difficult to show that this text was influential on the major pro-Nicenes of the 360s and 370s.[6] Hence for

---

[5] The text survives in a number of versions, though the earliest surviving text of the profession of faith is that of Theodoret, *eccl. hist.* 2. 8. For one version of the Latin, see *EOMIA* 1/2, 651–3.

[6] For a reading of Serdica as the fundamental point of reference for understanding Latin theology at this time, see Jörg Ulrich, *Die Anfänge der Abendländischen Rezeption des Nizänums* (Berlin: De Gruyter, 1994). Christoph Markschies, 'Was ist lateinischer "Neunizanismus"?' *ZAC* 1 (1997), 73–95, offers an account which places less weight on Serdica, but which assumes that the development of Latin pro-Nicene theology (he uses the more traditionally German 'Neo-Nicene') was a result of Latin imitation of Greek developments. For a challenge to this view, see Michel

the purposes of this argument I have bracketed this text. Chapter 3 will outline a number of very different Latin theological dynamics that can be securely traced to the third century; in this chapter I will focus on exploring some principles of Latin pro-Nicene theology as they are apparent in the 358–81 period.

Some of those fundamental principles, as they appeared in Italy in the 370s and 380s, can be seen clearly in the surviving letters of Pope Damasus:

> For when some time ago, as now again, the heretics' venom began to creep in, and the Arians' blasphemy especially had begun to emerge, our predecessors, 318 bishops together with legates from the city of the most holy bishop of Rome, were brought together in council at Nicaea ... and drove out the deadly cups with this antidote, so that it was proper to believe that the Father, the Son and the Holy Spirit are of one Godhead, one power, one form, one substance [*ut Patrem, Filium, Spiritumque Sanctum unius Deitatis, unius virtutis, unius figurae, unius credere oporteret substantiae*].[7]

> For we all say with one voice that the Trinity is of one power [*virtus*], one majesty, one Godhead, one substance so as to be an inseparable power [*inseparabilis potestas*]. We assert, however, that there are three persons [*personas*], that they do not turn back into themselves, or less, as many blaspheme, but that they always remain [*semper manere*], that they are not certain stages of power and disparate occasions of origin [*potentiae gradus quosdam ortusque tempora disparate*] ... We assert that the Son is not dissimilar in operation, not dissimilar in power, or in anything at all dissimilar ... Let us also confess that the Holy Spirit is uncreated but of one majesty, one substance, one power with God the Father and our Lord Jesus Christ.[8]

The first text here offers a clear example of the manner in which pro-Nicenes identified the creed and judgement of Nicaea as identical in content with the assertion that Father, Son and Spirit are unified in power, majesty and substance – an assertion which had emerged clearly only in the 358–60 period. The second text spells out at more length one of the central themes of this pro-Nicene theology: the unity that the three possess as one power involves their inseparable activity. In its claim that the persons 'do not turn back into themselves' we see a strong assertion of the persons' irreducibility. As we shall see in Chapter 3, such

---

Barnes in 'The Other Latin Nicenes of the Second Half of the Fourth Century', in Lewis Ayres (ed.), *Unity and Diversity in Nicene Theology* (forthcoming). The text may, however, witness to the prevalence in Latin theology at this time of a type of Spirit-Christology that impeded development of pneumatology until the 360s.
[7] Damasus, *ep.* 1 (*Confidimus quidem*) (Field, 10–12).
[8] Damasus, *ep.* 2 (*Ea gratia*) (Field, 14–16).

language draws on a long tradition of anti-Monarchian expression in Latin theology.⁹

For the moment I will focus on the doctrines of common and inseparable operation in order to show some of the fundamental principles and argumentative cruces in Latin pro-Nicene tradition. Inseparable operation states that all three divine persons work in each divine act. This doctrine moves beyond the argument that all three persons must have the same ontological status because each is described in Scripture as performing the same acts, the doctrine of *common* operations. Both doctrines are fundamental for Latin anti-Homoian polemic; their importance becomes even clearer when we note that they also appear in a variety of catechetical texts.¹⁰

In his anti-Donatist *Contra Parmenianum* – written in the mid-360s and then revised in the early 380s – Augustine's younger African contemporary Optatus offers much uncharitable reading of his opponent. In the fifth book, for example:

If you slander us, at least show respect for God, who holds first place in the Trinity [*qui in Trinitate prior est*], who with his own Son and the Holy Spirit performs and fulfils all things, and even in the place where no human being is present. But you, brother Parmenianus, in your praise of water from the readings in Genesis, said that waters first brought forth living souls. What, were they able to generate of their own accord? What, was the whole Trinity not there too? Certainly the Father was there too, as he deigned to give an order, saying 'let the waters bring forth swimming creatures, flying creatures', etc. [Gen. 1.20]. But if what happened happened without an agent [*sine operante*], God would say 'bring forth, waters' [Gen. 1.2]. So the Son of God was also there as an agent, there was the Holy Spirit, as we read, 'and the Spirit of God was moving above the waters'.¹¹

Optatus's argument combines elements of common operation – insisting that Father, Son and Spirit all create – with hints towards inseparable operation – in his initial statement that the Father performs all things

---

⁹ On Marcellus, see Ayres, *Nicaea and its Legacy*, 62–9; Joseph T. Lienhard, *Contra Marcellum: Marcellus of Ancyra and Fourth-Century Theology* (Washington DC: Catholic University of America Press, 1999). On Photinus, see Hanson, *The Search*, 235–8.

¹⁰ For example in the short *Explanatio symboli ad initiandos* which may well originate in lectures given by Ambrose himself, see *Symb.* (PL 17. 1157–8). This may provide us with a window onto Augustine's own catechesis during the spring of 387. Cf. Rufinus, *Comm.* 10. Quodvultdeus, *Cat. hom.* 1. 3.1–4.28 offers both an excellent example of the doctrine in a catechetical context and an excellent example of the 'in' language that we will discuss shortly, including use of John 14.10. While these homilies, delivered *c.*435, are dependent on Augustine, they also perhaps reveal an independent reading of prior Latin Nicene tradition.

¹¹ Optatus, *c. Don.* 5. 2 (SC 413. 244).

with Son and Spirit. Arguing that all of the divine three create is a common argument among pro-Nicenes; the activity of creating *ex nihilo* was understood to be the preserve of God and, thus, if all create, all must possess the power of divinity.

The importance of arguing that Father, Son and Spirit all participate in activities that are the preserve of divinity is evident in the following passage from Ambrose's *De spiritu sancto*:

> God has the power to raise up the dead. For, 'as the Father raises the dead and gives life, so the Son also gives life to whom he will' [John 5.21]. Moreover the Spirit also raises up, through whom God raises up, for it is written, 'He shall quicken you in your mortal bodies, because of his Spirit dwelling in you' [Rom. 8.11]. Yet, so that you may not think this a weak grace, hear that the Spirit also raises up, for the prophet Ezekiel says 'Come Spirit and blow upon these dead, and they will live. And I prophesied as he had commanded me; and the Spirit of life came into them, and they lived, and they stood upon their feet, an exceedingly great assembly'. And below, God says 'You shall know that I am the Lord, when I shall open your sepulchres, to bring my people out of their graves, and I shall put my Spirit in you, and you shall live' [Ez. 37.9–10, 13–14].[12]

Ambrose uses God's statement at Ezekiel 37.13 ('And you shall know that I am the Lord') to emphasize that the power of raising the dead is one reserved to divinity, and hence that the Spirit's raising must be taken as an indication of the Spirit's divinity. The argument that all three persons raise the dead is part of a wider shift, beyond our purview here, in which as Greek and Latin pro-Nicenes emphasize that all three persons undertake the work of sanctification, they also emphasize that sanctification itself is an immediate participation in the divine life.[13] This passage again argues mostly from common operations, but it also hints at inseparable operation in its use of texts that emphasize that God, the Father, raises through and by imparting his own Spirit.

In these quotations we already see the most obvious question that the doctrine provokes: *how* do the persons work inseparably? While the attribution of distinct roles to each of the divine three is a common tactic, pro-Nicenes cannot accept such language at face value, insisting that there remains one God. But insisting on the indivisible unity of God, even as the three persons are irreducible, renders the idea of the three

---

[12] Ambrose, *spir.* 3. 20.149 (CCSL 79. 213–4).
[13] For the joint action of the three in salvation, see, for example, Ambrose, *spir.* 1. 13.131. For discussion of the wider shift I mention see my 'The Holy Spirit as the Undiminished Giver: Didymus the Blind's *De Spiritu Sancto* and the Development of Nicene Pneumatology', in Janet Rutherford and Vincent Twomey (eds.), *The Theology of the Holy Sprint in the Fathers of the Church* (Dublin: Four Courts Press, forthcoming).

working inseparably particularly difficult to explain. Both Ambrose and Optatus hint at one standard element shared among Latin pro-Nicenes when they speak of the Father working 'through' the Son and Spirit, but this very particular style of apportioning roles still begs many questions.

In *De spiritu sancto* 2, Ambrose attempts to refute Homoian exegesis of 1 Corinthians 8.6 ('yet for us there is one God, the Father, from whom are all things and for whom we exist, and one Lord Jesus Christ, through whom are all things and through whom we exist'). Distinguishing between 'from whom' and 'through whom' Homoians claim that the Son is an instrument in the hands of the Father who is the true creator.[14] Ambrose compares the verse with Romans 11.36 ('for of Him and through Him and in Him are all things'), which he sees as referring to the Son. On the basis of this comparison Ambrose argues that the particular prepositions 'from' and 'through' in 1 Corinthians 8.6 should not be taken to indicate any necessary status, because both may be used of Father and of Son (as he also claims for the Spirit); the prepositions are intended to teach, he asserts, that Father, Son and Spirit are other (*alius*) only in 'an unconfused distinction'.[15]

In the same discussion, however, Ambrose also insists that the Father works all things through the Son, who is the Father's 'operating wisdom' (*operatrix sapientia*: Wisd. 7.21) and that all things are 'in' the Spirit.[16] Thus Ambrose still assumes a fundamental order of divine operation (the Father working all things through the Son and in the Spirit) even as he denies that the prepositions 'from' and 'through' indicate an ontological hierarchy. He does so, in part, by arguing that each of these prepositions is true of each person in a particular way:

> If you speak also regarding the Father, then 'of' him because of him was the 'operative wisdom' [*ex ipso operatrix sapientia*], which of his own and the Father's will gave being to all things which were not; 'through him', because through his Wisdom all things were made; 'in him', because he is the source of the vivifying substance [*vivicatoriae fons substantiae*], in whom we live and are and move. Of the Spirit also, so that, having been formed through Him, established through Him, strengthened in Him, we receive the gift of eternal life.[17]

---

[14] The sort of Homoian reading that he faced at the Council of Aquileia itself can be seen, for example, at *scol. Aquil.* 306r (CCSL 87A. 162), and 346r (CCSL 87A. 191). The latter text is particularly interesting because 1Cor. 8.6 is deployed against the doctrine of inseparable operation. In our surviving texts Homoians noticeably do not mention John 14.10. The one exception I have been able to locate is at *ep. Cand.* 1. 10, but this is perhaps only further evidence that the text was composed by Victorinus as a foil.

[15] Ambrose, *spir.* 2. 9.89 (CSEL 79. 121).

[16] Ambrose, *spir.* 2. 9.92 (CSEL 79. 123). [17] Ambrose, *spir.* 2. 9.92–3 (CSEL 79. 123).

Things are 'of' or 'from' the Father not only because he creates, but because of his role within the Trinity as the generator of his Wisdom who also creates; all things are 'of' or 'from' the Spirit in a different manner because the Father creates through the Spirit, and in the Spirit things receive permanence and eternal life (I return to this pneumatological theme later in the chapter). Comparing this passage with the previous quotation, we see a strategy found in many Latin pro-Nicenes, the use in close proximity of different terminologies and emphases to address the same question. In the first passage Ambrose makes central language which emphasizes the individual agency of Father, Son and Spirit; in the second he makes central the Father's working through Son and Spirit. Both passages also contain hints of the other terminology. This practice of supplementation, which builds on different aspects of scriptural language, places side by side and interweaves principles which must be upheld in Nicene contexts, but contributes little towards any formal discussion of the modes of distinction, unity and causality implied. We can progress a little further by noting the importance of a further terminology.

In the initial paragraphs of *De spiritu sancto* 3, Ambrose comments on the Spirit remaining 'upon' Christ at Luke 4.18, emphasizing that this is true only of the Son of Man:

For according to the Godhead the Spirit is not upon Christ but in Christ [*nam secundum divinitatem non super Christum est spiritus, sed in Christo*], because, just as the Father is in the Son, and the Son in the Father, so the Spirit of God and the Spirit of Christ is both in the Father and in the Son, for he is the Spirit of his mouth. For he who is of God abides in God, as it is written, 'Now we have received not the spirit of this world, but the Spirit that is of God' [1Cor. 2.12] … He is not then over Christ according to the Godhead of Christ, because the Trinity is not over itself, but over all things: it is not over itself, but in itself [*quia non super se est Trinitas, sed supra omnia, supra se autem non est, sed in se est*].[18]

Ambrose's analysis of prepositions finds parallels in other Latin pro-Nicenes and in the famous discussions of Basil on whom Ambrose also draws, but his use of 'in' language to qualify the traditional Trinitarian *taxis* or order of Father, Son and Spirit represents a distinctively Latin pro-Nicene discussion.[19] Latin pro-Nicenes draw on the use of such language

---

[18] Ambrose, *spir.* 3. 1.6 (CSEL 79. 151–2). Cf. the same language in the final summary passage at the end of *fid.* 5. 11.133.

[19] See Basil, *spir.* 3ff. The 'in' language I am considering here has varying utility in the Greek authors Ambrose used: for example, at *Serap.* 2. 3 Athanasius uses John 14.10 to argue that whatever is in the Father is in the Son. This reading follows extensive discussion in *c. Ar.*, most clearly at 3. 3, where Athanasius uses the text as a reinforcement for his insistence that the Son is proper to the Father as sun and radiance. The same text is, however, used by Basil just once in *spir.* at

by Tertullian and Novatian. Both of these earlier authors argue that for Father and Son to be 'in' one another implies their distinct existence but also that a unique continuity exists between them without any material separation or distinction.[20]

At *De trinitate* 8. 52, Hilary writes:

> What more fitting words could he have employed ... that we might believe in their unity, than those by which ... it is declared that whatever the Son did and said, the Father said and did in the Son? This says nothing of a nature foreign to himself, or added by creation to God, or born into Godhead by a partition [*ex portione*] of God, but it betokens the divinity of one who by a perfect birth is begotten perfect God [*sed perfecta nativitate in Deum perfectum genitae divinitatis*]. Of whom there is so confident an assurance of his nature that he says 'I in the Father and the Father in me' [John 14.10].[21]

Hilary is not implying that the Son lacks full individuation or the power of initiating action, as might seem to be the case if he had only stated that the Father was in Son and Spirit enabling them to act. Rather, this language qualifies continuing pro-Nicene use of the traditional Trinitarian order or *taxis* by insisting that the Father's speaking of the Word and breathing of the Spirit eternally gives rise to three who exist incomprehensibly 'in' one another.

---

[18]. 45 to show that the Son has all that the Father has. Latin pro-Nicenes make use of the language far more consistently and extensively. We should also note its use in the 'Western' creed at Serdica, Theodoret, *eccl. hist.* 2. 6.

[20] For example, Tertullian, *adv. Prax.* 24. There Tertullian argues against Monarchians who claim that John 14.9 ('He who has seen me has seen the Father') implies the identity of Father and Son. Tertullian suggests that John 14.10 'makes manifest the conjunction of the two persons' and 'from this very fact it is apparent that each person is himself and none other'. Cf. *adv. Prax.* 8 where the same language (with reference to John 14.11) is used against the idea that the Son is any quasi-Gnostic 'emanation'. The same terminology also appears at Novatian's *trin.* 31, its final summary, but there Novatian argues that the Son must somehow have been eternally 'in' the Father 'before' his generation, even though no temporal language is appropriate.

[21] Hilary, *trin.* 8. 52 (SC 448. 462). In this passage Hilary twice invokes the theme of the Son's perfect birth, a favourite of his. While this is distinctively his and not found, for example, so extensively in Ambrose, this distinction only highlights the common use of 'in' language. Besides the mention of Hilary, Phoebadius and Gregory of Elvira in what follows, see also Faustinus, *trin.* 10–14, esp. 11 (CCSL 69. 304): 'Cum enim omnia quae sunt paternae virtutis et deitatis, habentur in Filio, Pater in Filio est et Filius in Patre'. The remainder of the long passage in Faustinus that I note offers a particularly extensive discussion, partly dependent on Hilary. Victorinus is a further witness to the utility of this language. His statement at *adv. Ar.* 1. 7 (CSEL 83/1. 64): 'Quos substantia patris Christus: ego in patre et pater in me', follows lines identified in our discussion (see also the extended discussion at *adv. Ar.* 2. 6). At *adv. Ar.* 1. 11 we also find a Tertullianesque inference that John 14.9–10 demands confession of Father and Son as distinct. But at *adv. Ar.* 3. 6–7 we find the text quoted as part of a list all of which are then explained by Victorinus's account of the relationship between Being and Life. This explanation of the language by means of a philosophical model is precisely what is not found in other Latin pro-Nicenes. Cf. *adv. Ar.* 4. 10.

Phoebadius makes particularly clear the extent to which this existence 'in' one another indicates its incomprehensibility when he writes,

'Who will recount his birth?' [Is. 53.8] This is to say: let no one dare to recount what he cannot. But why will no one be able to? Because indeed the one who lacks birth is not only 'from Him' and 'with Him' but also 'in Him' [Rom. 11.36].[22]

It is also, as Ambrose and his Latin peers all assert, *because* Father and Son are 'in' each other that they share a nature:

for it is written 'God was in Christ, reconciling the world to himself' [2Cor. 5.19], that is to say [in Christ was] 'eternal godhead' [Rom. 1.20]. Or, if the Father is in the Son even as the Son is in the Father, then their unity in both nature and operation is plainly not denied.[23]

While Ambrose argues that Father, Son and Spirit are all agents with uniquely divine power, he also maintains a traditional Trinitarian order in which the Father works through the Son and in the Spirit. Both of these languages are further qualified by his insistence that Father, Son and Spirit exist 'in' each other. The notion of existence 'in' one another is used both to argue that Son and Spirit are dependent on the Father, and to show that the Father's acts of generation and spiration without division result in a true sharing of existence.

While some Latin pro-Nicenes occasionally do use directly philosophical language to found the doctrine of inseparable operations in an account of shared power and substance, for the most part this language is used to demonstrate only that the exercise of identical power indicates unity of substance. We far more commonly find assertion of the principle of unity of substance, the use of multiple scriptural languages, the ruling out of inappropriate ways of understanding, and perhaps deployment of the language of the divine three being 'in' one another. With Augustine we will see the same fundamental doctrine, but rather different forms of expression and exploration. Augustine's idiosyncrasy will, in part, stem from the anti-Manichaean (and anti-Sceptical) shape of his developing theology. Similarly, in Latin pro-Nicenes before Augustine, the notion of a unified causal activity (such as we occasionally find in Gregory of Nyssa, for example) is at most only implied behind accounts of inseparable operation. With Augustine we will find a slow but significant development of such conceptual resources.

---

[22] Phoebadius, *c. Ar.* 9. 7 (CCSL 64. 33).
[23] Ambrose, *fid.* 3. 11.89 (CSEL 78. 140). Cf. *fid.* 5. 11.136, Hilary, *trin.* 8. 51, and Gregory of Elvira, *fid.* 53 (CCSL 69. 233): 'id est unius substantiae … cum patre, sicut ipse Dominus ait: Ego in Patre et pater in me'.

AN ANTI-MANICHAEAN TRINITARIANISM I:
DE MORIBUS ECCLESIAE CATHOLICAE

Let us, then, turn back to Augustine and examine a text that will reveal, first, how Augustine's Trinitarian theology developed in the 387–9 period and, second, what it means to speak of that theology as 'anti-Manichaean'. The *De moribus ecclesiae catholicae et de moribus Manichaeorum* ('On the Catholic and Manichaean Ways of Life') is a text whose parts are difficult to date. It was begun at Rome in 387, but completed when Augustine arrived back in Thagaste during 389. In the first book Augustine offers an anti-Manichaean argument which presents God as the one object of our love and us as having fallen away by the corruption of the mind. We can return to God only by a reformation of our love. At *De moribus* 1. 12.21, Augustine writes

> [The soul] should believe that its Creator, as he truly is, always remains in the inviolable and immutable nature of Truth and Wisdom [*sicuti est inuiolabili et incommutabili semper manere natura ueritatis atque sapientiae*], but it should admit that folly and falsehood can overtake it, at least because of the errors from which it desires to be set free. But again, it should be aware that it is not separated by love for another creature, that is, for this sensible world, from the Love of God himself, by which it is made holy in order that it may remain most blessed. Since we ourselves are a creature, no other creature, therefore, 'separates us from the Love of God, which is found in Christ Jesus our Lord' [Rom 8.39].[24]

This passage is immediately followed by another, much more clearly Trinitarian passage which, it has been plausibly suggested, was added as the work was redacted. If so, it may have been intended to clarify the rather vague references of the passage just quoted.[25] Augustine speaks of the creator of the soul 'remaining in the inviolable and immutable nature of Truth and Wisdom', but it is unclear whom Augustine is indicating by the term 'creator'. He does not at this stage usually speak of the Son as creator without qualification. But if we rightly read 'as he truly is' as an allusion to 1 John 3.2 ('we shall be like him, for we shall see him as he truly is'), and if we remember that in the next paragraph Augustine will identify sanctification as being conformed to Christ, then Augustine's comment indicates that the Creator remains 'in' Wisdom and Truth, the Son, and that we are conformed to that Wisdom by the Love of God, the Spirit. If

---

[24] *mor.* 1. 12.21 (CSEL 90. 25–6).
[25] See Kevin Coyle, *Augustine's De Moribus Ecclesiae Catholicae: A Study of the Work, its Composition and its Sources* (Fribourg: The University Press, 1978), 241–59.

so, the passage is a witness to the continued presence of the dynamics we saw in the very earliest works. The section is, however, confusing.

But then Augustine adds:

(22) Let this same Paul tell us who is this Christ Jesus our Lord. 'To them that are called', he says, 'we preach Christ the power of God, and the wisdom of God' [1Cor. 23–4]. And does not Christ himself say, 'I am the Truth?' [1John 14.6]. If, then, we ask what it is to live well – that is, to strive after happiness by living well – it must assuredly be to love virtue, to love wisdom, to love truth, and to love with all the heart, with all the soul, and with all the mind virtue which is inviolable and immutable, wisdom which never gives place to folly, truth which knows no change or variation from that which it always is. Through this the Father himself is seen, for it is said, 'No man cometh unto the Father but by me' [John 14.6]. To this we cling by sanctification. For when sanctified we burn with full and perfect love, which is the only security for our not turning away from God, and for our being conformed to him rather than to this world; for 'he has predestined us', says the same apostle, 'that we should be conformed to the image of his Son' [Rom. 8.29].

(23) It is through love, then, that we become conformed to God; and by this conformation, and configuration, and circumcision from this world we are not confounded with the things which are properly subject to us. But this is done by the Holy Spirit. 'For hope', he says, 'does not confound us; for the love of God is shed abroad in our hearts by the Holy Spirit, who has been given to us' [Rom. 5.5]. But we could not possibly be restored to perfection by the Holy Spirit, unless he himself continued always perfect and immutable. And this plainly could not be unless he were of the nature and the substance of God [*nisi dei naturae esset ac substantiae*], who alone is always possessed of immutability and invariableness. 'The creature', it is affirmed, not by me but by Paul, 'has been made subject to vanity' [Rom. 8.20]. And what is subject to vanity is unable to separate us from vanity, and to unite us to the truth. But the Holy Spirit does this for us. He is therefore no creature. For whatever is, must be either God or the creature.

(24) We ought then to love God, a certain triune unity [*deum ergo diligere debemus trinam quandam unitatem*], Father, Son and Holy Spirit; because I can say nothing other than that he is 'to be' itself. For it is said of God, truly and in the most exalted sense, 'of whom are all things, by whom are all things, in whom are all things' [Rom. 11.36].[26]

We do not here have a clear argument from common and inseparable operations, but we do have one that, I suggest, is dependent on such arguments. Augustine first argues that *because* Christ is always immutable and perfect Wisdom and Truth who makes visible the Father, we can come to

---

[26] *mor.* 1. 22–4 (CSEL 90. 26–8).

a true contemplation of the Father in the Son. On the basis of Romans 5.5 Augustine then argues that it is the Spirit who so conforms us and that the Spirit could not undertake this work unless the Spirit were also always perfect and immutable. The Spirit must thus be of the nature of God (*Dei naturae*). Augustine then moves into his brief Trinitarian summary, which we shall consider in a moment. This argument about the Son and Spirit is set up for us as an answer to the question 'who is Christ?', and takes the form of a description of the roles of both Son and Spirit as possible because they possess the full characteristics of divine existence.

The Trinitarian summary at the end of this passage pushes the argument further. In a number of texts from his early writings Augustine uses Romans 11.36 as a Trinitarian summary which also demonstrates the persons' inseparable operation.[27] He first does so in the *De quantitate animae*, probably written in Rome during 388, and thus either contemporary with *De moribus* I, or slightly preceding it:

> He alone is to be adored who is the Creator of all things that are, from whom all things come, by whom all things are made, in whom all things exist; that is, the unchanging Source, unchanging Wisdom, unchanging Love [*inconmutabile principium, inconmutabilem sapientiam, inconmutabilem caritatem*], true and perfect, who never was not, never will be … Nothing is more hidden than he, nothing more present.[28]

As in the *De moribus* text we are considering, Augustine here takes each term of the verse to refer to a distinct person. Over the next few years we see Romans 11.36 used a number of times to describe how the three persons work inseparably in creation, for example, in the *De fide et symbolo* of 393 (discussed in the next chapter) and in the *Contra Adimantium* of 394. These arguments reveal some of the main ways in which Augustine adapted existing Nicene arguments into his anti-Manichaean polemic.

In the *Contra Adimantium*, for example, Augustine begins by confronting Adimantus's argument that there is a discrepancy between Genesis's ascription of creation to the Father and John's ascription of creation to the Son. Augustine cites Romans 11.36 as evidence that even though the Son is not named he must be understood, just as the Son must be understood to be working when Genesis tells us only that the Father spoke and created.[29] For this Manichaean challenge, originally anti-Homoian

---

[27] In a useful appendix Du Roy, *L'Intelligence*, 479–85, lists all of the pertinent texts in Augustine's corpus. It should be noted that Du Roy lists them in chronological order, but his dates are not always those that would now gain majority support among scholars.

[28] *an. quant.* 31. 77 (CSEL 89. 225–6).   [29] *c. Adim.* 1.

arguments in favour of inseparable operation are perfectly suited. Indeed, we should also note that Manichaeans in the fourth century used some of the very same verses that appealed to non- and anti-Nicenes to argue for their account of the distinctions between Father, Son and Spirit. Augustine's first-hand knowledge of Manichaeanism enables him to combine the use of anti-Homoian arguments with a critique of Manichaean attempts to co-opt Trinitarian language into a very different mythical framework. Thus, most famously at *Contra Faustum* 20 (written *c*.398–400) when Faustus appeals to 1 Timothy 6.16 and 1 Corinthians 1.24 in his presentation of the Father as inhabiting the highest light and the Son as a twofold reality inhabiting a second light, Augustine first suggests that Faustus's appeal to Trinitarian language hides commitment to a fourfold account of divinity within a cosmogonic narrative very different from that of orthodox Christianity. Augustine then offers an account of those verses as together presenting Father, Son and Spirit as one divine light operating inseparably – an argument of clearly anti-Homoian provenance.[30] It is important to note, however, that in both the *Contra Faustum* and the earlier *De moribus* Augustine links an appropriate understanding of God not only to recognition that the Scriptures speak of realities that transcend the material connotations of the language they use, but also to a wider need to recognize that the created order is intelligible and is designed (and used) by God to lead the soul towards contemplation.

In *De moribus* 1, for example, Augustine defends Catholic morality by arguing that it is possible for the soul to achieve happiness because the immutable and perfect God is immediately present to and sustains the created order in such a way that human beings who submit themselves to God may grow in knowledge and love of God.[31] It is at the culmination of this account, in the very passage we are considering here, that Augustine places much weight on the manner in which all things exist 'from', 'through' and 'in' the divine three.[32] The same perspective is found developed with particular clarity in the *De vera religione*.[33] Augustine's account of the created order's intelligibility is, then, closely linked to an account of the Trinity as inseparably sustaining and using that of which it is (triune) cause. We will see further dimensions of this theology in the next section of the chapter, but enough has been delineated for me to say

---

[30] *c. Faust.* 20. 2 (passage from Faustus's *Capitula*), 20. 7–12. Cf. *c. Faust.* 15. 6.
[31] See *mor.* 1. 10.16–12.20. It is this discussion that then leads up to the Trinitarian discussion that we are considering, beginning at 1. 12.21.
[32] See especially *mor.* 1. 14.24.   [33] See esp. *vera rel.* 7. 14, 34. 64, 55. 113.

that it is these themes and this set of links to which I refer when I speak of an 'anti-Manichaean Trinitarianism'.

But let us return to the long passage quoted on p. 53. Augustine's exegesis of Romans 11.36 is distinct in the clarity and persistence with which he applies each term of the verse to a distinct person of the Trinity. While the verse is used by a number of Latin pro-Nicenes before Augustine, it is usually used with reference to the relationship between Father and Son: thus Hilary, Phoebadius and Gregory of Elvira.[34] It seems, however, most likely that Ambrose is the origin of Augustine's particular exegesis. Previously we saw Ambrose discussing this text in his *De spiritu*, and primarily reading the verse as a statement about the relationship between Father and Son. At the same time, however, Ambrose adds reference to the Spirit to round out a more fully Trinitarian account of the persons all possessing divine power.[35] In the same passage he also maintains a clear sense that the Father works through Son and in Spirit:

> Therefore, as we read that all things are of the Father, so, too, we read that all things can be said to be of the Son, through whom are all things, and we are taught by testimonies that all things are of the Spirit, in whom are all things.[36]

In fact, Ambrose reads the verse thus only in this passage, but it is one of a very few parallels to Augustine's practice of directly linking each person of the Trinity to a clause of the verse in preceding Latin tradition.[37] Ambrose also foreshadows Augustine in using a variant of Romans 11.36, 'Ex quo omnia, per quem omnia in quo omnia' in addition to the more normal 'Quoniam ex ipso et per ipsum et in ipso sunt omnia'.[38] Augustine, then, probably adapts Ambrose, and does so in ways that help to bolster his account of an intelligible cosmos immediately sustained by the triune life.

---

[34] Hilary, *trin.* 11. 16 and 46; Phoebadius, *c. Ar.* 26; Gregory of Elvira, *fid.* lines 262 and 595. For Ambrosiaster see n. 37 below. The text did not play a role in the earlier Latin anti-Monarchian controversies, and makes its appearance in Latin theology only with these writers.

[35] Cf. the similar discussion at Ambrose, *fid.* 4. 11.139–53.

[36] Ambrose, *spir.* 2. 9.96 (CSEL 79. 124). It is possible that both here and in *fid.* 4 Ambrose is dependent on Basil, *spir.* 5. 7ff. Even after writing these texts Ambrose easily reverts to a more traditional exegesis in which the 'through' and 'in' of Romans 11.36 are both taken to apply to the Son or all three prepositions to the Father: for example *Hex.* 1. 5.19.

[37] See Ambrosiaster, *quaest. test.* 122. 26–7. Ambrosiaster's account of the differences in authority and cause is not mirrored in Augustine. A similar account is to be found at Ambrosiaster, *ad Rom.* 11. 36 (CSEL 81/1. 390–1). Cf. Eusebius of Vercelli, *trin.* 4. 21–4.

[38] The only other example of an author using this variant before Augustine's usage is Victorinus, and his exegesis of Romans 11.36 follows the pre-Ambrosian Latin tradition described above: see Du Roy, *L'Intelligence*, 483–5.

The next aspect of the long quotation from *De moribus* I that demands attention is Augustine's use of Romans 5.5 to describe the Spirit's function.[39] Augustine builds on themes we have already seen. He has previously hinted that the third person admonishes and effects our return to wisdom, our gradual conformation to the wisdom that is the Father's image. As we saw above, in the *De quantitate animae* he already attributes the title *caritas* to the Spirit in parallel with 'Source' and 'Wisdom' for the Father and Son, but *De moribus* I is the first time Augustine quotes Romans 5.5. He does so in order to identify love as the Spirit's (economic) *proprium*, and as the organizing principle for the other activities attributed to the Spirit. Two aspects of his later exegesis are, however, not clearly present here. Augustine does not indicate how the title of love helps us understand the Spirit's relationship to Father and Son. Augustine also offers no clear indication that he sees the Spirit as the substance of the gifts he gives (while we could read the sentence following his quotation of Romans 5.5 as indicating a paralleling of the Spirit and the Love of God in us, Augustine offers no warrant for so doing). Elsewhere in *De moribus* I, however, Augustine uses threefold formulae in which *sumum bonum* and *summa sapientia* are paralleled with *summa concordia* ('the highest harmony') and *summa pax* ('the highest peace').[40] All seem to be titles for the Spirit and, given Augustine's clear sense that the Spirit inspires love for God (or perhaps *is* the Love of God in us) because of the Spirit's perfection, we may see here the beginnings of Augustine's account of the Spirit as eternally concord, peace and love within the Trinitarian life. Augustine, thus, identifies the Spirit as a co-equal to Father and Son, but we can glean only the barest sense of how he understands the Spirit's relationship with Father and Son.[41]

---

[39] See A. M. La Bonnardière, 'Le verset paulinien Rom., v. 5 dans l'oeuvre de saint Augustin', *AugMag* 2. 657–65.

[40] *mor.* 1. 15.25 and 1. 24.44, respectively. *Concordia* is also that which the Spirit brings about as inspirer of the unified canon of Old and New Testaments, see *mor.* 1. 30.62 and Kevin Coyle, 'Concordia, The Holy Spirit as the Bond of the Two Testaments', *Aug(R)* 22 (1982), 427–56. See also the more general reference to *concordia* at *sol.* 1. 4. Cf. *vera rel.* 11. 21, *div. qu.* 18.

[41] When he treats *De moribus* I, Du Roy (*L'Intelligence*, 215ff.) argues that Augustine's vision of the Trinity here is fundamentally 'economic', dependent on a model in which the Spirit leads us to the Son who provides knowledge of the Father. Du Roy places the scriptural discussion of *De moribus* 1. 14.22ff. in the wider context of Book 2's account of the fall away from Being and the conversion towards it that Augustine uses to counter Manichaean understandings of evil. The scriptural discussion of these passages is by this means 'revealed' to be only a thin veil over Augustine's fundamentally Platonic concerns. With reference to *De moribus*, Du Roy argues that while Augustine demonstrates a deeper understanding of Nicene Trinitarian language an account of the creation as exhibiting triune structures forms the basis for all ascent towards and understanding of the Trinity as such. Du Roy thus treats as surface ornament the evidence of Augustine's engagement with his theological peers.

The sources for this pneumatological discussion are not known with certainty. Du Roy's argument that Augustine makes use of Gregory Thaumaturgus's *Confession* in addition to Ambrose has received little support.[42] La Bonnardière suggested a range of general possibilities – anti-Manichaean *florilegia*, anti-'Arian' professions of faith and some catechetical lectures – but ultimately admitted defeat.[43] Kevin Coyle offers what remains the most extensive analysis to date, arguing for the possibility of Augustine using both Ambrose's *De spiritu sancto* and Jerome's translation of Didymus the Blind's *De spiritu sancto*. Coyle suggests a number of possible parallels, but Didymus remains unlikely, given that Jerome only seems to have finished his translation in 389.[44] The presence of Ambrose is likely, given that his fairly frequent use of Romans 5.5 in the first book of the *De spiritu* is the most plausible source for Augustine's usage.[45]

Before moving on from this work entirely, we should note *De moribus* 1. 30.62 where Augustine writes,

> Catholic Church, truest mother of Christians ... you propose no creature for us to adore, which we might be commanded to serve, and you exclude everything that has been made, that is, subject to change, and that falls under time from that incorruptible and inviolable eternity, to which alone a human being should be subject and by adhering to which alone the human soul is not unhappy. You do not confuse what eternity, what truth, and finally what peace itself distinguishes, nor do you separate what one majesty joins together.[46]

The use of *aeternitas* to describe the Father here is striking – the only clear parallel it finds in earlier Latin tradition is in Hilary's famous description of Father, Son and Spirit as 'infinity in the eternal, the form in the image and the use in the gift', a passage Augustine will discuss at length in *De trinitate* 4. If this passage is the first evidence that Augustine has been reading Hilary, then we must note that Hilary's use of *aeternitas* is preceded by a set of allusions to 1 Corinthians 8.6 in which all things

---

[42] Du Roy, *L'Intelligence*, 227 (Rufinus's translation dates from 402 at the earliest).
[43] A. M. La Bonnardière, *Biblia Augustiniana. A. T. Le Livre de la Sagesse* (Paris: Études Augustiniennes, 1970), 33–4.
[44] Coyle, *Augustine's De Moribus*, 241–59. On Augustine's knowledge of Didymus, see Berthold Altaner, 'Augustinus und Didymus der Blinde', in *Kleine Patristische Schriften* (Berlin: Akademie-Verlag, 1967), 297–301.
[45] The question of the sources for this whole passage of *De moribus* 1 is further complicated by the appearance of what may be Augustine's first uses of texts from Wisdom (the alternative is *lib. arb.* 2: the relative dating of these two works is uncertain). In the following decade Augustine clearly engages earlier uses of Wisdom, but his earliest discussion may result primarily from his own reading. See La Bonnardière, *Le Livre de la Sagesse*.
[46] *mor.* 1. 30.62 (CSEL 90. 65–6).

are 'from' the Father, 'through' the Son, and in which the Spirit is 'in' all.⁴⁷ Hilary does not use Romans 11.36 in a Trinitarian fashion, but his Trinitarian reading of 1 Corinthians 8.6 – whose exegesis Augustine, Ambrose and Victorinus all understand to be interrelated with that of Romans 11.36 – may have provided further impetus towards Augustine's reading of the Romans text.

Our examination of some passages from the *De moribus* enables a number of conclusions. First, Augustine already knows the doctrine of inseparable operations. Second, Augustine continues his engagement with his Latin peers and predecessors, but he engages in an appropriation of them that is highly personal and shaped by his anti-Manichaean polemic. That shaping is particularly evident in Augustine's linking of the Trinity as a causal sequence in which the Father, through Son and Spirit, acts to create, maintain and then redeem an intelligible order. Third, while Augustine's presentation of Father as source, and the Son as Wisdom (which follows easily enough from his allusions to the Son as *intellectus* in the earliest works), is stable, his description of the Spirit remains in development – the Spirit's economic role is reasonably clear, but we see only hints of how Augustine imagines the Spirit's eternal *proprium*. Considering a further text will reinforce these conclusions and offer further clarity about Augustine's idiosyncratic adaptation of Latin Nicene theology.

AN ANTI-MANICHAEAN TRINITARIANISM II: *EPISTULA* 11

Augustine's *Epistula* 11 was written to his ever-curious and constantly badgering friend Nebridius sometime between 388 and 391.⁴⁸ Nebridius had written asking how it can be that the Son is said to assume humanity but not the Father. Augustine's reply begins with a direct assertion:

according to the Catholic faith, the Trinity is proposed to our belief and believed – and even understood by a few saints and holy persons – as so

---

⁴⁷ Hilary, *trin.* 2. 1 (SC 443. 276): 'unus est enim Deus Pater ex quo omnia. Et unus unigenitus Dominus noster Iesus Christus per quem omnia. Et unus Spiritus, donum in omnibus. Omnia ergo sunt suis virtutibus ac meritis ordinata: una potestas ex qua omnia, una progenies per quam omnia, perfectae spei munus unum. Nec deesse quicquam consummationi tantae repperietur, intra quam sit in Patre et Filio et Spiritu sancto infinitas in aeterno, species in imagine, usus in munere.'

⁴⁸ The uncertain dating of the letter means that it may pre-date or be contemporary with *mor.* 1, and thus reinforce my reading of that book, but our lack of certainty leads me to discuss it as a separate and probably subsequent text.

inseparable that whatever is done by it must be thought to be performed at the same time by the Father and by the Son and by the Holy Spirit.[49]

The question that faces us in analysing this letter is, then, not whether Augustine understood the centrality of the doctrine, but *how* he understood the doctrine. At the same time, this letter is also significant for our story because in it we find pneumatological themes and patterns of analogy that appear for the first time. Augustine's understanding of inseparable operation and his developing pneumatology are intertwined, and it will be clearest if we begin with the latter, and then return to the question of inseparable operation.

After the statement of inseparable operation quoted above, Augustine offers an analogy:

> There is no nature, Nebridius, and no substance whatsoever that does not have in itself and does not display these three things: first, that it exists; second, that it is this or that; and third, that it remains as it was to the extent it can [*primo ut sit, deinde ut hoc uel illud sit, tertio ut in eo quod est maneat, quantum potest*]. That first element reveals the very cause of nature from which all things come; the second reveals the form by which all things are fashioned and somehow or other formed; the third reveals a certain permanence [*manentiam quandam*], so to speak, in which all things exist.[50]

Augustine then, somewhat rhetorically, states that were it possible for any one of these three dimensions, or perhaps 'activities', that constitute each thing not to be present, then it would be possible for one person of the Trinity to act apart from the others. So far the analogy is intended to help Nebridius understand the doctrine of inseparable operation.

Augustine now explains that the form (*species*) properly ascribed (*propria ... tribuitur*) to the Son may also be understood as a discipline, a skill and an understanding which informs the mind.[51] The three features of any thing are now also described as three questions that one may ask.

---

[49] *ep.* 11. 2 (CCSL 31. 26–7). Michel Barnes and I have discussed this text in a number of pieces in recent years, see his 'Re-reading Augustine's Theology of the Trinity', in Stephen T. Davis, Daniel Kendall and Gerald O'Collins (eds.), *The Trinity: An Interdisciplinary Symposium on the Trinity* (Oxford: Clarendon Press, 1999), 145–76, and my '"Remember that you are Catholic" (*serm.* 52,2): Augustine on the Unity of the Triune God', *Journal of Early Christian Studies* 8 (2000), 39–82.

[50] *ep.* 11. 3 (CCSL 31. 27). The text here is complicated; I have used that of Daur's new CCSL edition, for the older text, see CSEL 34. 26–7.

[51] When he reads *Epistula* 11 (*L'Intelligence*, 391ff.) Du Roy has virtually nothing to say about the principle of inseparable operation; he focuses on arguing that Augustine's attempt to explain the doctrine by means of the inseparable nature of the three aspects of any reality – that it exists, that is something determinate and that it endures – reveals Augustine's dependence on a vision

The intention (*intentio*) of the one asking often singles out one question in response to the peculiar character of an object, even though the others are inseparable. Thus the Incarnate Christ focuses our intention towards one of the persons, even though all three must be there:

> we, first of all, desire to know both the means by which we might attain some knowledge and that in which we might remain. We had first, therefore, to be shown a certain norm and rule of discipline. This was done through that divine dispensation of the assumed man, which is properly to be ascribed to the Son [*quae proprie filio tribuenda est*], so that there follows through the Son both a knowledge of the Father, that is of the one principle from whom all things come [*unius principii ex quo sunt omnia*], and a certain interior and ineffable sweetness of remaining in this knowledge and of scorning all mortal things, which gift and function is properly attributed to the Holy Spirit. Though all these actions, then, are done with the highest unity and inseparability [*cum agantur omnia summa communione et inseparabilitate*], they still had to be shown to us distinctly on our account, for we have fallen from that unity into multiplicity.[52]

Taken together the two passages I have just quoted summarize Augustine's 'order pneumatology',[53] which ascribes to the Spirit the function of maintaining created things in their particular individuated and formed existence. Augustine links this new account seamlessly with his picture of the Spirit separating us from the world and conforming us to God. The 'interior and ineffable sweetness' that the Spirit provides here is probably synonymous with the love for God that the Spirit is described as inspiring in *De moribus* I. Augustine has thus linked the Spirit's work in sanctifying to the Spirit's role in sustaining the creation.

It will be helpful to explore the place of this theme in Augustine's early texts a little more extensively. This account of the Spirit appears first in Augustine's *De Genesi adversus Manicheos* written at Thagaste, probably in 389. Here Augustine makes use for the first time of Wisdom 11.21 ('you have ordered all things in measure, number and weight') to identify the factors that make any body into a harmonious unity.[54] At the same time,

---

of the Trinitarian structure of creation. *Epistula* 11 also provides Du Roy with the chance to rail against the doctrine of appropriation, which he argues is the result of Augustine interpreting the Trinity on the basis of the Trinitarian ontology. I briefly discuss the doctrine of appropriation in Chapter 8; see also the discussions of inseparable operation at the end of this chapter and in Chapter 9.

[52] *ep.* 11. 4 (CCSL 31. 28). The text quoted in this note is the same in both CCSL and CSEL versions.

[53] The title 'order pneumatology' is Chad Gerber's.

[54] Augustine's use of texts from Wisdom during this period may owe to hints found in Ambrose, but the unique use to which he puts them bears further witness to a personal appropriation: see La Bonnardière, *Le Livre de la Sagesse*, 19–34.

Augustine presents this harmonious, beautiful and intelligible structuring of the creation as the result of it having been caused by 'the supreme measure and number and order which are identical with the unchanging and eternal sublimity of God himself'. The Trinity is not openly invoked, but the allusion is highly likely.[55]

At around the same time, in the eighteenth of his *De diversis quaestionibus LXXXVIII*, Augustine reflects directly on a similar parallel:

> For every existing thing there is something responsible for its existing, something responsible for its distinguishing marks, and something responsible for its coherence [*omne quod est aliud est quo constat, aliud quo discernitur, aliud quo congruit*] ... [Accordingly] it requires a threefold cause [*causam ... trinam*] ... But the cause that is the author of every created thing is God. Therefore it is fitting that he be a Trinity ... For this reason also, in the search for truth, there can be no more than three kinds of question: Does a thing exist at all? Is it this particular thing or something else? Should it be approved or disapproved? [*utrum omnino sit, utrum hoc an aliud sit, utrum adprobandum improbandumue sit*].[56]

Lastly, the theme is most extensively developed in the *De vera religione*, written in 390. Near the beginning of the text Augustine summarizes the Catholic faith for Romanianus, the dedicatee of the treatise:

> Not that the Father should be understood to have made one part of the whole creation and the Son another and the Holy Spirit yet another, but that each and every nature has been made simultaneously by the Father through the Son, in the Gift of the Holy Spirit. Every particular thing, you see, has simultaneously about it these three: that it is one something, and that it is distinguished by its own proper look or species from other things, and that it does not overstep the order of things [*simul habet haec tria: ut et unum aliquid sit et specie propria discernatur a ceteris et rerum ordinem non excedat*].[57]

Most of the terminology and thought here mirrors the passages already examined. In *Epistula* 11, however, Augustine says that the gift of the 'interior and ineffable sweetness' is appropriately attributed to the Spirit; here he simply uses *Donum*, Gift, as a title for the Spirit. We previously saw Augustine use Hilary's *Aeternitas* to describe the Father: now we see him make use of Hilary's favourite title for the Spirit.[58] Augustine also

---

[55] *Gn. adv. Man.* 1.16.26.
[56] *div. qu.* 18 (CCSL 44A. 23). For the dating of the various questions of the work, see Gustave Bardy in BA 10. 12–36. Much of Bardy's discussion is summarized by Davis Mosher at FoC 70. 2–20.
[57] *vera rel.* 7. 13 (CCSL 32. 196).
[58] It is interesting that while Hilary links *aeternitas* and *Pater* in a number of places, Augustine would have found one of the clearest examples in precisely the same passage (*trin.* 2. 1) to which we saw him allude earlier.

repeats 'simultaneously' (*simul*) twice to emphasize that the action of the persons in creation is not sequential.

Towards the end of the *De vera religione* Augustine writes:

> (112) So there you are: I worship one God, the one Principle of all things, and the Wisdom by which is made wise any soul that is wise, and the very Gift by which is blessed any soul that is blessed … (113) All things, nonetheless, would not have been made by the Father through the Son unless God were supremely good, so good that he is not jealous of any nature's being able to derive its goodness from him and has given them all the ability to abide in this good. That is why it is incumbent on us to worship and confess the very Gift of God, together with the Father and the Son unchanging – a Trinity of one substance, one God from whom we are, through whom we are, in whom we are … the Source … the Form … the Grace by which we are being reconciled.[59]

This quotation only hints at the full complexity of Augustine's threefold structuring of this passage, but it does enable a view of the main dogmatic lines that Augustine follows. Once again the Spirit is Gift, that which enables us to remain as we are created, that which moves us towards the Good *and* that which enables us to remain in the Good when we are purified.[60] In this new clarity about the Spirit's roles we perhaps see the barest hints of Augustine's later understanding of the Spirit's role as the one who preserves the union of Father and Son. We will see further early hints towards this theology in the next chapter, but much will remain inchoate.

The origins of this 'order pneumatology' are complex. While a number of Latin pro-Nicenes argue that the Spirit inspires and remains in the faithful, leading them towards knowledge of God through Christ, only Ambrose among the Latin theologians (and among Augustine's likely sources at this time) articulates such accounts as part of a wider account of the Spirit's particular role in creation. In other writers, assertions that the Spirit was involved in creating and is thus divine sit alongside discussion of the Spirit's roles in sanctifying Christians without these themes being drawn together.[61] Near the beginning of *De spiritu* 2 Ambrose writes,

---

[59] *vera rel.* 55. 112–13 (CCSL 32. 259–60).

[60] Both in this text's assertion of God's (and the Spirit's) absolutely generous goodness and in the assertion of *De moribus* 1 that the Spirit sanctifies because the Spirit is immutable we may see echoes of the doctrine of the undiminished giver, the doctrine that God bestows his enlightening presence without any diminishment. This doctrine is particularly associated with Greek pro-Nicene pneumatology in the late fourth century and Ambrose adopts it from Athanasius and Didymus the Blind. It may also be that Augustine's account here owes to Plotinian use of the same doctrine, for example, Plotinus, *Enn.* 5. 1.6, 4. 9.5, 4. 8.4, 3. 5.2. On this theme see my 'The Holy Spirit as the Undiminished Giver'.

[61] By the time of writing *Gn. litt.* c.400, Augustine will also have read Basil's *Hex.*, most probably in the translation of Eustathius (for an edition of this text, see TU 6). Cf. *Gn. litt.* 1. 18.36 and Basil, *Hex.* 2. 6. Ambrose himself had made extensive use of Basil's homilies.

(33) So, when the Spirit moved over the waters, there was no grace in creation, but after the creation of this world also received the operation of the Spirit, it gained all the beauty of that grace with which the world is illumined. Finally, the prophet declared that the grace of the universe cannot abide [*manere*] without the Holy Spirit, when he said [Ps. 103: 29–30] … (34) And who will deny that the work of the Holy Spirit is the creation of the earth, whose work it is that it is renewed? … (36) Thus [gentile writers] do not deny that the power of creatures stands firm [*subsistere*] through the Spirit.[62]

The same theology is present in more opaque form in Ambrose's *Hexameron*, written *c.*386/7, although there has been considerable argument about whether Augustine knew this text or only its basic contents from Ambrose's preaching. In the *Hexameron* Ambrose speaks also of the 'will' of God as that which enables the creation to remain. Augustine similarly speaks of the Spirit as the will of God in his first anti-Manichaean Genesis commentary, written in 389.[63]

While these passages provided Augustine with a stimulus towards his order pneumatology, the prominence of the theme during these years is only explained by also noting the prominent function of order in his earliest writing.[64] Augustine frequently hypostasizes *ordo* as that which enables our return to contemplation: 'order is that which, if we hold to it in life, will lead us to God.'[65] These early discussions of *ordo* may well adapt something of Plotinus's understanding of the ordering function of his third *hypostasis*, even if Augustine never interpreted it as the Holy Spirit.[66] Plotinus accords a significant role to appropriately ordered love in the existence not only of *Nous* and *Psuche* but of all things as they attend to their particular source.[67] Augustine's use of *concordia* in *De moribus* 1 shows the interwoven nature of love and order throughout his earliest writing, suggesting that his turn to a more overt 'order pneumatology'

---

[62] Ambrose, *spir.* 2. 5.33–6 (CSEL 79. 99–100).

[63] See Ambrose, *Hex.* 1. 62.22, 1. 5.19; Augustine *Gn. adv. Man.* 1. 7.12.

[64] This order pneumatology is also a fundamental theme in Augustine's emerging account of creation. Augustine presents the creation's achievement of form as a conversion towards God. See, for example, *Gn. adv. Man.* 2. 15.22, 1. 25.43. On this theme, see Marie-Anne Vannier, *'Creatio', 'Conversio', 'Formatio' chez S. Augustin* (Fribourg: Editions Universitaires Fribourg Suisse, 1991).

[65] *ord.* 1. 9.27 (CCSL 29. 102): 'Ordo est, quem si tenuerimus in vita, perducet ad deum'. For an example of its status, see Licentius's reference to 'occultissimum divinumque ordinem' at *ord.* 1. 11.32 (CCSL 29. 106) and Augustine's own use of identical language at *ord.* 2. 7.24. For extensive discussion of the theme of order in creation, see Anne-Isabelle Bouton-Touboulic, *L'Ordre Caché: La notion d'ordre chez saint Augustin* (Paris: Études Augustiniennes, 2004), Part 1, chs. 1–7 and Part 3, ch. 2.

[66] See, for example, the passage from *Enn.* 3. 2 quoted in the first chapter. That passage can be usefully compared with *Enn.* 3. 3.1's description of the activity of the world-soul as producing a harmonious order.

[67] For example, Plotinus, *Enn.* 5. 1.6–7, 5. 2.1–2, 6. 7.35.

in these years is an emphasizing of a theme already latent in those earlier reflections. Once we reject the idea that behind these discussions of order lies Plotinus's third *hypostasis*[68] in favour of admitting Augustine's fundamental uncertainty about the nature of the Spirit at this stage, then it is most plausible that Augustine has made use of a pneumatological theme from Ambrose to give new theological density to his earlier speculations. Augustine has used Ambrose's insistence that the work of the Spirit in redemption mirrors the work of the Spirit in creation to draw together his developing sense of the relationship between creation and redemption. Augustine has perhaps begun to see the Spirit's role in sustaining the creation and leading it towards contemplation of God as pointing to the core of the Spirit's eternal *proprium*.

We can, however, press further: examining some key themes of the analogies Augustine proffers here will take us towards a better grasp of the Trinity's inseparable operation at this stage, and the ability of the created order to mirror that triune activity. The three questions that one may ask of anything have their origins in the Latin rhetorical tradition's discussion of *status*, or 'issues', the general headings under which any case should be approached, or the bases on which cases rest. There are a variety of ways of breaking these down, but Cicero opts for three: 'Is it? What is it? Of what sort is it?'[69] Quintilian, in a survey of the various systems for organizing *status*, both presents threefold theories as the most common and persuasive and provides evidence that some rhetoricians also saw these questions as involving judgements of value. A little later he states that the threefold division is best because it is suggested by nature, perhaps even following the process by which things come to be.[70] In the fifth century Martianus Capella witnesses to the continued centrality of the threefold division, and the *De rhetorica* sometimes ascribed to Augustine himself offers further indications of a tendency to read the threefold structure as reflecting a natural ordering.[71] While this rhetorical tradition fills in

---

[68] For discussion of this theme, see Chapter 1. I also discount the suggestion of Robert O'Connell that *ordo* refers to the Son. For discussion and rejection of this possibility, see Gerber, *The Spirit of Augustine's Early Theology*, ch. 3, 'Excursus A'.
[69] Cicero, *orat*. 15. 45: 'aut sitne aut quid sit aut quale sit' For a parallel division of theology into four parts, the final two of which concern the Gods' governance of the world and their concern for humanity, see *Nat. deo*. 2. 1.3. On this rhetorical background, see the helpful discussion of Du Roy, *L'intelligence*, 385ff.; Lausberg, *Handbuch*, para 134ff.
[70] Quintilian, *inst*. 3. 6.45. Cf. 3. 6.80.
[71] Martianus Capella, *nupt. phil*. 5. 444. Cf. Ps. Augustine, *rhet*. 9 (Giomini 50–1). In his discussion of *essentia* and *substantia* Hilary offers distinctions that may at least further demonstrate that Augustine systematizes a distinction that can be found less well put in other contemporary Latins. See *synod*. 12 (PL 10. 490).

a little more of the background to Augustine's picture, there is no clear parallel to Augustine's Trinitarian appropriation of it in Latin Christian literature.[72] Augustine's adaptation reflects his personal predilection for reinterpreting Latin educational and rhetorical traditions in the light of his Neoplatonic-inspired understanding of the intelligibility of the created order.

At the beginning of the previous paragraph I spoke of Augustine's 'analogies' in *Epistula* 11. This term is inappropriate insofar as Augustine does not use a technical term to describe the likenesses he finds in the created order, nor for the related process of reasoning that he deploys. When, many years later, he does use analogy as a term for his procedure, he does so in order to deny its appropriateness.[73] Nevertheless, we are seeing something distinctly Augustinian coming into view. I have already rejected Du Roy's view that the first stage of Augustine's Trinitarian theology is entirely founded in reason's ability to progress in contemplation because of our participation in a threefold Plotinian system of ultimate realities. I am similarly unconvinced by the manner in which Du Roy casts the second stage of his thesis, in which Augustine's Trinitarianism is now increasingly driven by an account of the soul ascending towards contemplation through reflection on the Trinitarian structures of the created order. Du Roy's description still gives insufficient weight to Augustine's engagement with Latin pro-Nicene theology, and it still fails to recognize ways in which Augustine's theology is not purely economic.

Nevertheless, Du Roy's emphasis on the importance to Augustine of an account of the creation as intelligible and as a site for reflection on the Trinity is correct and it is here that we find one of Augustine's most distinctive contributions to reflection on the Trinitarian mystery. At the heart of Augustine's account of this intelligibility is a belief that God uses the creation to draw us towards a restored contemplation, a belief that the creation is intelligible towards a clear end. In *Epistula* 11 – and in the anti-Manichaean works more generally – Augustine sees the created order itself as prompting the threefold sets of questions that the rhetorical and philosophical traditions he values have come to ask about the nature of reality.

Because these questions are prompted by the created order itself, Augustine's thinking seems to run, they may be read as pointing to the

---

[72] That one might turn to these questions in order to structure a response (and give a sense of forensic proof to the following argument) is shown by Tertullian, *adv. Prax.* 5. 1.
[73] *serm.* 52. 23. On Augustine's analogical practice see also ch. 5, pp. 133f. and ch. 11, pp. 288f.

triune cause of the created order. Reflection on triune structures in the creation is then to be found at a variety of levels. Threefold accounts of how the good student is to be educated reflect the cause and end of the created order. In *Episula* 11 Augustine sees the Son's status as form reflected not only in the formed nature of created realities, but also in the need for form or discipline in life. This latter observation then leads him to our need for a desire to remain in this knowledge or discipline, a desire given by the Spirit. These examples delineate two of the most basic analogical sites with which Augustine is concerned during these years: the created order, and the interplay between form or knowledge and desire or love in intellectual life understood as a key expression of the soul's nature and power. We find these two sites examined in increasingly complex forms through the *De vera religione* and on into the *Confessions*. In his mature work, as we shall see in Chapter 5, Augustine will draw a third from these two.[74]

In these 'analogical' reflections, however, Augustine is not merely using the rhetorical-philosophical traditions on which he draws to fill out an account of the Trinity otherwise shaped only by a formal acknowledgement of the 'rule of faith'. Augustine is engaged in a far more complex process, using his growing understanding of Nicene theology to offer an interpretation of some traditional rhetorical and philosophical material read in a broadly Platonic fashion. This can be seen in Augustine's argument that the three questions one may ask of something are inseparable and thus help to illustrate the doctrine of inseparable operation. Here the doctrine guides what one should find within the created order. As we shall see again when we return to Augustine's analogical practice, however he tries to separate at a formal level the distinction between reason and authority during these years, his accounts are considerably complicated by his actual analogical practices.

This leads us, at last, back to Augustine's presentation of inseparable operation in *Letter* 11. Two features of Augustine's account should draw our attention. First, Augustine's analogy attempts to explain the doctrine of inseparable operation by deploying a model in which Father, Son and Spirit work in creation with a threefold causal action. At least initially, Augustine accords each of the divine three a role in that creative action. The Father is the ultimate cause, the Son is the form (or forming reality) of all, the Spirit maintains all in existence. I say 'at least initially' because Augustine qualifies the temporal succession implied in

---

[74] See pp. 133–7 (cf. p. 280). That discussion also offers further reflection on the question of Augustine's sources.

the analogy. He argues that if one sees that it is necessary that whatever exists must in consequence also be of a particular sort and remain thus, then we understand the divine inseparable operation. This qualification suggests that Augustine may see the utility of the analogy partly to rest in the fact that although the creative act may be presented sequentially, the effects of the causal activity are distinguishable only logically because of human inability to grasp the unity that obtains between Father, Son and Spirit.

Second, and against a reading that would see Augustine's language of a 'threefold cause' as semi-modalist, there is evidence that Augustine understands the unity of the divine three as a harmonic unity in which the three remain irreducible. This is apparent when Augustine speaks of the three questions one may ask of an object. Because of the interest of the one questioning, he tells us, a particular question appears to take prominence. This illustrates the general principle that 'quamvis multa insint, aliquid tamen eminet' ('although many are present, one thing nevertheless stands out'). The prominence of a given question thus reflects a real plurality, not only the partial focus of the onlooker. Similarly, Augustine speaks of the divine actions being done with 'the highest degree of mutual association and inseparability' (*cum ... summa communione et inseparabilitate*). Now, one might think that Augustine's contrast in *Epistula* 11 (and elsewhere in his early work) between our multiplicity and the unity that is the source of all and from which we have fallen, as well as his occasional use of Plotinian-sounding titles such as 'the One' to refer to God, would argue against this emphasis on the irreducibility of the divine three. Yet, in *De vera religione*, which may be contemporaneous with *Epistula* 11, just as Augustine casts the Christian life as a search for 'the One, than which there is nothing more simple' (*unum ... quo simplicius nihil est*), he also argues that the One has a perfectly realized likeness that is identical to it (*ita simile sit, ut hoc omnino impleat ac sit id ipsum*), that is the Word who is God from God.[75] The 'One' is actually the Father and Augustine has already at least attempted to adapt this Plotinian language to Trinitarian use. He interprets the notion of the Son as 'God from God' by reference to the Word's status as an image that is also identical to that which it images. Augustine says little here about how or whether he also understands the relationship between Father and Son in terms of any philosophy of substance. There is, then, a parallel between speaking of the image's perfect similarity to that which it images and speaking of the divine actions as

---

[75] *vera rel.* 36. 66 (CCSL 32. 229–30).

happening with 'the highest degree of mutual association': in both cases these intentionally non-reductive harmonies are taken to be compatible with the divine unity and simplicity.

Augustine's *Epistula* 14 enables us to push a little further. In this text, again addressed to Nebridius, Augustine struggles with a number of questions concerning the nature of individuation. The first question asks how it is that we may still be distinct individuals if we do the same thing. Augustine's answer begins with the observation that all appearance of identical activity not only hides differences invisible to the naked eye, but ends with the positing of a fundamental distinction based on our possession of an individual motion (*motus*).[76] It is most plausible that Nebridius has asked about the unity of the two natures in Christ, although there is room for debate. Nevertheless, the answer bears on Augustine's understanding of inseparable operation. For the persons to exemplify perfect unity they must exhibit one motion or activity. Augustine should not, however, be taken as indicating that for the Trinity to be truly one the divine must be most fundamentally one entity with its own *motus*; the evidence from the preceding paragraph indicates that Augustine understands the unity of the three to be such that they exhibit a unified causal *motus*. Further evidence comes from Augustine's reference to everything possessing a threefold cause in *De diversis quaestionibus*, no. 18. Augustine's use of *trinam ... causam* there is not only a *hapax legomenon* within his corpus, it finds no clear parallel in preceding or contemporary Christian (or non-Christian) literature.[77] Thus, *trinam ... causam* probably represents not the application of an accidental adjective to a fundamentally unitary concept, but Augustine's desire to find a way to express a concept for which he could find few parallels in the Christian or non-Christian literature available to him.

I suggest, then, we find three themes in Augustine's account of inseparable operation between 388 and 391. First, Augustine sees Father, Son and Spirit as joined in a harmonic and inseparable unity that exhibits many of the features that we would normally attribute to a unified agent (the paucity of evidence does not enable us to specify further the precise sort of unity Augustine envisages). Second, Augustine envisages this unity of action as an ordered unity initiated by the Father. The paradigmatic

---

[76] *ep.* 14. 2 (CCSL 31. 33–4).

[77] There is also some evidence from later decades that Augustine's choice not to use the alternative adjective *triplex* may have been an intentional avoidance of a term that he saw as indicating 'tripartite', see Chapter 8, p. 223.

operation Augustine has in mind is that of creating, but *Epistula* 11 makes clear that the same unity of action is apparent in the work of salvation. As I indicated in the initial section of this chapter, pro-Nicene accounts of inseparable operation frequently move beyond asserting merely that each of the divine three is involved in every act, by emphasizing the Father works through Son and in Spirit. Such assertions both emphasize the fact of Trinitarian order, and they begin to specify how we may conceive of the three as unified. Throughout his career, as we shall see, Augustine strongly emphasizes this ordered sequence, and his explorations of the doctrine may almost be read as a series of attempts to spell out how the Father's working through Son and in Spirit provides the key to understanding it. Once again, however much his work follows original lines, its foundation remains the principles of Latin Nicene theology.

Third, Augustine seems already to see a connection between the manner in which Father, Son and Spirit operate inseparably and their eternal relationships. Augustine's account of the Son as form and image in the causal analogy that he deploys shows that he envisages the Son's role in creation as reflecting his eternal status as form and image. The Father works inseparably with the Son because he always works through the Son who is image and that in which all things find their form. If we assume the same logic obtains in the case of the Spirit (and here we are on far less certain ground), then we have an even stronger hint that he already sees the Spirit's eternal role as the unity and love between Father and Son. This set of links will become far clearer in his mature work: here we can only extrapolate towards an account Augustine himself never offers. Interestingly, in the discussions of this period Augustine does not invoke the scriptural description of the persons being 'in' one another that we saw in the first section of the chapter.[78] Indeed, in the texts from 389–91 we do not even find clear parallels to Augustine's very early description of the Son as *Intellectus* resting 'in' the *Principium*. This aspect of previous Latin Nicene Trinitarianism will remain largely absent from Augustine's thought. As we shall see, he later provides some evidence that he is unhappy with the language, but here it may simply be that he has not yet seen its significance.

In any case, we would be foolish to try and nail down Augustine's understanding of inseparable operation too tightly at this stage. His account defies easy summary in part because he is simply not yet clear. At the same time, the texts covered in this chapter offer a snapshot of a period

---

[78] Augustine first quotes John 14.10 *c*.404 at *cons. ev.* 1. 4.7.

during which there is considerable development. We have not yet reached the point at which Augustine's mature summaries and more extended discussions have begun to appear. Nevertheless, it will eventually become clear that what we have seen shows that those mature accounts were, for the most part, linear developments of themes from these early texts. It is time now to move to a text that shows significant development.

CHAPTER 3

Faith of our fathers: De fide et symbolo

In the autumn of 393, all the bishops from the province of Africa assembled in council at Hippo. In a sign of his growing intellectual reputation the recently ordained Augustine was asked to address the council and offered a discourse on the creed that reveals significant shifts in his Trinitarian theology.[1] In this discourse, the *De fide et symbolo*, Augustine does not articulate his Trinitarian theology in a primarily anti-Manichaean context, and he far more openly and extensively invokes terminologies and themes typical of Latin pro-Nicene theology. He speaks in terms he thought his Episcopal audience would recognize, and reveals a significant amount of preparatory re-reading in his Latin sources. It should, however, be no surprise that Augustine's account is also very much his own and in a number of cases we see him starting down paths of interpretation that will result in the development of some of his most distinctive mature themes.

One of the most important aspects of the *De fide* is the debt that Augustine reveals to Latin anti-Monarchian and anti-Sabellian traditions of Trinitarian definition that are barely mentioned in traditional characterizations of Latin theology. Latin Trinitarian theology was born in the anti-Monarchian conflicts of the late second and third centuries and Latin theologians of the fourth century continued to write in a theological dialect shaped by those conflicts. This 'theological dialect' is apparent in particular exegetical concerns, and in a broad field of terminologies for asserting the irreducibility of the divine three. Modern scholarly concern for the terminology of 'person', 'substance' and 'nature' has tended to miss the significance of the wider linguistic patterns that

---

[1] See *retr.* 1. 17. For other surviving records of this council, see CCSL 149. 20–53. A useful point of departure for considering this text is E. P. Meijering, *Augustine: De Fide et Symbolo. Introduction, Translation, Commentary* (Amsterdam: J. C. Gieben, 1987). Meijering, however, offers little on Augustine's relationship to his Latin pro-Nicene sources.

Faith of our fathers: De fide et symbolo

formed the context for these particular terms.[2] One of my central goals in this chapter is thus to place Augustine's new Trinitarian language within its broader historical context. Doing so may give some discussions here the feel of relentless cataloguing, but only such an exercise will lay the foundations for our later explorations. My aim is, however, not to describe a new theological dialect that replaced Augustine's anti-Manichaean concerns, but to describe one into which those earlier concerns were now woven: to understand Augustine's mature work we need to see how he melded and interwove the various terminologies and dialects described in these first three chapters.

AUGUSTINE AND LATIN ANTI-MONARCHIANISM

At the end of his discussion of the Spirit, Augustine offers a brief summary of Trinitarian orthodoxy:

> we must maintain a faith which is unshakeable, so that we call the Father God, the Son God and the Holy Spirit God. Also, there are not three Gods, but that Trinity is one God, not with different natures, but of the same substance [*neque diuersas naturas, sed eiusdem substantiae*]. Nor is the Father sometimes the Son and another time the Holy Spirit, but the Father is always the Father, the Son always the Son and the Holy Spirit always the Holy Spirit [*sed pater semper pater et filius semper filius et spiritus sanctus semper spiritus sanctus*].[3]

The first item of note here is the form of summary definition used by Augustine, the application of 'always' (*semper*) to each of the divine three.

There are only two precedents for applying this language thus. The 'Tome' of Damasus, a Roman synodal document with a number of anathemas attached and dating from 377/8 or 382, has as its first anathema: 'whoever does not say the Father always is, the Son always is and the Holy Spirit always is, is a heretic'.[4] Also, Ambrose, in *De fide* 4,

---

[2] For recent discussions of Latin anti-Monarchian theology, see Michel René Barnes, 'Latin Theology up to Augustine', in Peter Phan (ed.), *The Cambridge Companion to the Trinity* (Cambridge: Cambridge University Press, forthcoming) and *idem*, 'The Other Latin Nicenes'. See also Daniel H. Williams, 'Monarchianism and Photinus of Sirmium as the Persistent Heretical Face of the Fourth Century', *HTR* 99 (2006), 187–206. The best guides in English to Monarchianism remain the introduction and commentary in Evans, *Tertullian's Treatise Against Praxeas*, and Ronald Heine, 'The Christology of Callistus', *JThS* 49 (1998), 56–91. The latter offers an important account of the possible differences among Monarchian theologies.
[3] *f. et symb.* 9. 20 (CSEL 41. 26).
[4] Damasus, *Tom*. ln. 75 (*EOMIA* 1. 2.1.288): 'Si quis non dixerit semper Patrem, semper Filium, semper Spiritum sanctum esse: hereticus est'. My own preference is for 382, following the arguments of Lester Field Jr., *On The Communion of Damasus and Meletius: Fourth-Century Synodal Formulae in the* Codex Veronensis LX (Toronto: Pontifical Institute of Medieval Studies, 2004), ch. 5.

writes c.380, 'in this divine and wonderful mystery, we accept that the Father always remains, the Son always, the Holy Spirit always [*semper accepimus patrem, semper filium, semper spiritum sanctum*], not two Fathers, not two Sons, not two Spirits. For there is one God and Father, from whom are all things. [1Cor. 8.6]'.[5] Although we cannot be certain about the extent of Ambrose's influence over the 'Tome' it is clear that there was some.[6] One or both of these earlier statements seems to be Augustine's source.

This language presents us with the first of a series of terminologies that were in origin anti-Monarchian. Writing against Praxeas, Tertullian uses this language to emphasize that the Son is 'always' with the Father and 'always' the one who is heard and seen, revealing the Father: 'it was the Son always who was seen, and the Son always who conversed, and the Son always who wrought, by the authority and will of the Father'.[7] In his anti-Sabellian *De trinitate* (c.250) Novatian uses the same language, but in a manner closer to that of our fourth- and fifth-century examples. He writes of the Son:

Since he is begotten of the Father, he is always in the Father. I say 'always', however, not in such a manner as to prove that he is unborn, but to prove that he is born ... He is always in the Father, lest the Father be not always the Father [*ne Pater non semper sit Pater*].[8]

In the fourth century, this language begins to appear with Hilary. Once in his commentary on Matthew (written in the early 350s) Hilary insists that the names Father and Son indicate the referents of those names exist 'always'.[9] A few years later, c.359 or 360, in the first book of the *Adversus Arium*, Victorinus uses this terminology to insist on the eternal existence of Father and Son, combining it with his account of the persons eternally existing 'in' one another.[10] A little later he repeats the terminology, again paralleling it with an insistence that the two are 'in' one another and that 'the Father is not the same (*idem*) as the Son, nor is the Son the same as the Father' – this last style of summary being one that we will consider at more length in Chapter 4.[11] It is noteworthy that

---

[5] Ambrose, *fid.* 4. 8.91 (CSEL 78. 188).
[6] See Christoph Markschies, *Ambrosius von Mailand und die Trinitatstheologie* (Tubingen: J. C. B. Mohr, 1995), 42–165; Field, *Damasus and Meletius*, 176–88.
[7] Tertullian, *adv. Prax.* 15 (Evans, 108).
[8] Novatian, *trin.* 31. 3 (PL 3. 949). Cf. Tertullian, *adv. Prax.* 8.
[9] Hilary, *In Matt.* 16. 4. [10] Victorinus, *adv. Ar.* 1. 34. [11] Victorinus, *adv. Ar.* 1. 41.

this terminology only appears in the first book of the work, that which is most traditional in its argumentation and most makes use of traditional Latin exegesis. In *De trinitate* 12, c.358–60, Hilary insists that the Father must eternally be Father and the Son eternally Son.[12] Gregory of Elvira, in his *De fide* of c.358–9 (or possibly early 360s), argues that the Son is eternally with the Father, but that there are not two principles because the Son is eternally born from the Father. The name of Father implies the existence of a Son and vice versa, 'and hence the Son is always because the Father is always'.[13] In *De fide* 1 (c.378), Ambrose similarly uses the same language to insist on the eternity of Father and Son.[14] In Book 5 we find the use of the language extended to all three persons quoted above.[15]

The examples in the previous paragraph link 'always' language, used to assert that the divine three are 'always' themselves and thus irreducible, to a more well-known fourth-century argument that the term 'Father' implies the existence of a child and, thus, Father and Son must be coeval realities. In fourth-century Greek texts this language makes an early appearance in the Trinitarian debates in Arius's famous accusation that Alexander was teaching 'always God, always Son'.[16] Not surprisingly, the argument then appears occasionally with positive evaluation in Athanasius, and once in a threefold form: 'it is impossible to exchange the names: the Father is always Father, and the Son always Son, and the Holy Spirit is and is said to be always Holy Spirit'. Interestingly, Athanasius makes it clear earlier that he is adapting Greek traditions of anti-Sabellian polemic.[17] Nevertheless, this language appears only rarely in other Greek Nicene theologians. Thus, while Ambrose's application of *semper* to all three persons *may* be copying the Athanasian text just quoted, this language had its own history and a far more widespread presence in Latin theology.

---

[12] Hilary, *trin.* 12. 23.
[13] Gregory of Elvira, *fid.* l. 220 (CCSL 69. 227): 'quia nec pater potest umquam sine filio nominari nec filius sine patre vocari; ac per hoc semper filius, quia semper pater'.
[14] Ambrose, *fid.* 1. 8.55 and 1. 9.61.
[15] One of the most extensive discussions of *semper* terminology is to be found in the anonymous commentary on the Nicene creed (of 325) edited by Turner at *EOMIA* 1. 2.1. 330–47, esp. 330–1. The author (and I agree the piece most likely dates from between 360 and 400) sees this terminology as both anti-Monarchian and anti-Arian.
[16] Arius, *ep. Evs.* 1. 2 (U 1. 1–2); for Alexander's assertion of the principle, see *ep. Alex.* (U. 14. 26–7).
[17] Athanasius, *Serap.* 4. 6.64 (PG 26. 645). For the anti-Sabellian context of such language see *Serap.* 4. 5.56ff. Cf. Epiphanius, *pan.* 62. 3.7ff.

A little before the passage from the *De fide* that we are now discussing Augustine writes:

> this Trinity is one God: not that the Son and the Spirit are identical to the Father, but that the Father is the Father and the Son is the Son and the Holy Spirit is the Holy Spirit, and thus this Trinity is one God.[18]

Once again this language originates in Tertullian's anti-Monarchian polemic.[19] The language then appears in the 'Western' statement of faith from Serdica (343) and extensively in Latin pro-Nicenes, including Hilary, Victorinus, Eusebius of Vercelli and Victricius of Rouen.[20] Augustine himself uses the terminology again in his *Contra Adimantum*, a text which is virtually contemporary with the *De fide*, and in a number of later texts.[21]

Hilary reveals something important about both these anti-Monarchian modes of expression when he writes,

> For this Son, who is the way, the truth and the life, is not playing a theatrical role [*mimis theatralibus ludit*] here by changing his name and appearance, so that in the manhood which he assumed he calls himself the Son of God, but he calls himself God the Father in his nature, and he who is one and alone now falsely represents himself as someone else by a change of disguise [*et unus et solus personali demutatione se nunc in alio mentiatur*] ... The simple sense of the words is quite different, for the Father is the Father and the Son is the Son [*Nam et Pater Pater est, Filius Filius est*].[22]

Latin anti-Monarchian terminologies are intended to defend the principle that the divine names must be understood as implying the real existence of the agents and relationships they name.[23] Against Monarchian charges that their opponents were teaching ditheism, anti-Monarchian theologies argued that Scripture's presentation of two (or three) divine agents could be understood as not contradicting Scripture's simultaneous insistence on the unity of God. The original generations of anti-Monarchians argued also that this unity is founded in the Son or Word's existence as

---

[18] *f. et symb.* 9. 16 (CSEL 41. 18): 'ista trinitas unus est deus: non ut idem sit pater, qui est filius et spiritus sanctus, sed ut pater sit pater et filius sit filius et spiritus sanctus sit spiritus sanctus, sed haec trinitas unus deus'.

[19] See Tertullian, *adv. Prax.* 10 (Evans, 98): 'Ita aut pater aut filius est, et neque dies eadem et nox neque pater idem et filius, ut sint ambo unus et utrumque alter, quod vanissimi isti monarchiani volunt'. There may be some echoes of the language at Novatian, *trin.* 31.

[20] For Serdica, see Theodoret, *eccl. hist.* 2. 8. For pro-Nicene use, see Hilary, *trin.* 1. 33, 6. 43, 7. 59; Victorinus, *adv. Ar.* 1. 19, 1. 41, 1. 33; Eusebius of Vercelli, *trin.* 2. 25; Victricius, *laud.* 4. 10.

[21] *c. Adim.* 1; cf. *Io. ev. tr.* 36, 37 and 39; *c. Max.* 12.

[22] Hilary, *trin.* 7. 39 (SC 362–4).

[23] Such a perspective is integral to Tertullian's fuller argument at *adv. Prax.* 10, a section of which is discussed below.

'the Father's' and a conception of the Father extending to the Son a share in his own divine substance or power.

These anti-Monarchian traditions emphasize the irreducibility and non-identity of the 'divine three' without making use of technical 'count nouns' such as *persona*. While Latin theologians from the third to fifth centuries certainly make use of terminologies such as *persona*, *natura* and *substantia*, it is often the case that summary statements rely as much on the anti-Monarchian traditions we have begun to explore as they do on those terminologies. As we shall eventually see in the case of Augustine, reticence to use those terminologies may also reflect a belief that the philosophical questions they always beg may be circumvented, or at least better approached, by means of other summary styles. The prevalence of these traditions should warn us that attempts to summarize Latin tradition by an etymological focus on a particular term – such as the oft-repeated claim that *persona* originally means 'mask', an etymology which is then taken to reveal something essential about Latin tradition – have little cogency. Individual elements of such terminology in Trinitarian definition must be considered within the wider fields of which they are part.[24] In the case of *persona*, it is worth adding, this unhelpful mode of terminological genealogy is further complicated by a failure to attend to the actual semantic range of the term. The quotation from Hilary in the previous paragraph offers a good example of a Latin theologian denying that Son and Spirit are 'masks' for the Father. Hilary's denial not only sits squarely within anti-Monarchian tradition, it also reflects a long-standing use of *persona* to mean 'irreducible individual'.[25] It is interesting to note that in the *De fide* Augustine knows this language to be anti-Monarchian (or anti-Sabellian) in intent: we say that the persons persist *semper*, lest we think that 'the Father is sometimes the Son and another time the Holy Spirit'. We do not know if Augustine had, at this stage, read Tertullian or Novatian first hand, or whether his knowledge was mediated through others.

---

[24] A similar case might be made with respect to texts in the fourth century which simply equate *ousia* and *hypostasis* – such as the statement of faith from the so-called 'Western' council of Serdica in 343 (see above, n. 20). Only in context can one judge whether this indicates a particular view of the divine unity or simply the lack of a meaningful distinction between the two terms.

[25] See, for example, the discussion in Ernest Evans, *Tertullian's Treatise Against Praxeas* (London: SPCK, 1948), 46–50. See also G. L. Prestige, *God in Patristic Thought* (London: Heinemann, 1936), 157–9, on both *persona* and the Greek *prosopon*. The idea that *persona* 'means' mask and that hence Latin theology was condemned to semi-modalism by the inherent failures of its terminology is a fascinating example of the extent to which an easily conveyed but highly erroneous statement can persist in teaching and in textbooks decades after its scholarly rejection!

The next noteworthy aspect of the passage from the *De fide* with which we began is Augustine's insistence that all three persons are to be termed *Deus*.[26] The application of *Deus* to all three begins with Tertullian, again in anti-Monarchian context. Against Praxeas's charge that the Catholics should consistently teach the two Gods that their teaching implies, Tertullian argues:

> [we] do indeed specify two ... Yet two Gods or two lords we never let issue from our mouth: not but that both the Father is God and the Son is God and the Holy Spirit is God ... Consequently I shall in no case say either 'gods' or 'lords', but shall follow the apostle, with the result that if the Father and the Son are to be mentioned together, I call the Father God and name Jesus Christ 'the Lord'. But Christ by himself I shall be able to call God, as does the same apostle when he says 'of whom is Christ, who is God over all, blessed for evermore'. For also the sun's beam, when by itself, I shall call 'the sun': but when naming the sun, whose beam it is, I shall not immediately call the beam 'the sun'. For though I make two suns, yet the sun and its beam I shall count as two objects, and two manifestations of one undivided substance, in the same sense as I count God and his Word, the Father and the Son.[27]

Tertullian conditions his use of the term 'Deus' by emphasizing that our ability to name the Son thus depends on our belief in his substantial connection to and generation from the Father: the Son is truly named God only because the Father is the one God who shares his being with Son and Spirit.

The application of *Deus* to both Father and Son can subsequently be found in a number of first-generation Latin Nicenes, such as Phoebadius and Hilary. Both of these authors insist on the Son's unique mode of generation from the Father and take an account of the Son as 'in' the Father to guarantee that Father and Son can both be termed *Deus* without the implication that there are two *dei*.[28] In neither do we find Tertullian's argument that the terminology is only appropriate under certain circumstances. For both, Nicaea's language of 'God from God' and 'light from light' provides a clear foundation for such speech. It is, however, only with the 'Tome' of Damasus that we find the threefold language reappearing, and Augustine's use of this phrasing probably represents a debt to that document (perhaps a further debt, given the discussion above of *semper*

---

[26] My concern here is primarily with the background to Augustine's terminology; in Chapter 4, I treat the particular question of whether Latin pro-Nicenes effect a shift from thinking of the Father as the one or true *Deus* to thinking of the Trinity as such.
[27] Tertullian, *adv. Prax.* 13 (Evans, 103–4).
[28] Hilary, *trin.* 2. 4; Phoebadius, *c. Ar.* 25. 1. Cf. *c. Ar.* 27. 4.

language).²⁹ Such a phrasing appears only once in Ambrose, and he does not even parallel *Pater Deus* and *Filius Deus*.³⁰

Whereas so far I have argued that Augustine is dependent on his Latin Nicene predecessors (and through them inherits Latin anti-Monarchian traditons), we can now be a little more precise. The evidence suggests that Augustine quickly identified Ambrose as a key source. We have already seen Augustine possibly using Ambrose as a guide to what was and was not acceptable in Victorinus in 386–7. Augustine then seems to have come to see Damasus and the Roman synodal documents of the 370s and early 380s as key points of reference in his attempt to formulate the basic lines of Catholic Trinitarian belief.

PERSONA, NATURA, SUBSTANTIA

Augustine does not, in fact, use *persona* in the passage from the *De fide* quoted at the beginning of the chapter. Indeed, only once and without Trinitarian import does he use the term in the *De fide* as a whole. Although he uses the term in a variety of other contexts in his early work, it is not until the 393–5 period that we first see him use the term in Trinitarian contexts.³¹ Nevertheless, this is a good juncture at which to discuss the background to these three terms in Latin tradition, before commenting on Augustine's particular use of *natura* and *substantia* in the *De fide*.

The use of *persona* and *substantia* as a pairing in Trinitarian theology originates in Tertullian:

And if he himself is God, as John says – 'the Word was God' [John 1.1] – you have two, one commanding a thing to be made, another making it. But how you must understand 'another' [*alium*] I have already professed, in the sense of person, not of substance, for distinguishing, not for dividing [*personae non substantiae nomine, ad distinctionem non ad divisionem*].³²

---

²⁹ Damasus, *Tom.* ln. 133–5 (*EOMIA* 1. 2.1.232): 'Quod si quis putat [Christi] Patrem Deum dicens et Deum Filium eius et Deum Sanctum Spiritum'. I say 'probably' because this language is used in the *De trinitate* sometimes ascribed to Eusebius of Vercelli, see *trin.* 6. 15.4 (CCSL 9. 85). Gaudentius of Brescia, *Tract.* 21. 14.21, also uses the language. It is also of note that the first of the 'Arian' fragments from the Bobbio manuscript attributes, with disgust, precisely such an application of *deus* to each person to Phoebadius, see CCSL 87. 230.

³⁰ *Luc.* 10. 4 (CCSL 14. 346): 'Et non duo Domini, sed unus Dominus; quia et Pater Deus, et Filius Deus: sed unus Deus; quia Pater in Filio, et Filius in Patre. Unus Deus, quia una deitas'. There has been much discussion of when Augustine read this text. While Cipriani has argued that Augustine did so early, many others have suggested that he did not do so until *c.*412. See Hombert, *Nouvelles recherches*, 56ff.

³¹ The first two uses are at *lib. arb.* 3. 21.60 and *div. qu.* 69. 1 and 2. I comment on these texts below.

³² Tertullian, *adv. Prax.* 12 (Evans, 102). I comment on Augustine's use of *substantia* outside this pairing in Chapter 8.

The sentences before this quotation tell us that Tertullian uses *persona* primarily to identify a distinct individual, but that he also draws on a Roman literary sense of *persona* as a distinct speaking agent.[33] This passage also gives us an example of the main use of this opposition: in the third and fourth centuries it is primarily used to distinguish, in the course of argument, between ways of speaking about unity and distinction in God. It is only very infrequently used in summary Trinitarian statements.

Novatian makes no use of this opposition and it does not recur until the very late 350s. Our knowledge of Latin theology between 250 and 350 is, however, patchy. In the case of most of these traditional Latin terminologies we do not know if the controversies of the late 350s stimulated a *ressourcement* from Latin sources in aid of new battles, or whether the adaptations of anti-Monarchian terminologies that we are tracing were part of a continuity hidden from us by the paucity of surviving Latin material from the previous century. Whichever it was, Phoebadius of Agen, probably adapting Tertullian's terminology to his own theological context, writes *c*.358, 'he taught that the Father and Son are not one person as Sabellius says or two substances as Arius says, but as the Catholic faith acknowledges, that there is one substance and two persons'.[34] At around the same time Gregory of Elvira similarly uses Tertullian's distinction, and Zeno of Verona – who may have been writing in the early 360s – offers another example of a subsequently widespread usage.[35]

Interestingly, Hilary uses this opposition only once, and Ambrose only four times and never in the *De fide* or *De spiritu sancto*.[36] Victorinus, in a particularly clear example of his idiosyncratic relationship to previous Latin tradition twice denies the opposition's appropriateness.[37] Augustine uses the opposition directly in *De diversis quaestionibus* 83, n. 69, a long discussion of 1 Corinthians 15:28 dating from around the same time as the *De fide*. In that passage Augustine also speaks of the *proprietates* of a *persona*.[38] This terminology, which has occasional play in Latin rhetorical

---

[33] The literary/rhetorical use of *persona* has been most fully traced by Hubertus R. Drobner, *Person-Exegese und Christologie Bei Augustinus* (Leiden: Brill, 1986). Drobner's concern is Christological, but his account is equally applicable to Trinitarian usage.

[34] Phoebadius, *c. Ar.* 14 (CCSL 64. 39).

[35] Gregory of Elvira, *fid.* ln. 678; Zeno, *tract.* 1. 4. ln. 59, 2. 8. ln. 35. For the terminology in other pro-Nicenes, see also Filastrius, *haer.* 64, 93 and 110; Ambrosiaster, *ad Eph.* (α and γ) 5. 28, *ad Thess.* (α and γ) 3. 10, *quaest. test.* 97. 8; Faustinus, *trin.* 9; Jerome, *ad Gal.* 2. 3. v.6, *Lucif.* 9; Potamius, *ad Ath.* (PL 8. 1417–18).

[36] Hilary, *trin.* 4. 42; Ambrose, *Hex.* 6. 7.41, *in Psalm* 35. 22.3, *Luc.* 7. ln. 1226, *incar.* 7. 77.

[37] Victorinus, *adv. Ar.* 1A. 11, 41.

[38] Augustine, *div. qu.* 69. 1. At *lib. arb.* 3. 21.60 (CCSL 29. 310) Augustine writes: 'de cuius trinitatis unitate et aequalitate et singularum in ea personarum quadam proprietate non hic locus est

Faith of our fathers: De fide et symbolo

tradition (though not in Cicero), is prominent in Tertullian but plays only a very limited role in pro-Nicene theology until Augustine.[39]

The opposition between *persona* and *natura* is far more common in the fourth century than that between *persona* and *substantia* – although it is not found in Trinitarian contexts in third-century writers – but again is rarely used in short summary statements. This opposition is used in phrases which state that distinction between the 'persons' does not mean that the 'nature' is divided. In this sense the terminology is found a number of times in Ambrose's *De fide* and Hilary's *De trinitate*.[40] A number of other pro-Nicenes, such as Gregory of Elvira, Ambrosiaster and Jerome, also use the language.

The passage that we are considering from the *De fide* is, however, not an example of either of these pairings, but a reference to Nicaea's ὁμοουσίος. *Eiusdem substantiae* is one standard translation of the term in Latin, the other being *unius substantiae* – and this latter eventually becomes more common in Augustine's writing.[41] Nicaea's creed did not yet have liturgical or direct catechetical use and reference to the persons being *einsdem substantiae* was a convenient way of identifying oneself with its

---

disserendi'. In his Latin predecessors the adjective *singuli* and the abstract noun *singularitas* are occasionally used to emphasize the irreducibility of *persona* and *proprietas* as a category. Thus Ambrose, *fid*. 5. 3.46 (CSEL 78. 234): 'Evidens est igitur quia, quod unius est substantiae, separari non potest, etiamsi non sit singularitatis, sed unitatis. Singularitatem dico, quae graece monotes dicitur. singularitas ad personam pertinet, unitas ad naturam'. This is a particularly interesting passage for those used to standard portrayals of Latin theology because of its claim that *monotes* is only true of each person not of God as one. Contemporary Greeks, in fact, do apply the term in this way: Ambrose may be unaware of its flexibility. For the use of *singuli*, *persona* and *proprietates*, see also the final sentence of Tertullian, *adv. Prax*. 26; Isaac, *fid*. 1; Faustinus, *trin*. 12; Ambrosiaster, *ad Rom.* (rec. γ) 8. 34. The last passage referenced here, but in very different language and with Ambrosiaster's usual insistence on the persons' disparate authority, replicates Ambrose's insistence that *singularitas* is really only true of the persons.

[39] Particularly clear at Quintilian, *inst*. 11. 3.179. Cf. Ps. Augustine, *rhet*. 21, and Victorinus, *in Cic. rhet*. 1. 53. It appears at Novatian, *trin*. 27, but in Latin pro-Nicenes I have been able to locate only Hilary, *Psalm*. 63. 1, 69. 1, *In Matt*. 22. 1; Gregory of Elvira, *fid*. ln. 46, *tract*. 3, ln. 96; Didymus, *spir*. 30; Ambrose, *Abr*. 1. 5.38.

[40] Hilary, *trin*. 4. 35, 5. 10, 5. 35, 6. 8, 7. 39, 7. 40, 9. 14; Ambrose, *fid*. 3. 15, 5. 3, *spir*. 3. 13.

[41] The two versions appear an almost equal number of times in Augustine and he speaks a number of times of 'unius eiusdemque substantiae'. For evidence of the relative prominence of these translations see *EOMIA* 1. 2.1.298–307 (and the collation on 321). Turner gives twelve versions of the creed from the fourth century (and some later from Africa): all of these use some version of 'unius substantiae cum Patre (quod Graeci dicunt homoousion)' (for the African uses, including at the council of Hippo in 393 itself, see CCSL 149. 30–1). Alternative translations appear in the fifth century in connection with the Christological controversies; at the same time the parenthetical reference to *homoousios* also disappears. At *EOMIA* 1. 1.2.174ff. Turner provides further examples of the creed some of which may also be of appropriate date: these demonstrate that some version of 'homoousion Patri hoc est eiusdem cum Patre substantiae' was the second most important translation. The same picture emerges from an LLT search.

judgements and giving to more traditional formulations a Nicene cast.[42] In the Trinitarian discussions of the *De fide* Augustine uses *natura* as a synonym for *substantia* and, despite having already used the term *essentia* of the *summa essentia* in the *De vera religione* of 390, Augustine seems to avoid using a term that was not traditionally used by Latins in Trinitarian definition.[43]

The detailed terminological discussions of the last few pages show how terms such as *persona*, *substantia* and *natura* were, for Latin tradition since Tertullian, inseparable from a wider matrix of anti-Monarchian terminologies. The *De fide* shows that Augustine himself adopted this tradition and moved within it. As a corollary we should note that Latin tradition does not assume that the most appropriate way of explaining these terminologies was a discussion of genus, species and individual language. Indeed, in the case of both *substantia* and *persona*, Augustine's exploration in *De trinitate* 5–7 is the first surviving extended discussion in Latin theology.

'MOST FITTINGLY CALLED HIS WORD'

Early in the *De fide*, Augustine attempts for the first time to explain the title Word in detail. Long before his mature discussions of Word terminology in the *De trinitate*, this passage shows us something of their origins. Ending an anti-Manichaean argument for the creation's dependence on its one source, Augustine writes that because all was made through the Word, only the Father could generate the Word:

And because he created everything through the Word, he alone was able to generate that Word, through whom all things were made and through whom he made all things. This particular Word is also described as 'Truth' [John 14.6] and 'the Power and Wisdom of God' [1Cor. 1.24] [*virtus et sapientia dei*] and by many other terms and is presented for our belief as Jesus Christ the Lord, our redeemer and ruler, the Son of God [*liberator scilicet noster et rector filius dei*].[44]

The following paragraphs of his exposition turn directly to this Word. Augustine is still concerned with the Manichaean challenge – he ends

---

[42] Marius Victorinus is an exception here. While concurring with these judgements in general, Michel Barnes, in his 'Latin Theology', suggests that there is a distinct fourth-century tradition, in Potamius of Lisbon and Ossius of Cordoba, which has a more complex philosophical account of substance language.

[43] For the equation of *natura* and *substantia*, see *f. et symb.* 9.17. For the use of *summa essentia* see, for example, *vera rel.* 40. 76; for the equation of *essentia*, *natura* and *substantia*, see *vera rel.* 7. 13. I return to Augustine's use of *essentia* in Chapter 8.

[44] *f. et symb.* 2. 3 (CSEL 41. 6).

Faith of our fathers: De fide et symbolo

by drawing out the conclusion that the Son's existence as the Father's Word shows rather than denies the impossibility of any nature existing in opposition to God – but the 'meat' of his argument involves a more direct invocation of Latin anti-Homoian theology than we have so far seen.

For the first time Augustine places the title Word centre-stage. It is this title that, he says, is 'most fittingly' used of the second person. And yet, this sentence subtly misrepresents Augustine; he actually describes the 'Wisdom which God the Father has begotten' as 'most fittingly called his Word'.[45] Augustine has made the terminology of Word central, but his explanation of why Word is central is dependent upon his understanding of what it means to talk of God's Wisdom. Augustine's invocation of 1 Corinthians 1.24 as a verse intended to enable expansion of our understanding of another title goes back to *De libero arbitrio* 1 in 387, and in both cases Augustine seems to use the verse because of its reference to Wisdom.[46]

Augustine now uses the link between Word and Wisdom to argue that the Word is beyond change and thus cannot in one central respect be likened to the words that humans speak:

But that Word remains, beyond change. What was predicated of Wisdom is applicable to the Word: 'Herself unchanging, she renews all things' [Wisd. 7.27]. He is called the Word of the Father, because through him the Father makes himself known [*uerbum enim patris ideo dictum est, quia per ipsum innotescit pater*].[47]

Augustine offers an analogy. Our use of words is an attempt to reveal the contents of our mind through signs. Through his Wisdom, which he has begotten, the hidden Father makes himself known (to those who desire to know God).[48] Our words involve not a begetting, but a making, and they are made by means of the body, not the mind. Nevertheless, even this making is an attempt to imitate the begetting of the Word. God begets 'what he himself is' [*id quod est ipse genuit*] and 'from himself' (*de seipso id quod est ipse*). When we 'make' words we remain within ourselves (*in nobis ipsi quidem maneamus*) but as far as our power allows we construct something like 'another mind' (*quasi alter animus*) as a sign (*indicium*) that will enable us to be understood. Interestingly, Augustine sees our 'words' as involving also our facial and bodily gestures.[49] Of course, the bringing forth of such another mind inevitably fails and the mind of

---

[45] *f. et symb.* 2. 3 (CSEL 41. 7).   [46] *lib. arb.* 1. 2.5.   [47] *f. et symb.* 3. 3 (CSEL 41. 7).
[48] *f. et symb.* 3. 3.   [49] *f. et symb.* 4. 4.

one speaking is always hidden. Only the Father can beget another beside himself through which such revelation is possible.

The following passage takes us further:

> But God the Father, who both wills and can reveal himself most truly to souls who would know him, begot the Word in order to reveal himself, a Word which is what he himself, the begetter, is [*hoc ad se ipsum indicandum genuit, quod est ipse qui genuit*]. It is also described as his Power and Wisdom [1Cor. 1.24], for through the Word he is at work governing all things.[50]

These dense sentences reveal a number of interactions in Augustine's developing thought. As in his anti-Manichaean works, Augustine treats the created order as an intelligible act of divine revealing. The identification of Wisdom and Word shows us that Augustine now understands the eternal generation of the divine Wisdom as also the Father's eternal revelation of himself through the generation of another in whom all that might be exists. Second, we already see here in inchoate form Augustine's mature method of linking revelation and creation: the Incarnation draws us towards the existence of all in the Word and thence to the informing Word itself.

Scholarship on Augustine has long debated Augustine's early use of *verbum* terminology. This controversy mirrors that over the compatibility of Christianity and Platonism explored in Chapter 1. For a number of scholars, Augustine's understanding of Word was primarily shaped by his early Platonism (to which they accommodated his interest in the title Wisdom). For others, Augustine understood *verbum* as speech and hence truly saw the Word as divine proclamation.[51] I mention this debate only to reject its most unhelpful elements: Augustine's interest in Wisdom is both a 'biblical' interest, in the language of Wisdom and Proverbs at the very least, *and* it is a 'philosophical' interest in the sense that Augustine's earliest use of Wisdom language is shaped by a Plotinian understanding of *intellectus*. It is, however, true that we do not yet see in the *De fide* an analogy between the 'inner Word' of human beings and the eternal Word of the Father: the analogy here is only between our spoken words and the Father's eternal speech.[52]

A further example of Augustine's adherence to traditional Latin understandings of the Father/Son relationship is his discussion of the term 'Son'.

---

[50] *f. et symb.* 4. 4 (CSEL 41. 8).
[51] The debate is usefully summarized in D. W. Johnson, '*Verbum* in the Early Augustine (386–397)', *RecAug* 8 (1972), 25–53.
[52] For a history of this analogy, see Chapter 7, pp. 194–6.

The only-begotten Son has no brothers and is the 'natural son' (*naturalis filius*) of the Father, thus sharing His substance:

> As a natural Son, he was born the only-begotten Son from the substance of the Father [*de ipsa patris substantia unicus natus*], existing as the Father, God from God, light from light.[53]

The phrase *de patris substantia* ('from the substance of the Father') is another allusion to the Nicene Creed of 325. Augustine's phrasing here corresponds to the translation of that creed found in the *Breviarium Hipponense*, a collection of material stemming from the 393 council in Hippo. At the same time, although neither Hilary nor Ambrose focuses on this formulation, it is presented as a key marker of orthodoxy in Damasus's 'Tome' and is to be found in a number of other Latin pro-Nicenes.[54] The language of the Son as 'natural' or as sharing the Father's substance 'naturally' may well indicate a debt to Hilary,[55] and it points to a key way of expressing the Nicene claim that the Son's generation from the Father is a unique event in which the nature of the one generating is shared with the one generated. This theology is related, of course, to the claim that the names Father and Son are mutually entailing, but it focuses on the metaphysical core of the relationship articulated in such language.[56]

The language of the Son being generated from the Father's substance will persist throughout Augustine's career.[57] That language begins in the *De fide*, and should be considered the baseline for Augustine's mature

---

[53] *f. et symb.* 4. 6 (CSEL 41. 10).

[54] See, for example, Victorinus, *adv. Ar.* 2. 1.10, *hom. rec.* 4; Ambrosiaster, *quaest. test.* 97; Gregory of Elvira, *fid.* ln. 1.143; Filastrius, *her.* 66; Damasus, *Tom.* ln. 78ff. Cf. Phoebadius, *c. Ar.* 25. For the *Breviarium hipponense*, see CCSL 149. 30.

[55] The only clear parallel to the expression is Hilary, *trin.* 9. 41 (SC 462. 100): 'Natiuitas enim non nouae neque alienae naturae Deum fecerat, sed naturalis Filius Patri naturali generatione substiterat'. Cf. *trin.* 9. 2, 7. 39; Faustinus, *trin.* 19 and 49. Something of the same language is also to be found in Ambrose, for example *Spir.* 3. 16.113. For Hilary the language of the Son's *nativitas* is also central, see e.g. Hilary, *trin.* 6. 10ff. See also Ambrosiaster, *quaest. test.* 97. 1, 8, who is possibly dependent on Hilary.

[56] The *Ur* text in Latin theology is probably Tertullian, *adv. Prax.* 8, which combines the imagery of the shoot of a plant which comes from a root, the river from the spring and the beam of the sun. The dynamic force of this language is seen in *adv. Prax.* 29, where Tertullian attempts to explain how the Son suffered in his flesh, but the Father did not, by arguing that mud which gets into a river does not pollute the spring from which the river flows.

[57] See, for example, *cons. ev.* 2. 3, *Io. ev. tr.* 17. 16, *serm.* 46. 11, *serm.* 92. 3, *serm.* 214. 5, *trin.* 15. 20.38. At *c. Max.* 15. 14, Maximinus accuses Augustine of saying that both Son and Spirit are *de substantia Patris*. Augustine had not used this phrase, but it seems likely that here we should see Maximinus accommodating Augustine to his expectation of a Nicene argument. Augustine has, however, spoken of the Son as born from the father and therefore sharing a nature and substance with him (see note 61, below): it is probably this that Maximinus is glossing. Augustine does not quibble with him over this.

understanding of the Son's generation – however he eventually nuances his account. Oddly, the argument that just as each species generates offspring that share a nature, so too the Father generates a 'natural' Son who shares his nature, is not found fully developed in Augustine until his latest anti-'Arian' works, works in which he seems to be consciously turning back to the anti-'Arian' polemic of his forebears.[58] This is another intriguing sign that Augustine was an attentive reader of his forebears, but one whose interpretations of them were frequently very much his own.

As we note the appearance of themes that will occupy much of Augustine's mature reflection, we should also note what does not yet appear. As we saw above, Augustine does not yet attempt to illustrate the notion of the Word through reference to the 'interior Word' in the human mind.[59] Augustine also treats the divine Wisdom as eternally with the Father without showing signs he is worried this implies that the Father is wise only because his Wisdom is eternally with him: in other words, he still accepts without question a fairly standard pro-Nicene account that he will later question and modify.[60]

SPIRITUS, DEITAS, COMMUNIO

Later in the *De fide*, Augustine comes to the Spirit. Here for the first time we find Augustine offering a detailed account of the Spirit's eternal relationship to Father and Son. Augustine seems to have been searching for such a sense of the Spirit's inner Trinitarian 'role': he tells us that earlier interpreters have not applied themselves sufficiently to the Spirit and that such an application would enable us 'to understand his *proprium*, that which he uniquely is'.[61] *Proprium* here is virtually interchangeable with some senses of *proprietas*. Both terms, like so many we have considered, go back to Tertullian, but are also extensively used in late fourth-century Latin theology. In Tertullian, 'the *proprietas* of each Person is not that which he specifically possesses but that which he specifically is'.[62] To identify the *proprietas* is thus also to identify that which distinguishes one person from another.[63] Augustine's translation of Romans 8.32 ('who spared not his own Son') reads *Qui Filio proprio non pepercit*, and in this sense

---

[58] See *c. s. Ariann.* 2.3; *c. Max.* 14.
[59] For the evolution of this concept see Chapter 7, pp. 194–6.
[60] See Chapter 8.
[61] *f. et symb.* 9. 19 (CSEL 41. 22): 'ut intellegi facile posit et eius proprium, quo proprio fit'.
[62] Evans, *Tertullian's Treatise Against Praxeas*, 257.
[63] For example Tertullian, *adv. Prax.* 27 and Novatian, *trin.* 27.

the term provided grist to the mill of all Nicenes who wished to argue that the Son was necessarily the Father's true Son, the Father's own Son associated with Him in nature and power, rather as Athanasius understands the implications of the Greek term ἴδιος.

Late fourth-century Latin Nicenes use the terms similarly. Victorinus, in an extensive discussion of Romans 11.34–6, argues that 'from whom are all things' is proper to the Father because he is the source, while 'in whom' must be proper to the Son because He is Logos and the 'receptacle' in whom all things exist. Within Victorinus's theology, where the persons are differentiated by having their own act or movement within the divine substance, that which is *proprium* to a person is what a person is.[64] Hilary uses similar language to describe the import of the Father's words at Matthew 3.17 'this is my beloved Son': 'but if "this is my Son" is proper and unique to him [the Son], why do we criticize God the Father for confessing that he is his proper Son?'[65] A few paragraphs later Hilary even sums up the Catholic faith in these terms: 'this faith is the gift of the Father's revelation, that Christ should not be misrepresented as a creature from nothing, but confessed as the Son of God according to a nature that is his own [*secundum proprietatis naturam*]'.[66] Ambrose follows similar patterns of usage. Somewhat differently, however, at the beginning of *De fide* 2, he divides scriptural titles (*indicia*) into three types, the first of which 'reveal that which is proper to the divine nature [*quae proprietatem deitatis ostendant*]'.[67]

Thus, *proprium* and *proprietas* are used in discussions to identify that which is distinctive of and proper to individual persons (and occasionally divinity). No clear association between identifying a 'person's' *proprium* and identifying their relationship(s) of origin is yet apparent, although there is already an implicit connection, in that many of the standard things that are 'proper' to the Son are precisely those which indicate that the Son is both a subsistent being and yet uniquely so because of his unique relationship to the Father. Thus, with the discussion of the Spirit that we have been examining we can compare Augustine's summary of what *docti et spirituales viri* have said about Father and Son a little later in

---

[64] Victorinus, *adv. Ar.* 1. 37 (CSEL 83/1. 122): 'Hoc autem ex quo omnia patri dedit Hoc igitur patri ut proprium. Filio autem istud ut proprium: in quo omnia, quod lo/goj et locus est.' Cf. *ad Cand.* 31 (CSEL 83/1. 47): 'Qui quidem spiritus sanctus propria sua actione differt a filio, filius cum ipse sit, sicuti filius actione est differens a patre'.
[65] Hilary, *trin.* 6. 23 (SC 448. 214): 'Sin uero proprium ac singulare ei est Hic est Filius meus, quid calumniam Deo Patri professae de Filio proprietatis adferimus?'
[66] Hilary, *trin.* 6. 37 (SC 448. 246).   [67] Ambrose, *fid.* 2. pro. 2 (CSEL 78. 58).

the *De fide*. The learned and spiritual have shown that Father and Son are *unum* (one) but not one thing (*unus*) and that it is proper to the Father to be begetter (*genitor*) and source (*principium*) of the Son while it is proper to the Son to be begotten from the Father, and image (*imago*) of the Father, while completely equal.[68]

Augustine's initial attempt to define the Spirit's *proprium* is couched as the opinion of his predecessors:

> Some have even dared to believe that the Holy Spirit is the *communio* or, so to speak, the *deitas* (which the Greeks call θεότητα) of the Father and the Son. So as the Father is God and the Son is God, that very *deitas* by means of which they are joined together – the one by generating the Son and the one by cleaving to the Father [*qua sibi copulantur et ille gignendo filium et ille patri cohaerendo*] – is equated with him from whom [the Son] is born. This divinity, which they also interpret as the mutual love and charity of each to the other, they say is called the Holy Spirit and that many scriptural texts exist to support their view [including Rom. 5.5] … whenever there is mention in Scripture of the Gift of God, they want to interpret it above all else as meaning that the charity of God is the Holy Spirit. For it is only through love that we are reconciled to God and through it that we are called children of God, no longer like servants living in fear, 'because perfect(ed) love drives out fear' [1John 4.18], and that we have received the Spirit of freedom, 'in which we cry: Abba, Father' [Rom. 8.15].[69]

This passage has long puzzled commentators seeking to find its sources, and for good reason. Du Roy was, I think, right to suggest that Augustine makes use of a variety of sources, but combines them into a personal synthesis that he is nevertheless keen to present to the assembled bishops as bearing the weight of tradition. There is some evidence for this in the last sentence of the passage just quoted: the emphasis on the restoration of love as that which enables our return to God clearly builds on Augustine's previous work, as does his reference a few sentences later to the Spirit enabling us to be united to the divine *Wisdom*. The argument is also partly buttressed by reference to 1 John 4.18, a text used by none of the Latin pro-Nicenes we can show him to have read up to this point.

Nevertheless, what are the sources Augustine has drawn together? Du Roy rightly begins with the third book of Ambrose's *De spiritu sancto*.[70] Commenting on Peter's speech to Ananias in Acts 5, Ambrose draws attention to Peter's claim that Ananias has lied to the Holy Spirit and, a little later, to God. Ambrose writes:

---

[68] *f. et symb.* 9. 18.   [69] *f. et symb.* 9. 18 (CSEL 41. 22).
[70] Du Roy, *L'Intelligence*, Appendix 6, 486–7.

Not only does the Scripture in this place clearly bear witness to the θεότης of the Holy Spirit, that is the *deitas*, but the Lord himself also said in the Gospel: 'for the Spirit is God' [John 3.6].[71]

The relevance of this passage is enhanced when we notice that Ambrose also turns to John 4.24 within a few paragraphs, a text that Augustine links with John 3.6 in his discussion in the *De fide*. To Du Roy's account we should add that in *De spiritu* 3 Ambrose interprets Romans 1.20's mention of God's 'eternal Power and Divinity' as a reference to the Son and the Spirit: 'just as the Son is called the eternal Power of the Father, so too the Spirit, because he is divine [*divinus*], may be believed to be His eternal Godhead [*sempiterna divinitas*]'.[72] Although this text refers only to the *Father's* divinity, Augustine may, in part, be using this text to interpret Ambrose's reading of Acts 5 earlier in the same book.

Beyond Du Roy, we should note that Ambrose's discussion offers a window onto developments in Latin theology that are the broader context for Augustine's arguments. Let us begin by noting some of the basic questions that faced Latin Nicene pneumatology in the late fourth century. In the first place, there is a distinction between asserting *that* the Spirit is co-eternal with Father and Son and articulating *what* distinguishes the Spirit from Father and Son. After 360, Latin theologians had become good at doing the former, but (like their Greek counterparts) found the second task far more difficult. Arguments from common operations served only to highlight the problem: asserting that all three persons perform the same activities easily leads to the classic anti-Nicene question 'are the Son and the Spirit brothers?' Arguments from inseparable operation may contain the germ of an answer insofar as they frequently at least insinuate that within each action the Son and Spirit perform distinct roles.

In the second place, Latin theologians also contended with a long history of treating *spiritus* as a synonym for divinity. When Tertullian, for example, describes the Incarnation he often treats *spiritus* as a term for the Word that was in Christ (on the basis, lest this terminology should be thought unscriptural, of Romans 1.3 and John 3.6).[73] At the same time, Tertullian (like many before and after him) treats the *spiritus* who overshadowed Mary at the Incarnation as the Word.[74] Thus not only is *spiritus*

---

[71] Ambrose, *spir.* 3. 10.59 (CSEL 79. 174). [72] Ambrose, *spir.* 3. 3.13 (CSEL 79.155).
[73] For example, Tertullian, *adv. Prax.* 27.
[74] For example Tertullian, *adv. Prax.* 26. For a description of this exegesis and its history, see Evans, *Tertullian's Treatise Against Praxeas*, 63–70. To Evans's discussion we should add, at least, Hilary's *trin.* 8. 23. Although Hilary does not discuss the annunciation here, he offers a small catena of other texts that may be read similarly – Luke 4.18, Matt. 12.18 and Matt. 12.28. The

taken as a synonym for the divine substance, but some of the most significant passages for interpreting the Spirit's roles are attributed away from the third person.

Hilary was probably the first Latin to point towards a clearer theology of the Spirit's relationship with Father and Son. He does so by building on the established Latin concerns that we have sketched. Thus, in *De trinitate* 8 Hilary asks whether the Spirit comes from Father or Son. Hilary's response is particularly interesting, not simply because of its possible relationship to Augustine's theology, but because of the way it uses earlier exegeses which treat Spirit as a title of either Father or Son. The Spirit of God is, Hilary argues, the Spirit of the Father *and* the Spirit of the Lord who is 'upon' Christ sending him to preach (Matt. 12.28).[75] But the Spirit of Christ, who makes us 'spiritual', is identical to the Spirit of God, on the basis of Romans 8.9–11, and the Spirit's casting out of demons (Matt. 12.28) seems to reveal that the Spirit possesses the 'power of the [divine] nature'.[76] In the middle of this discussion Hilary asks whether the Spirit is a nature (*natura*) or 'of' a nature (*res naturae*).[77] Hilary's answer is complex and I must quote two passages to draw it out:

> I think that the term 'the spirit of God' is applied to both, therefore, in order that we may not conclude that the Son is in the Father or the Father in the Son in a corporeal manner, that is to say, we may not believe that God remains in a place and never seems to be anywhere else apart from himself ... But God, the living power of incalculable strength, who is present everywhere and is absent from nowhere, shows himself completely through his own and gives us to understand that his own is nothing else than himself [*se omnem per sua edocet et sua non aliud quam se esse significant*].[78]

> If we realize that Christ is in us through the Holy Spirit, we still recognize that the latter is just as much the Spirit of God as the Spirit of Christ. And since the nature itself dwells in us through the nature of the thing, we must believe that the nature of the Son does not differ from that of the Father, since the Holy Spirit, who is the Spirit of Christ and the Spirit of God, is made known as the thing of one nature [*Et cum per naturam rei natura ipsa habitet in nobis, indifferens natura Filii esse credetur a Patre, cum Spiritus sanctus, qui et Spiritus Christi et Spiritus Dei est, res naturae esse demonstretur unius*]. Accordingly, I now ask in what manner are they not one by nature? The Spirit of truth proceeds from the Father; he is sent by the Son and receives from the Son. But, everything that the Father has belongs to the Son. He who receives from him, therefore, is the Spirit

---

same ambiguities about the referent of spirit language we have also noted in the 'Western' statement from Serdica (343).

[75] Hilary, *trin.* 8. 24. [76] Hilary, *trin.* 8. 21, 23. [77] Hilary, *trin.* 8. 22ff. (SC 448. 412ff.).
[78] Hilary, *trin.* 8. 24 (SC 448. 414).

of God, but the same one is the Spirit of Christ. The thing belongs to the nature of the Son, but the same thing also belongs to the nature of the Father.[79]

We see here a number of traditional Latin *topoi*. That the persons are 'in' one another is foundational in the first quotation, enabling Hilary to suggest that the mutual interpenetration of the persons is equivalent to saying that God (meaning the Father) is present everywhere and reveals himself through himself. Thus the Spirit is the Father's spirit and is 'of' his nature, proper to that nature. Hilary adheres to the Latin tradition of reflecting on the equivocal naming by which 'Spirit' seems to name both Father and Son, but he has taken that tradition further, interpreting it alongside the twin themes of the Spirit's irreducibility and the mutual existence of the persons 'in' one another.

Hilary's combination of *natura* and *spiritus* language here is not repeated directly by his successors. Nevertheless, Hilary has taken significant steps towards an account of the Spirit as that which the Father gives to the Son, constituting him as one in nature with the Father. Ambrose's reading of Romans 1.20 discussed above hints at a similar line of argument. Both are, perhaps, drawing on the traditional ambiguities of Latin theology to speak (still hesitantly) of the Spirit's *proprium* as an irreducible one of the divine three. Augustine's discussion in the *De fide* follows similar lines and he may understand (at some level) the ambiguities that shape those earlier arguments and is pursuing his own version of them.

At the same time, even before the *De fide*, Augustine had already developed the idea (in part adopted from Hilary) that the Spirit is called the Gift because the Spirit enables us to return in love to God. In the *De moribus* we saw him insist that the Spirit was able to be such a gift because of the Spirit's perfection: here Augustine is moving hesitantly towards the position that the Spirit as love is the substance of the gifts he gives. This position will appear fully developed only in his mature work. Augustine probably also linked that which he learnt from Ambrose and/or Hilary to the language of Victorinus's *Hymns*, describing the Spirit as the *copula*, *conexio* and *complexio* of Father and Son.[80] These same *Hymns* speak of the Trinity as a communion of mutually entailing *caritas*, *gratia* and

---

[79] Hilary, *trin.* 8. 26 (SC 448. 418).
[80] Victorinus, *hymn.* 1. 3 (CSEL 83. 285): 'Adesto, sancte Spiritus, patris et filii copula'; 3. 242–7 (CSEL 83. 303): 'Tu, Spiritus sancte, conexio es: conexio autem est, quidquid conectit duo, ita ut conectas omnia, primo conectis duo, esque ipsa tertia complexio duorum, atque ipsa complexio nihil distans uno, unum cum facis duo: o beata Trinitas'.

communicatio.⁸¹ If something like this picture is correct then we can see both why Augustine's sources are so difficult to trace with accuracy, and that Augustine has engaged in an intense period of reading and thinking in order to fill out his earlier account of the Spirit's function into an account of the Spirit's eternal *proprium*. Interestingly, when Augustine finally sets out his mature pneumatology, the language of the Spirit as the 'Spirit of Christ' and the 'Spirit of God' that we see Hilary using in the texts quoted above will be a central resource.⁸²

TAKING STOCK

The *De fide* is a significant turning point. In this text we see Augustine use for the first time a variety of terminologies from Latin pro-Nicene and anti-Monarchian tradition to define Catholic Trinitarianism. Drawing attention to these terminologies helps to undercut still-common presentations of Latin tradition as insufficiently attentive to the irreducibility of Father, Son and Spirit. Noticing the range of terminology involved – and that the terms *persona* and *natura* or *substantia* function within this wider field – suggests a number of questions about the nature of summary definition and the relationship between such definition and the text of Scripture. Augustine's extensive use of these terminologies also lays a foundation for discussing his mature accounts of that irreducibility.

Beyond these terminologies, the *De fide* documents the appearance of two themes that will figure prominently in Augustine's mature account of the relations between Father, Son and Spirit: a reading of the Son as *Verbum* and the Spirit as the love between Father and Son. It is particularly worth noting that while the emergence of these two themes marks a real step forward in his attempt to think the eternal relations between the Trinity, Augustine gives no hint here how his account of *verbum* as *imago* and Spirit as *communio* and *caritas* are related.

---

[81] Victorinus, *hymn*. 3. ln. 35–42. Augustine may also have been familiar with Victorinus *adv. Ar*. 4. 4 (SC 68. 510): 'Spiritus Deus est; et adorantes eum, in spiritu et veritate adorare oportet. *Deus*, inquit, *spiritus est*, hoc est Dei, quod est esse: ergo substantia Dei spiritus est, eadem substantia, hoc est quod vivens.'

[82] See Chapter 10. In Chapter 8, pp. 210f., I discuss Augustine's attempt to defend his notion of the Spirit's existence between Father and Son in the *De fide*.

PART II

Ascent

Take away all bodily things. See simplicity, if you are simple. But how will you be simple? If you do not entangle yourself [in the world], you will be simple. And if you can, see what I am saying; or, if you cannot, believe what you do not see.[1]

---

[1] *Io. ev. tr.* 23. 8.

CHAPTER 4

The unadorned Trinity

With this chapter a new section of the book begins, one that focuses upon the ascent from belief to understanding that is central to Augustine's mature vision of our attempts to grow in knowledge of the Trinity. I will attempt to sketch key aspects of the relationship between belief and understanding as they are apparent between 400 and 410, although I will occasionally range more widely. This chapter begins in the period during which Augustine most likely began writing the *De trinitate*. My initial concern will be with the summary of Trinitarian belief that Augustine offers near the beginning of *De trinitate* 1 and which I suggest dates from the earliest stratum of the work. My first goal is to explore some of the new vocabulary and new methods of summary apparent in this text. At its end, however, we find a statement of the persons' inseparable operation that is highly austere in form, articulating relationships without any explanatory terminology of a philosophical or analogical nature. The linguistic austerity of this statement parallels that intrinsic to the Latin anti-Monarchian traditions on which we have seen Augustine draw, but it also suggests the need for a wider investigation into how Augustine understands the relationship between the text of Scripture and doctrinal summary statement. To understand this relationship is to understand much about how Augustine sees the task of doctrinal exegesis and the basic statement of Christian faith prior to the work of understanding proper. This concern will occupy the remainder of the chapter.

TRINITAS QUAE DEUS EST

The initial summary of Trinitarian faith that Augustine offers in the *De trinitate* – after a preface almost certainly added years later – deserves to be quoted in full:

(A) The purpose of all the Catholic commentators I have been able to read on the divine books of both testaments, who have written before me on the Trinity which God is [*de trinitate quae Deus est*], has been to teach that according to the Scriptures Father and Son and Holy Spirit make known a divine unity in the inseparable equality of one substance [*unius substantiae inseparabili aequalitate divinem insinuent unitatem*]; and therefore there are not three gods but one God; (B) although indeed the Father has begotten the Son, and therefore he who is the Father is not the Son; and the Son is begotten by the Father, and therefore he who is the Son is not the Father [*et ideo filius non sit qui pater est*]; and the Holy Spirit is neither the Father nor the Son, but only the Spirit of the Father and of the Son, himself co-equal to the Father and the Son, and belonging to the unity of the Trinity [*ad Trinitatis pertinens unitatem*]. (C) It was not however this same three (their teaching continues) that was born of the Virgin Mary, crucified and buried under Pontius Pilate, rose again on the third day and ascended into heaven, but the Son alone. Nor was it this same three that came down upon Jesus in the form of a dove at his baptism, or came down on the day of Pentecost after the Lord's ascension, with a roaring sound from heaven as though a violent gust were rushing down, and in divided tongues as of fire, but the Holy Spirit alone. Nor was it this same three that spoke from heaven, You are my Son, either at his baptism by John [Mark 1.11], or on the mountain when the three disciples were with him [Matt 17.5], nor when the resounding voice was heard, I have both glorified it [my name] and will glorify it again [John 12.28], but it was the Father's voice alone addressing the Son; although just as Father and Son and Holy Spirit are inseparable, so do they work inseparably [*inseparabiliter operunt*]. This is also my faith inasmuch as it is the Catholic faith.[1]

While some commentators have divided the text into four sections, I suggest a threefold division best captures Augustine's argument. In Section A Augustine argues that Scripture reveals Father, Son and Spirit to be equal, inseparable and to have the equality and inseparability that follows on from their being one substance. Section B expands on what it means for the three to be one God by stating the logical irreducibility of the three. Section C expands on the final phrase of B, which refers to the unity of the Trinity, by emphasizing that even though the doctrine of inseparable operation is a central Catholic principle we must still follow Scripture and accord each of the divine three a specific role (in some sense). I will discuss, first, the terminological innovations apparent in sections A and B of this statement.

As we saw in the *De fide*, Augustine alludes to Nicene language, but the creed itself plays little overt role. Augustine uses *unius* rather than

---

[1] *trin*. 1. 4.7 (CCSL 50. 34–6). We should also note that this text is the first time Augustine names the doctrine of inseparable operation by speaking precisely of the divine three as *inseparabiliter operunt*. From now on this will be his standard terminology.

eiusdem substantiae but the two versions are used equally through the *De trinitate*.² Augustine's references to the creedal language of Christ being born 'of the Virgin Mary', 'crucified and buried under Pontius Pilate' and 'rose again on the third day and ascended into heaven' are not references to Nicaea but to the creed of Milan which Augustine had received at his baptism and used for most of his career, even with catechumens in Hippo.³ Nowhere in this summary does Augustine use the term *persona*.

At the heart of Section B Augustine states the irreducibility of the three using yet another form of originally anti-Monarchian language: 'he who is the Son is not the Father; and the Holy Spirit is neither the Father nor the Son'. This is probably the first appearance of this style of statement in Augustine's corpus, but from this point on Augustine uses it frequently and in all the genres in which he wrote, homiletic and non-homiletic, from a work such as the *De trinitate* aimed at a very small audience to the records of his public debate with the Homoian bishop Maximinus.⁴ One or two other forms of anti-Monarchian language also persist, but this is by far the most common. Augustine has thus made a significant choice.

Once again, Tertullian's *Adversus Praxean* offers the earliest examples of this language:

(8) Everything that proceeds from something must of necessity be another besides that from which it proceeds, but it is not for that reason separated ... (9) Remember at every point I have professed this rule, by which I testify that Father and Son and Spirit are unseparated from one another, and in that case you will recognize what I say and in what sense I say it. For look now, I say that the Father is one, and the Son another, and the Spirit another ... not however that the Son is other than the Father by diversity, but by distribution, not by division, but by distinction, because the Father is not identical with the Son,

---

² *Eiusdem substantiae* is to be found at *trin.* 1. 6.9, 5. 6.7, 5. 8.9, 11. 2.2; *unius substantiae* at 1. 4.7 (NBA, reading disputed by CCSL), 2. 12.22, 9. 4.7.

³ The creed of Nicaea 325, for example, makes no mention of Pontius Pilate (versions of this creed as it was known and confessed at the Council of Hippo in 393 are available at CCSL 149. 30–1). The options which remain are the Milanese creed (see August Hahn, *Bibliothek der Symbole und Glaubensregeln der Alten Kirche* (Breslau: Morgenstern, 1877), §§20 and 21: this is a form of the old Roman creed, see Hahn, *Bibliothek*, §14ff.) and the North African creed of Hippo (see Hahn, *Bibliothek*, §§ 30 and 31). The phraseology here is closest to the Milanese creed. On Augustine's credal practice, see Caelestis Eichenseer, *Das Symbolum Apostolicum beim Heiligen Augustinus* (St Ottilien: Eon, 1960).

⁴ For other examples in different genres and over the remaining quarter-century of Augustine's literary career see, for example, *serm.* 212. 1; *Io. ev. tr.* 105. 3; *c. Max.* 11. The only fly in the ointment here is *Sermon* 214, one of his sermons 'at the handing over of the creed'. The creed uses the formula we have been discussing, but Augustine begins the sermon with what appears to be a reference to the recent nature of his ordination. Pierre Verbraken, 'Le Sermon CCXIV de Saint Augustin pour la Tradition du Symbole', *RevBen* 72 (1962), 7–9, offers good reasons why it may well date from some decades later.

they even being numerically one and another [*non tamen diversitate alium filium a patre sed distributione, nec divisione alium sed distinctione, quia non sit idem pater et filius, vel modulo alius ab alio*].⁵

In the mid-third century Novatian not only demonstrates participation in the same tradition but also anticipates Augustine's own phraseology. At *De trinitate* 27, arguing against a Sabellian reading of John 10.30 ('I and the Father are one'), Novatian writes:

> And because he is of the Father, whatsoever he is, he is the Son; the distinction however remaining that he is not the Father who is the Son, because he is not the Son who is the Father.⁶

Most of the terminologies considered in the last chapter re-emerged in the first generation of Latin pro-Nicenes during the late 350s. In this case we find far fewer cases of pro-Nicene usage. Commenting on John 14.16 ('I will ask the Father, and he will give you another Paraclete'), Phoebadius writes *c*.358:

> Thus the Spirit is other than the Son, just as the Son is other than the Father. Thus the third is the Spirit, as the second person is the Son: and so all are one God because the three are one.⁷

Phoebadius may be using Tertullian at this point, but the passage only approaches Augustine's summary statement in its emphasis on Father and Son being 'other' than one another. We find no parallel this close in Hilary or Ambrose, and there is nothing (other than the use of *semper* language discussed in Chapter 3) in the 'Tome' of Damasus. Only two direct contemporaries parallel Augustine's usage, both authors with Roman connections.

Faustinus was a priest under Liberius in Rome (pope 352–66) and later an anti-pope during the reign of Damasus. Exiled to Egypt by the latter he joined the party of Lucifer of Cagliari (*fl.* 360s). Like the Novatians, the Luciferians seem to have met with some acceptance under Theodosius, and Faustinus even wrote a *De trinitate* at the request of Flacilla, Theodosius's wife. There also survives a short 'confession' which Simonetti has argued is best attributed to Faustinus and which may have

---

⁵ Tertullian, *adv. Prax.* 8–9 (Evans, 96–7).
⁶ Novatian, *trin.* 27 (PL 3. 938): 'Et quoniam ex Patre est; quidquid illud est, Filius est: manente tamen distinctione, ut non sit Pater ille qui Filius; quia nec Filius ille qui Pater est'.
⁷ Phoebadius, *c. Ar.* 27. 4 (CCSL 64. 51): 'Sic alius a Filio Spiritus, sicut alius a Patre Filius. Sic tertia in Spiritu, ut in Filio secunda persona: unus tamen Deus omnia quia tres unum sunt'. For Tertullian's discussion of John 14.16, which similarly argues that it reveals the distinction between the persons, see *adv. Prax.* 9.

The unadorned Trinity

been presented to Theodosius sometime between 379 and 381.[8] This text specifically sets out to defend Faustinus against charges of 'Sabellianism' and near the beginning we find:

We believe in the Father, who is not the Son ... and we believe in the Son, who is not the Father ... and we believe in the Holy Spirit, who is truly the Spirit of God.[9]

There also survive two short confessions of faith from Isaac, a converted Jew who was involved in the disputes between Damasus and Urbinus in the mid-370s, only to suffer exile to Spain where he may have reverted to his ancestral faith. The *Fides Isatis* articulates an account of the three persons as distinguished by their *proprietates*: the Father is not *natus*, *factus* or *genitus*; the Son is *unigenitum*; the Spirit is *ex Patre*. They are truly three because they have individual 'properties', even though they are also *una natura* or *substantia*, and there is only one *nomen Dei*.[10] This is summed up as:

the Father is not the Son, nor the Holy Spirit, whom we call the Paraclete; the Son is not the Father nor the Paraclete because the Son said [John 15.26] ... nonetheless [following quotation of John 15.26 to show that the one who sends and the one who is sent are two distinct agents], in our faith concerning his divinity it is and ought always to be that God the Father, God the Son and God the Spirit-Paraclete are of one and a triune substance.[11]

The shorter *Confessio fidei Catholicae* repeats the same formula and links the non-identity of the persons to their *propria*. This text offers the closest parallel we have to Augustine's own phrasing:

that is, so that we would believe that the Father is not the Son, and certainly we do believe that the Son is not the Father, and certainly the Holy Spirit is neither the Father nor the Son, because the Father is ingenerate, the Son is certainly

---

[8] Manlio Simonetti, 'Note su Faustino', *Sacris Erudiri* 14 (1963), 92–8. We know that Faustinus was eventually granted the toleration for Luciferians for which he asked, from the rescript to Cynegius appended to the longer confession (known as the *Libellus precum*) composed by Faustinus (and a certain) Marcellinus and addressed to Valentinus II, Arcadius and Theodosius in 383/4 (*CPL* 1571).
[9] Faustinus, *fid.* (CCSL 9. 357): 'Nos Patrem credimus, qui non sit Filius, sed habeat Filium de se sine initio genitum, non factum; et Filium credimus, qui non sit Pater, sed habeat Patrem, de quo sit genitus, non factus; et Spiritum Sanctum credimus, qui sit vere Spiritus Dei'.
[10] Isaac, *fid.* 1 (CCSL 9. 338).
[11] Isaac, *fid.* 3 (CCSL 9. 342): 'et patrem non esse filium, neque spiritum sanctum, quem paracletum dicimus; filium non esse patrem neque paracletum; paracletum non esse patrem neque filium, quia filius dicat. Deum tamen patrem et deum filium et deum paracletum spiritum unius substantiae et trinae substantiae eius divinitatis in fide nostra esse et manere debere'.

generated from the Father without beginning, and the Holy Spirit proceeds from the Father and receives from the Son.[12]

It is possible that Augustine's usage independently parallels these two authors or that his formula represents a personal construction (perhaps after reading Tertullian and/or Novatian). Nevertheless, even though the route of transmission remains conjectural, it seems most likely that Augustine encountered the formulae of Faustinus and Isaac in a collection of texts associated with Damasus or with imperial legislation defining orthodoxy. We have previously seen Augustine adapt – often in a highly personal manner – themes from his predecessors, and among these Ambrose and Damasus were particularly significant. That he would use so frequently a style of definition so uncommon in those predecessors (even if he encountered it in a context associated with them) further illustrates the idiosyncratic nature of his dependence on Latin tradition.

This summary of Trinitarian belief also offers us Augustine's first use of the phrase *Trinitas quae Deus est*, a phrase not found in his predecessors. Interestingly this phrase is only once used by Augustine in his homiletic corpus, but it is used frequently in the *De trinitate*, in two letters closely connected with that work and in his later anti-'Arian' works. Its absence from sermons, and from the record of his public debate with Maximinus, suggests that Augustine saw the phrase as, at the least, needing careful explanation because of its direct identification of *Trinitas* as *Deus*. While Augustine's standard practice seems to have been to refer to the Father when *Deus* is used without further qualification, he also uses a number of innovative phrases which speak directly of the Trinity as God and which identify Son and Spirit by (scriptural) titles and phrases that his predecessors were reticent to apply to any other than the Father without qualification.

To place Augustine's innovations in context, we can begin with polemic over John 17.3 ('[Father] ... and this is eternal life, that they may know thee, the only true God, and Jesus Christ whom thou hast sent'). The verse is one that anti-Nicenes across the Mediterranean claimed as their own, and we have ample evidence of its use by Latin Homoians.[13]

[12] Isaac, *exp.* (CCSL 9. 347): 'id est ut patrem credamus non esse filium, filium vero credamus non esse patrem, spiritum autem sanctum nec patrem esse nec filium; quia pater est ingenitus, filius vero sine initio genitus a patre est, spiritus autem sanctus processit a patre et accipit de filio'.

[13] The text is used three times, for example, in the Homoian scholia: *scol. Aquil.* 24 (304v), 66 (339v), 87 (346v). It also occurs in the first few sentences of the 'Arian Sermon' (*serm. Ar.* 1. 1) and we find the Homoian bishop Maximinus quoting it against Augustine (*conl. Max.* 15. 15). *Trinitas quae est deus* is used at *retr.* 2. 15.1; *ep.* 120. 6 and 17; *ep.* 174. *pro*; *Io. ev. tr.* 6. 5; *c. Max.* 1. 19, 2. 10.2, 2. 22.3, 2. 26.7; *c. s. Arrian.* 4 and 9; *trin.* 1. 4.7, 9. 1.1, 13. 20.26, 15. 4.6, 15. 6.9, 15. 6.10, 15.

The unadorned Trinity

Pro-Nicene defence against the charge that Christ cannot also be 'true God' reveals much about the ways in which pro-Nicenes were and were not willing to speak simply of the Trinity as the 'only' or 'true' God. In *De trinitate* 9 Hilary argues from the character of the Son's 'true birth' that Christ shares in the Father's status as 'only' and 'true' God. The mysterious birth of the Son never implies, Hilary argues, that Christ becomes 'God' in separation from the one divine nature.[14] Thus even the truth (*veritas*) of the Father's nature abides in him.[15] Not surprisingly, Hilary also quotes John 14.9–12 to emphasize the existence of Father and Son 'in' each other.[16] At the same time, the mystery of the birth enables the Father to remain the source and the Son to remain the only-begotten even though all that the Father has is the Son's.[17] On this basis Hilary then tries out a number of summary statements: 'he was the true God in the nature of the one true God';[18] 'if the one God the Father does not deprive Christ of being the one God, so the only God the true Father does not take anything away from Christ so that he is not the true God'.[19] Hilary also contrasts our assumptions that anything that is *solus* is also *solus sibi* ('alone by itself') with the Father who is alone Father but alone with his true Son.[20] Throughout this exposition Hilary asserts the unity of the divine nature, but does not say without qualification that the Son is also *solus verus Deus*.

Ambrose, writing around twenty years later, offers a good point of contrast. In *De fide* 5 Ambrose begins discussion of the verse by emphasizing that as Christ is the Truth (John 14.6) then he must be equal to the Father who is 'true'. At the same time, even though Isaiah 44.24 says 'I alone stretched out the heavens' we know that the Son was also there from texts such as Proverbs 8.27 ('When he prepared the heavens I was there').[21] Ambrose argues that 'alone' is an indication that the Son and not the Father, for example, became incarnate and walked on the sea even though the Father was there. Without using any technical terminology Ambrose argues that 'alone' in reference to Father, Son and Spirit identifies the 'person' acting even though the three also act

---

17.28, 15. 26.45, 15. 27.49; *civ.* 16. 6; *ench.* 56; *praed. sanct.* 13. It is interesting to note that Latin Nicene allusion to the Son being both 'God' and 'true God' begins with the definition of Serdica (343).

[14] Hilary, *trin.* 9. 22ff. Cf. 9. 26. [15] Hilary, *trin.* 9. 24.
[16] Hilary, *trin.* 9. 29. [17] Hilary, *trin.* 9. 27.
[18] Hilary, *trin.* 9. 29 (SC 462. 72): 'se in unius Dei veri natura Deum verum professus esse'.
[19] Hilary, *trin.* 9. 34 (SC 462. 82): 'Quodsi unus Deus Pater Christo non adimit ut unus sit Dominus, ita solus Deus Pater verus Christo Iesu non aufert ut Deus verus sit'.
[20] Hilary, *trin.* 9. 36 (SC 462. 84–6). [21] Ambrose, *fid.* 5. 2.29.

inseparably.²² On this basis Ambrose argues that 'the Son, therefore, is 'only and true God', for this prerogative also must be awarded him'.²³ But then he writes:

> Since no created thing can be compared with the divinity of the Father and the Son and the Holy Spirit (which is alone, not among all things, but above them) … as the Father is said to be 'alone true God', because he has nothing in common with others, so also the Son is alone the Image of the true God, he alone is at the right hand of the Father, alone the Power and Wisdom of God.²⁴

Ambrose thus pushes a little further than Hilary in arguing that the title 'only true God' may also be directly accorded the Son because of the unity of nature, and speaks more directly of the Trinity as the one God than (most) earlier Latin Nicenes. For example, in *De spiritu* 3 Ambrose says both 'therefore God is one, the majesty of the eternal Trinity being preserved' and 'But does anyone deny that the divinity of the eternal Trinity is to be worshipped?'²⁵ I added 'most' in parentheses because Victorinus's *Hymn* 3, addressed to the Trinity, says 'this is our God / This is [the] one God / This is [the] one and only God / O Blessed Trinity'.²⁶

Both Hilary and Ambrose link John 17.3 to 1 Timothy 6.15–16 ('The King of Kings and Lord of Lords, who alone has immortality and dwells in unapproachable light'), a verse of great significance in the earliest phases of the Trinitarian controversies, and still in dispute through Augustine's lifetime. Hilary treats the text *en passant* alongside John 17.3, arguing that to assume 'alone' implies that the Son does not possess those things attributed to the Father denies the mysterious birth indicated by the name Father. In fact, 'alone' exalts the Father in order that we may also recognize that the Son's possession of them through his generation gives further glory to the Father.²⁷ Ambrose is again more willing to speak directly of the Son as sharing the adjectives attributed to the Father. In *De fide* 3 he argues that the 'alone' in 1 Timothy 6.16 actually concerns 'God' which is a name common to Father and Son.²⁸ When we compare

---

²² Ambrose, *fid.* 5. 2.30–1.
²³ Ambrose, *fid.* 5. 2.32 (CSEL 78. 228): 'Est ergo "solus et verus dues" filius; haec enim et filio praerogativa defertur'.
²⁴ Ambrose, *fid.* 5. 2.34 (CSEL 78. 229).
²⁵ Ambrose, *spir.* 3. 14.94, 3. 12.86. Cf. Eusebius of Vercelli, *trin.* 1. 11–12 (CCSL 9. 6): 'Cur solus deus? utique quia solus deitas in trinitate … Cur unus uerus deus? procul dubio, dum una sit natura trinitatis, propterea unus uerus est deus'.
²⁶ *hymn.* 3. 270–3 (SC 68. 652): 'Hic est deus noster; / hic est deus unus; / hic unus et solus deus; / O beata trinitas'.
²⁷ Hilary, *trin.* 4. 9–11.   ²⁸ Ambrose, *fid.* 3. 2.11–12.

this reading with that of John 17.3 we see that Ambrose envisages a fairly complex typology of referents for 'alone' in Scripture, but his intention is clear. That which might seem to indicate only the Father, in fact speaks of the divine nature and power present in both Son and Spirit.[29] Augustine is thus the heir both to a trajectory of increasingly direct descriptions of the Trinity as the one God and of the divine nature as the object of worship, and to an older tendency emphasizing that the Father is the source of the Trinity such that titles like 'only' and 'true' can only be applied to Son and Spirit with care.

In the initial chapters of the *De trinitate* Augustine speaks directly and without qualification of the Trinity as the one God. He is also the first Latin to state simply that the *solus verus Deus* is the Trinity, and he begins to do so in these pages.[30] His use of *Trinitas quae est deus* is probably to be understood as a related move, adopting a style of speech only adumbrated by previous Latin Nicene theology. Whether these shifts represent a fundamentally new conception of Trinitarian theology – as some have alleged – and whether they undermine his equally strong assertions of the Father's status are questions that can only be approached slowly over the course of the book as a whole.

Lastly, in Section A, we should note Augustine's statement that to understand the Scriptures is to understand that Father, Son and Spirit slowly reveal themselves to be a unity: *divinem insinuent unitatem*. Augustine's decision to put the matter thus is not, I suggest, accidental, but the announcement of a programme that will run through the first books of the *De trinitate*. At the core of our response to scriptural material describing Father, Son and Spirit should be attention to the ways in which the text insinuates the ineffable unity of those agents who might initially appear to be distinct in the manner that human agents are distinct. This account of Scripture's manner of teaching demands of Augustine an account of how we are to follow the path down which Scripture draws us. It is to this we will turn in Chapter 5.[31]

---

[29] Cf. Ambrose, *fid.* 3. 2.13.
[30] Augustine, *trin.* 1. 6.10 (CCSL 50. 40): [following quotation of 1Tim. 6.14–16] 'In quibus uerbis nec pater proprie nominatus est nec filius nec spiritus sanctus, sed beatus et solus potens, rex regum et dominus dominantium, quod est unus et solus et uerus deus, ipsa trinitas'. This text may be paralleled with a number of other places where he describes the Trinity as 'unus et solus deus', for example *trin.* 2. 17.32.
[31] In Chapter 10, I discuss the pneumatological innovations in this introductory statement, see pp. 251f.

THE UNADORNED TRINITY

Section C of the summary expands on Augustine's comment at the end of Section B that the Spirit belongs to the 'unity of the trinity' (*ad Trinitatis pertinens unitatem*), and offers a concessive explanation of what *unitas Trinitatis* should *not* be taken to mean. In form it is austere, merely laying out the logic of three narrative episodes from the New Testament. The three were not born of Mary, but the son alone; the three did not descend on Jesus in the Jordan, but the Spirit alone; the three did not speak from heaven, but the Father alone (*tantummodo*). Nevertheless, just as the persons are inseparable, they work inseparably. Augustine's summary thus identifies a series of principles about the three agents of the scriptural passages to which he refers and offers no explanation or analogy. One thing that should immediately strike the reader of this passage is its similarity to the anti-Monarchian styles of summary definition that we have considered. From both, philosophical terminologies are absent. In both, emphasis is placed on clarity of logical relationships. Through the remainder of this chapter I will offer an explanation of why Augustine prefers these austere styles of summary. The key to answering this question lies, I will suggest, in understanding the links between this style of summary and Augustine's wider approach to the task of expounding and defending Trinitarian faith as scriptural.

In the very next paragraph he points to the fact that some are disturbed (*perturbantur*) about their faith. The problems he identifies involve the difficulties of *understanding* (*intellegere*) inseparable operation once it has been clearly stated.[32] Thus the summary itself is not intended to offer understanding, merely a clear statement of the faith that one seeks to understand. The distinction between understanding and a preliminary faith or belief founded in appropriate authority is fundamental throughout Augustine's career. The following passage from the *De vera religione* reveals some of the fundamental principles behind the distinction:

> So let us then ... not confuse what trust we should place in historical narrative [*historia*], and what trust we should place in understanding [*intellegentia*] – what we should commit to memory without knowing that it is true but still believing it is, and where the truth is that does not come and go but always remains in the same way.[33]

---

[32] *trin.* 1. 5.8 (CCSL 50. 36–7). [33] *vera rel.* 50. 99 (CCSL 32. 251).

The use of 'historical narrative' rather than 'faith' follows from the passage's concern with God's speech to us through Scripture – paralleled here with the pillar of fire or cloud that led the Israelites through the desert – and with the varying responses that Scripture's different ways of teaching should elicit. This passage also glosses the distinction as being between that which is committed to the memory and believed, and that which is understood because it is seen or judged in the light of eternal unchanging truth. 'Understanding' here carries a sense that ties it closely to the progress of the Christian towards the final vision of God. Understanding grows as one learns to 'see' with increasing clarity in the Truth which makes all true judgement possible.[34]

So far I have been concerned with anti-Monarchian styles of summary and with Augustine's austere summary of inseparable operation in *De trinitate* 1. With these we should link a key feature of Augustine's preaching on the Trinity (and, indeed, other doctrinal topics). While we do frequently find exhortation to purify our minds and think beyond the material imagery that is now our natural home, and while we do also find the use of extended explanatory analogies, at the heart of his preaching and teaching is an attempt to draw attention to the logic of the scriptural text. Doing so frequently moves Augustine towards summary statements which directly parallel those we have just seen. One example will suffice:

Just as the Father himself and the Son himself are inseparable, so also the works of the Father and the Son are inseparable. How is it possible that the Father and the Son are inseparable? Because he himself said 'I and the Father are one' [John 10.30] … So, look, we have now heard the gospel when he answered the Jews who were boiling with rage 'because he not only broke the Sabbath but also said God was his Father, making himself equal to God' [John 5.18]. For so it was written in the previous section. Therefore when the Son of God and the Truth replied to such mistaken indignation of theirs, he said, 'Amen, amen, I say to you, the Son cannot do anything of himself, but only what he sees the Father doing' [John 5.19]. As if he were to say 'Why were you scandalized because I said God is my Father, and because I make myself equal to God? I am equal in such a way that he begot me; I am equal in such a way that he is not from me, but I am from him.' For this is understood in those words, 'The Son cannot do anything of himself, but only what he sees the Father doing'. That is, whatever the Son has to do, of the Father he has it to do.[35]

---

[34] The distinction between faith and understanding does not imply that faith lacks its own modes of thinking. On this question, see Basil Studer, 'History and Faith in Augustine's *De Trinitate*', *AugStud* 28 (1997), 7–50.

[35] *Io. ev. tr.* 20. 3–4 (CCSL 36. 204).

A number of times here Augustine states doctrinal principles in simple and logical language, and offers scriptural proof for these principles. To break up the discourse he resorts to a very common rhetorical device of a question-and-answer format (for example, 'How is it possible that the Father and the Son are inseparable? Because he himself said "I and the Father are one"'). At one point he also argues that a scriptural passage is proof for his formulations by rephrasing it ('As if he were to say ...'); in this case the summary statement of principles is embedded in his account of what the scriptural passage is supposedly saying. Throughout, Augustine offers no analogy or explanation – that will follow later in the sermon – his goal is a drawing out of principles. Understanding the context and rationale for this exegetical style will provide us with the key to Augustine's preference for austere styles of doctrinal summary.

Our best point of departure is Augustine's discussion of Cicero's three *genera dicendi* or 'styles of speech' in the fourth book of *De doctrina christiana*. Augustine, following Cicero, links these three styles to the three traditional functions of oratory: the unadorned style (*subtilis* or *submissa dictio*) is linked to teaching, the moderate to persuading and the grand to delighting.[36] In what he presents as a contrast to Cicero, Augustine emphasizes that one should not assume too rigid a link between style and function. True eloquence consists not in adherence to a textbook scheme, but in knowing how to apply style in aid of the *overall* goal of one's speaking.[37] Despite this warning Augustine assumes a link between teaching and the unadorned style throughout the book. Thus when, a little later, he offers examples of the various styles, Ambrose's *De spiritu sancto* provides the first example of the unadorned style:

> St Ambrose, although treating the important subject of the Holy Spirit, so that he may show his equality to the Father and Son, nevertheless uses the unadorned style of speaking. For the thing discussed does not need verbal ornaments, nor motions of the affections to persuade, but clear proofs of the matters at issue [*documenta rerum*].[38]

---

[36] *doctr. chr.* 4. 12.27.74ff.; Cicero, *orat.* 21. 69–70. See also Adolf Primer, 'The Function of the *genera dicendi* in *De doctrina christiana* 4', in Duane Arnold and Pamela Bright (eds.), *De doctrina christiana: A Classic of Western Culture*, vol. 1 (Notre Dame, IN: University of Notre Dame Press, 1995), 68–86.

[37] *doctr. chr.* 4. 15.32.87ff.; 4. 19.38.104ff. Cf. *doctr. chr.* 4. 19.38.105.

[38] *doctr. chr.* 4. 46.21.127 (CSEL 80. 155). Augustine argues that the imitation of Scripture in the speech of a preacher is inappropriate when it would hinder understanding. Preachers are not – in a wonderfully worded injunction – to 'offer themselves to be interpreted as if they had similar authority' by making their sermons as difficult to understand as the hardest parts of Scripture, *doctr. chr.* 4. 8.22.62 (CSEL 80. 133–4): 'Non ergo expositores eorum ita loqui debent, tanquam se ipsi exponendos simili auctoritate proponant'.

Earlier in the book Augustine uses the same language. He asserts that, when teaching, the expositor must be ready to offer *narratio* and, when doubtful things must be confirmed, the same expositor must draw out evidence from the materials that have been given (in Scripture) (*documentis adhibitis ratiocinandum est*).³⁹

Augustine here, then, associates the task of teaching and the proving of doctrine with particular classical rhetorical styles of speech. We can make further progress by asking ourselves whether he also associates these styles with one of the three traditional divisions of rhetoric: forensic, epideictic and deliberative. Commenting a little earlier on Cicero's suggestions that one should use the three *genera dicendi* in relation to the lesser or greater significance of the subject matter, Augustine remarks that while Cicero could certainly do this in forensic cases it is not so in ecclesiastical questions because what seems small in court is of great significance for the life of the soul.⁴⁰ This *en passant* comment hints that Augustine's frame of reference for the rhetorical styles and figures he is discussing through much of Book 4 is not deliberative or epideictic, but forensic.

Caroline Humfress's recent *Orthodoxy and the Courts in Late Antiquity* makes clear the extent to which modern scholars have neglected the importance of forensic training and practice in the lives of a surprising number of the key figures in fourth- and fifth-century ecclesial life. In Augustine's case, even though he did not practise as an *advocatus* or *causidicus* (both terms may be translated by 'advocate'), he presents this as being both his original goal as a student of rhetoric and the likely career of those he taught in Carthage.⁴¹ As a bishop Augustine spent a considerable portion of his day dealing with legal disputes, and Humfress shows that dealing with these cases involved a fairly deep knowledge of court procedure. As she notes, the recently discovered Divjak letters reveal that Augustine was even willing to assist some members of his congregation in preparing dossiers for secular court cases.⁴² One sermon in particular not only shows Augustine openly linking the task of defending Catholic teaching and the advocacy of legal causes in court, it also suggests that his choice of certain rhetorical styles and figures in doctrinal exegesis follows

---

³⁹ *doctr. chr.* 4. 4.6.14–15 (CSEL 80. 121).
⁴⁰ *doctr. chr.* 4. 18.35.97.
⁴¹ Caroline Humfress, *Orthodoxy and the Courts in Late Antiquity* (Oxford: Clarendon Press, 2007), 189ff. See *conf.* 3. 3.6–4.7. I am grateful to Humfress for sharing chapters of her book before publication. Our readings of *serm.* 52 were produced independently, but concur to a remarkable degree.
⁴² *ep.* 24* and 28*.

traditional Roman rhetorical assumptions about what is best suited for the exposition of cases and the production of evidence.[43]

Augustine's *Sermon* 52 concerns the seeming paradoxes involved in Scripture's (and the creed's) witness to the action of Father, Son and Spirit. A short *exordium* – an initial statement which presents the topic of a speech in a form aimed to gain sympathy[44] – sets out the problem and calls on the congregation to pray for him as he works through the difficulty he describes.[45] The baptism of Jesus in the Jordan seems to show the three working separately, but Catholics should believe (Augustine tells us) that the three are one Godhead working inseparably. A section of *narratio* – a style of speech setting out the facts that will need to be proved in the body of the argument – follows.[46] Taking the example of Father and Son, Scripture provides us with evidence that the Father does all things through the Son and that the two work together, but our faith states that the two are really irreducible and that only the Son became incarnate. At the core of this *narratio*, Augustine identifies a precise problem (*quaestio*) and a *propositio* – one traditional term for a summary of an advocate's case[47] – in austere form: 'the Son indeed, and not the Father, was born of the Virgin Mary; but this birth of the Son, not the Father, from the Virgin Mary was the work of both Father and Son'.[48] Augustine then moves into what he, again following standard rhetorical divisions, describes as the

---

[43] Exploration of the forensic background to Latin styles of doctrinal argument has been pursued in a number of other cases. See, for example, Pierre Hadot, '*De lectis non lecta componere*' (Marius Victorinus, *adversus Arrium* II 7). Raisonnement théologique et raisonnement juridique', *SP* 1 (= TU 129) (1957), 209–20. Hadot then draws attention to the use of legal language in connection with some creedal texts of the fourth century – especially those stemming from the attempts of the Emperor Constantius to enforce a settlement during the 350s (p. 217). Perhaps, he suggests, the entanglements between emperor and bishops during the post-Constantinian period gave increased impetus to a *rhetor* turned Christian polemicist such as Victorinus to make use of techniques of forensic interpretation against his opponents.

[44] Lausberg, *Handbook*, §263ff. The table setting out the different ways in which ancient handbooks described the parts of a speech at §265 is helpful in giving a sense of the constants and yet the great flexibility with which these terms could be used.

[45] *serm.* 52. 3.

[46] Lausberg, *Handbook*, §289. Aristotle's *Rhetoric* (1414a30ff.) closely identifies the Greek precursor of *narratio* as essential to and peculiarly part of forensic rhetoric because without the clear statement of a case no argument can be made to the court. Roman writers such as Cicero or Quintilian, even though they recognize that *narratio* could be found in many styles of rhetorical performance, continue to assume that forensic *narratio* is the foundational type.

[47] Lausberg, *Handbook*, §346. As a parallel to the senses of *propositio* I explore in this chapter, we might note Martianus Capella's use of the term in both dialectical and rhetorical contexts: see *nupt. phil.* 4. 328, 422; 5. 439. Augustine uses the term directly at *serm.* 52. 14, and at 52. 8 he describes his preceding statement by the corresponding verb *propono*.

[48] *serm.* 52. 8.

The unadorned Trinity

presentation of proofs or argument (*probationes* or *argumentum*).⁴⁹ At this point Augustine clarifies the context he is assuming for his sermon:

> Let us prove each point. You are listening as judges; the case has been stated, let the witnesses step forward [*iudices auditis, causa proposita est, testes procedant*]. Let's suppose you, the justices, say to me what is usually said to pleaders, 'Bring forward the witnesses to your proposition'. I certainly will, and I will also read out to you the text of the heavenly law. You have listened carefully to my statement of the case; listen even more carefully now to my proof of it [*intente audistis proponentem, audite intentius iam probantem*]. The first thing I have to bring proof of concerns the birth of Christ, how the Father effected it and the Son effected it, although what Father and Son effected together belongs only to the Son. I refer you first to Paul as a suitable counsel learned in divine law. Plaintiffs [*causidici*] today, you see, also have a Paul who declares the laws for litigants [*Paulum dictantem iura litigatorum*], not for Christians.⁵⁰

Augustine not only speaks of the texts that he will bring forward as witnesses or proofs drawn from a heavenly law, but he is probably paralleling Paul as a Christian *iurisperitus* or *causidicus* with Julius Paulus, the Roman Jurist of the third century.

In the paragraphs that follow Augustine teases out scriptural evidence for his case. These paragraphs include many features paradigmatic of those passages throughout his sermons where his goal is to extract from Scripture basic principles of Christian belief:

> (9) Let the holy apostle show us how the Father brought about the birth of the Son. But when the fullness of time, he says, had come, God sent his Son, made of a woman, made under the law, to redeem those who were under the law [Gal. 4. 4–5]. You have heard it, and because it is clear and straightforward, you have understood it. There you have the Father causing the Son to be born of the virgin. For when the fullness of time had come, God sent his Son, that is, the Father sent Christ. How did he send him? Made of a woman, made under the law. So the Father made him of a woman under the law. (10) Or perhaps you are bothered because I said 'of the virgin' and Paul says 'of a woman'. Don't let it bother you; don't let's linger on it; I'm not, after all, speaking to illiterate people. You get each thing said in Scripture, both 'of a virgin' and 'of a woman'. Of a virgin, how and where? Behold, a virgin will conceive and bear a son [Isa. 7.14]. Of a woman, as you have just heard. They don't contradict each other. It's an idiom of the Hebrew language to mean by 'women' not those who have lost their virginity, but just females. You have the evidence of a text in Genesis, when Eve was first fashioned: He fashioned her into a woman [Gen. 2.22]. It also says somewhere else in Scripture that God ordered the women to be set apart who

---

⁴⁹ Lausberg, *Handbook*, §348.
⁵⁰ *serm.* 52. 8 (*RevBen* 74 (1964), 21). The text of this sermon is also available at PL 38. 354–64.

had not known the bed of a man. So that's something we all ought to know. We mustn't let it hold us up, so that we can have time to explain, with the Lord's help, other things that are more likely to do so. (11) So we have proved that the birth of the Son was brought about by the Father; now let us also prove it was brought about by the Son. What is the birth of the Son from the Virgin Mary? It is certainly the taking of the form of a slave. Now hear that the Son too brought this about: *Who, when he was in the form of God, did not think it robbery to be equal to God, but emptied himself, taking the form of a slave* (Phil. 2.6–7). *When the fullness of time had come, God sent his Son made of a woman* (Gal. 4.4), *who was made for him of the seed of David according to the flesh* (Rom. 1.3). So we see the birth of the Son made by the Father. But because the Son emptied himself, taking the form of a slave, we see the birth of the Son also made by the Son. This has been proved. Let's pass on to the next point. Please concentrate on grasping it as it follows in due order.[51]

Augustine uses an unadorned style and repeats the relevant section of his case frequently, especially after he has offered a piece of scriptural evidence. In so doing Augustine again follows standard practice. The sections of a speech known as *narratio* and *probatio* were closely linked and the traditional virtues of *narratio* – brevity, clarity and plausability – followed on from the centrality of *docere* (teaching) to *narratio*.[52] Augustine attends to the same virtues throughout his production of evidence. He not only makes the function of *docere* central to the task at hand as a matter of Christian principle, he uses styles of proof that depend on deduction from written statements and the application of logical principles. These bear closest relation to what the rhetorical handbooks term *argumenta*, argued by means of *ratiocinatio*, and having their force not through grand or emotional rhetorical flourishes, but through the power of rational argument.[53]

At a number of points in the passage Augustine anticipates objections and attempts to answer them through close attention to relevant

---

[51] *serm.* 52. 9–11.
[52] For the links between *narratio* and *probatio*, see Lausberg, *Handbook*, §§324 and 348, and Quintilian, *inst.* 4. 2.79. For the virtues of *narratio*, see Lausberg, *Handbook*, §294 and esp. Cicero, *inv.* 1. 20.28.
[53] For the centrality Augustine accords *docere* see *doc.* 4. 11.74ff. For *argumenta* and *ratiocinatio*, see Lausberg, *Handbook*, §366ff. and Cicero, *inv.* 1. 34.57: 'ratiocinatio est oratio ex ipsa re probabile aliquid eliciens quod expositum et per se cognitum sua se vi et ratione confirmet'. See also the extended example of this figure at *Her.* 4. 16.23. For Augustine's own use of *interrogatio*, see, for example, the particularly clear *serm.* 12. 3 and 11. See also *doctr. chr.* 4. 20.39.07–10: here, as an example of the *submissa dictio*, Augustine cites Gal. 4.21–6. His brief commentary on the passage lauds Paul's success in anticipating objections and rhetorically posing questions beginning to arise in the minds of a sceptical audience. Paul 'raises objections' and 'offers propositions': the tools are those of dialectic (as we shall discuss below), but the language in which Augustine describes Paul's practice and imagined context is that of the law court.

The unadorned Trinity

scriptural texts. The anticipation of objections is a standard figure used in forensic *narratio* and *argumentatio*.⁵⁴ The use of questions both enlivens an otherwise dense and dull exposition and it enables Augustine to direct that exposition. For example, he asks 'what is the birth of the Son from the Virgin Mary?' and his answer, that it is 'the taking of the form of a slave', allows him to bring into play one of his favourite texts – Philippians 2.5–7 – for distinguishing between the *forma Dei* and *forma servi* and to argue that, as *forma Dei*, the Son is the author of his own incarnation. Augustine thus directly offers the analogy of forensic argument to cast his exposition, and he uses a range of figures and styles that Roman rhetorical tradition would have immediately recognized as appropriate for that context.

Augustine concludes this section of *Sermon* 52:

> I've carried out my promise; I have proved my propositions, I think, with the strongest documentary evidence [*propositiones nostras firmissimis, ut arbitror, testimoniorum documentis probauimus*]. Hold on to what you have heard. I shall repeat it briefly, and so commend to your minds' safe keeping something that is in my humble opinion exceedingly useful. The Father wasn't born of the virgin, and yet this birth of the Son from the virgin was the work of both Father and Son. The Father did not suffer on the cross, and yet the passion of the Son was the work of both Father and Son. The Father did not rise again from the dead, and yet the resurrection of the Son was the work of both Father and Son. You have the persons quite distinct, and their working inseparable ... What I have said is plain enough, it only needed to be said. We don't have to work at understanding it, only to take care to remind ourselves of it [*non laborandum ut intellegerentur, sed curandum ut commemorarentur*].⁵⁵

Augustine again reinforces the forensic analogy in which he has cast his activity as preacher. But as he repeats his case or *propositio*, concluding his presentation of evidence, we should note the striking parallel with the summary we have been studying in *De trinitate* 1. Augustine's summary statements of doctrinal positions, and their appearance amid passages of careful, unadorned, exposition of the scriptural text, echo the advocate offering a *propositio*, a summary of a case to be defended and proved.

---

⁵⁴ For the relevant types of *interrogatio*, see Lausberg, *Handbook*, §§771–5. Quintilian's comment at *inst.* 9. 2.6 – 'Quid enim tam commune quam interrogare vel percontrari?' – could be Augustine's own about his doctrinal preaching. See M. Inviolata Barry, *St. Augustine the Orator: A Study of the Rhetorical Qualities of St. Augustine's Sermones ad populum* (Washington: Catholic University of America Press, 1924), 145ff. It is important to note that in the contexts with which we are concerned, Augustine eschews emotive questions in favour of those which enable him to guide and hone a line of argument.

⁵⁵ *serm.* 52. 14 (*RevBen* 74 (1964), 25).

But if doctrinal summaries draw out propositions embedded in the text, the propositions must be provable from the text and little is gained from using terminology not to be found in those texts.

We must, however, to use the evidence offered by *Sermon* 52 with care: it is one of only a very few texts where the forensic analogy is openly pressed. That Augustine can so easily cast this rhetorical style as a forensic exercise here shows it is a resonance that others would hear in that style, but the use of 'resonance' seems important: homiletic rhetoric was already developing as an independent tradition. Augustine was a member of a generation that gradually adapted traditional rhetorical forms for Christian homiletic use. At the heart of this project was the creation of a Latin that was both stylish and yet consciously simpler than anything rote adherence to classical norms would have encouraged. Augustine made his own contribution to this emerging tradition and yet had many models for emulation.[56] Thus, what we see in *Sermon* 52 is better viewed as Augustine revealing one of the main resonances that doctrinal preaching had for someone with his rhetorical background, and (coupled with the evidence of *De doctrina*) one of the main contexts on which he drew as he made his own the Christian homiletic, polemical and catechetical tradition. Indeed, a fuller picture only emerges when we look at some of the other techniques Augustine brought to bear on this task. By far the most important here, is dialectic.

Dialectic was the skill of arguing logically, and the set of techniques used towards this end. Much of its content consists in the principles of logic, aimed towards the task of identifying key distinctions and offering precise definitions as well as identifying the consequences that followed from given propositions. The process of question and answer – either between student and teacher or in a written dialogue form – was one of the central ways in which dialectic was exhibited or taught. At the

---

[56] This style made only rare use of complex prose rhythms; it used vocabulary and expression familiar to his audience even if it broke the rules of 'good' Latin, and the wordplays and figures of speech that he knew delighted his audiences are common. On this theme, see Christine Mohrmann, *Études sur le latin des chrétiens*, 3 vols. (Rome: Edizioni di Storia e Letteratura, 1961–3). For her general reflections, see 'Saint Augustine and the Eloquentia', I, 351–70, and 'Augustin Prédicateur', I, 391–402, here 396: 'La langue de la prédication augustinienne n'est pas le latin vulgaire de son époque, c'est plutôt une forme très stylisée du latin tel qu'il se parlait dans un milieu cultivé mais qui était, dans sa simplicité, facile à comprendre, meme par l'homme du peuple. Sans descendre au niveau du peuple, il parle une langue qui lui reste accessible.' See also Steven M. Oberhelman, *Rhetoric and Homiletics in Fourth-Century Christian Literature* (Atlanta: Scholars Press, 1991).

same time, as we see, Augustine in himself extended examples of such reasoning to take the form of continuous exposition.[57]

The relationship between the disciplines of dialectic, grammar and rhetoric was the subject of much debate in the ancient world.[58] Grammar was the discipline that lay at the foundation of all subsequent education in the late antique world, teaching a wide range of practices from being able to read a text (for example, understanding sounds, their combinations, punctuation, good word inflection) to basic literary criticism (identifying a text's argument or plot and its moral lessons).[59] Like most ancient commentators, Augustine sees grammar as a distinct discipline insofar as it is concerned with questions of sound and questions of basic linguistic inflection, but dependent on dialectic for its principles insofar as it is also concerned with questions of definition and distinction.[60] The relationship between rhetoric and dialectic is more complex. Classical authors envisaged the good orator making use of dialectical skills only within a broader rhetorical concern for keeping the audience's attention and carrying them along (thus, for example, the orator was allowed to make use of far looser syllogistic rules because tightness of one's logic was not the only goal being sought); for the dialectician the figures of rhetorical ornament were of no value.[61] Thus to suggest that Augustine sees the task of doctrinal exposition both as parallel to an exercise in forensic rhetoric *and* as an exercise in dialectic is not particularly surprising, but we must exercise some care in examining precisely what role Augustine imagines for dialectic within his overall vision of Christian argument.

Augustine's earliest valuations of dialectic follow Plotinian lines in presenting it as a revelatory tool which uncovers the very structure of reality.[62] As Johannes Brachtendorf has argued, however, the *De magistro*,

---

[57] Whether or not one is convinced by his argument for strong continuity in Augustine's positive valuation of dialectic, Pépin's *Saint Augustin et la dialectique* remains the point of departure for modern study. For Augustine's definitions of dialectic and accounts of its content, see pp. 161–87 (of particular note are *Cresc.* 1. 13.16, 2. 2.3, *sol.* 2. 11.19–21, *ord.* 2. 13.38 and *doctr. chr.* 2. 35.53). Lacking Pépin's precision but still useful is Marrou, *Saint Augustin*, 240–8.

[58] I discuss Augustine's attitudes to the Liberal Arts in Chapter 5.

[59] The scholarly literature on the influence of the grammarian and the discipline of grammar on Christianity has grown considerably in the last twenty years. See the discussion of and bibliography in Catherine M. Chin, *Grammar and Christianity in the Late Roman World* (Philadelphia: University of Pennsylvania Press, 2008).

[60] See, for example, *sol.* 2. 7.14ff.

[61] See the discussion of Pépin, *Saint Augustin et la dialectique*, 191–210.

[62] I discuss these earliest accounts, and Augustine's changing attitudes to dialectic, further in Chapter 5.

which was probably written in 389, already shows a revision of this earliest attitude. Although the *De magistro* does not mention dialectic as such, a number of factors seem to indicate that there has been a re-evaluation. For example, whereas Augustine earlier asserts with enthusiasm that dialectic enables the resolution of ambiguity in words, he now hesitantly argues that this may not be possible.[63] Augustine now also begins to treat dialectic as a tool which may be used for ill or good. In *De doctrina* 2, even though the validity of syllogisms is 'not something instituted by humans, but observed and recorded by them' and is part of the 'permanent order of things',[64] Augustine is now clear that the propositions to which people hold, and from which they reason, may be faulty and that logical skill in such a context may only lead to pride.[65] Thus, those who have argued for the continued centrality of dialectic in Augustine's thought – especially Henri-Irénée Marrou and Jean Pépin – are fundamentally correct, but only when we note the new context within which Augustine evaluates dialectic.[66]

We should also note how Augustine approaches dialectic in two key texts that date from the years during which he began writing the *De trinitate*. In *Contra Cresconium* 1, written *c.*405, Augustine defends the role of dialectic alongside a defence of eloquence. He speaks of eloquence as a combination of ornamented and truthful speech, and dialectic as a combination of subtle logic with truthfulness.[67] He even presents Christ himself as a model of appropriate dialectical practice.[68] Chronologically, this distinction follows shortly after the discussion of dialectic in *De doctrina* 2.[69] There Augustine specifically identifies certain types of inference and syllogistic reading as appropriate for teasing out the precise meaning and implications of scriptural teaching, as long as one does not become overly entranced by valid rules of deduction at the expense of the truths

---

[63] *mag.* 13. 43. Johannes Brachtendorf, 'The Decline of Dialectic in Augustine's Early Dialogues', *SP* 38 (2001), 27–9.

[64] *doctr. chr.* 2. 32.50 (CCSL 32. 67): 'ipsa tamen ueritas conexionum non instituta, sed animaduersa est ab hominibus et notata, ut eam possint uel discere uel docere; nam est in rerum ratione perpetua et diuinitus instituta'.

[65] *doctr. chr.* 2. 34.52.

[66] On this topic, see also Joseph T. Lienhard, 'Augustine on Dialectic: Defender and Defensive', *SP* 33 (1997), 162–6. Philip Burton, 'The Vocabulary of the Liberal Arts in Augustine's Confessions', in Karla Pollman and Mark Vessey (eds.), *Augustine and the Disciplines: From Cassiciacum to Confessions* (Oxford: Oxford University Press, 2005), 151–5, traces interesting variations in Augustine's vocabulary.

[67] Cf. *Cresc.* 1. 13.16 and 1. 16.20.

[68] *Cresc.* 1. 14.17–1. 19.23.

[69] Dialectic is referred to periphrastically as 'disputationis disciplina' at *doctr. chr.* 2. 31.48.117 and as 'scientia definendi, dividendi atque partiendi' at *doctr. chr.* 2. 25.53.129.

of scriptural propositions.[70] In Book 4, written twenty-five years later, Augustine discusses the traditional threefold division of oratorical function: *docere, delectare, flectere*.[71] But he distinguishes between the first and the remaining two, and by implication between the unadorned and the other two styles. *Docere* pertains to the subject matter, the *res* of which we speak, and in keeping with his theological goal, Augustine both lauds the value of *delectare* and *flectere* but emphasizes that instruction is a *sine qua non* and that the uncovering of truth itself may delight and move.[72] The basic distinction is still that of the *Contra Cresconium*, allowing us to see the perduring links between the unadorned style, the office of teaching and the use of dialectic as a tool for revealing the structure of scriptural teaching. In Augustine's austere style of summarizing doctrinal principles as well as in his style of doctrinal exposition, we should hear the voice of a preacher who, even in his mature work, continues to value dialectic.[73]

In a number of earlier publications I have spoken of the 'grammar' of Augustine's Trinitarian thought, referring to the 'matrix of principles and rules for theological discourse that Augustine inherited and developed'.[74] Drawing analogies to the grammar of a language is, of course, a widely used device in recent writing, and one used with varying degrees of clarity. Invoking the language of a forensic *propositio* or the style of a dialectical exercise enables us to move beyond the over-used language of 'grammar' while still retaining its helpful sense of the 'rules' of speech. In his preaching and methods of summary, then, Augustine sees Scripture as susceptible to an analysis that extracts from it the basic rules of relationship between the agents, activities and objects we find in its texts. The doctrinal content of faith is founded in these rules and the scriptural imagery and terminology used to speak of them; understanding begins as we try to imagine what it means to predicate those relationships of the immaterial and simple reality that is God. Of course, Augustine treats Scripture as a repository of the basic language and imagery for Christian

---

[70] For the discussion see esp. *doctr. chr.* 2. 31.48.117ff., and for Augustine's insistence on appropriately valuing the art, *doctr. chr.* 2. 34.52.128. Marrou, *Saint Augustin et la Fin de la Culture Antique*, 422ff., offers a very useful exposition of Augustine's 'exégèse grammaticale' (he uses the term following Marie Comeau).

[71] *doctr. chr.* 4. 12.27.74, quoting Cicero, *orat*. 69.

[72] *doctr. chr.* 4. 12.27.74–13.29.80.

[73] Note also Studer's discussion of the dialectical connotations inherent in Augustine's description of *trin.* as a *dissertatio*, and his direct discussion of dialectic in that work, *Augustins De Trinitate*, 64–66, 130–2.

[74] for example 'The Grammar of Augustine's Trinitarian Theology', in Robert Dodaro and George Lawless (eds.), *Augustine and his Critics* (London and New York: Routledge, 1999), 52.

thought and speech about God, and he accepts that one's use of this speech and its embedded rules should be governed by the faith of the Church as summarized in its creeds and catechesis. We have seen this demonstrated in practice through his early work, and will continue to see the same pattern throughout his corpus.

TOWARDS UNDERSTANDING

In the sections of *Sermon* 52 that I have followed here, and in the summary statement from the beginning of *De trinitate* 1 with which we began the chapter, Augustine makes no use of analogies. For Augustine the *rhetor* and *advocatus*, analogy would divert attention away from his focus in such texts, the shaping and reinforcing of faith's principles. This avoidance of analogy is also part of a clear distinction between faith and understanding, the exploration of analogical resources being part of the movement towards the latter. *Sermon* 52 also well illustrates this shift and is, in fact, one of the rare examples in which Augustine does offer an extended analogical reflection to illustrate inseparable operation. It is, in fact, the *only* sermon in which he offers the analogy of memory, intelligence and will. Immediately after his comment that we need only to bear the principles that he has laid out in the memory, Augustine says:

There's still something else I want to say, for which I really do require both your keenest attention and your intercession with God. Well then, it's only bodies that are contained by and occupy local space. The godhead is quite beyond material localization. No one should go looking for it, so to say, in space. It is present everywhere, invisible and inseparable; not more in one part, less in another, but everywhere whole, nowhere divided. Who can see this, who can grasp it? Let us be modest in our aims; let us remember who we are that are talking and what we are talking about. This and that, whatever it is that God is, must be believed with piety, reflected on in a holy manner, and as far as possible, as much as is granted us, it must be understood in a way beyond telling. Let words be stilled, the tongue cease from wagging; let the heart be stirred, the heart be lifted up thence.[75]

Augustine sets a new backdrop for the sermon: no longer are we in a courtroom judging the sacred 'law', the backdrop is the relationship between the intelligible and the sensible and the need for ascent towards the brilliance of the truth (*fulgor ueritatis*), a brilliance on which we are

---

[75] *serm.* 52. 15 (*RevBen* 74 (1964), 25–6).

yet too weak to gaze.⁷⁶ Augustine now calls for a process of *cogitatio* and, at the same time, for an attitude of humble longing for the sight of God. No longer does Augustine sell himself to the congregation as the advocate able to marshal irrefutable evidence from the text: now he invokes his unity with the congregation as 'we' attempt in modesty to move forward and pray for grace. That Augustine is now engaged in a new enterprise is also apparent in the shift in rhetorical style: Augustine's outline of the analogy that follows is peppered with questions in a far grander style – 'how long, O Man, will you go round the creation?'⁷⁷ These exhortations seek to move his audience, to elicit from them a movement towards the mystery of God. To understand this movement is the task of Chapters 5 and 6.

---

⁷⁶ *serm.* 52. 16. For a parallel use of this sermon to illustrate two styles in Augustine's discourse, see Studer, *Augustins De Trinitate*, 78ff. Studer here hints also at something like the epistemological concerns in the first half of *trin.* that I will draw out in Chapter 6.
⁷⁷ *serm.* 52. 17.

EXCURSUS 1

THE DATING OF THE *DE TRINITATE*

All subsequent chapters include discussion of texts from Augustine's *De trinitate*. Dating the individual books of this work and their various levels of authorial redaction, of which we know a little and frequently suppose we know much more, is a highly complex task. I do not need here to offer an account of all the relevant dating questions, but given my desire to trace some lines of development in Augustine's thought, it is important that I indicate the general lines of scholarship that I have followed. As noted in the Introduction, the argument of this book culminates in discussion of texts I take to have been produced in the 410–20 period. These texts reveal the basic lines of Augustine's mature vision of the Trinitarian life, lines that do not significantly change in the last decade of his life (even as various themes and exegeses do change). Accordingly I have focused here on questions relating to dating those sections of the *De trinitate* up to 420: I have not discussed in any detail when, in the early to mid-420s, the work was concluded.

We are certain that the *De Trinitate* was a long time in composition, and we are certain that an incomplete version of the work, ending at some point in Book 12, was stolen from Augustine. In response he finished the work, and edited the earlier books, adding substantial discussions to the beginnings of the early books.[78] Beyond this, much is in doubt: the evidence provided by his entry in the *Retractationes* and in various letters is all open to multiple interpretation. The discussion of Anne-Marie La Bonnardière and the supplement offered by Pierre-Marie Hombert are the points of departure for all scholars considering these questions today. Roland Kany's recent discussion of La Bonnardière and Hombert is a particularly significant commentary on their work.[79]

La Bonnardière's work offered a wholesale and broadly persuasive critique of earlier assumptions that the bulk of the work was written between 399/400 and 410/15 (with a slightly later date of 411–16 sometimes being offered for Books 5–7). La Bonnardière's characteristic methods were to note parallels in exegesis of particular verses between more and less easily datable works, and combinations of verses that emerge at distinct points during Augustine's career. An

---

[78] See *retr.* 2. 15. *ep.* 174 is also fundamental, and is the basis on which we know the work had reached some point in Book 12 when it was stolen.
[79] Older scholarship defended earlier dates for the work. See, for example, Hendrikx in BA 15. 557–66 where *trin.* 1–12A can be dated to between 400 and 410. For a summary of the older dating and its problems, see Pierre-Marie Hombert, *Nouvelles recherches de chronologie augustinienne* (Paris: Études Augustiniennes, 2000), 45–51. See Kany, *Augustins Trinitätsdenken*, 31–46.

The unadorned Trinity

initial collection of dating suggestions, published in 1965, was supplemented by a series of later and less well-known discussions of the *De trinitate* during the 1970s. Her final suggestions are:

(1) after 404 Augustine began the work;
(2) between 411 and 414 Augustine wrote the bulk of *De trinitate* 2–4 as a literary unity, except the prefaces and later additions which she identifies;
(3) commencing in 416–17 Augustine wrote or redacted *De trinitate* 5–7 (at the same time as *civ.* 11) after he acquired some knowledge of Eunomian doctrine;
(4) in 417–18 Augustine compiled *De trinitate* 8–12a (ending at 12. 14. 23);[80]
(5) in a final period beginning in 419 Augustine finished the work, ending sometime between 420 and 425.[81]

Hombert's more recent suggestions are a series of supplements to La Bonnardière's work, and concern only the first four books. He tabulates them as follows:

(1) 400–03, *De trinitate* 1;
(2) 411–13, *De trinitate* 2–3;
(3) 414–15, *De trinitate* 4.[82]

Hombert offers little comment on the particular passages in these first four books that La Bonnardière identifies as the product of Augustine's final redaction; he generally agrees with her suggestions but tends to be more hesitant about the certainty with which we can distinguish the different layers of the early books. La Bonnardière's conclusions about the various redactional layers in these books, and my views of her suggestions, can be tabulated as follows:

> *De trinitate* 1: This book is particularly hard to analyse. La Bonnardière argues that 1. 1.1–6.13 is late, but admits that in many cases Augustine is probably adapting material that is much older. My own sense is that her arguments for ending the insertion at 1. 6.13 do demonstrate the probability that this chapter is indeed late, but they offer no proof that the earlier summary, beginning at 1. 4.7, is not part of the original work, even if it has been edited.[83] Accordingly I assume that the earlier summary belongs to the earliest layer of the work.

---

[80] For discussion of where the break in *trin.* 12 occurred, see A.-M. La Bonnardière, *Recherches de chronologie augustinienne* (Paris: Études Augustiniennes, 1965), 168–9.

[81] *Recherches*, 165–77; La Bonnardière, 'Le *De trinitate* de saint Augstin, confronté au livre XI de la Cité de Dieu', *AÉPHÉ* 85 (1976–7), 346.

[82] *Nouvelles recherches de chronologie augustinienne*, 638.

[83] For her arguments, see La Bonnardière, *Recherches*, 83–7. Augustine's use there of Phil. 3.3, 1Cor. 6.19 and Deut. 6.13 all seem to fit most plausibly with a set of other texts from 419–21, all of which seem dependent on *c. s. Arrian.* 20. 9 and 29. 27. The fact, however, that *trin.* 1. 6.13 begins by speaking of 'collecta sunt testimonia quibus ante nos qui haec disputaverunt …' and seems to interrupt the flow of the argument with a section on the Spirit, may suggest that it is this small section that is interpolated rather than that it brings to an end a much longer section.

De trinitate 2: 2. *proem.* 1–2. 5.8 is, for La Bonnardière, a late addition. Her argument here certainly shows that the text appears to have been heavily edited in line with the theology of the 415–20 period, but I am not convinced that we can be certain about the date of initial composition. The dating of 2. 5.8–2. 7.12 is even more problematic, but La Bonnardière argues that it is also late. Her arguments here again seem to me to show convincing signs of later editing, even as her conclusion that the whole argument is later may not be necessary (and her certainty about the break between this and the previous section seems unwarranted). The core of the original book consists of 2. 7.13–18.35 (the end of the book). I am convinced by this argument even as I think that it remains unsettled whether Augustine's addition of his second exegetical rule earlier in the book belongs to initial composition or later redaction.

De trinitate 3: The later preface consists of 3. *proem.* 1–3. The rest of the book, 3. 1.4–11.27, is original. By this I am convinced.

De trinitate 4: The later preface consists only of 4. *proem.* 1. By this I am also convinced.

For my purposes I do not need to adjudicate between La Bonnardière's and Hombert's different dating of the beginning of the work. Hence, I assume only that the *De trinitate* was begun in the 400–05 period. I assume also that the bulk of Books 2–4 was written between 411 and 414. In my discussion of these books, however, I note a number of parallels in significant material that can be found in texts from the 400–10 period. While these parallels do not necessarily add to arguments about dating, they do add to the difficulty of tracing clear developments in Augustine's Trinitarian theology during the first decade of the fifth century.

I am not convinced by the need to place Books 5–7 after 416 because of the assumption that they must follow Augustine's knowledge of Eunomian doctrine, but other reasons suggest dates after 414, although it is very difficult to know if the version of these books we possess has been substantially redacted.[84] Thus, without absolute certainty, I assume a date for Books 5–12a somewhere between 414 and 418. The final books then date from some period between 419 and 427.[85] As will become clear during Chapter 9, the complexity of dating the variety of texts thus probably composed between 411 and 418 means that it is as difficult to trace the precise development of some key ideas during the second decade of the fifth century as it was during the first decade!

---

[84] See, for example, Kany, *Augustins Trinitätsdenken*, 45.
[85] Kany, *Augustins Trinitätsdenken*, 42–6, offers a very good discussion of the possible dates at which Augustine may have completed the work.

CHAPTER 5

Per corporalia ... ad incorporalia[1]

The previous chapter ended with the transition that occurs in *Sermon* 52 between Augustine's exposition of the faith that must be believed and his exhortation to the task of understanding that faith. The next two chapters concern the character of this 'understanding'. In this chapter I begin by arguing that Augustine's early appropriation of a Platonist reading of the Liberal Arts tradition provided the foundations for his account of understanding Trinitarian faith. Between the years 386 and 400, however, we can trace a shift in Augustine's approach to this tradition, but one that should be read as a rejection of that early appropriation only with caution. Many of the intellectual practices that stem from his Platonizing reading of the Liberal Arts tradition remain at the heart of how Augustine conceives the practice of thinking beyond the material and towards the divine. Throughout his mature corpus the search for understanding remains, at its heart, a process of reflecting on the principles of Trinitarian belief, and the scriptural evidence pertaining thereto, attempting to think how these principles and this evidence draw us towards sight of a God who transcends the temporal and material categories with which they are imbued. At the end of this chapter I consider briefly some of the analogical explorations of Trinitarian doctrine found in the *Confessiones*. In Chapter 6 I turn to the manner in which Augustine adds further theological and Christological density to the task of seeking to understand God in the initial books of the *De trinitate*.

ASCENT AND THE LIBERAL ARTS

One frequent assumption about Augustine's early enthusiasm for the Platonists is that it instilled in him a desire for ascent towards contemplative vision of the Plotinian One, for experiences that would take him

[1] *retr.* 1. 6 (CCSL 57. 17).

beyond the material world towards its source. And many have taken just such an experience to be described in *Confessiones* 7.[2] Such assumptions about how Platonism affected Augustine are overly simplistic, and attending in a little detail to the complexities of the language of 'ascent' will show why and provide a good foundation for considering Augustine's account of 'understanding'. My point of departure is not Augustine, but non-Christian Neoplatonic use of the term ἀναγωγή and its cognates insofar as they are used to describe the mind being led up towards or ascending towards contemplative vision of the One.

In broad terms, Neoplatonic authors use the language of ascent in two ways. In the first place, the language is used to describe the process that results in immediate vision. But even here we must be careful. Plotinus, for example, in *Ennead* 5. 7, describes the One as 'beyond being' (quoting *Republic* 509B), and yet to say this is only to issue a denial. If the name 'One' has a positive function, Plotinus continues, it is in its indication that the One is truly such and thus beyond multiplicity and form. Turning to the question of our ascent to intellect, Plotinus likens *Nous* to the Sun: if one looks beyond what is illuminated then one moves towards the sight of light itself. But the intellect only moves towards seeing the One when another light springs out from itself, not a light that is different from itself. This light springs out even when one lowers one's eyes before its brightness: 'then in not seeing it sees, and sees then most of all: for it sees light'.[3] Thus, Plotinus insists:

> So one must not chase after it, but wait quietly till it appears, preparing oneself to contemplate it, as the eye awaits the rising of the sun, and the sun rising over the horizon ['from Ocean' as poets say] gives itself to the eyes to see.[4]

Thus, in one sense, the final stages of this ascent do not depend on an active seeking to see, but on one's skill at resting in *Nous* until the One reveals itself.

---

[2] At *conf*. 7. 10.16, if not also at 9. 10.24 in his last conversation with Monnica. One of the key points of reference for discussion of the first of the passages remains Pierre Courcelle, *Recherches sur les Confessions de Saint Augustin* (Paris: E. De Boccard, 1950), 157–67. For a good recent discussion of Augustine's 'mysticism', see John Peter Kenney, *The Mysticism of Saint Augustine: Rereading the Confessions* (London: Routledge, 2005). I discuss *conf*. 7. 10.16 at the end of this chapter. There is a brief but helpful discussion of Augustine's understanding of ascent and its sources at Studer, *Augustins De Trinitate*, 140–7.
[3] *Enn*. 5. 5.7: Τότε γὰρ οὐχ ὁρῶν ὁρᾷ καὶ μάλιστα τότε ὁρᾷ· φῶς γὰρ ὁρᾷ.
[4] *Enn*. 5. 5.8: διὸ οὐ χρὴ διώκειν, ἀλλ' ἡσυχῇ μένειν, ἕως ἂν φανῇ, παρασκευάσαντα ἑαυτὸν θεατὴν εἶναι, ὥσπερ ὀφθαλμὸς ἀνατολὰς ἡλίου περιμένει· ὁ δὲ ὑπερφανεὶς τοῦ ὁρίζοντος – ἐξ ὠκεανοῦ φασιν οἱ ποιηταί – ἔδωκεν ἑαυτὸν θεάσασθαι τοῖς ὄμμασιν.

Against this background it is not surprising that Plotinus also uses the language of ascent to describe the long process of learning the intellectual disciplines that train the mind to distinguish the character of intelligible reality, the necessary preliminary to resting in *Nous*. In *Ennead* I. 3 ('On Dialectic') Plotinus describes the process of training both philosophers who already grasp something of the intelligible and those who love beauty and form but cannot yet move beyond particular beauties. For both, dialectic is necessary.[5] But, whereas in Chapter 4 we discussed dialectic as a technique for argument, here we see something of the ancient disputes about the relationship between dialectic and the structure of reality. Plotinus engages this debate by arguing against Aristotelian understandings of logic. For Plotinus, Aristotelians treat logic and dialectic as merely tools used by the philosopher to enhance precision in language. For Plotinus, following Plato, dialectic is rooted in the very structures of the intelligible world and is capable of revealing knowledge about the distinctions and unities therein.[6] Our approach towards dialectic and the mysteries it may reveal must, then, be a careful progression. The musician must learn the idea of beauty itself by learning to separate the material from the intelligible, and thus imbibe the doctrines of philosophy.[7] But even the philosopher must undertake mathematical studies and further perfection of the virtues before turning to dialectic itself – dialectic may then lead to the philosopher's *nous* resting in a unified vision of the intelligible.[8] This turn to dialectic does not imply its absence at the lower levels of ascent, but rather a full flowering of dialectical skill and the centrality of dialectic in the formed *nous*. And so Plotinus speaks of ascent here as the extensive forms of training that are the preliminaries to ascent in the first sense.

Plotinus's discussion of dialectic not only provides background for discussion of Augustine's own initial understanding of this discipline; it also offers us a small window on to some of the ways in which the language of ascent was a tool in the debate among and within ancient philosophical schools about the appropriate ordering of disciplines that structured one's 'ascent' in this longer-term sense. An understanding of the end and nature of ascent allows Plotinus to indicate the relative positioning of various disciplines and the character of the order through which a student should move – which, for example, can be left behind, which have

---

[5] For Plotinus's definition of dialectic, see *Enn.* I. 3.4.
[6] For Plato's views, see esp. *Rep.* 531Cff., *Sophist* 253Bff.
[7] *Enn.* I. 3.1.   [8] *Enn.* I. 3.3.

lasting significance. For many late antique Platonists, ascent language similarly proved a helpful tool in appropriating ancient educational traditions. Thus, to give one more example, Ammonius, head of the school in Alexandria at the turn of the sixth century, uses his commentary on the *Categories* as an occasion for insisting on an initial education in ethical practice, followed by the reading of texts concerning logic, ethics, physics, mathematics and finally theology. Progress occurs in this order because of the demands of ascending to the one true goodness from the many things of which goodness may be predicated.[9]

One of the main ways in which non-Christian Platonists could use the notion of ascent to reflect on ancient educational theory and practice was through engaging the Liberal Arts tradition which developed out of earlier notions of ἐγκύκλιος παιδεία or 'well-rounded education'. This tradition may have begun with Plato, who lists dialectic and mathematical disciplines. During the second and first centuries BC the list was expanded to include grammar and rhetoric, in a move which may represent attempts by philosophers in that period to co-opt existing educational disciplines into an order which pointed towards goals that then could be defined by the various philosophical schools. This process continued throughout the imperial period in Middle and Neoplatonic contexts. At the same time, for authors such as Cicero, the Liberal Arts provided an appropriate foundation for the ideal orator/politician/philosopher that he saw as the very perfection of the elite male.[10] It is important to bear in mind that while we have a number of accounts, we are unclear as to how far such lists of disciplines represent curricula actually followed. It is far more plausible that the vast majority of such systems represent ideal visions of the purpose and order of disciplines taught in more piecemeal fashion or engaged on the basis of personal reading.[11]

It is against this background that we can now turn to Augustine himself. It is striking that Augustine's initial enthusiasm for the Platonists very quickly inspired a desire to produce texts on each of the Liberal Arts. Such a decision both fits within well-established Platonic traditions and

---

[9] Ammonius, *in cat.* 5. 31ff. Cf. Marinus's description of Proclus's education, *vit. Procl.* 13.

[10] Marrou's *Saint Augustin et la fin de la culture antique*, 187–327, is still unsurpassed as a basic guide to the development of models for organizing the Liberal Arts in antiquity and Augustine's place in that tradition. The table on pp. 216–17 offers a summary list of the disciplines included by different authors. See also the works mentioned below in n. 15.

[11] On this complex topic, see the remarks of Teresa Morgan, *Literate Education in the Hellenistic and Roman World* (Cambridge: Cambridge University Press, 1998), 67–89. On the book as the whole, however, one should note the cautionary remarks of Raffaella Cribiore in *Bryn Mawr Classical Review* 1999.05.22 (http://bmcr.brynmawr.edu/1999/1999-05-22.html).

is a sign of how much Augustine saw his conversion to Platonism as culminating his search (inspired by Cicero's *Hortensius*) for a way to integrate his rhetorical and philosophical readings into a path towards the *beata vita*. Between the autumn of 386 and spring of 387 Augustine produced works on grammar and music, and notes for other volumes. For many scholars none of these survive, although short texts on dialectic, rhetoric and grammar have each received strong argument in favour of their authenticity.[12]

During the same period, however, Augustine also wrote the *De ordine*, a text from which a number of passages considered in the first chapter were drawn. The work is concerned with the question of evil and divine providence, and its solution for our inability to perceive God's omnipresent ordering hand is to recommend a dialectical practice of education that will teach us to recognize the distinction between the sensible and the intelligible, and hence point us towards the character of the divine. In *De ordine* 2, Augustine offers an extended account of the function and interrelationship of the Liberal Arts that tells us much about Augustine's attitude to them as a whole.[13] The passage focuses around *ratio*'s natural organization of the disciplines as it seeks its own end in eternal contemplation of 'divine things'. By the use of dialectic, *ratio* learns its own power and thus is admonished to attend to itself as the path for further ascent.[14] *Ratio* then constructs a series of steps (*gradus*) necessary if it is to persevere in the contemplation at which it aims.[15]

We cannot identify with certainty the immediate model that Augustine had in mind for the encyclopaedia of the Liberal Arts that he decided to compile. While Ilsetraudt Hadot argued that Porphyry's lost *De regressu animae* was the model, Virgilio Pacioni and Danuta Shanzer have argued strongly for the older scholarly judgement that Cicero's discussions and the lost *Disciplinarum libri* of Cicero's contemporary Marcus Terrentius Varro were his basic models.[16] The passage from the *De ordine*

---

[12] For Augustine's own note about this unfinished project, see above n. 1. The authenticity of each text has been the subject of controversy. For the *De rhetorica*, see the edition and introduction of Remo Giomini, 'Aurelius Augustinus "De rhetorica"', *Studi latini e italiani* 4 (1990), 7–82; for the *De dialectica* see B. Darrell Jackson, *Introduction to Augustine's 'De Dialectica'* (Dordrecht and Boston: Reidel, 1975) and Pépin, *Saint Augustine et la dialectique*, ch. 2; for the *De grammatica*, see Vivien Law, 'St. Augustine's "De Grammatica": Lost and Found?' *RecAug* 19 (1984), 155–83.

[13] *ord.* 2. 12.35–16.44. For the encyclopaedic nature of *ord.*, see Ubaldo Pizzani, 'L'enciclopedia agostiniana e i suoi problemi', in *Congresso Internazionale su S. Agostino nel XVI centenario della conversione, Roma, 15–20 settembre 1986* (Rome: Augustinianum, 1987), 331–61.

[14] *ord.* 2. 13.38.   [15] *ord.* 2. 14.39.

[16] See Ilsetraut Hadot's *Arts libéraux et philosophie dans la pensée antique* (Paris: Études Augustiniennes, 1984); Virgilio Pacioni, *L'unità teoretica del* De Ordine *di S. Agostino* (Rome: Millenium

discussed in the previous paragraph, however, offers us a clear example of a Platonizing – and perhaps Plotinian – interpretation of the Liberal Arts: we are perhaps on firmest ground when we see Augustine drawing heavily on earlier Latin educational traditions, but drawing on those traditions in a context marked by his Platonic concerns and allegiances. Thus, in clearly Platonist fashion, the Augustine of the *De ordine* insists that the *artes* find their unity in reason's uncovering of the harmonic and numerical form of all that enables an ascent towards contemplation, and that dialectic is a skill which attends to the order and structure of reality itself.

In the *De ordine* Augustine not only discusses the Liberal Arts in the abstract, he also models for his readers fundamental intellectual practices that one who has learned from them can undertake. The examples Augustine gives almost all fall into two broad sets: one which focuses around analysis of the soul's nature and progress as the best site available to us for trying to think beyond the material towards that which informs all (though at this point, as I noted in Chapter 2, Augustine's concern is not yet with the soul itself understood as a threefold *imago*);[17] one which focuses around observation of the ordered and mysterious qualities of the creation as a preliminary to recognizing the existence of more than what one sees. In both cases Augustine makes use of his dialectical skills. Given the brief exploration of Augustine's earliest analogical practice in Chapter 2, this basic division should not surprise. It is these practices that form the core of the exercises Augustine recommends and displays when he speaks of 'understanding' throughout his corpus.

In the first place, again in *De ordine* 2, Augustine reflects on his twofold division of philosophy into knowledge of the soul and God. He attempts to show how focusing attention on the synthesizing and unifying activity of the soul in the body (whether in the synthetic judging of sense data or in the seeking of unity with other people) may lead to a recognition of

---

Romae, 1996). Pacioni builds both on the much earlier work of Adolf Dyroff and on Nello Cipriani's much more recent 'L'influsso di Varrone sul pensiero antropologico e morale nei primi scritti di S. Agostino', in *L'etica cristiana nei secoli III e IV: eredità e confronti* (Rome: Augustinianum, 1996), 369–400. Cf. Danuta Shanzer, 'Augustine's Disciplines: *Silent diutius Musae Varronis?*', in Karla Pollman and Mark Vessey (eds.), *Augustine and the Disciplines: From Cassiciacum to Confessions* (Oxford: Oxford University Press, 2005), 69–112. Oddly, Shanzer does not cite Pacioni. Neither Pacioni nor Shanzer denies that Augustine's interpretation of the Liberal Arts is also shaped by his Platonism and by his Christianity. Some basic indication of the importance of Varro in 386–7 is given by his being named at *ord*. 2. 12.35 and 2. 20.54, the beginning and end of Augustine's outline of the *artes*. If the Varro mentioned at *ep*. 26. 6 is this Varro then we have a further important indication of his significance.

[17] See p. 67.

the harmonious unity of the cosmos and the importance of a life ordered according to the intrinsic measure or number of the soul.[18] Reflection on this order prepares the soul for the sight of God.[19] Similarly, in *De musica* 6, the 'Teacher' leads the 'student' through a complex process of reflection on the functions of the soul in the body.[20] Recognition of the soul's ability to judge according to harmonic principles is propaedutic to reflection on the soul's ability to turn towards or away from God, and thus to be also rightly or wrongly ordered towards the creation. The same reflection also enables clearer thought about the nature of God.[21] In the second place, in *De ordine* 2 Augustine also describes the soul reflecting on the unity and harmony apparent (or to be desired) in the natural world, in architecture, in music and in society. Such reflection leads the soul to attend again to its own ability to make these judgements and then to the possibility of ascending towards vision of the One whose informing activity has created such an order.[22] These two sets of intellectual practices are thus closely interrelated.

The text on which I drew to give an example of my second set of exercises demands more attention. It occurs a few paragraphs after the extended description of the *artes* that we examined above, and in it Augustine speaks of the soul that has been educated in the *artes* and then 'handed over to philosophy' as the one able to recognize form in the material world and the power of the soul to ascend beyond it.[23] Here it is not so much the *artes* themselves that teach the soul how to ascend (and the practices we have examined) but the transcendent discipline of philosophy. This observation provides further evidence for the claim that Augustine's account represents a Platonizing view of the *artes*: Augustine incorporates the disciplines into an account of the soul's recognition of form and thence of its own power to judge form and to ascend towards the source of all that both sits comfortably alongside other descriptions of the principles he learnt from his non-Christian Platonic readings, and could be simply copied from the classic discussion of a text like *Ennead* 1. 6.

While it is clear that Augustine had considerable training in grammar and rhetoric, some training (supplemented by much reading) in dialectic and had read a good deal about some aspects of number and harmonic

---

[18] *ord.* 2. 18.48–19.50.   [19] *ord.* 2. 19.51.   [20] *mus.* 6. 2.2–5.12.
[21] Further good examples of these practices are provided by *an. quant.* 22. 40ff. and 31. 71–3, *imm. an.* 1. 6, *lib. arb.* 2. 20–4.
[22] *ord.* 2. 18.48–19.51.   [23] *ord.* 2. 18.48.

theory, his knowledge of what he terms 'philosophy' was much weaker. Augustine had not studied with any living philosopher and his initial readings in Platonism do not seem to have been extensive. Thus, while his accounts of 'philosophical' exercises that help one grasp the intelligible make use of some dialectical principles and material from other disciplines, they seem either to be dependent on just a few literary models, or to be his own adaptations thereof.[24] This may help to explain why, throughout his early works, Augustine tends to model very similar intellectual practices that both relate only in rather general terms to those we see reported in non-Christian Platonic literature and reflect the basic and fundamental insights Augustine reports he gained from his encounters with non-Christian Platonist texts. In his mature writing – especially in the *De civitate Dei* and *De trinitate* – we see Augustine demonstrating the fruits of an increasing knowledge of Platonism in his reflections especially on the character of mental life, but outside these few contexts he still tends to deploy the two basic sets of practices identified here. There are, however, significant shifts that occur in Augustine's understanding of the Liberal Arts over his first decade as a Christian and to those we must now turn.

CHANGING ATTITUDES TO THE *ARTES*

The *De ordine* demonstrates a great optimism about what the soul may learn by its self-examination. In the same work, however, in the very first winter after his conversion, we also see tensions. One of the most important examples concerns the role of memory. In a revealing exchange, Licentius argues that memory is of significance only with reference to the material world and irrelevant to the blessed life – the wise man has the objects of his knowledge present to his mental 'eyes'.[25] Although it would be difficult for him to refute this view given his account of reason's own powers a little later, Augustine is clearly not convinced by Licentius's likening of memory to a maidservant; the servant seems to have enabled Licentius to speak. After a brief attempt to argue against Licentius, Augustine defers further argument.[26] Around eighteen months later, in the *De quantitate*

---

[24] And, as we shall note in Chapter 11, his discussions frequently make as much use of Ciceronian material – from texts such as *fin.* or *Tusc.* – as they do of Plotinian or Porphyrian material.
[25] *ord.* 2. 2.7 (CCSL 29. 110).
[26] *ord.* 2. 2.7. On Augustine's uncertainty here, see Catherine Conybeare, 'The Duty of a Teacher: Liminality and the *disciplina* in Augustine's *De ordine*', in Mark Vessey and Karla Pollman (eds.), *Augustine and the Disciplines* (Oxford: Clarendon Press, 2005), 49–65.

animae (written 388), this early uncertainty begins to resolve: Augustine now locates even the principles of logic and number that he has learnt through the Liberal Arts in the memory, even though memory is surpassed as we learn to ascend through the various 'levels' of the soul.[27] As we see from *Epistula* 7 (*c*.388–91), it is around this time that Augustine also states clearly that the act of remembering through the production of images is central to our thinking even about ideas such as eternity.[28] Thus over only a few years memory has come to play a far more central role in the intellectual and the Christian life.

For our purposes a detailed story of the shifts that can be traced over the next decade is unnecessary, we can look instead to one of the texts that best represents the results of those shifts: *Confessiones* 10 (written *c*.400).[29] Here, all that one learns from the Liberal Arts is contained in the memory, or rather the Liberal Arts appear to bring to light and organize that which is somehow already present.[30] 'Somehow' is an important word here: Augustine offers little in the way of technical vocabulary, relying on the metaphorical to insinuate the mysterious depths in which such knowledge is somehow hidden. Augustine's employment of this tone is central to the message he wishes to convey. His famous statement that he has become a mystery to himself culminates an assertion of memory's necessary but near incomprehensible self-presence.[31] This emphasis on the difficulty of understanding memory is the context within which we should understand how Augustine views the classical and somewhat commonplace language of memory as storehouse – that metaphorical language is used to highlight the difficulty of conceiving memory's power, not

---

[27] *an. quant.* 33. 71–2. Cf. *conf.* 10. 12.19–13.20. It is important to note that Augustine sees even these memories as the result of learning (10. 13.20): 'et quomodo ea didicerim memoria teneo'. One of the nicest indications of the change that occurs in Augustine's thought may be seen in his use at *an. quant.* 33. 76 of the metaphorical language of 'milk' and 'meat' or 'food' used by Paul at 1Cor. 3.2. Here we move beyond the 'milk', but still deign to thank 'mother' Church for providing it. In his mature exegesis Augustine emphasizes that both 'milk' and 'solid food' are to be found in the one reality of Christ, for example *Io. ev. tr.* 1. 17. The clearest account of his mature reading of the texts is at *Io. ev. tr.* 98. 6 where he says that the metaphor of a 'foundation' is more apt than that of 'milk', because the crucified Christ is the foundation of a building that cannot be removed.

[28] *ep.* 7. 1.1.

[29] The literature on this book of *conf.* is extensive. Two good ways into this material are the commentary provided by James O'Donnell in his *Augustine: Confessions*, 3. 174ff. and Aimé Solignac's 'note complémentaire' on memory at BA 14. 557–67.

[30] *conf.* 10. 9.16–10.17, esp. 10.17.

[31] *conf.* 10. 15.25 (CCSL 27. 167): 'ego certe, domine, laboro hic et laboro in me ipso: factus sum mihi terra difficultatis et sudoris nimii'. The high point of the discussion which leads to this asssertion is the statement that memory's knowledge of itself defeats analysis: *conf.* 10. 15.24 (CCSL 27. 167): 'et hoc quis tandem indagabit? quis comprehendet, quomodo sit?'

merely its ordered nature. Augustine even speaks about memory in active terms, suggesting that memories put themselves forward, frustrating our attempts at controlled recollection.[32]

The highpoint of the discussion is Augustine's consciously non-technical celebration of the presence of Truth to the mind. The turn inward towards the memory enables the discovery that God is the truth who illumines and yet transcends the memory in a manner that renders our knowledge constantly mediated and yet constantly puzzling.[33] The discussion of the function of memory has thus changed considerably since the early works. Augustine's discussion of memory's function is now inseparable from his mature sense of memory's deceptive ability. At the same time, the central problems for any analysis of the role of memory in the life of faith revolve around the memory's necessary existence *in* that which it seeks, and about which it may slowly gain knowledge. The discussion of memory, thus, finds its high point not so much in a celebration of memory's complexity, but in an articulation of the tension between the complex character of the mind's self-knowing in the context of fallen desire, and the divine presence to the mind enabling it to know and judge even as fallen. As we shall see, this tension also shapes much of his mature analogical reflection on the mind and on our search to understand the divine.

In parallel fashion Augustine also changes how he presents the stages that mark the Christian life. Laying out the basic lines of this shift will draw us back to the intellectual practices I examined above. In the *De quantitate animae* Augustine describes seven levels (*gradus*) of the soul's activity (*actio*), levels that lay bare simultaneously the structure of the soul and the route by which one attains to true vision.[34] Memory is the act of the third level; at the fourth level the soul begins to separate itself from material concerns. Augustine speaks of the importance of the soul struggling towards a tranquillity that comes from recognition of divine providence. The soul seeks to overcome the fear that God will not approve of it in judgement. This level is surpassed, at the fifth and sixth levels, by the joy of true self-possession without fear and an advance towards

---

[32] *conf.* 10. 8.12.
[33] *conf.* 10. 27.37–8 (CCSL 27. 174–5): 'ubi ergo te inueni, ut discerem te? neque enim iam eras in memoria mea, priusquam te discerem. ubi ergo te inueni, ut discerem te, nisi in te supra me? et nusquam locus, et recedimus et accedimus, et nusquam locus. ueritas, ubique praesides omnibus consulentibus te simulque respondes omnibus etiam diuersa consulentibus ... sero te amaui, pulchritudo tam antiqua et tam noua, sero te amaui!'
[34] *an. quant.* 33. 70ff.

contemplation of God. Contemplation involves a vision of all things in the Truth, both the ordering of the cosmos and the truth of doctrine. This series of steps is the context for those practices of thought that enable us to think the intelligible. Augustine begins the series with a wish – both rhetorical and yet reflective of Augustine's own relationship to such subjects – that he and Evodius might be able to consult someone learned who would explain by teaching and dialectical reasoning (*dicendo ac disputando*) the powers of the soul.[35] Augustine then offers his own account despite his lack of formal education (*indoctus*). The account contains none of the inductive exercise through which Augustine leads Evodius elsewhere in the dialogue, but we have already seen enough to imagine with some accuracy the exercises that he sees as giving form to the ascent he has described.

During the early 390s Augustine develops a very different account of the soul's ascent. This can be seen for the first time in his *De sermone Domini monte* of c.393. The beatitudes are here read as eight stages (*gradus*) in the soul's progress.[36] This series does not parallel that of *De quantitate animae* directly; there is no overt reflection here on the various powers of the soul. But we do find the same contemplative goal, and the same progress through stages in which the soul accepts counsel from others and gradually learns to distinguish itself from that which is essentially 'below' it. The initial stages, however, are very different. Augustine describes a pious submission to the text of Scripture as the second stage, following a humble submission to divine authority. The third stage, of knowledge, comes from the reading of Scripture and focuses on the identification of the chains by which we are bound. Rather than identifying lower levels of activity that the introspective soul may fairly easily differentiate from the higher, Augustine has located the soul's progress wholly within a Christian and ecclesial *schema* in which humility, desire for divine mercy and attention to the Scriptures are the *sine qua non* for being led towards contemplation.

The same themes can be seen even more clearly in a similar series of *gradus* in *De doctrina christiana* 2, written c.397. This text has frequently been seen as the archetypal statement of a move away from the Liberal Arts.[37]

---

[35] *an. quant.* 33. 70 (CSEL 89. 217).
[36] *s. dom. m.* 1. 3.10–11. Eight because of eight sentences, immediately paralleled with the seven gifts of the Spirit.
[37] See, for example, Karla Pollman's excellent *Doctrina Christiana: Untersuchungen zu den Anfängen der christlichen Hermeneutik unter besonderer Berücksichtigung von Augustinus* De doctrina Christiana (Fribourg: Universitätsverlag Freiburg Schweiz, 1996), 192–6.

Augustine describes some of the *artes* as a useful propaedutic to the work of exegesis, but he also strongly cautions against the pride that follows from placing too much store in one's knowledge of them.[38] Among those he lists here, as we have seen, is dialectic. Against this possible pride, *De doctrina* 2 outlines appropriate modes of humility in thinking and speaking before the divine mystery revealed in Scripture. Near the beginning of the book Augustine offers a seven-stage account of ascent to wisdom, in which knowledge that we walk in faith is the central thread. At the first stage, fear of God inspires reflection (*cogitatio*) upon our mortality and possible punishment, thus inspiring holiness (*pietas*) and deference to Scripture. Augustine presents the third stage – that of knowledge and that at which the Liberal Arts begin to serve their revised propaedutic function – as founded in awareness of our entanglement in love of this world and failure to exhibit the love that Scripture describes.[39] At this stage Augustine also emphasizes that our prayer is answered by grace so that we might not despair.[40] Just as the steps of *De quantitate animae* provided the context within which the exercises Augustine models in the early works can be understood, this new account of the soul's progress provides a new context for many of the very same practices.

Thus, to take one example, in *De doctrina* 1, Augustine explains that all humanity attempts to imagine God, but only those who attempt to understand God through the intellect and as life itself are not simply mired in material imagery. Augustine then tells us *how* such people proceed in their thinking:

Whatever corporeal form occurs to them, they establish that it either lives or does not live; and they esteem what lives more highly than what does not … Then they proceed to examine that life, and if they find it has energy but not sense (as in the case of trees) they subordinate it to a sentient form of life, and they subordinate that in turn to an intelligent form of life (like that of humans). Realizing the mutability of human life, they are obliged to subordinate that too to some unchangeable form of life, namely the life which is not intermittently wise but rather is wisdom itself.[41]

---

[38] The clearest summary statements of his position can be found at *doct. chr.* 2. 39.58, 2. 41.62. Note also his discussions of what may and may not be usefully learnt from various disciplines. The disciplines of rhetoric, dialectic and number are discussed at *doct. chr.* 2. 31.48–40.60 and astronomy at 2. 29.46.

[39] *doct. chr.* 2. 9.16–10.19.

[40] *doct. chr.* 2. 10.20. In many ways, *De doctrina* 2 is the epistemological counterpart to the contemporary but more poetic account of Scripture as the 'firmament' set above us at *conf.* 13. 15.16–18.

[41] *doct. chr.* 1. 8.8.17–18 (CCSL 32. 11).

These techniques are then located as useful within the purification that is also a journey to our homeland made possible by Wisdom itself becoming visible in the flesh and laying down for us an *exemplum vivendi*, an example or pattern of living.[42]

Similar examples of these practices are apparent throughout his mature work, as we shall see through the rest of the book. But before we begin to encounter them, let us return to *Confessiones* 10. Here we see some of those practices interwoven with a particularly clear emphasis on their new context. Augustine locates his examination of the memory within a series of steps which ascend towards God.[43] He begins by modelling appropriate attention to the beauty and form of the created order, an attention which questions and distinguishes, separating that beauty from its creator.[44] But the journey goes by way of the soul, and again new questions and dialectical divisions are necessary, the mind understanding its own role in the assessment of sense data and yet recognizing that such judgement requires a higher informing truth or standard.[45] And yet the memory is now not surpassed in a further exercise of dialectic but becomes, as we have already seen, the site for confessing the mysteriousness of the mind to itself. At the same time Augustine exhorts us to ever deeper personal confession of our sinfulness to the God who is immediately present and yet hidden, a confession that may be best couched in the words God has given us in the Psalms.[46]

Again, then, Augustine adheres to the same basic set of intellectual practices, but now locates them within an understanding of human progress and nature that reflects a modified understanding of the possibilities offered by the Platonists. It is against this background that we must place the exhortations to think beyond the material that we have begun to encounter in texts written in or after 393, and will encounter as we move into Augustine's mature Trinitarian discussions.

ANALOGY IN THE *CONFESSIONES*

I want to end this chapter by considering a text written between the *De fide* and the passage from the beginning of the *De trinitate* (c.400–05)

---

[42] *doct. chr.* 1. 10.10.22–3. As we shall see, the same practices appear in more or less complex forms in a wide variety of genres. For a very useful recent discussion of the relationship between his homiletic practice and the longer treatises, see John Cavadini, 'Simplifying Augustine', in John Van Engen (ed.), *Educating People of Faith: Exploring the History of Jewish and Christian Communities* (Grand Rapids: Eerdmans, 2004), 63–84.
[43] *conf.* 10. 8.12.   [44] *conf.* 10. 6.9.   [45] *conf.* 10. 9.9 and 7.11.   [46] *conf.* 9. 4.8ff.

considered in Chapter 4, but one which shows that some of the main concerns of the latter work were already present in Augustine's mind in the late 390s. The same text also provides an important link between his earliest and his mature analogical practice.

In *Confessiones* 13 (*c*.398–400) Augustine writes:

> I wish that people would reflect upon this triad in themselves [*haec tria ... in se ipsis*]. These three are very different from the Trinity, but I make the observation that on this triad they could well exercise their minds and examine the problem, thereby becoming aware how far distant they are from it. The three I mean are being, knowing, willing. For I am and I know and I will. Knowing and willing, I am. I know that I am and I will, I will to be and to know. In these three therefore, let him who is capable of so doing contemplate how inseparable in life they are: one life, one mind and one essence, yet ultimately there is distinction, for they are inseparable yet distinct.
>
> Certainly each is present to himself [*certe coram se est*]. Let him consider himself, see for himself and tell me. When, however, through his investigation of these three, he has found something out and made his report on it, he should not suppose that he has discovered the immutable that transcends them, that which immutably is, immutably knows, immutably wills. And whether these three are there the Trinity, or whether the three are in each so that the three belong to each, or whether, in ways beyond finite understanding, both in simplicity and in multiplicity, it is itself an unbounded boundary in itself to itself by means of which it knows itself and is immutably the self-same because of the overflowing greatness of the unity: who can think this?[47]

With the appearance of the triad existing–knowing–willing (soon we find also the virtual synonym 'loving' used for the third term) in this text we see the foundation of Augustine's mature 'analogical' practice appear. Augustine offers many variations on his vocabulary and, especially in the later books of the *De trinitate*, tries out many triadic 'likenesses'. But most of them stand in more or less complex but fairly direct relationship to this.

Tracing the background to the triad of existing–knowing–willing presents a number of problems. Augustine makes use of a triadic language to describe the character of the knowledge that we may have about our own existence at least as early as the second book of the *Soliloquia*. His purpose in that text is not Trinitarian, but anti-Sceptical. Nevertheless,

---

[47] *conf.* 13. 11.12 (CCSL 27. 247–8): (quoting only the last convoluted sentence) 'et utrum propter tria haec et ibi trinitas, an in singulis haec tria, ut terna singulorum sint, an utrumque miris modis simpliciter et multipliciter infinito in se sibi fine, quo est et sibi notum est et sibi sufficit incommutabiliter id ipsum copiosa unitatis magnitudine, quis facile cogitauerit?'

he identifies in all people a desire to exist, to live and to know.[48] This famous triad of being–life–mind has Platonic origins, available to Augustine in Plotinus, but also through a number of other sources, including Victorinus.[49] These three terms identify three levels of existence in *De libero arbitrio* 1 and the same is implied in *De trinitate* 6 where the identity of these three in the Word defines it as the *prima et summa vita*.[50] In *De trinitate* 10 we find a parallel to his usage in the *Soliloquia*: the triad names three aspects of existence about which we may be certain and all of which must be true of the mind's intellectual existence.[51] However, while this triad thus plays a fairly consistent role through Augustine's career, we do not find him developing it – as Marius Victorinus had extensively done – as a specifically Trinitarian analogy. For Victorinus, the three terms name the three constitutive moments or aspects of perfect self-knowing living being, knowledge and life coming forth as distinct and yet as each necessarily containing the others. Usually Victorinus treats the Son as Life and the Spirit as Understanding. For Augustine, perhaps because he never does other than treat the triad as naming three levels of existence, the higher always encompassing the lower, the terms do not suggest themselves as a Trinitarian analogy.[52]

Nevertheless, this Platonic triad is not unrelated to the triad of existing–knowing–willing. In the *De duabus animabus* of 392, Augustine uses an account of the soul as knowing, living and willing against Manichaean duality.[53] Du Roy plausibly suggests that this is a variation on the more famous triad of being–life–mind. The change Augustine has made is probably easily explained. Let us note, first, that in *De libero arbitro* 3, a text roughly contemporary with *De duabus animabus*, we find him asserting that nothing more can be said to be our own than our will.[54] Second, at around the same time, we also find Augustine beginning to reflect on the necessary intertwining of knowledge and love in the search

---

[48] *sol.* 2. 1.1 (CSEL 89. 45). See the discussion at Du Roy, *L'intelligence*, 173–7 (where he also lists various possible precursors in Augustine's earliest texts). For his discussion of *conf.* 13. 11.12, see *L'intelligence*, 432–4.
[49] Plotinus, *Enn.* 6. 6. 8; Victorinus, *adv. Ar.* 1. 58, 4. 5. The origin of the triad is to be found at *Sophist* 248–9. For discussion of this triad, see Pierre Hadot, 'Etre, vie, pensée chez Plotin, et avant Plotin', in *Les Sources de Plotin*, Entretiens sur l'Antiquité classique V (Geneva: Fondation Hardt, 1960), 107–57 (including subsequent discussion of the paper). Mark J. Edwards, 'Porphyry and the Intelligible Triad', *Journal of Hellenic Studies* 110 (1990), 14–25, offers an important critique of Hadot's view of the significance of the triad in Porphyry.
[50] *lib. arb.* 1. 3.7; *trin.* 6. 10.11 (CCSL 50. 241).   [51] *trin.* 10. 10.13.
[52] It is uncertain whether Augustine's use of this triad occurs in response to Victorinus. On this question, see further Chapter 11, pp. 293–6.
[53] *duab. an.* 10. 13–14.
[54] *lib. arb.* 3. 3.7. The statement is in the mouth of Evodius, but Augustine congratulates him for it.

for happiness and in contemplation of the eternal.⁵⁵ Third, in his anti-Manichaean and anti-Sceptical works Augustine combines an interest in *cogito*-type arguments – arguments that enable us to be certain of our existence within an intelligible and ordered cosmos – with a strong desire to show the unity of the human will and *mens* against Manichaeism. In this context, and given Augustine's lack of commitment to (and, in many cases, knowledge of) traditional Platonic discussions, it is not surprising that Augustine felt free to adapt the triad without clear precedent:⁵⁶ first, adding willing/loving as a key term and then, second, focusing on the mind's act as intellectual life as the site for his own analogical investigations.⁵⁷

In none of the relevant texts from the *Soliloquia*, *De libero arbitrio* or *De duabus animabus*, however, does Augustine treat this triad as an analogy for the Trinity. Nevertheless, that further shift seems to have been prepared for in the 389–95 period. The short and enigmatic 38th of his *De diversis quaestionibus*, which is difficult to date but which certainly pre-dates the gathering together of the work following Augustine's Episcopal ordination, is the first text where Augustine reflects directly on triads within the soul as images of the Trinity. *Natura*, *disciplina* and *usus* as well as *ingenium*, *virtus* and *tranquilitas* are described as existing in a soul without diversity of substance (*substantia*). Augustine most probably knew the first of these triads from Latin rhetorical literature, although he may also have known it from contexts where it had been given Platonic purpose.⁵⁸ In its rhetorical context the triad described three

---

⁵⁵ *div. qu.* 35. 2. The necessity of knowing and loving for the contemplation that defines the blessed life is noteworthy (CCSL 44. 52): 'omnium enim rerum praestantissimum est quod aeternum est; et propterea id habere non possumus nisi ea re qua praestantiores sumus, id est mente. quidquid autem mente habetur noscendo habetur; nullumque bonum perfecte noscitur, quod non perfecte amatur'. The text is undatable, but certainly prior to 395. Du Roy, *L'intelligence*, 303–6, offers a useful discussion, noting both ways in which this text prepares the way for the arguments of *trin*. 8 and seems to represent a process of reflection very much Augustine's own. Du Roy also sees in the text an at least implicit triad and Trinitarian analogy of life–knowledge–love. These latter conclusions, however, seem to rest mostly on extrapolations from what is true in *trin*. 8 and should be regarded with caution.

⁵⁶ As a much later example of this felt freedom we might note Augustine's rejection of Cicero's triad *memoria*, *intellegentia* and *providentia* in favour of his own *memoria*, *intellegentia* and *voluntas* based on purely theological reasons. See *trin*. 14. 11.14 and Chapter 11.

⁵⁷ The one scholarly attempt to argue that Augustine depends on Platonic precedent is Willy Theiler who, in his controversial *Porphyrios und Augustin* (Halle: M. Niemeyer, 1933), 52, argues that Porphyry *sent*. 40 makes use of a triad of οὐσία, γνῶσις and φιλία which prefigures Augustine's *mens*, *notitia* and *amor*. Although the three terms are deployed, there is no indication Porphyry intends them as a triadic structure, and Theiler himself has to admit this is his one witness. Very few scholars have followed Theiler here.

⁵⁸ See Cicero, *orat*. 3. 88–91. See also Seneca *ep*. 11. 2. Augustine also probably encountered the triad in Victorinus's commentaries on Cicero's rhetorical works: see e.g. *in Cic. rhet*. 1. 2, 1. 24. Du Roy, *L'intelligence*, 299–303, offers an excellent discussion of sources.

features of a well-educated orator; an orator must be appropriately gifted by nature, trained by the appropriate discipline and possess appropriate zeal for learning. The second of these triads – *ingenium, virtus* and *tranquilitas* – is probably Augustine's own concoction and intended, as Du Roy suggests, as a commentary on the first.

With this text from *De diversis quaestionibus*, however, we should link *Epistula* 11 itself. There, as we have seen, Augustine identifies Son and Spirit as the authors of the discipline or knowledge that we need in order to progress towards God and the desire for God that we need to remain in that desire; already, here, Augustine has begun to meditate on the ways in which Son and Spirit create, and maybe imagined on the basis of the knowledge and love that constitute our movement towards God. In both of these texts we see Augustine reflecting not so much on triads within the soul *qua* soul, but on the soul as (being) formed for or capable of being formed for attention to God. We thus see Augustine treat the soul in the same way as he treats the creation's intelligibility more widely: it is intelligible for a purpose and as it turns towards its Creator. These texts also deserve our attention because in them we see Augustine turning to triads which place knowing in second place – a natural location given his emerging Christology – and desire, love or will in third place – again a natural location given his emerging pneumatology. Thus to the account developed so far, we need to add that even at this early stage Augustine's developing Trinitarian theology seems itself to have influenced the development of these noetic triads.

In *Confessiones* 13 Augustine pushes a step further, reflecting directly on the soul engaged in cognitive action as imaging something of the Trinitarian life: a new third analogical site has emerged out of the two that have been his central concerns up to this point.[59] No one reason accounts for Augustine's increasing interest in images found within the human *mens*. Augustine's strong, early and commonplace belief that intellectual life represents the 'highest' part of the created order combines with a strong belief in that order's intelligibility. From one perspective, then, it should surprise us that he does not turn towards mental analogies earlier. That he does not may, in part, result from his early ambiguity about whether the image has been lost in fallen humanity. It is only really between 411 and 413 that Augustine comes to state with certainty that the image which rests in human rationality remains even after the fall.[60] But

---

[59] For these two, see also p. 67 and p. 280.
[60] The best survey of this theme is that of Albrecht Schindler, *Wort und Analogie in Augustins Trinitätslehre* (Tübingen: J. C. B. Mohr, 1965), 63–73.

the emergence of this mature position is as much the emergence of clarity from confusion as a simple change of mind, and the text we consider here from the *Confessiones* shows how much may be said even if the question of the *imago* as such is not discussed.

Augustine's gradual development of triadic structures in the mind's life that we have traced back to 388–91 reaches, in the *Confessiones*, a point that already prefigures significant aspects of what we will see developed far more extensively in the *De trinitate*. Du Roy is quite right to emphasize that Augustine's turn to 'psychological' analogies occurs as part of his general interest in the intelligibility of the created order.[61] Nevertheless his suggestion that this 'turn' results from Augustine recognizing the failure of his earlier models based on a Trinitarian anagogy and on a Trinitarian metaphysics of creation lacks warrant. As I argued in Chapter 1, it is not clear that the model of 'Trinitarian anagogy' actually exists in the form Du Roy proposes; Augustine's anti-Manichaean account of the created order, and then these psychological triads, seem rather to emerge within and from his earliest reflections. At the same time, and again following the lines sketched in Chapter 1, it is not the case that these patterns of analogy simply determine his understanding of the Trinity – his early and developing pro-Nicene commitments already shape what he thinks may be found in analysis of the creation. In the cases of these emerging triads in mental life, the picture follows similar lines, but raises questions that seem ultimately unanswerable. It seems likely that Augustine's developing sense of the Son as intellect/wisdom and the Spirit as love played a significant role in shaping the analogical triads he finds in mental life. At the same time, Augustine already demonstrates a keen interest in the interplay of knowledge and love that we see in his discussions of the human search for the *beata vita* and which owes much to Latin rhetorical and philosophical discussion. This interest certainly also shapes his developing reflections on the Trinity and on the analogical triads he describes in mental life. As we shall see in discussion of the *De trinitate*, the intertwining of these different dynamics only becomes more complex in his mature writing.

We should note one further feature of the *Confessiones* that anticipates the *De trinitate*. In Book 7 Augustine famously describes the inward turn and initial 'ascent' prompted by his reading of the 'Platonic books'. When Augustine first describes the nature of the 'light' that illumines the mind, he tells us:

[61] Du Roy, *L'intelligence*, 420–1.

The person who knows truth knows it, and he who knows it, knows eternity. Love knows it. Eternal Truth and true Love and beloved Eternity [*o aeterna ueritas et uera caritas et cara aeternitas*]: you are my God.[62]

The triad of eternity, truth and love is (with variations in vocabulary) found a number of times in Augustine and throughout his career.[63] Augustine has, only a few sentences before, stated that he could enter into himself because God was his *adiutor*, his helper (probably alluding to Ps. 29.6, but cf. Ps. 62.8, 17.3, 18.15). Now he suggests to us that we know that of which he speaks if we know truth. This is so, of course, because truth is a participation in the Word, the Wisdom and the Truth, and to know Truth is to know Eternity and Love which are inseparable from it. This is the first example of a style of Trinitarian argument in which Augustine suggests that one of the great paradoxes of our seeking to know God is that we cannot but know God if we possess a rational and desiring life. Moreover, because we know and love through the presence of God to us, it becomes possible, as here, to use the language of Trinitarian faith as a guide to that which is but is not known as it is. Not only is this practice consonant with the account of God's mysterious presence that I explored in *Confessiones* 10, it also further shows us how the shifts we have been exploring have shaped Augustine's complex analogical practice. We will encounter this style of argument again in discussion of *De trinitate* 8 in Chapter 10.

The long passage from *Confessiones* 10–13 quoted above is, however, not noteworthy only because of what it reveals about Augustine's developing analogical practice. The same text also shows us a new dimension of Augustine's reflection on the Trinity itself. In the *De fide* we saw Augustine insisting that each of the divine three is God but that together they are not three Gods. Here we see Augustine first asking a question that we will find repeated a number of times in his mature expositions. Augustine asks whether the three aspects of mental life he has identified may be directly mapped onto the divine being, each of the divine three being somehow constituted by an immutable version of the activity in question. The answer to this question comes in the form not of a denial or a direct statement that each of the divine three must possess each mental activity, but of a third offered possibility. Perhaps, he suggests, each of the

---

[62] *conf.* 7. 10.16 (CCSL 27. 103).
[63] For details see O'Donnell, *Augustine: Confessions*, 2: 439–40. O'Donnell notes also the plausible echoes of John 4.7, 'if you knew me, you would know my Father', which is itself preceded by the threefold 'I am the way, the truth and the life'.

divine three somehow immutably mirrors a function of rational life *and* is also in themselves all three. The final clauses of Augustine's statement add a little more, but we should note that some of his key vocabulary in this passage – his contrast between the adverbs 'simply' and 'multipicitly' (or however one might put this in English), his discussion of the unbounded boundary – are never repeated again in Trinitarian contexts. These clauses advance the picture because they show Augustine attempting to find a way of envisaging the boundaries of the persons – their individual possession of all aspects of the divine immutable mental life – as being of a paradoxically unbounded quality such that the Trinity is also one life. Augustine grounds this paradox in what he terms the 'overflowing greatness of the unity' between the divine three. What he means is not fully clear, and we will have to wait for the work of the next two decades for Augustine's answers to progress significantly.

Let us end by noting the ways in which the Trinitarian discussions of the *Confessiones* should be read against, and are partly products of, the shifts in approaches to thinking the divine that we have explored in the earlier sections of this chapter. Augustine offers us a developed version of a pattern we saw in Chapter 2: he suggests to us a triad in the created order that we may see as reflecting the divine three and their unity. He suggests that reflection on this triad may aid in the exercise of our minds towards imagining God. He suggests that reflection on the soul and its life may draw us away from projecting the mutable and the temporal onto the divine. Augustine even shows us how reflection on this analogical site enables some ways of speaking about the Trinity itself. And yet, the passage is, first, framed by Augustine's insistence not only that the intelligible created order is so because the Spirit turns it towards its creator, but also that we must call upon the same Spirit to turn us back towards our source. Acceptance of divine aid is now essential to the task of turning towards God.[64] The passage is framed, second, at the end by Augustine's parallel insistence that now we live only through faith and lack sight of God. Our life must be one shaped by hope and by sighing for that which lies beyond our vision.[65] In this connection we might also note Augustine's account towards the end of the book of the 'spiritual' soul who 'judges all things' (1Cor. 2.15) and who understands the unity and diversity of the Trinity, but who does not attempt to judge the Scripture, the firmament placed above us.[66] In our text from *Confessiones* 13, Augustine emphasizes that the mind is exercised in part by being taught how far distant it is

---

[64] *conf.* 13. 9.10–10.11.   [65] *conf.* 13. 12.13   [66] *conf.* 13. 22.32–23.33.

from understanding. When Augustine moves from reflection on this analogical site towards the Trinity itself he is clear that now he is attempting to speak of that which defeats speech. Moving from the created analogue towards the Trinity is done well, then, when it is recognized as, and performed as, a move towards that which defeats the exercised mind. The advance towards understanding is one that is only appropriately founded in humility before the divine mystery.[67]

The most important transition in Augustine's analogical practice is thus not a turn from focusing on analogies in the created order towards internal analogies; it is the gradual shift narrated in this chapter towards a conception of ascent that is always a building on faith in humility, always a process of reflection that sees Scripture as inviting its readers into the mystery of God, just as Christ taught in the language of a temporal and spatial universe about a reality transcending such conditions. But this is to anticipate the argument I will pursue through the next chapter.

---

[67] It is in part because of the way in which Augustine marks the shift from reflection on the analogical site to reflection on the Trinity itself that we must be cautious about the ways in which we assume Augustine projects onto the Trinity that which he finds in the analogical site itself.

CHAPTER 6

A Christological epistemology

The previous chapter suggested that Augustine's account of thinking the divine is founded on themes learnt through his encounters with Platonizing conceptions of the Liberal Arts. The present chapter takes forward my argument by showing that the initial books of the *De trinitate* bring Augustine's adaptation of practices for thinking the intelligible to a new focus. They do so by describing the movement of the attention and understanding necessary for interpreting Scripture's speech about Father, Son and Spirit as mirroring the process by which the incarnate Word speaks of divine realities in spatial and temporal terms. As we shall see, this relationship is not only extrinsic: Augustine views the process by which the mind moves from obsession with the material towards contemplation of the divine as a constitutive part of the purification that is salvation, and as occurring *in* the two-natured Christ, through participation in Christ's body.

I term Augustine's account of this movement an 'epistemology' because it constitutes a major part of Augustine's mature account of how God may be known. This is to use the term rather differently from its standard post-Enlightenment philosophical sense, but doing so emphasizes the extent to which Augustine presents this account of knowing as the condition of possibility for understanding what it is that Scripture teaches. This 'epistemology' could also be termed an anthropology insofar as it is founded on an account of the human being as a desiring rational creature set within an intelligible cosmos. I use the adjective 'Christological' because Augustine argues that this movement is precisely that which Christ models and teaches by using his fleshly appearance as a revelation of the invisible God.

Augustine treats his Christological epistemology as that which is lacking in all anti-Nicene exegesis. Previous Latin Nicene writers had offered frequent but piecemeal critiques of anti-Nicene failure to read beyond the letter of Scripture, and they had presented such failure as the result of an anti-Nicene materialism. But it is only with Augustine that we see these piecemeal observations transformed into a tool for critiquing anti-Nicene theology as a whole and setting out the global structure of Nicene faith. In fact, Augustine uses his Christological epistemology as a tool for critiquing a wide range of tendencies in thought, including what he takes to be the failures of the Platonic tradition.[1]

Thus, just as the Cappadocians are rightly seen as placing epistemological concerns front and centre in the Trinitarian controversies of the East, so Augustine is the first Latin to make the same concerns central in the West. Yet, there are significant differences. The Cappadocians needed to counter Heterousian accounts of the strong correspondence between names and reality, and in this context developed detailed accounts of theological language. Their solutions developed a long-standing philosophical and theological discussion of terms such as *epinoia* and *ennoia*.[2] In his context, Augustine deals with opponents who have little precise to say about the origins and referential nature of theological language, and he himself seems to know nothing beyond highly formal accusations about Eunomian and Heterousian theology.[3] It may even be that previous generations of scholars have tended to overlook the manner in which he makes epistemological concerns central because he does so in a way that looks so unlike Cappadocian concerns.

An article published by Michel Barnes in 2003 is the point of departure for my account. Barnes explores Augustine's arguments that the Son's divinity must share the qualities of invisibility that Homoian theology reserves to the Father and that, consequently, the Son's human visibility must be intended to draw us towards recognition of his divine invisibility.[4] Augustine reads 1 Corinthians 15.24–8 as an eschatological narrative in conjunction with Matthew 5.8 ('the pure in heart shall see God') to show that there is a progress towards vision at the end, when the pure

---

[1] I return to the manner in which Augustine links these two in Excursus 2, at the end of this chapter.
[2] On this theme, see Andrew Radde-Gallwitz, *Basil of Caesarea, Gregory of Nyssa and the Transformation of Divine Simplicity* (Oxford: Oxford University Press, 2009).
[3] See *haer*. 19. 54. This is so whether or not Augustine knows in general terms that Heterousians see names of the divine as revealing essence.
[4] Michel René Barnes, 'The Visible Christ and the Invisible Trinity: MT. 5:8 in Augustine's Trinitarian Theology of 400', *Modern Theology* 19 (2003), 329–55. See also his 'The Arians of Book V, and the Genre of *De Trinitate*', *JThS* 44 (1993), 185–95; Kari Kloos, 'Seeing the Invisible God: Augustine's Reconfiguration of Theophany Narrative Exegesis', *AugStud* 26 (2005), 397–420. This question has also been the subject of debate in German scholarship. Barnes's account of the nature of faith finds parallels in Johannes Arnold's dense 'Begriff und heilsökonomische Bedeutung der göttlichen Sendungen in Augustinus *De Trinitate*', *RecAug* 25 (1991), esp. 38–46.

144 *Ascent*

in heart gaze upon the form of a servant, and see 'through' that form the form of God in equality with Father and Spirit. Neither the Old Testament theophanies nor the Incarnation itself make God available to sight; they enable a faith that knows it will become sight and knowledge only at the end. Barnes writes,

> Salvation came from faith – this is faith's 'utility'. Such a judgment is not merely one about discipline, as though the virtue of faith was primarily the act of obedience. The utility of faith for salvation lies in the fact that it marries an epistemology with a moral anthropology, and then grounds them both in Christology: 'Everything that has taken place in time … has been designed to elicit the faith we must be purified by in order to contemplate the truth, [and] has either been testimony to this mission or has been the actual mission of the Son of God'.[5]

With this argument Augustine attempts to undermine all Homoian exegesis of passages which apparently suggest the ontological subordination of Christ to the Father. All such exegesis should be seen, according to Augustine, as misunderstanding the role of the Incarnation in the shaping of faith and thus misunderstanding the very nature of the Incarnate Word. In what follows I build on Barnes's argument to show how Augustine develops the 'Christological epistemology' that will be foundational for his mature Trinitarian theology. We must begin by turning back to the first book of the *De trinitate*.

AUGUSTINE FINDS HIS PANZER

Immediately after his introductory summary, Augustine begins the main argument of *De trinitate* 1 by arguing that the Son must be 'true God' and co-equal with the Father.[6] In these few paragraphs Augustine offers his interpretation of a number of the most famous contested verses in Trinitarian debate – John 1.2–3, 1 Timothy 6.16, 1 Corinthians 8.6 – and in so doing he mainly summarizes the work of his predecessors. In every case Augustine emphasizes that the Christ who seems subordinate to the Father is also the co-eternal Word. John 1.2–3 only says, Augustine tells us, that 'all things that were made' were made through the co-eternal Word. The verse offers no warrant for thinking that Christ must be among the things that were made. The argument may be an adaptation

---

[5] Barnes, 'Visible Christ', 342–3. At the end Barnes is quoting *trin*. 4. 19.25.
[6] *trin*. 1. 6.9–13. In line with my comments in Excursus 1, I treat these paragraphs as part of the earliest stratum of Book 1.

from Ambrose, but if so Augustine adds to it 1 John 5.20 as a proof for the Son's divinity.[7] The referent of 'who alone has immortality' at 1 Timothy 6.16 is not the Father but the Trinity. John 5.19–21, in what we can call its original Nicene usage, demonstrates that the Son does what the Father does, including raising the dead.[8] Here an Ambrosian source is likely,[9] but Augustine has added a reference to Sirach 24.5's 'alone I have made the circuit of the vault of heaven' to undermine the significance of the Father being 'alone' immortal in 1 Timothy 6.16.[10] Augustine reads 1 Corinthians 8.6 alongside Romans 11.36, arguing that while the from/through/in sequence of the latter might seem to indicate three distinct actions, and hence three distinct beings, the doxology with which the verse concludes refers to the proceeding three in the singular, thus revealing their unity. This final singularity should be added to 1 Corinthians 8.6's distinction between Christ and the one God, the Father. Again Ambrose is the likely source for Augustine, but Augustine brings home the argument with more force, and does not follow Ambrose in citing John 5.22 only to argue about variant readings of that text.[11] Augustine ends this section by turning to the Spirit and emphasizing that the 'worship' of the Spirit commended by Paul at Philippians 3.13 is the same as the worship of God recommended at Deuteronomy 6.13. The Spirit is one with Father and Son. Here the dependence on Ambrose is the most certain of all the parallels suggested in this paragraph.[12]

---

[7] *trin.* 1. 6.9. Cf. Ambrose, *spir.* 1. 2.27–9. Hilary does not seem familiar with anti-Nicene use of this text. The argument, however, is to be found in the mouth of Victorinus's 'Candidus', *ep. Cand.* 1. 11. Victorinus's responses (e.g. *adv. Ar.* 1. 3) are somewhat cursory and do not parallel those of Augustine and Ambrose.

[8] *trin.* 1. 6.10–11. I discuss Augustine's interpretation of John 5.19 in Chapter 9.

[9] At *fid.* 5. 2.36, Ambrose links 1Tim. 6.16 with John 5.26; Augustine parallels 'alone has immortality' with Christ being 'eternal life'. Ambrose prefaces this discussion by quoting John 5.19 at 5. 2.34. Cf. *fid.* 3. 3.17ff. The discussion is more extended, but the same three elements are present. The elements that Ambrose and Augustine share are not present in Hilary's few discussions of the text (most extensively at *trin.* 4. 8), and the text is not discussed in Phoebadius, Faustinus or Gregory of Elvira.

[10] The addition is in itself interesting. Although this verse is not, to my knowledge, quoted by *any* other Patristic Latin theologian, Sirach 24.5 ('I came forth from the mouth of the most high') is quoted a number of times by pro-Nicenes, including by Ambrose (e.g. *spir.* 1.11.120, *fid.* 4. 8.87). Perhaps, knowing the text from Ambrose, Augustine happened upon the significance of the 'alone' a few verses later in the course of research for *trin.* Augustine never refers to it again.

[11] *trin.* 1. 6.12. Cf. Ambrose, *fid.* 4. 11.138–56. Ambrose also interprets 1Cor. 8.6 by means of Rom. 11.33–6, partially in order to draw attention to the conclusion of the latter. Both Ambrose and Augustine also use 1John 1.3 in this context. Augustine ends by reference to the inseparable operation of Father and Son; Ambrose cites John 5.17 to the same end.

[12] *trin.* 1.6. 13. Cf. Ambrose, *spir.* 2. 5.46 and 3. 18.142ff.

Suddenly Augustine cuts through these disparate arguments and identifies an architectonic problem with those who misread texts which suggest the Father's superiority to the Son. Such readers do not consider each text in the light of 'the whole sequence of the Scriptures' (*universam seriem Scriptuarum*), which describes how the Incarnation took place *pro salute nostra*, for our salvation.[13] Scripture itself sets out a *regula* or rule for our reading, speaking sometimes of Christ insofar as he was a human being, sometimes with reference to his *substantia*, to his status as eternal. The division, it should be noted, is not simply between the two 'natures' of Christ, but relies on an understanding of Christ as one subject who may be spoken of as he is eternally and as he is having assumed flesh.[14] For Augustine, Paul's narrative in Philippians 2.6–7 ('though he was in the form of God ... [he] emptied himself taking the form of a slave') summarizes the rule. Without ceasing to be in *forma Dei* the Son assumed the *forma servi*: because he himself is both we can even say:

> Who does not perceive that in the form of God he himself is even greater than himself, but in the form of a slave even less than himself? ... because the form of God took the form of a slave, then both is God and both is man [*utrumque Deus, et utrumque homo*]. But both God on account of the God who takes, and both man on account of the man who is taken. By that taking he one was not turned and changed into the other.[15]

The late Alois Grillmeier SJ described his own division of early Christologies into *logos-sarx* or *logos-anthropos* types as his 'Panzer' because of its ability to drive all before it and organize innumerable Christologies into fundamental categories. With this interpretation of Philippians 2.6–7, Augustine has found his own Panzer to use against Homoian theology.[16] The Panzer, however, is misunderstood if it is understood as only an exegetical rule for distinguishing between two types of text. It is a rule which Augustine presents as implying and revealing a comprehensive conception of what it means to read Scripture at this point in the life of faith, at a point when we should seek to see what is said and done

---

[13] *trin.* 1. 7.14 (CCSL 50. 45).
[14] Some account of the history of this division can be found in Michael Slusser, 'The Exegetical Roots of Trinitarian Theology', *TS* 49 (1988), 461–76.
[15] *trin.* 1. 7.14 (CCSL 50. 45–6). On Augustine's use of this text, see Albert Verwilghen, *Christologie et Spiritualité selon Saint Augustin. L'hymne aux Philippiens* (Paris: Beauchesne, 1985); Verwilghen 'Le Christ médiateur selon Ph 2,6–7 dans l'oeuvre de saint Augustin', *Aug* (*L*) 41 (1991) 469–82. Unfortunately Verwilghen locates Augustine's usage only against African sources.
[16] Alois Grillmeier, *Jesus der Christus*, viii: 'Manche Kritiker haben gefordert, entweder einzelne Väter anders zu deuten oder diesen "Panzer" als solchen bei einer Neubearbeitung des Werkes abzustreifen. Doch ließ eine erneute Überprüfung erkennen, daß man nicht darauf verzichten kann'. I am grateful to Michael Slusser for the reference.

in *forma servi* as a drawing of our desires and intellects towards the *forma Dei* that will remain hidden until the *eschaton*.[17]

FAITH AND CONTEMPLATION

Our first task is to see the character and clarity of the distinction that Augustine draws between contemplation and faith. This distinction begins to appear as soon as Augustine's Panzer trundles into action, and it does so first against Homoian readings of a text long in dispute: 1 Corinthians 15.28 ('But when all things are made subject to him, then shall the Son himself also be made subject to the one who subjected all things to him'). The foundation of Augustine's reading of 1 Corinthians 15.28 is an interpretation of what it means for Christ to 'hand over' the kingdom:

> The fact is that 'the man Jesus Christ, mediator of God and men' [1Tim. 2.5], now reigning for all 'the just' who 'live by faith' [Heb. 2.4], is going to bring them to that sight which the Apostle calls 'face to face' vision [1Cor. 13.12], that is what is meant by 'when he hands the kingdom over God and the Father'. as though to say 'when he brings believers to a contemplation of God and the Father [*ad contemplationem dei et patris*]'.[18]

A central aspect of Augustine's rule is used here as the hermeneutic key to 1 Corinthians 15.28: 'the man Jesus Christ' has his purpose in leading the just towards contemplation of the Trinity – his incarnate materiality draws us towards his nature as the immaterial and fully divine Son. Thus, his 'handing over' of the Kingdom cannot reveal an ontological deficiency, but must be read as the accomplishing of his drawing Christians. Augustine immediately offers a catena of texts to justify his understanding of contemplation as the goal: 1 John 3.2 ('it has not yet been manifested what we shall be; we know that when he is manifested we shall be like him, for we shall see him as he is'); John 17.3 ('but this is eternal life, that they may know you the only true God and him whom you have sent, Christ Jesus'); Psalm 5.4 ('In the morning I will stand before you and contemplate'); Romans 8.25 ('if we hope for what we do not see, we wait for it through patience'); Psalm 15.11 ('You will fill me with joy with your countenance'). This list combines texts whose language is that of sight with those that speak of knowing, but the language of sight has clear

---

[17] It is for this reason that I do not think Jaroslav Pelikan's otherwise helpful and frequently cited 'Canonica regula: the Trinitarian Hermeneutics of Augustine', in Joseph C. Schnaubel and Frederick van Fleteren (eds.), *Collectanea Augustiniana*, I, *Augustine: 'Second Founder of the Faith'* (New York: Peter Lang, 1990), 329–43 offers a sufficient reading.

[18] *trin*. 1. 8.16 (CCSL 50. 49).

predominance. Augustine offers this catena not because he is inventing a theme alien to his pro-Nicene predecessors, but because he is giving that theme a centrality and purpose absent from their accounts. Most importantly, Augustine's clarity about the nature of this contemplation casts all knowing and seeing prior to that state as faith and not sight, albeit a faith heading *towards* sight.

The character of this final contemplation, and thus what we now lack, will become clearer if we turn to the discussion of three types of vision found *De Genesi ad litteram* 12, composed only a few years after Augustine had begun the *De trinitate*. The first kind is vision by means of the eyes; the second is *per spiritum hominis*, through the human spirit, 'by which you think of your neighbour even though he is not there'; the third *per contuitum mentis*, through the gaze of the mind.[19] Augustine tells us that he uses the term *spiritualis* for his second kind on the basis of 1 Corinthians 14.14–15 ('if I pray in a tongue, my spirit prays but my mind is unfruitful. What am I to do? I will pray with the spirit and I will pray with the mind also') to designate a 'seeing' that involves the awareness or articulation of signs or images without the understanding that comes from intellectual vision. Spiritual vision by itself may mislead; coupled with intellectual vision it may lead to true contemplation. Eventually Augustine insists that corporeal vision always involves spiritual insofar as any seeing of bodies involves the production of images.[20] Spiritual vision may, however, occur without involving the body. Similarly spiritual vision, if it is also to involve judgement about what is seen, must involve the intellectual, but intellectual vision need not involve the lower kinds.

Augustine terms the third kind of vision *intellectualis* because of the link between the *mens* as the highest part of the soul and the *intellectus*.[21] And yet he struggles to describe this third vision. In one sense it is easy: intellectual vision is never deceived because it is a direct sight in 'the light of the mind'; its objects include the virtues by which we are purified and, in some sense, God (insofar as the divine may be seen even by the purified mind) in whom are all things.[22] And yet, because Augustine

---

[19] *Gn. litt.* 12. 6.15ff. On this division, which first appears *c.*392–6 at *c. Adim.* 28. 2, see the helpful notes by Agaésse and Solignac at BA 49. 575–81.
[20] *Gn. litt.* 12. 24.51.
[21] *Gn. litt.* 12. 7.16, 12. 10.21. For Augustine's use of *mens* and *anima*, see below, p. 286, n. 25.
[22] *Gn. litt.* 12. 24.50 (cf. 12. 31.59). The objects of intellectual vision also include the forms of material bodies, see *trin.* 12. 14.23. In his debate with the Homoian bishop Maximinus in 427, Augustine suggests in passing – presumably because of the pressure of scriptural warrant for talking about 'seeing' God, language that Maximinus uses to argue for the Son's visibility – that because the true seeing of God occurs in the *intellectus* or *intellegentia* we 'see' something that is by nature

is increasingly convinced of the fallen mind's inability to escape from images of bodies, he presents pure intellectual vision as accessible only through a divine rapture away from the world of images to a direct sight, love, possession and rest in the intellectual, the Truth itself, the Light that informs all understanding.[23] This vision is of the 'Glory of the Lord', and is a vision also described as a speaking 'face to face' with the mind. Thus, 'intellectual vision' is misunderstood unless it is also seen as a participation in the Word himself.[24] The poetry with which Augustine describes 'intellectual vision' masks a deep uncertainty about its character. The power of the bodily image over the fallen mind, intellectual vision's virtually eschatological or rapturous quality (coupled with the question of how we will see even as we still possess a resurrected *body*), and the mystery of this form of participation in God conspire to render any description beyond the formal or the poetic highly difficult.

Augustine does not make much use of his threefold distinction in the extensive discussions of vision in the *De trinitate*, nor in *epistulae* 147 and 148, texts that have much to say on the topic. Nevertheless, there is great continuity between these various texts: all that Augustine says about intellectual vision remains at the heart of his understanding of contemplation, and all that he says about the difficulty of understanding it is, if anything, enhanced in those discussions.[25] In *Epistula* 120, Augustine describes the three kinds of vision, but suggests that our ultimate contemplation of the Trinity is either of the third kind or simply transcends all three.[26] That intellectual vision involves at its highest a turn from seeing the virtues towards seeing the Truth which renders them possible and illumines all judgement remains clear. How this 'seeing' is to be spoken of remains intensely problematic, and we will meet the problem in a number of guises throughout the book.

I will look a little later in the chapter at the relationship of Augustine's 'Panzer' to his Latin predecessors' use of Philippians 2.5–7 and 1 Corinthians 15.28, but even before that wider discussion, Augustine's use of the term *contemplatio* is revealing in itself. From his earliest works Augustine uses this vocabulary fairly consistently to describe

---

'invisible', *conl. Max.* 14 (PL 42. 723): 'ecce intelligendo conspiciuntur inuisibilia dei, et tamen inuisibilia dicuntur'.

[23] *Gn. litt.* 12. 31.59. Note also the allusion to 1Cor. 8.6 at the end of 12. 24.50.

[24] *Gn. litt.* 12. 26.54 (CSEL 28. 419–20). This passage combines a remarkably rich combination of terminologies and it deserves close attention.

[25] See, for example, *ep.* 148. 5.16–18, *ep.* 147. 21.49. Both of these texts focus around the problems that follow from trying to imagine seeing in the resurrected body.

[26] *ep.* 120. 11–12.

contemplation of divine realities, truth and beauty.[27] The term is used by his Latin theological predecessors, but often in a far more general sense to describe a consideration of or reflection on something. Ambrose presents numerous examples, Victorinus virtually none. Hilary distinguishes between 'spiritual' and 'corporeal' *contemplatio*, but this only provides further indication that he does not immediately identify the term with contemplation of the divine.[28] It seems then plausible that Augustine's understanding of *contemplatio* comes to him from his early readings in non-Christian Platonism (or is his own term for one used there). Augustine's use of the adjective *intellectualis* does not follow the same pattern; the term does not occur until the *De vera religione*, *c.*390. Among Latin pro-Nicenes only Victorinus uses it and, once again, it seems most likely that Augustine adopted the term from a non-Christian Platonist source.[29]

Thus, in the vocabulary he uses, Augustine reveals himself to be developing a notion of contemplation (of the divine), that is Platonist in origin, but pro-Nicene in purpose. While his Latin pro-Nicene contemporaries certainly consider the vision of God to be non-corporeal, Augustine outlines a non-corporeal vision beyond any bodily image, attainable (except in fleeting instances) only at the end of the process of purification, and this clear sense of such contemplation may allow him to focus the distinction between faith and sight with peculiar clarity.[30] In general terms, then,

---

[27] For example, *ord*. 2.14; *imm. an.* 6.10; *an. quant*. 35. 79; *lib. arb*. 2.9.

[28] For example, Ambrose, *fid*. 5. *pro*. 26; Hilary, *in Ps*. 118, *lamed*. 2, *phe* 12. Victorinus does not use the term. The term is used in a manner more like Augustine's in Rufinus's translation of Origen's *De principiis* (e.g. 2. 6.1, 3. 1.1), which postdates Augustine's early usage.

[29] For example Victorinus, *adv. Ar*. 1. 61 (CSEL 83/1. 162). Here the soul which is not fully *Nous* is the *potentia vitae intellectualis* and when it looks towards *Nous* it is as if it were *Nous*. In *Nous* itself *visio ... unitio est*. When the soul looks away from *Nous* it becomes only *intellegens* not also *intelligibile*. *Intellectualis* is used in Jerome's translation of Didymus (e.g. *spir*. 10. 31), but it is most likely that Augustine's knowledge of that text postdates the *De vera religione*. Augustine's discussion of the relationship between *intellectuale* and *intelligibile* at *gn. litt*. 12. 10.21 has stimulated much discussion about possible Plotinian or Porphyrian sources for the vocabulary. The discussion is nicely summarized in the note at BA 49. 566–8. Little has been added since the publication of this note in 1970.

[30] One particularly interesting point of comparison is Ambrose's *De Isaac vel anima*. In the discussion of the ultimate vision and participation, when the purified soul's knowledge is its beauty, and the soul disregards all except the supreme good that is the cause of all (8.78–9), Ambrose here seems to make use of *Enn*. 1. 6 as does Augustine in *conf*. 7, and the latter may even be also using this very passage of Ambrose (see Courcelle, *Recherches*, chs. 3–4). Ambrose does not, however, make use of *contemplatio* terminology; he does little to define the type of vision involved (which may be due to the possibly catechetical nature of the work); he makes no use of a clear distinction between faith and sight. Augustine seems both to have taken more precise language from his non-Christian Platonist sources and he seems more thoroughly to have Christianized it in

A Christological epistemology

this discussion of intellectual vision provides the basic dynamics of how Augustine understands the highest level of understanding and ascent: it is both that in which faith culminates and the goal of the intellectual exercises we discussed in Chapter 5. As we will see more fully towards the end of this chapter, it is also that to which grace draws us.

Having offered his catena of texts in favour of contemplation as the Christian's goal, Augustine further specifies what is seen in that final vision, and its relationship to the faith that we may now have. Philip's comment 'Lord, show us the Father and we shall be satisfied' (John 14.8) demonstrates that Philip did grasp contemplation of the Father as our goal,

but he did not yet understand [*intellexerat*] that he could just as well have said the same thing like this, 'Lord, show us yourself and it suffices us'. To make him understand [*intellegeret*], the Lord answered, 'Have I been with you all this time and you do not know me? Philip, whoever has seen me has seen the Father'. But he wanted him to live by faith [*ex fide uiuere*] before he could see that, and so he went on, 'Do you not believe that I am in the Father and the Father is in me?' (John 14.9–11). For, 'as long as we are in the body we are abroad from the Lord. For we walk by faith, not by sight' [2Cor. 5.6].[31]

Christ, here, does not only provide Philip with extra information that enables him to understand the unity of Father and Son. Christ simultaneously helps Philip to grasp that faith stands in for sight until the *eschaton* and that what may be seen in the body does not enable us to understand what is or what will be seen at the end. The question of John 14.11 invites Philip to recognize that while he *should* believe he has 'seen' the Father, he believes correctly only when he understands that faith must stand in for sight until the unity of Christ in *forma Dei* with the Father is apparent. Augustine thus sees a direct link between accepting that contemplation of Father, Son and Spirit is the goal of Christian life, and recognizing that faith entails a discipline in our seeing and imagining of the material (and of the material insinuations embedded in the language of faith), a discipline in which we learn not to take the material for that towards which it should draw us.

Trinitarian faith, then, requires a constant negotiation between the language of temporality, materiality and division intrinsic to Scripture

---

the sense that the language of intellectual vision is incorporated into the systematic account of the movement from faith to fulfilment that we are examining here.

[31] *trin.* 1. 8.17 (CCSL 50. 51). The remainder of this paragraph and much of the next (*trin.* 1. 8.18) emphasize the Trinitarian nature of that final vision: wherever the seeing of one person is indicated the presence of the others must be understood.

and our ability to grasp the character of the final vision. It is of note in this passage that it is Christ who teaches us in such a way that we embrace this negotiation, and thus are drawn down the path towards greater understanding of the mysteries that Scripture describes. But note that Christ here does not teach only that the reality of the divine transcends all that we may say about it in human speech; Christ teaches that the Christian should attempt to clarify her faith, believing that there is a correspondence between the language of faith and the reality that awaits. Philip should believe (although he cannot *see*) that to see the Son is to see the Father because this belief will be fulfilled. One of the constitutive tasks of our journey down the path towards understanding of faith is, then, to grow in the ability to hone these correspondences, identifying and applying the principles that allow us to 'look' beyond the created categories within which Scripture speaks.

FAITH, DESIRE AND CHRIST

A few sentences after the last passage quoted above, Augustine turns to Christ's relationship to the Spirit. Attending to this passage will allow us to see the extent to which Augustine identifies the core of the life of faith (and the core of what Christ teaches) as a movement of the attention.

'For if I do not go, the advocate will not come to you' [John 16.7]. But he said this, not because of any inequality between the Word and the Holy Spirit; but as if the presence of the Son of Man among them would be a hindrance to the coming of him, who was not less, because he had not 'emptied himself', as the Son had done, by 'taking the form of a slave' [Phil. 2.7]. So it was necessary for the form of a slave to be removed from their sight, since as long as they could observe it they would think that Christ was only that which they saw. The words which he spoke also refer to this: 'If you loved me, you would indeed rejoice since I am going to the Father, for the Father is greater than I' [John 14.28]. That is to say, it is, therefore, necessary for me to go to the Father, because while you see me as I now am, you conclude from what you see that I am less than the Father. You are so engrossed with the creature and the habit that I have assumed, as not to perceive the equality that I have with the Father. This is also the meaning of his words: 'Do not touch me, for I have not yet ascended to the Father' [John 20.11]. For touch sets as it were a limit to knowledge [*Tactus enim tamquam finem facit notionis*]. And, therefore, he did not want the intention of their heart, which was directed towards him, to be limited, so that he would be considered only what he appeared to be [*Ideoque nolebat in eo esse finem intenti cordis in se ut hoc quod uidebatur tantummodo putaretur*]. But his ascension to the Father meant that he should be looked upon as he is, the equal to the Father, so that they should at last see the vision which suffices for us.[32]

The ascension of his body, placing it beyond our touch, was an essential part of Christ's teaching and revealing. The 'touch' of which Augustine speaks refers, first, to the touch that the apostles (paradigmatically Thomas) sought as a reinforcement for their faith. But, second, this touch also stands for our 'touching' in faith. Christ wished that the only limit set to our faith be the eschatological sight of the Trinity, and thus that we 'touch' in faith only in order to confess what lies beyond sight and touch. Christ teaches in the body in such a way that the body becomes the means of directing our attention away from itself. And so, just as appropriate faith can only be formed when the heart of the one who believes moves away from the visible Christ towards the unity with the Father that he preached, so too the Spirit can only be recognized in faith when he is understood not to have a visible form in the way that the Son had a visible form, and to be one with Father and Son.

The movement of attention, which follows from Christ's own teaching, is the context within which exegesis of texts apparently presenting Christ as less than the Father should take place. Here, in the case of John 14.28, Augustine suggests we read Christ's statement that he is less than the Father not merely as a statement about his human form ('The Father is greater as regards my human nature, but not my divine'), but – in the light of the first half of the verse – also a statement about the necessary movement of the attention if correct faith is to be formed and progress towards that final vision begun.

A little later Augustine reinforces the point:

What do the words mean: 'I came forth from the Father' [John 16.28], if not, I have not appeared in that form in which I am equal to the Father, but in another form, that is as one less than Him on account of the creature that I have assumed? And what is the meaning of: 'I have come into the world' [John 16.28] if not, I have shown the form of a slave, which I took by emptying myself, even to the eyes of sinner who loves that world? And what do the words mean: 'Again I leave the world' if not, I am taking away from the sight of the world that which they have seen? And what is the meaning of: 'I go to the Father' if not, just as I am equal to the Father, so I teach my faithful ones that they must regard me as such? Those who believe this will be considered worthy of being brought from faith to sight, that is, to the vision itself.[33]

---

[32] *trin.* 1. 8.18–9.18 (CCSL 50. 53–4).   [33] *trin.* 1. 10.21 (CCSL 50. 58–9).

Christ himself here, speaking in Augustine's interpretation, shows us that Philippians 2.5–7 functions as an exegetical rule when it is seen as a summary of the incarnate mission itself. Acceptance of a partitive exegesis in which Scripture speaks of the Son in *forma servi* and in *forma Dei* is also to accept (if, indeed, it is not better to say that the partitive exegesis follows from accepting …) a narrative of salvation in which Christ comes to purify and reshape the attention of human beings towards eternal contemplation of and in the incorporeal and invisible divine three.

Let us return for a moment to Christ shaping the 'intention of the heart'. The same theme appears again when Augustine comments on texts in which Christ appears to deflect attention away from himself towards the Father, such as John 12.44's 'He who believes in me does not believe in me':

> How is such a self-contradiction to be believed? … unless you take it like this: he who believes in me does not believe in what he sees, lest our hope be in something created, but in him who assumed the creature in which he would appear to human eyes, and would thus purify our hearts by faith in order that they might be able to contemplate him as the equal of the Father. And, therefore, when he turns the attention of the faithful [*intentionem credentium*] to his Father by saying 'He does not believe in me, but in him who sent me', he certainly did not intend to separate himself from the Father, that is, from him who sent him, but that we might so believe in Him as in the Father to whom he is equal.[34]

Once again, appropriately formed faith finds its end in understanding that the co-equal Son assumed flesh in order to lead us to contemplation and union, drawing our *intentio* to its true end.

Intentio cordis and *intentio credentium* are phrases with which Augustine seems to have experimented in the decade between 395 and 405. In the final paragraphs of *De libero arbitrio* 3, Augustine speaks of the various objects of the *intentio animi*: formally ruling out the idea that the *intentio* of the mind includes the Trinity because of the divine transcendence, he nevertheless suggests that something like this must be so. *Intentio* here has the senses of both 'attention' and 'affinity' but, in a typically Augustinian sense, it also seems to involve elements of desire and love.[35] Once Augustine begins to link *intentio* to the theological vocabulary of the 'heart' the term takes on a wider range of resonances. In the one other use of *intentio credentium* in his corpus Augustine speaks of those who subvert the gospel with and for their personal glory at Galatians 1.6–7 as

---

[34] *trin.* 1. 12.27 (CCSL 50. 67–8).   [35] *lib. arb.* 3. 25.75 (CCSL 29. 320).

A Christological epistemology

drawing the *intentio credentium* from spiritual things to carnal (*ab spiritualibus ad carnalia*).³⁶ In a number of other texts around this period Augustine speaks of the *intentio cordis* as an internal and incorporeal shout for the help of God,³⁷ and as the desire for understanding (often of scriptural complexity) that is aided by God.³⁸ But this desire is also the moral intent – the light within us – that must become simple in attention to only one master.³⁹ Augustine's invocation of the *intentio credentium* thus contributes to his discussion of Christ's departure from visible gaze by emphasizing that such a departure is intended to shape our attention and desire.

In the texts we have been considering, Augustine is still experimenting with his language, but the basic lines of his mature position are now clear and will be filled out in his later treatments of the relationship between faith, hope and love, especially insofar as Augustine there insists that one of the main functions of faith is the formation and encouragement of hope and love.⁴⁰ This section of the chapter has added more detail to our picture by showing some of the links Augustine makes between recognizing that our faith (and hence our theological exploration of it) is not yet sight, and the drawing of the attention that lies at the heart of Christ's teaching. Understanding Christ's teaching about the divine is thus inseparable from following the path of the attention that Christ also teaches – and failure to see that Christ teaches and draws the attention beyond the material is a failure that renders good conception of the Trinity impossible. This theme will eventually enable us to note some of the ways in which what might seem to be a certain intellectualism in Augustine – his linking of understanding the Trinity to the complex task of thinking the intelligible – is much complicated by his emphasis on the priority he gives to the formation of desire for God and confession of divine mystery.

INTERLUDE: AUGUSTINE'S PANZER AND THE LATIN TRADITION

Before taking our sketch of this Christological epistemology further, I want to offer a brief consideration of Augustine's relationship to earlier Latin use of Philippians 2.6–7 and 1 Corinthians 15, an exercise that will

---

³⁶ *exp. Gal.* 4. 4. Cf. *en. Ps.* 16. 10.   ³⁷ *en. Ps.* 4. 5.
³⁸ *en. Ps.* 25 (2). 12; 33 (1). 1; *Io. ev. tr.* 12. 1.
³⁹ *s. dom. m.* 2. 13.46–14.48. This text includes the discussion of humility and ascent examined in Chapter 3.
⁴⁰ The archetypal text being the late *ench.* 5–8.

make clear the elegance and distinctive qualities of Augustine's Panzer. Only two Latin pro-Nicenes offer Philippians 2.6–7 to stave off the seeming subordinationist force of 1 Corinthians 15.28.[41] Hilary uses Philippians 2.6–7 in the last third of his *De trinitate*, and from then on it takes on great importance as Hilary seeks to defend the idea that the mystery at the heart of Christianity is the 'double birth' of the one Son of God.[42] Hilary, however, seems uncertain about how to understand the term *forma*, suggesting that while Christ eternally has the essence of deity, he gives up the *forma Dei* in assuming the *forma servi*.[43] Nevertheless, one key similarity with Augustine is his reading of Philippians 2.6–7 as providing a pattern for the drama of redemption as a whole, describing Christ's post-resurrection ascent and the course of our own ascent towards God. In this context Hilary sees the ascent of the *forma servi* as the restoration of Christ's status as *forma Dei*[44] and he reads the handing over of the kingdom at 1 Corinthians 15.28 as a sharing in the glory of Christ's heavenly body by those united to him.[45] In its details Hilary's account differs considerably from that of Augustine – in his account of *forma*, and in the fact that the theme of contemplation is at most a muted undertone – but we do see here the beginnings of a significant Latin attempt to draw out of Philippians 2.5–7 a narrative of Christ's descent and ascent (and our ascent) to counter Homoian use of 1 Corinthians 15.28.

---

[41] Of the other Latin Nicene writers, Phoebadius, *fid.* 26. 1, uses Phil. 2.5–7 to show that the Word possesses the 'whole power of God' even as he assumes flesh, but he does not draw the text into his attempt to refute Homoian exegesis of 1Cor. 15.28 at *fid.* 16. 1. Gregory of Elvira defends a subordinationist reading of Phil. 2.7 by arguing that the emptying and taking of the *forma servi* did not involve any change in his divine status, see *fid.* 88, *tract.* 7. 23. Faustinus, in his *De trinitate*, follows some of the same general principles that we see in Hilary and Ambrose. While he does not discuss 1Cor. 15.28, he uses Phil. 2.5–7 both to demonstrate that Christ remains *in forma Dei*, assuming the *forma servi* to teach *humilitas*, and to free Adam from his servitude and bring him to glory (*trin.* 37–8). The same assumption also shows the Word working to shape our faith (*trin.* 17). The *De trinitate* often attributed to Eusebius of Vercelli again does not discuss 1Cor. 15.28, but uses Phil. 2.6–7 to emphasize that being in *forma Dei* the Christ must share complete equality with the Father, see esp. *trin.* 3. 3–10. While Phil. 2.6–7 and 1Cor. 15.28 occasionally occur in proximity in Victorinus, he gives no indication of seeing the former as a tool against subordinationist reading of the latter. He generally uses elements of theses verses as proof texts for the Son's equality to the Father and taking of flesh: the former is explained by reference to the Father as 'inactive action' and the Son as 'act' (*adv. Ar.* 1. 9, 1. 13), while the latter is treated as a sensible manifestation of the perfect life possessed by the Word (e.g. the extended discussion of *adv. Ar.* 1. 22–6). Ambrosiaster does not link the two verses.
[42] See the use of the text in summary of Christian faith at Hilary, *trin.* 11. 6. For emphasis on the unity of the one subject of Phil. 2.6–7, see *trin.* 9. 14, 10. 7, 15–16.
[43] Hilary, *trin.* 9. 51–3.
[44] Hilary, *trin.* 9. 53.
[45] Hilary, *trin.* 11. 38–9.

Ambrose uses Philippians 2.6–7 throughout his *De fide* and parallels Hilary in treating the text as a summary of Christ's mission and of Christian life as a whole. Unlike Hilary, Ambrose does not interpret *forma* as indicating appearance.[46] Ambrose's extensive discussion of 1 Corinthians 15.28 in *De fide* 5 argues that the Son 'subjects' his *assumed* body to the Father, but the focus of the account is on the unity of the assumed body with those who are 'in' Christ. Ambrose links the parable of the rich man who goes into the far country of Luke 19.12 with 1 Corinthians 15. Thus the kingdom that Christ comes in order to receive is that Kingdom which Christians *are* (twice citing to this end John 17.21's 'the Kingdom of God is within you'), which is gathered by the Father's drawing (John 14.6), and which is then subjected to the Father.[47] Ambrose applies Philippians 2.6–7 both to Christ in his incarnate nature, and to us before we too are 'stripped' and see the glory of Christ, although the unity of power and godhead means that the Father reigns in the Son and the Son in the Father.[48] Ambrose hints here at our contemplation of the divine as the goal of Christian life, but he makes only a little more of the theme than Hilary. Far more than Hilary, and to some extent anticipating Augustine, Ambrose emphasizes the importance of not being misled by Christ's visible form.[49]

While Augustine is likely to have drawn on both Hilary and Ambrose, the distinct character of Augustine's account is striking. Most importantly, Augustine has made his vision of Christian life as a movement towards contemplation central. But the account of *De trinitate* itself develops an earlier extensive reading of 1 Corinthians 15.28 in *De diversis quaestionibus* 69 (*c.* 394–5), making use of a variety of elements apparent in piecemeal form in the works of the late 390s. In *De diversis quaestionibus* 69 Augustine interprets Christ's 'handing over' of the kingdom as his manifestation (*manifestatio*) of the Father's rule, a confounding of those who do not know or obey that rule.[50] While Augustine is clear that only those who constitute Christ's kingdom live eternally, he does not yet distinguish well, as he will in *De trinitate* 1, between the visions given to the just and the unjust at the judgement. The blessedness of the just consists

---

[46] For example, Ambrose, *fid.* 2. 8.70ff., 3. 14.121.
[47] Ambrose, *fid.* 5. 12.146ff. The importance of the pairing 1Cor. 15.28 and Phil. 2.5–7 is further seen when the pairing crops up in the final paragraphs of the work, see *fid.* 5. 18.225.
[48] Ambrose, *fid.* 5.12.152. On the unity between Christ and Christians, see also 5. 13.169.
[49] For example, Ambrose, *fid.* 2. 8.63 and 5. 14.171 and 5. 15.184.
[50] *div. qu.* 69. 4.

158 *Ascent*

in the contemplation of the Father,[51] and towards the end of the exposition this theme takes centre stage when Augustine asks for what purpose 'the Lord reigns now during the dispensation of his mystery through the incarnation and passion?'[52] This dispensation effects humility in those who are to be saved, and the purpose of such humility is a purification such that 'he will lead the faithful nourished by faith in his incarnation to the vision of his equality with the Father ... through himself the only-begotten, he will cause the Father to be seen by sight'.[53]

Elements of Philippians 2.6–7 occur three times in this text. At the beginning it is one of five texts whose meaning is elucidated by the rule that distinguishes between statements about the Son as God and about the Son having assumed flesh. A little later Philippians 2.6's 'equality' is used as a proof text for the Son's equality with the Father. In the third use Augustine presents Christ's being in the form of a servant as the means by which he reigns by faith in believers.[54] Only the last of these citations indicates that Augustine is beginning to envisage the verse as a key summary of the Son's mission, and it is noticeable that he does not offer any discussion of the Son's ascension and the taking away of the *forma servi*, and thus no discussion of the manner in which this taking away shapes desire.[55] The account of the journey from faith to contemplation that we have been exploring thus seems to have achieved its mature form in the writing of the earliest stratum of the *De trinitate*.[56]

When we read Augustine's emphasis on contemplation against the background of the discussion of the soul's ascent that we explored in earlier chapters, we can see how clearly this area of Augustine's theology has been shaped by his appropriation of non-Christian Platonism. And yet, at the same time we can see that that appropriation has also enabled him to

---

[51] *div. qu.* 69. 5. For his standard mature presentation of the judgement, see, for example, *trin.* 1. 30–1. In that account (following John 19.37) both the just and the unjust see the *forma servi*, but only to the just is the *forma Dei* revealed. This account is nicely consonant with the general approach explored in this chapter, the final and full vision of Christ is only granted those who have learnt to see in faith the *forma servi* as it should be seen.

[52] *div. qu.* 69. 9 (CCSL 44A. 192): 'dispensatione sacramenti sui per incarnationem atque passionem'.

[53] *div. qu.* 69. 9 (CCSL 44A. 193).

[54] *div. qu.* 69. 1, 1 and 9.

[55] *f. et symb.* 4. 5–6 and *conf.* 7. 9.14 offer further good examples of the ways in which, prior to *trin.* 1, Augustine already uses Phil. 2.5–7 as a key text for summarizing Christological principles, even if he does not yet there articulate that text as revealing the journey from faith to contemplation in the way that he does in *trin.*

[56] This is not to say that no further development took place. For example, Augustine's account of the Pauline food and drink metaphors in *Io. ev. tr.* 98 (see below) represents a further increase in clarity, if not a fundamental change.

draw out and develop Christian theological themes inchoate in his Latin Christian predecessors.

CORRESPONDENCE AND MYSTERY: THE EXAMPLE OF MOSES

I now turn directly to the consonance Augustine sees between the language of faith and the sight in which faith is fulfilled. Discussion of the Old Testament theophany texts – texts such as Genesis 18, Exodus 33 and Daniel 7 – occupies a good deal of space in the initial books of the *De trinitate*, primarily because Augustine has much invested in refuting any account in which such texts are said to reveal the Son (or the Spirit) to be by nature visible to human eyes and hence distinct in mode of existence from the Father. As is well known, Augustine rejects the certainty of earlier traditions that it was the Word who appeared, instead building on some hints in his immediate predecessors to argue that the theophanies are a mode of communication in which one of the divine three or the Trinity as a whole speaks or is signified by the assumption of a created form.[57] In general the theophany texts make very infrequent appearances in Augustine's corpus outside directly anti-Homoian polemical contexts. The only exception is Moses's request to see God at

---

[57] Latin tradition is consistent in seeing the Son as the one revealed in the theophanies, but from its inception offers a number of ways round assuming that this is consequent on the Son's visibility. A fundamental point of departure is Tertullian, *adv. Prax.* 14–15. In an anti-Monarchian argument Tertullian accepts that the second person is the subject of the theophany at Exodus 33 – and hence there must be two divine persons, one who appears and one who does not. But while Tertullian argues that there must be some way in which Father and Son are distinguished in their capacity to be seen (following the analogy between the Sun and its beam), he still insists that the Son is not seen face to face, but by means of a vision or in a dream. Novatian, *trin.* 18, follows Tertullian's reading, but is less concerned to emphasize that Christ is not truly seen. In Latin pro-Nicene theology the theophanies continue to serve as a way of indicating that there is 'God from God', but now with the twist that these two are eternally so. See, for example, Hilary, *trin.* 4. 23. The discussion here follows on from Hilary's exegesis of the Son's role in creating. While Hilary continues to see the Son as the subject of the theophanies, *en passant* he states that the second person must have taken a bodily form to be seen and is not inherently visible, *trin.* 5. 17. Ambrose takes a step closer to Augustine's exegesis. In the passage from Ambrose's *Commentary on Luke* which Augustine quotes at *ep.* 147. 6.18ff., Ambrose makes central the insistence that the Son was made visible. But at the same point, while Ambrose adheres to the idea that it was the second person who became visible in the Old Testament theophanies, he also offers a general principle that *any* divine person who appears does so through a created form, *Luc.* 1. 26. Ambrose also prefigures Augustine in asserting that the divine cannot be seen with human eyes, and that when any of the divine persons are seen it is through an act of divine will which makes use of a created form. The true 'seeing' which occurs in such events is an inner seeing dependent on purity of heart. By 412/13 Augustine cites a wide range of authors in favour of (at least parts of) his interpretation: see *ep.* 148. 10 (Ambrose, Athanasius, Jerome and Phoebadius).

Exodus 33. 11–23 and his consequent vision of God's 'back parts': verses from this chapter make a number of appearances in Augustine's mature corpus.[58] The interpretation of this text found in *De trinitate* 2 is not the first in Augustine's corpus to make a number of the points we will discuss, but it is one of the most developed of a number produced during the 412–14 period, and it is one that reveals much about the relationship between faith and the final vision – and hence about the nature of interpretation prior to that vision.[59]

It may be helpful, however, to begin with the only surviving extended Homoian discussion of the theophanies.[60] In his 427 debate with Augustine, the Homoian bishop Maximinus makes two points. First, he argues that it is the Son who appears in the theophanies. It is the Son who walks with Adam in the Garden, it is the Son who was seen by Abraham, who wrestled with Jacob and whose glory was seen by the apostles (John 1.14). The whole list is introduced by pairing Moses's statement at Exodus 33.20 that 'No one can see God and live' with 1 Timothy 6.16's 'No human being has seen him or can see him'. Maximinus even claims that Augustine's reading not only denies Scripture's clear statement that it was the Son who was seen, but even implies that the Father himself can be seen and hence 'all the Scriptures are for you filled with lies'.[61] But this is only half of the picture for, second, Maximinus also offers his own account of the Father and Son as differently invisible. The Son cannot be seen by bodily eyes, being naturally more invisible than the soul and the angels created through him. The Son cannot even be seen in his substance by the angels, but only by that which is superior to him, just as we cannot see the angels who see and penetrate us. Thus the Father alone is truly invisible and infinite, being seen by none above him and seen by the Son as incomprehensible.[62]

In the actual debate Augustine does not even acknowledge these complex doctrines.[63] In his response to Maximinus composed after the public

---

[58] For example, through the whole of *serm.*, *Io. ev. tr.* and *en. Ps.*, only *serm.* 7 discusses the appearances to Abraham at Mamre in Gen. 18. I suspect, however, that this should not surprise us. Whereas, in anti-Monarchian contexts, the theophanies were very useful in demonstrating the pre-existence of the Word as a separate reality, in pro-Nicene context where the Word's pre-existence was not at issue, the theophanies offered little that obviously spoke of the Son's eternal status and were thus more naturally appealed to by anti-Nicenes.

[59] For discussion of dating and (incomplete) lists of other texts see Hombert, *Nouvelle recherches*, 60–2.

[60] A number of other shorter references survive. See *coll. ver.* 14. 3 (fol. 97v) (CCSL 87A. 116); *scol. Aquil.* 71 (fol. 340r) (CCSL 87A. 182).

[61] *conl. Max.* 15. 26.   [62] *conl. Max.* 15. 9.

[63] Perhaps they are among the things described as 'beside the point' at *c. Max.* 1. 15.

debate, however, Augustine returns twice to his opponent's claims. In the first book he argues that Scripture offers no warrant for Maximinus's theology of hierarchical seeing. In the second, Augustine addresses his opponent's statement that in the theophanies it was always the Son who was seen. Augustine offers an extensive treatment of the key passages, arguing that the referent of the theophany is by no means clear. At the end of the list he cites Moses's words at Exodus 33.11, 'if I have found favour before you, show me yourself clearly'. Augustine takes this text, which Maximinus had not mentioned, as proof that Moses understands the divine nature to transcend the visible form that he has seen.[64] How Augustine understands Moses's attitude to this visible form is more fully revealed in *De trinitate* 2.

There Augustine's exegesis concerns the whole of Exodus 33.11–23, and focuses initially around the challenge presented by the contrast between Exodus 33.11 describing Moses as speaking to the Lord 'face to face', and Exodus 33.13 reporting Moses's request to God, 'show yourself to me openly'. Augustine argues that Moses knew his conversation with the Lord in verse 11 occurred through some form of physical manifestation, and that in verse 13 he is asking to receive a vision of the Lord's substance, a true spiritual vision.[65] The importance of Moses here, however, is that he models for us the link between desire for true vision and the love of God when he qualifies his expression of desire with 'if I have found favour in your sight': Moses knows that the purer the soul, the more the vision is desired. And yet even those whose vision rises towards the spiritual have only the sight of the 'back' of Christ, the flesh.

Augustine then shifts to a more directly figural reading of the text. Belief in the resurrection of Christ makes our faith effective: believing in this, we hope that we, as Christ's body, will ascend where our head has already gone. It is to shape this faith that Christ does not wish to be seen until he has 'passed,' that is, ascended. Until this point the 'hand' of Christ lay upon the eyes of the Israelites who were to believe; when Christ 'passed' they were able to 'see' by means of true faith in Christ:

> We must stand on the solid foundation of the faith which the rock signifies, and gaze upon it from such an impregnable watch-tower, namely in the Catholic

---

[64] *c. Max.* 1. 3 and 2. 26.1ff., Ex. 33.11 at 2. 26.12.
[65] *trin.* 2. 16.27. I am grateful here for the discussion of Robert Dodaro, *Christ and the Just Society in Augustine* (Cambridge: Cambridge University Press, 2004), 139ff. It should be noted that the sections of *trin.* 2 to which I turn here probably date from the earliest stratum of the book and thus can be fairly placed alongside the passages from book 1 considered earlier in the chapter. See Excursus 1.

church, of which it is said 'and upon this rock I will build my church' [Matt. 16.18]. For, the more certainly we love the face of Christ which we desire to see, the more we recognize in his back parts how much Christ has first loved us. (29) But with regard to the flesh itself, faith in his resurrection saves and justifies us … For even his enemies believe that that flesh died on the cross of his passion, but they do not believe that it rose again. And we believe it most firmly, and view it as it were from the solidity of a rock, where we are waiting with a certain hope for our redemption, namely, the resurrection of our body.[66]

Augustine calls us to firmness in the true faith (it is this that constitutes our 'seeing'). True faith here includes belief that Christ died and rose, and belief that God first loved us. It is this faith that leads to increased love or desire for the true face of Christ and hope that we too shall rise. But, Augustine argues, the desire true faith stimulates is in tension. On the one hand this faith is a trust in the correspondence between what happened to Christ and what will happen to us, and a trust that our 'sight' of Christ in faith *will* be fulfilled in eternal and true sight. On the other hand, Moses is paradigmatic *because* he desires a vision of that which he knows to transcend him. Faith thus results in a desire to enter into that which is known as mysterious. Augustine sees humility (and the desire for grace) as an essential component of this desire, both because of his (by this stage) well-established sense that only God can give the understanding that is identical to participation in the divine life, and because such humility is the only faithful response to recognition of the divine transcendence. As Robert Dodaro writes in his discussion of this passage,

Faith … exercises a purifying effect on the soul by continuing to remind it that it cannot understand the realities disclosed by God by relying on its own efforts. This self-knowledge, achieved in humility, draws the soul into a deeper love of God.[67]

Two sermons, probably preached a few years after the first sections of *De trinitate* 2 were drafted, provide further clarity. In *Sermon* 23 (*c*.413 or 415/16) Augustine turns to Exodus 33 to demonstrate that God appears while being hidden. God must appear, otherwise the text would not describe Moses as speaking with God 'face to face' (Ex. 33.11), and yet God must be hidden, otherwise Moses would not ask for God to show himself (Ex. 33.13). God certainly uses some created reality to be present – God does not change God's nature, making himself visible – but he is

---

[66] *trin*. 2. 17.28–9 (CCSL 50. 119).   [67] Dodaro, *Christ and the Just Society*, 143.

A Christological epistemology

truly present even as the divine nature is hidden.[68] In consequence we must imitate Moses and be inflamed by the 'earnest' that is this presence and desire the true vision of the divine nature beyond any created reality.[69] God's self-disclosure is thus trustworthy and a product of his choosing; our response must be to search through and beyond that appearance towards the reality and mystery of God.

The next day Augustine preached *Sermon* 53. Here our preacher turns to Matthew 5.8 ('the pure in heart shall see God'), but links it with Ephesians 1.18 ('having the eyes of your heart enlightened'), 2 Corinthians 6.5–7 ('for we are walking by faith and not by sight') and 1 Corinthians 13.12 ('we see now through a glass in an enigma; but there it will be face to face'). This combination sets up sight as a promise and faith as an anticipation of that sight, but one that grows only as the 'eyes of the heart' grow.[70] We must seek God's face, Augustine continues, following the command of Psalm 27.8, but we must do it with the heart (following Wisdom 1.1). Thus we must not imagine God's 'face' to have any corporeality. Scripture speaks in material terms of God's being (God's 'hand', 'face', 'feet'), but in reality these are aspects of the divine life (God's 'power', 'knowledge' and 'presence') that may only be known through purification of the soul, through the emergence of the just soul that is the 'temple of God' (1Cor. 3.17).[71] Thus when Augustine speaks of Scripture accommodating itself (and of Christ accommodating himself) to our fallen and material imaginations, he also intends us to recognize that such speech necessarily involves the choosing of correspondences, the exploring of which constitutes the core task of the attempt to understand the life and unity of the divine three.[72]

A little later he writes:

> And now, what does faith itself actually do? [*et modo ipsa fides quid agit?*] With so many testimonies from Scripture, so many different readings, such a plentiful variety of sermons and exhortations, what does it actually do, if not ensure that we see now by mirror in a riddle, later on face to face? But not so that you should turn your thoughts back again to that face of yours. Think of the face of the heart. Force your heart to think about divine matters, compel it, drive it on [*coge cor tuum cogitare diuina, compelle, urge*]. Anything that occurs to it in

---

[68] *serm.* 23. 14–15.   [69] *serm.* 23. 16.   [70] *serm.* 53. 6.   [71] *serm.* 53. 7.
[72] *serm.* 53. 8 (*RevBen* 104 (1994), 26). As an example, Augustine speaks here of the manner in which the works and rewards of the Sermon on the Mount match or harmonize (*congrueret ... et consonaret*). We are commanded to mourn; we receive consolation. We are commanded to be merciful; we will receive mercy. In the same sequence, we are commanded to purify the heart; we receive sight. Moreover, these commands do not mark out different rewards for different activities, but identify different aspects of a unified practice and a unified reward. And thus only through the unity of faith, hope and love can we move towards sight.

its thinking which is like a body, fling it away. You cannot yet say 'this is what he is'; do at least say 'this is not what he is'. When, after all, will you say 'This is what God is'? Not even when you see him, because what you will see is inexpressible [*ineffabile*].[73]

Learning to look beyond the temporal and corporeal language of Scripture towards God is to look towards that which remains inexpressible. And yet the task of seeking the purification of the eyes of the heart – through the shaping of love and humility before God – remains, as does the task of trying to think towards the divine. The sermon thus beautifully illustrates how Augustine holds together two themes: first, because humility before God is at the core of a true approach to God the unlearned Christian may be as 'spiritual' as the one most able to follow Augustine's speculative flights;[74] second, the understanding of doctrinal faith is a task of speculative improvisation, a drawing together of scriptural hint and dialectical skill to look towards the outer rim of what may be grasped as we attempt to think how Scripture's speech about God is true, but is true of a reality beyond the temporal and the material.

Augustine's focus at the end of *Sermon* 53 is not so much on playing out exercises that help us think the intelligible, but on recommending the transformation of the eyes of the heart through the practice of good works. But this recommendation suggests further types of correspondence for us to seek. Commenting on Ephesians 3.17–19,[75] Augustine suggests we read the 'breadth' of Christ's love as good works, the 'length' as long-suffering and perseverance, the 'height' as the expectation of rewards in heaven and the 'depth' as the mysterious grace of God. This interpretation is founded on an allegorical reading of Christ's crucifixion, where his outstretched hands and the cross-beam represents good works, the length of the main beam on which he 'stands' represents endurance, the piece of the upright which protrudes above the crossbeam represents hope, while that which is hidden in the ground represents grace, the hidden source of all that is seen.[76] The culmination of these correspondences is given by Ephesians 3.19 itself: whereas elsewhere we read of seeing 'face

---

[73] *serm.* 53. 12 (*RevBen* 104 (1994), 29).
[74] See the classic discussion of *conf.* 13. 23.33. But note also the principle articulated at 13. 31.46 (and quoted at the end of this book's Introduction) that any recognition of truth and appropriate delight is also God recognizing and delighting in us.
[75] For complementary readings of Augustine's discussion of Eph. 3.18–19 in his *ep.* 54–5 (*Ad inquisitionem Ianuarii, c.*400) and, especially, *ep.* 140 (*De gratia novi testamenti*, 412), see Dodaro, *Christ and the Just Society*, 123–33, 159–64.
[76] *serm.* 53. 16 (*RevBen* 104 (1994), 29): 'occulta est enim, in abdito latet; non uidetur, sed inde eminet quod uidetur'.

to face' in the final vision (1Cor. 13.12), the text here tells us that this seeing consists in being filled with the 'fullness of God' (*impleberis in omnem plenitudinem Dei*).[77]

Many of the correspondences that we have seen here concern divine actions or features described in corporeal terms. In these cases Augustine intimates through his suggestions ways in which we may use scriptural language to think a God who transcends the material and temporal categories Scripture often uses (while nevertheless offering a fully scriptural account of the divine existence – as we shall explore further in Chapters 8 and 9). At the same time corporeal language concerning human interaction with God is transposed into description of the soul's growing love for God and the soul's indwelling by God. Thus, while these paragraphs tell us very clearly that such seeking of correspondences lies at the heart of using Scripture to think towards God, the particular examples discussed reveal little about how we should interpret scriptural discussion of the relationships between Father, Son and Spirit that are tinted with the corporeal. We have, however, already seen Augustine suggest ways of so doing: in discussion of *Confessiones* 10–13, for example, we saw him both trying to make use of the soul as an analogical site to encourage us to think beyond the material, and then suggesting patterns of language for speaking directly about the divine unity and diversity. In the following chapters we will see Augustine offering far more extended attempts to think this correspondence but it is important to remember that those discussions are all framed by the dynamics we have seen here. All of those discussions are explorations of how we may imagine the correspondence between Scripture's language and the mystery of which Scripture speaks; but insofar as they are this, they are all also conceived as explorations of that which will only be 'seen' when faith gives way to the contemplation of the purified soul knowing itself and the three by whom it is filled.

The final paragraphs of *Sermon* 53 also bring us back to the way in which Augustine's account of the ascent to understanding is Christologically structured. Christ's crucifixion allegorically represents to us the structure of our ascent, grounded in grace and inseparable from humility and the practice of love; more literally, Augustine presents Ephesians 3.17–19 as teaching us that coming to know the love that is in Christ is the knowledge that surpasses all other knowledge. The perfection of love *in* Christ lies at the heart of the true ascent.

---

[77] *serm.* 53. 16 (*RevBen* 104 (1994), 33).

FAITH AND GRACE

These last sentences suggest both the importance of grace in the ascent Augustine describes and that ultimately Christ is not merely a model for, but the context within which, our ascent occurs. Earlier I quoted a passage from *De trinitate* 1. 10.21 to illustrate the manner in which Augustine uses Philippians 2.6–7 as a summary of the incarnate dispensation as a whole. Only a few sentences later we find:

> 'The Father himself loves you' [John 16.27] is so said as to be logically understood also of the Son and the Holy Spirit ... But through what merit on our part, if not that of faith by which we believe before we see that which is promised? For by this we shall arrive at sight, so that he may love us because we are such as he loves us to become, and are not such as he hates because we are, and he exhorts and enables [*hortatur ac praestat*] us to will that we may not always remain such as we are.[78]

The sight of contemplation is merited only by our faith and, Augustine suggests, it is through God's action that we are drawn into faith and towards contemplation. We need not conclude that this represents an addition during later redaction. The language of God exhorting externally and enabling us to follow that exhortation parallels Augustine's language in the *Ad Simplicianum* of 396.[79] And thus, the *De trinitate* may have been rendered increasingly anti-Pelagian during later redaction, or those passages which strongly espouse the pre-venience of grace may have been there from its inception – we cannot tell and for our purposes do not need to.[80] Throughout the writing of the work Augustine held to the principles that we see exemplified in the following passage from Book 4 (which is probably contemporary with *Sermones* 23 and 53), and the movement towards understanding that Augustine describes is thus misunderstood unless it is seen against the background of his theology of grace and, hence, as subsumed under his account of sanctification within the *corpus Christi*:

> There are certain ones, however, who think themselves capable by their own strength of being purified, so as to contemplate and to inhere in God [*ad contemplandum deum et inhaerendum deo*], whose very pride defiles them above all

---

[78] *Trin.* 1. 10.21 (CCSL 50. 59).

[79] See, for example, *Simpl.* 1. 2.21 (CCSL 44. 53). See also my 'Into the Poem of the Universe: *Exempla*, Conversion and Church in Augustine's *Confessiones*', *ZAC* 13 (2009), 263–81.

[80] The classic (but ultimately unconvincing) attempt to see the emphasis on grace (and Christologically mediated grace) as a product of the Pelagian controversy is Jean Plagnieux, 'Influence de la lutte antipélagienne sur le "De Trinitate" ou: Christocentrisme de saint Augustin', *AugMag* 2: 817–26.

others ... For they promise a purification of themselves by their own power, because some of them have been able to send their mind's eye [*aciem mentis ... transmittere*] travelling beyond all created things and to touch, though be ever so small a part, the light of the unchangeable truth, while many Christians, as they mockingly assert, who live in the meantime by faith alone, have not yet been able to do so ... [But] what harm is it for a humble man if he cannot see it from so great a distance, but yet is coming to it on the wood, by which the other does not deign to be carried?[81]

This passage (which combines anti-Homoian and anti-Platonic polemic) locates both Christians and Platonists as seeking the same goal – a final and enduring contemplation of and existence in divine truth. But this ascent towards contemplation is understood by Augustine to be facilitated for the Christian by acceptance in humility of the need to be carried on the 'wood' – a term which symbolizes both Church and the cross – towards a goal that he or she may not even grasp as yet. At the heart of Augustine's distinction between the humble Christian and the proud philosopher is the latter's pride in assuming that this passage can be made *virtute propria*, 'by their own strength'.[82]

The passage's contrast between the prideful philosopher and the humble Christian shows in allusive form some of the links between Augustine's understanding of our participation in Christ as the means of salvation and his understanding of the necessity of grace. Both halves of this pairing receive further discussion through Book 4. In the early chapters of the book, Augustine identifies the problem preventing our contemplation of God as our sinfulness, and thus our need as purification from sin.[83] God acts towards us by revealing to us the extent of his love for us (so that we do not despair) and our sinfulness (lest pride in our own merits leads us to refuse God's love). In this way God commends to us and perfects in us 'the power of love' in 'the weakness of humility'.[84] Commenting on Psalm 67.10 ('setting aside, O God, a free rein for your inheritance, and it was weakened, but you have made it perfect'), Augustine reads the rain as grace given out of love (the 'warmth of the Holy Spirit')[85] and the purpose of grace as the perfection of the Christian.[86] In the very first chapter of *De trinitate* 4 this theme is introduced by emphasizing the difference between an obsession with the world in its materiality (and consequent

---

[81] *trin.* 4. 15.20 (CCSL 50. 187).
[82] On Augustine's interpretation of Platonist pride, see now Giovanni Catapano, 'The Development of Augustine's Metaphilosophy: Col. 2:8 and the "Philosophers of this World"', *AugStud* 38 (2007), 233–54.
[83] *trin.* 4. 2.4.   [84] *trin.* 4. 1.2 (CCSL 50. 161).   [85] *trin.* 4. pro. 1.   [86] *trin.* 4. 1.2.

lack of self-knowledge), and a growing attention to oneself as sinful and in need of divine aid. The person consumed by the former lacks the tools necessary for true understanding of God, the humility that is the only final means of entry into God. And thus Augustine has located the movement from faith to understanding – his Panzer against the Homoians – as the movement of Christian attention and desire, a link we have already seen in discussion of *intentio*.

At the same time, to speak of grace as the necessary foundation of this movement is also to speak of membership in Christ as the context for grace.[87] In the passage from *De trinitate* 4 quoted above, Augustine identifies this contemplation or illumination (*inluminatio*) with *participatio verbi*, the participation in the Word that should be ours as beings created in and through the Word.[88] The one means of purification is Christ's sharing in our humanity so that we may share in his divinity.[89] The heart of *De trinitate* 4 explores how Christ's death and resurrection shape and effect our own death and resurrection in him. Augustine presents Christ's work as providing both an *exemplum* for the 'outer man' and a *sacramentum* for the 'inner man'. The death of Christ's body, for example, is an *exemplum* for us because it exhorts us not to fear those who can kill only the body (Matt. 10.28); the resurrection of the body is an *exemplum* because it confirms for us that we too shall rise. But the same events also reveal the *sacramenta* of the inner man. The crucifixion and death of Christ's body emphasize that we must undergo repentance and 'a certain agony of self-denial' which leads to the death of the godlessness, the interior putting away of lying that we might speak truth (Eph. 4.22–5). In Christ's injunction 'do not touch me, for I have not yet ascended to the Father' (John 20.17) the resurrection of the body also reveals a mystery of the inner resurrection: '[N]ot to touch Christ until he has ascended to the Father means not to think of Christ according to the flesh'. The heart of the inner resurrection is the return of the *intentio* towards God truly understood as he is.[90]

---

[87] I have explored this theme at more length in my 'The Christological Context of *De Trinitate* XIII: Towards Relocating Books VIII–XV', *AugStud* 29 (1998), 111–39.

[88] *trin.* 4. 2.4 (CCSL 50. 163): 'Inluminatio quippe nostra participatio uerbi est, illius scilicet uitae quae lux est hominum'.

[89] *trin.* 4. 2.4 (CCSL 50. 164): 'Non enim congruit peccator iusto, sed congruit homini homo. Adiungens ergo nobis similitudinem humanitatis suae abstulit dissimilitudinem iniquitatis nostrae, et factus particeps mortalitatis nostrae fecit participes diuinitatis suae'. Cf. *en. Ps.* 52. 6.

[90] *trin.* 4. 3.5ff. My understanding of the language of *sacramentum* and *exemplum* draws heavily on Dodaro, *Christ and the Just Society*, 147ff.

But this language of *exemplum* and *sacramentum* is misunderstood when conceived only as a set of extrinsic parallels in Christ for distinct events that occur in us. Christ's death and resurrection are 'administered to us … as a kind of medicine': Christ is himself the *sacramentum* and the *sacrificium* of our redemption because of our unity with him. Because Christ is our head and we are his members, we can have faith that what has happened to the 'head' is now begun in the members.[91] The members achieve unity of desire – they come to put aside lying and to speak truth, they come to attend to God as God is – only because they are one in the Christ who draws them towards blessedness. In the same passage, Augustine also hints at the Spirit's role as the 'soul' of Christ's body, as the love that draws into unity with God and each other.[92]

Jean-Marie le Blond's pioneering *Les Conversions de Saint Augustin* (1950) argued rightly that one of the fundamental movements of Augustine's Christology is towards the development of a series of parallels and analogies between Christ's unification of two natures in his person and the Christian's growth from faith towards contemplation, from the life of the 'old man' to the life of the 'new'. The Christological epistemology that we have seen here incorporates and develops a number of these parallels. Of course, it remains true that one essential difference between the head and the members, one at the heart of Augustine's Christological epistemology, is that what is accomplished in Christ is begun in us now through faith and only fulfilled as sight at the *eschaton*. Insofar as it stands in for sight, the gift of faith purifies by effecting a particular discipline of 'knowledge' that is always also a knowledge of mystery.

Through this chapter and the previous we have seen Augustine develop an account of understanding as a movement of thought which finds its end in contemplation of and participation in the divine life. This account draws on the work of his predecessors but is also peculiarly his. It is peculiarly his, however, for a surprising combination of reasons. It is his, because of the extent to which he makes the ultimate sight of the divine central to describing the character of Christian knowing *in via*. It is his, because of the emphasis on a correspondence between the language of Scripture and the reality of which Scripture speaks. It is his, because the Christian's progress in understanding is located within the Christological epistemology I have sketched here. It is, finally, peculiarly Augustine's

---

[91] *trin.* 4. 7.11.
[92] See *trin.* 4. 9.12. For a discussion of the Spirit as the soul of the Body of Christ, see my 'Augustine on the Spirit as the Soul of the Body of Christ', *AugStud*, forthcoming.

because this Christological epistemology allows him to unify the gradual transference of the affections that occurs in the unlearned Christian and the increasing understanding of the most learned Christian. These two are united by being incorporated into the one movement of the attention effected by grace within the body of Christ. What might seem initially, then, as a certain intellectualism in Augustine, is transformed into a peculiarly subtle linking (and joint celebration) of Christian piety and the Christian intellectual life.

EXCURSUS 2

POLEMICAL TARGETS IN THE *DE TRINITATE*

The summary of his predecessors' faith with which Augustine begins the *De trinitate* shows how clearly Augustine locates himself within Latin anti-Homoian theological traditions. Because of his location in this literary tradition, Augustine's articulations of Trinitarian theology have a clear polemical edge, and yet this observation suggests a question. Was Augustine's engagement with Homoian theology purely literary?

It is likely that for the first half of Augustine's literary career the answer is yes. We have little evidence that significant numbers of Homoians were present in North Africa during the late fourth and early fifth centuries. Nevertheless, Augustine was aware of continuing Homoian communities throughout his life and at a number of points between his conversion and the first decade of the fifth century Augustine had some encounters with anti-Nicenes, and perhaps with their texts.[93] In the second and third decades of the fifth century, Augustine had more extended encounters with Homoian theologians and texts.[94] The growing numbers of Homoians appearing in Africa in these decades stemmed partly from the influx of refugees after the Vandal incursions into Italy in the first decade of the fifth century (and the sack of Rome in 410), and partly from the increasing employment of Homoian troops in Roman Africa.

---

[93] At *conf.* 9. 7.15, Augustine tells us that his mother was involved in Ambrose's attempt in 386 to prevent Justina (the mother of Valentinian II) from getting the use of a basilica in Milan. Augustine himself did not take part. *ep.* 238 (*c.*405–10. Cf. Possidius, *vita*, 17) is addressed to Pascentius, a Homoian who had come to Carthage (for unknown reasons) and was prepared initially to debate with Augustine. In *serm.* 46. 18 (before 411?) Augustine claims, not surprisingly, that there are no Eunomians in Africa. It is noticeable that he says nothing about the wider category of 'Arians'.

[94] At *Io. ev. tr.* 40. 7 Augustine says that 'perhaps' there are Arians in his audience. If it is not a figure of speech it may reflect presence of Homoians appearing after 410. *ep.* 170 and 171/171A concern the conversion of Maximus, a physician from Thaenae in Byzacena. Others in his household have remained 'Arian'. (*ep.* 171 has a wonderful comment from Augustine to Maximus's bishop, telling the latter to make sure Maximus was not insulted by Augustine writing a long letter on paper [*charta*].) *ep.* 173A was sent to Deogratias and Theodore in Carthage offering proofs for the divinity of the Spirit, possibly reflecting argument over the issue in Carthage. In 418 or 419 Augustine wrote *c. s. Arrian.* From *ep.* 23*A. 3 and *retr.* 2. 52 we know he had received the 'Arian sermon' to which he responds from one Dionysius in Vicus Iuliani, far to the south. *serm.* 229O. 4 (*s. Guelf* 17: after 420?) records conversion of one of 'those four men' (he seems to mean four whom he had previously warned the congregation against). The men had anathematized Arianism and Eunomianism. Finally in 427 Augustine debated with the Homoian Bishop Maximinus and wrote his further response to the debate.

We need, however, to ask ourselves what it means to say that Augustine's engagement with Homoians as he began the *De trinitate* was primarily literary. It does not mean that his presentation of Homoian theology itself necessarily bore less relationship to the concerns of Homoian themselves. It is noticeable that when we do see him in extensive debates with actual Homoians, the basic lines of his attack remain fundamentally the same. Augustine has to respond to some exegetical thrusts he seems not to have expected (and to answer them he seems to return for inspiration to the work of his Latin pro-Nicene predecessors), and he avoids some of his more idiosyncratic themes. But his awareness of the shape of Homoian theology is, for example, at least every bit as great as that of Ambrose in the first two books of his own *De fide* which were written at a high point of north Italian debate with Homoians.[95] Thus while we can trace something of Augustine's encounters with living Homoians, this does not necessarily tell us much about the extent of his reading in anti-Homoian or actual Homoian writing.

Like the predecessors on whom he drew, Augustine understands Trinitarian theology to be an exercise that, however internally Catholic its audience, finds its most significant contemporary 'others' in the Homoian tradition. At the same time Augustine, again like many other Catholic writers of his period, treats heretical positions as also constant possibilities for the Catholic mind, and thus exposing what he sees as materialistic Homoian exegesis is also to expose the Catholic's constant temptation.[96] This tendency to link external heresy and internal temptation is matched by a vision of different heretical positions as sharing a failure to grasp the structure and necessity of the Word's descent into flesh.[97]

We see an excellent example of Augustine drawing these connections in the initial books of the *De trinitate*. The first three books attempt to refute Homoian 'demonstrations' of Christ's subordinate status because Christ is visible, is sent by and is obedient to the Father. Within this discussion, exegesis of the 'theophany' narratives of the Old Testament play a prominent role.[98] As the

---

[95] For the argument that Ambrose was prompted to develop a more immediate engagement with the actual theology of his opponents after the publication of *De fide* 1 and 2, see Daniel H. Williams, *Ambrose of Milan*, ch. 5.

[96] For a succinct version of this argument see *bapt.* 3. 20.

[97] See, for example, Robert Dodaro, '"Omnes haeretici negant Christum in carne venisse" (Aug., *serm.* 183.9.13). Augustine on the Incarnation as Criterion for Orthodoxy', *Aug Stud* 38 (2007), 163–74. See also my 'Augustine on the Rule of Faith'.

[98] The classic pieces of scholarship on Augustine's interpretation of the theophanies – Jacques Lebreton, 'Saint Augustin théologien de la Trinité. Son exégèse des théophanies', in *Miscelleanea Agostiniania* (Rome: Tipografia Poliglotta Vaticana, 1931), 2: 821–36; 2, 821–36; Jean-Louis Maier, *Les Missions divines selon saint Augustin* (Fribourg: Editions Universitaines Fribourg Suisse, 1960); and L. Johan van der Lof, 'L'exégèse exacte et objective des théophanies de l'Ancien Testament dans le "De Trinitate"', *Aug(L)* 14 (1964), 485–99 – represent a growing scholarly awareness of the anti-Homoian polemical context. Basil Studer, *Zur Theophanie-Exegese Augustins. Untersuchung zu einem Ambrosius-Zitat in der Schrift 'De videndo Deo' (ep. 147)* (Rome: B. C. Liberia Herder, 1971), set a new standard in discussing the precise relationship between Augustine's discussion of the vision of God (primarily in *ep.* 147, but also in *trin.*) and those of his Latin forebears.

discussion proceeds, however, and as we have seen, Augustine gradually treats the different anti-Nicene arguments he considers as variations of a common failure to understand what it means for Christ to have been a visible revelation of the invisible. To understand the character of and need for faith in a visible revealing of the eternally invisible co-eternal Son is, Augustine argues, to understand the purpose and integrity of Nicene exegesis. Defending the centrality of the Incarnation leads Augustine to incorporate and develop much of his refutation of Platonist pride and Platonist failure to understand the role of authority. He thus further interweaves polemical targets, linking Platonist pride with Homoian.

Thus Augustine's critique of Platonism (and his adaptation of it) is a constant background theme through the *De trinitate*, but I have resisted the urge to treat this work as primarily an engagement with the Platonist tradition. Such an assumption I take to be problematic because it ignores the extensive theological engagement with Homoian and Catholic positions evident through much of the work, and because it seems to stem from a scholarly world-view wherein the significant engagements are philosophical (and ontological). We are better founded, I suggest, when we note the skill with which Augustine interweaves a variety of critiques through an argument always theological in focus (however much the philosophical is thereby unavoidable and a constant companion).[99]

Michel René Barnes 'Exegesis and Polemic in Augustine's *De Trinitate* I', *AugStud* 30 (1999), 43–59, builds on this previous work.

[99] The thesis of Edward Booth, published in a number of articles (see the Bibliography) offers a clear example. While he offers much useful comment in the body of his work, he assumes that the 'real' challenge of 'Arianism' is recognized by Augustine to be ontological, and to be that of Platonism. This, then, offers a warrant for reading what Booth takes to be the most significant parts of *trin.* as a dense engagement with Neoplatonism and the Aristotelian tradition embedded within it. The most important assumptions here are about what constitutes 'real' argument!

PART III
Into the mystery

CHAPTER 7

Recommending the source

With this chapter a new section of the book commences. At the same time, the argument here will reveal more of the dogmatic foundations on which the Christological epistemology examined in Chapters 5 and 6 rests. In the first place I examine Augustine's account of the second exegetical rule that Augustine suggests at the beginning of *De trinitate* 2. Augustine's first rule, examined in Chapter 6, is not concerned only with the manner in which we should distinguish Scripture's statements about Christ, but also with the movement towards contemplation into which Christ and Scripture draw Christians. Similarly, while Augustine's second rule concerns scriptural texts that reveal only that Son or Spirit are 'from' the Father (and not ontologically subordinate to the Father), his exposition of the rule reveals the manner in which the sending of Son and Spirit, and their work in the created order, is founded in their manner of procession from the Father. Exploration of this topic both reveals the centrality of the Father's status in Augustine's mature Trinitarian theology, and suggests some initial questions about how Augustine envisages the Trinitarian communion that we will consider in Chapters 8, 9 and 10.

At the outset of my argument it needs to be noted that the texts considered here are, in many cases, extremely difficult to date with certainty. As I indicated in Excursus 1, I accord a high degree of probability to Anne-Marie La Bonnardière's suggestion that a long initial section of *De trinitate* 2 has been added after original composition. At the very least, much of Book 2 seems to have been the subject of extensive editing, and it is on these sections of the book that I focus my attention in the first half of the chapter. Thus, it is best for the reader to be cautious and treat the ideas I discuss here as the product of Augustine's mature thought: finally edited, if not simply composed, in the period between 415 and 420. Throughout, however, we may also be reading material originally sketched between 411

178   *Into the mystery*

and 414. The second half of this chapter concerns texts that date from the initial composition of Book 3 and before.

A SECOND RULE

At the beginning of *De Trinitate* 2, Augustine introduces a second exegetical *regula* in the face of a possible confusion about the first.[1] Some texts, while seeming to demonstrate the inequality of Son (or Spirit), actually show only that the Son (or the Spirit) is 'from the Father' (*de Patre*). This second rule emerges from a discussion of texts that seem problematic when interpreted according to the exegetical rule laid out at the beginning of Book 1. John 5.29 ('As the Father has life in himself, so he has given the Son to have life in himself') and John 5.19 ('for neither can the Son do anything of himself, but only what he sees the Father doing') are central among Augustine's first examples:

> certain among us, more unlearned and the least instructed in these matters, will be disturbed as long as they try to explain these texts according to the form of a slave, and so fail to grasp their true meaning. To avoid this, the rule we have just mentioned is to be observed, whereby it is intimated that the Son is not less, but that he is of the Father; in these words not his inequality but his birth is made known [*tenenda est et haec regula qua non minor filius sed quod de patre sit intimatur, quibus uerbis non inaequalitas sed natiuitas eius ostenditur*].[2]

Augustine argues that these texts should not be treated as speaking about the Son *in forma Dei* because they would then indicate dependence and inferiority. And yet, Augustine also refuses an interpretation that views them as speaking of the Son *in forma servi*. In the case of John 5.19, for example, this would mean that the incarnate Son walked on water only after he had seen the Father materially doing so.[3] Augustine's solution is to argue that the texts do speak of the Son *in forma Dei*, but that they indicate only that the Son is from the Father.

---

[1] Despite the late addition of this passage, the rule itself certainly pre-dates these passages of *De trinitate* 2. See *ep. Io. tr.* 7. 6 for a clear statement of the second rule from 407. Both rules are implied, in a somewhat confused manner, in *div. qu.* 69. 2 (BA 10. 286). There Augustine distinguishes statements that are written 'propter susceptionem hominis ... dum tamen divinae substantiae Patris et Fili deitas et unitas et equalitas manet' and those that are written 'propter personarum proprietates'. Thus, in the first case, Augustine sees some texts as speaking about the incarnate Word (who remains in union with the Father) while, in the second case, other texts serve only to identify relations between the divine three, or their personal characteristics. Texts of the second set include both those which speak of the Word as divine, and those which reveal the Word to be from the Father.

[2] *trin.* 2. 1.3 (CCSL 50. 84).

[3] *trin.* 2. 1.3. I discuss Augustine's interpretation of this verse at length in Chapter 9.

Augustine illustrates his point by commenting further on John 5.29:

> It remains, therefore, that these words were spoken in this manner, because the life of the Son, as that of the Father, is unchangeable, but nevertheless he is from the Father [*de patre*], and that the operation of the Father and the Son is inseparable, but yet that the Son's power to work so is given to him by him from whom he himself is, that is, from the Father … [*sed tamen ita operari filio de illo est, de quo ipse est, id est de patre* …][4]

In fact, Augustine's new rule does not teach that the texts which it governs reveal only *that* the Son is from the Father, but also *how* the Son is from the Father. The second rule necessarily operates against the background of Augustine's Nicene insistence that each of the divine three possesses the attributes of divinity. Thus, for example, the first quotation given in this section opposes the Son's (possible) *inaequalitas* and his (actual) *nativitas* – rather than simply his *aequalitas*. The language of *nativitas* suggests a possible debt to Hilary – other more compelling evidence is discussed later in the chapter – but it also reveals that Augustine's fundamental concern here is to point not simply to the Son's equality to the Father, but to the Son's dependence on the Father, his birth from the Father as one who is equal to the Father. Augustine thus reads these texts as revealing a clearly pro-Nicene picture of the Son and Spirit as dependent on the Father.[5]

The discussion of the Spirit which immediately follows shows us further dimensions of what Augustine understands by Son and Spirit being from the Father. Augustine begins with John 16.13–15:

> When the Spirit of Truth comes, he will guide you into all the truth: for he will not speak on his own authority, but whatever he hears he will speak, and he will declare to you the things that are to come. He will glorify me, for he will take what is mine and declare it to you. All that the Father has is mine; therefore I said that he will take what is mine and declare it to you.

The first two verses indicate that the Spirit will lead Christians into all truth, speaking only that which he 'hears'. If we had only John 16.15's 'he will not speak on his own authority … for he will take what is mine and declare it to you' we might suppose that the Spirit is born of Christ as Christ is from the Father. But, Augustine continues, Christ is clear that

---

[4] *trin.* 2. 1.3 (CCSL 50. 83).
[5] In thinking through Augustine's account of the Father's priority and the nature of the argument in *trin.* 1–4, I have been greatly helped by the recent exposition of Luigi Gioia, *The Theological Epistemology of Augustine's* De trinitate (Oxford: Oxford University Press, 2008), esp. chs. 5 and 6.

what *he* possesses is the Father's: this truth governs how we should understand the Spirit's role. John 15.26's 'the Spirit of truth who proceeds from the Father' is parallel to John 5.19's 'The Son cannot do anything of himself, but only what he sees the Father doing' in that both show that Son and Spirit are 'from' the Father, but neither reveals ontological inferiority. Further, in John 16.14 the Spirit takes what is Christ's in the sense that all the Spirit has is also the Father's and what he takes from the Son is that which is the Father's.[6]

Augustine follows up with a refutation of the Homoian reading of John 17.5's 'Father, glorify me'.[7] If the Son needs the Father to glorify him, then surely the Father is more powerful and ontologically superior? But, Augustine suggests, at John 16.14 the Spirit glorifies the Son in receiving from him. In so doing the Spirit receives what is the Father's and thus the Father glorifies the Son also:

> And, furthermore, if the Holy Spirit glorifies the Son for this reason, because he will receive what is the Son's and, therefore, will receive what is the Father's (because all things that the Father has are the Son's), it is evident that when the Holy Spirit glorifies the Son, the Father glorifies the Son. From this it follows that all things which the Father has are not only the Son's but the Holy Spirit's as well, because the Holy Spirit is able to glorify the Son whom the Father glorifies.[8]

This mutual glorification – and Augustine goes on to note also the Son's glorification of the Father at John 17.4 – is founded in the Father's gift of what he is to Son and Spirit, and is thus always a glorification and revelation of the Father. In Chapter 3, I argued that in the *De fide et symbolo* Augustine places Latin Nicene emphasis on the Son's being generated from the substance of the Father at the heart of his theology.[9] We see in these initial texts that such an emphasis is carried through to Augustine's mature work: the Son is what he is because he possesses what is the Father's, and he does so through being eternally 'from' the Father. At the same time this last text hints at a number of questions about Augustine's mature account of the character of the communion to which the Father has given rise. On the one hand, Augustine takes the principle that the Father gives all that he is to the Son to mean that Son and Spirit remain

---

[6] *trin*. 2. 3.5.
[7] Proof of Homoian use is not hard to find. The text is cited by Maximinus at the Council of Aquileia (*scol. Aquil.* 11 (CCSL 87A. 153)) and appears again in a series of fragments of a Homoian *De fide* at *frag. theol.* 14 (CCSL 87A. 251). Ambrose attempts to counter similar Homoian readings at *fid.* 2. 10.82–3. Hilary offers a far more extensive discussion at *trin*. 3. 13 (cf. 9. 31).
[8] *trin*. 2. 4.6 (CCSL 50. 87). [9] See pp. 85–6.

the Father's, remain constituted by being given all that is the Father's. On the other hand, While Augustine is clear that the Father is the source of Son and Spirit, in true pro-Nicene fashion Augustine also presents the dependence of Son and Spirit on the Father as resulting in their mutual glorification, a glorification only possible because they are a communion of three who are equal. An exploration of how Augustine articulates these relationships in his mature work must wait until the next two chapters: for the moment I want to turn back to the manner in which Augustine's account of divine *missio* or sending depends upon this account of the Father's position as source of Son and Spirit.

THE MEANING OF SENDING

In the next section of his argument, and in refutation of the Homoian objection that the one who sends must be greater than the one who is sent, Augustine offers what amounts to a short treatise on what it means to speak of Son or Spirit being sent. Quoting parts of John 16.28, Augustine says, 'To come forth from the Father and to come into this world means, to be sent'.[10] The importance of this initial definition is the role it accords the Father. For Son or Spirit to be sent (Augustine soon insists that the Father is never said to be sent) is to come from the Father into the world. In the words of his *Sermon* 71, 'the reason it says "[the Father] does the works" [John 14.10], is that the works have their origin in the one from whom the co-operating persons have existence'.[11]

The Son and Spirit are, however, always 'sent' to a place where they already are:

For he was everywhere who said 'I fill heaven and earth' [Jer. 23.24]. But if this was said of the Father, where could he be without his Word and Wisdom, 'who reaches from end to end mightily, and orders all things well'. But neither could he be anywhere without his Spirit. If therefore God is everywhere, then his Spirit is also everywhere. Consequently, the Holy Spirit was also sent to that place where he already was [*Illuc ergo et spiritus sanctus missus est ubi erat*]. [Augustine goes on to quote Ps. 138.7, 'whither shall I go from your Spirit?'][12]

Not only are the Son and the Spirit 'sent' to where they are, but this 'sending' is also governed by the doctrine of inseparable operations. Just

---

[10] *trin.* 2. 5.7 (CCSL 50. 88): 'a Patre exire et venire in hunc mundum, hoc est mitti'.
[11] *serm.* 71. 26 (*RevBen* 75 (1965), 94): 'et illud ideo dictum esse de patre "ipse facit opera", quod ab illo sit origo etiam operum, a quo est exsistentia cooperantium personarum'.
[12] *trin.* 2. 5.7 (CCSL 50. 88).

as the Father sends the Son into the world through Mary, the Spirit also sends the Son; indeed, the Son must in some sense send himself – just as the Son sanctifies himself (John 17.19).[13] Augustine attempts to explain this joint act of sending further by asking what it means for the Father to act through the Word:

> Perhaps what we are saying will become clearer, if we also ask in what way did God send his Son? Did he command him to come, and did he come out of obedience to him who commanded, or did he make a request or only a suggestion? But whichever of these it was, one thing is certain, it was done by a word, but the Word of God is the Son of God himself. Therefore, since the Father sent him by a word, it was brought about by the Father and his Word that he should be sent ... But in that Word of God itself, which in the beginning was with God and which was God, that is, in that Wisdom of God itself, it was certainly decided before time, at what time that Wisdom of God should appear in the flesh. Since the Word, therefore, was in the beginning, without any trace of a temporal beginning, and the Word was with God and the Word was God, it was in the Word itself apart from time at what time the Word should be made flesh and dwell among us.[14]

The Father's sending of the Son is intrinsic to the Father's eternal 'speaking' of the Word and Wisdom: there can be no importation of the language of 'command' because the Son eternally comes into existence as one who eternally shares in the decisions of the Father as the Father's Wisdom.[15]

That all things find their true existence and life in the Word eternally spoken by the Father is a theme we find in many of Augustine's exegeses of creation, and of the initial verses of John's Gospel. Towards the end of this chapter we discuss in some detail one such which probably dates from 407. As we shall see, during the second decade of the fifth century Augustine develops an account of inseparable operation in which the actions of the three are grounded in the Father's eternal generation of Son and spiration of Spirit. Here we see that account hinted at in Augustine's comment that the Son's sending was brought about by Father and Son because that the Son will be sent is expressed in the Word as the Father speaks the Word: common 'decisions' are not the result of a deliberative and temporal process, but rooted in the eternal generation of Son and Spirit. We will see this account much

---

[13] *trin.* 2. 5.8–9.   [14] *trin.* 2. 5.9 (CCSL 50. 91).
[15] Cf. the wonderfully succinct *Gn. litt.* 1. 5.11 (CSEL 28. 9): 'quod autem filius loquitur, pater loquitur, quia patre loquente dicitur uerbum, quod filius est, aeterno more, si more dicendum est, loquente deo uerbum coaeternum'. This text was probably written *c.*399–405.

more clearly in Chapter 9. This passage (which is separated by only a sentence or two from the passage I quote next) may, then, represent either an early version of the argument, or a later addition following the development of this account in the last decade or so of his life.[16]

REVEALING AND SAVING[17]

As Augustine sums up these arguments he writes:

And when this fullness of time had come, 'God sent his Son, made of a woman', [Gal. 4.4], that is made in time in order that the Incarnate Word might appear to men, while it was expressed in that Word itself, without time, at what time this should be done, for the order of times is certainly without time in the eternal Wisdom of God. Consequently since this was brought about by the Father and the Son, that the Son should appear in the flesh, it is proper to say of him who appeared in the flesh that he was sent. For those things done outwardly before fleshly eyes [*illa quae coram corporeis oculis foris geruntur*] arise from the interior ordering of the invisible nature [*ab interiore apparatu naturae spiritalis existent*].[18]

Thus we can say that the Son was 'sent' without implying that one has the authority to send, while the one sent is merely subordinate, because that the Son will be sent is intrinsic to the Son's generation from the Father. The visible life and ministry of the Incarnate Word is thus founded in the 'interior ordering' of the Trinity.

Augustine speaks also here of the sending of the Spirit at Pentecost as a manifestation *for the purpose of* moving people beyond that visible manifestation,

This operation [Pentecost], visibly manifested and offered to mortal eyes, has been called the sending of the Holy Spirit, not as if his substance itself had appeared in which he himself is invisible and unchangeable as the Father and the Son, but in the sense that the hearts of people, being moved by these external signs, might be turned away from the temporal manifestation of his coming to the hidden eternity of him who is forever present [*ad occultam aeternitatem semper praesentis conuerterentur*].[19]

Pentecost may, Augustine suggests, be appropriately called the *missio spiritus sancti*, the sending of the Holy Spirit, *because* it is an appearance providing signs which move people away from the temporal and the visible

---

[16] See Chapter 9, pp. 243f.
[17] Studer, *Augustins De Trinitate*, 171–9, insists very helpfully on the fundamentally soteriological concern of Augustine's doctrine of *missio*.
[18] *trin.* 2. 5.9 (CCSL 50. 91–2). [19] *trin.* 2. 5.10 (CCSL 50. 93).

towards the presence of the Father. We will examine Augustine's uncertainty about Pentecost later; here we need only note that Augustine sees this event as possibly the 'mission' of the Spirit because it is a salvific revealing that draws us to the ever-present Father.

The significance of this point becomes clearer at the end of *De Trinitate* 4. As that book draws to a close Augustine returns to the subject of what it means to speak of the Son's sending. He summarizes in a manner that brings out clearly the relationship between sending and revealing. Revealing enables faith which may become contemplation, and the movement towards contemplation is the content of the Christian's purification:

[19.25] Behold the purpose for which the Son of God has been sent, or rather behold what it means for the Son of God to be sent. Whatever things have been done in time for the sake of producing the faith, whereby we are cleansed for the contemplation of the truth, in things that had a beginning, have been brought forth from eternity and are referred back to eternity, and have been either testimonies of this mission or are the mission itself of the Son of God ...

[19.26] ... he was seen as the one who had been made and sent; he was not seen as the one through whom all things were made. Or why does he also speak as follows: 'He who has my commandments and also keeps them, he it is who loves me. And he who loves me will be loved by my Father, and I will love him and manifest myself to him' [John 14.21] when he had already been shown before the eyes of men, unless because he offered the flesh, which the Word was made in the fullness of time, to be accepted by our faith, but kept back the Word itself, through which all things were made, in order that the mind, cleansed by faith, might contemplate it in eternity?[20]

The Son is said to be sent because those of the Son's visible actions in time which are done to produce faith – the faith that begins and enables our purification[21] – come from eternity and are referred back to it. In other words, the visible human nature assumed by the Word is offered so that we might have a faith that may be consummated in the contemplation of eternity when we truly see that which the visible Christ represents.

Thus the Son being 'sent' from the Father indicates nothing other than that one is Father and begetter, while the other is begotten and Son:

[he said to be sent] not as though the one is greater and the other less, but because the one is the Father, the other is the Son, the one is the begetter, the other is the begotten, the one is he, from whom the one who is sent exists, the other is he,

---

[20] *trin.* 4. 19.25 (CCSL 50. 193, 195).
[21] See, for example, the medical language of *trin.* 4. 18.24.

who is from the one who sends. For the Son is from the Father, not the Father from the Son [*Filius enim a patre est, non pater a filio*].[22]

The idea of the Son's sending must, Augustine argues, be read against the background of his new exegetical rule – the Son is 'sent' only in a sense compatible with his being 'from' the Father.

On this foundation Augustine articulates the principle that one of the central purposes of this sending is the revealing of the Son and Word as Son and Word, that is a revealing of the Word as from the Father and as the Word with Father and Spirit. As he writes a little later:

For as to be born is for the Son to be from the Father, so to be sent is to know that the Son is from him.[23]

and:

And just as for the Holy Spirit his being the gift of God means his proceeding from the Father, so his being sent means his being known to proceed from him.[24]

The same final paragraphs of *De trinitate* 4 also clarify the distinction between the Incarnation and all other sendings. Wisdom is sent in one way to illumine prophets and the 'friends of God' (Wisd. 7.27), and in another when the Word and Wisdom himself is born of the virgin.[25] Thus all other 'sending' is prophecy of or testimony to the one true 'sending into the world' of John 16.28.[26]

This distinction, fairly easily offered in the case of the Son, begs the simple but important question: is there a unique sending of the Spirit to parallel that of the Son? Augustine struggles to give a clear answer. He treats Christ's 'breathing' of the Spirit at John 20.22 (which takes place after the resurrection but, because of its presence in John, in uncertain relationship to Pentecost) as a revelation of the Spirit's relationship to the Father. At the same time, however, prophets and apostles spoke by the Spirit and John 7.39 tells us that 'the Spirit had not yet been given, since Jesus had not yet been glorified'. It must be, then, that the true sending

---

[22] *trin.* 4. 20.27 (CCSL 50. 195). With this passage we should also read Augustine's very traditional Nicene invocation of Wisd. 7.25's description of Wisdom as 'a certain pure emanation of the glory of the almighty God' a little later at *trin.* 4. 20.27.

[23] *trin.* 4. 20.29 (CCSL 50. 199): 'Sicut enim natum esse est filio a patre esse, ita mitti est filio cognosci quod ab illo sit'.

[24] *trin.* 4. 20.29 (CCSL 50. 199): 'Et sicut spiritui sancto donum dei esse est a patre procedere, ita mitti est cognosci quod ab illo procedat'.

[25] *trin.* 4. 20.27.

[26] *trin.* 4. 20.28.

of the Spirit occurs only at Pentecost after Christ's glorification. But when Augustine describes Pentecost, he sees its uniqueness in the speaking in tongues which reveals that all nations would believe in Christ through the Spirit. Nevertheless, this reading offers no indication how Pentecost *uniquely* reveals the Spirit's relationship to the Father.[27]

Returning to Augustine's comments on John 20.22 towards the end of *De trinitate* 4, the same discussion also concerns Christ's breathing of the Spirit. That which Christ physically breathes into the faces of the apostles cannot be the Holy Spirit and thus the action must symbolize some other truth. Two premises shape Augustine's answer: the manifestation of the Spirit is always a revealing of his being from the Father; the Spirit is called the Spirit of the Father and the Spirit of the Son. On the basis of these premises, Augustine interprets John 20.22 as a reference to the Spirit proceeding also from the Son. He admits but bypasses the conundrum of the Spirit's double sending – at John 20.22 and then after the ascension – in order to push on to his conclusion: commenting on Christ's saying of the Spirit both 'whom I will send you from the Father' (John 15.26) and 'whom the Father will send in my name' (John 14.26). Augustine notes that Christ does not say 'whom the Father will send *from me*':

> thus he clearly showed that the Father is the principle of the whole divinity, or to speak more precisely, of the whole Godhead [*ostendens quod totius divinitatis uel si melius dicitur deitatis principium pater est*]. He, therefore, who proceeds from the Father and the Son, is referred [*refertur*] back to him of whom the Son was born.[28]

I quote this passage in part because it suggests further questions that we must face in Chapters 8, 9 and 10, questions about the relationship between Augustine's understanding of double procession and his account of the Father's status as *principium*. But I also quote the passage here as it further indicates Augustine's clarity that the purpose of the divine missions is the revelation of the Father. This is always also a revelation of the Father eternally speaking his Word and being with his Spirit. Augustine's final summary in Book 4 returns to the point:

> We should understand that these things are mentioned in Scripture on account of the visible creature, or better, in order to recommend the origin and source, not because of any inequality or disparity or dissimilarity of substance between the divine persons. Because even if God the Father had wanted to appear through a created reality bent to his will, only with absurdity would it be said

---

[27] *trin.* 4. 20.29. [28] *trin.* 4. 20.29.

that he had been sent by the Son whom he generated or from the Holy Spirit who proceeds from him.[29]

This section of the chapter has provided a fuller dogmatic foundation of or context for the Christological epistemology explored in Chapter 6. There we saw, in exposition of Augustine's first rule, that the movement towards contemplation is one that follows in reverse the movement by which the Word is manifest in the Incarnation, one that understands how the immaterial and transcendent Word manifests the divine mystery in flesh and in words adapted to fallen human comprehension. Augustine's second rule enables us to see, within this broader framework, that the manifestation of the divine Word is a manifestation of the eternal relationship of Father and Son and, hence, a making known of the Father. The manifestation of the Father by Son and Spirit is also both a drawing of believers to the Father, and founded in the Father's eternal generation and spiration of Son and Spirit (and is not the result of a temporal decision taken by Father and Son or Spirit).

AUGUSTINE'S NOVELTY?

Augustine's account of the relations between missions and processions is, once again, an idiosyncratic appropriation of themes already in play among his Latin forebears. A brief exploration of this relationship will help to highlight Augustine's particular contributions. Augustine's account shows striking parallels with Hilary's account of the Son's two nativities. In *De trinitate* 6, Hilary insists on the importance of the sequence and distinction between the nativities as following 'the order of the Gospel'.[30] He argues that the birth of the Incarnate Son is *for* the revelation of his eternal birth. Those to whom Christ says 'you neither know me, nor whence I am from' (glossing John 7.28) are the unbelievers who do not yet confess Christ, for to confess him is to confess his eternal birth.[31] And this confession is what merits the love of the Father.[32] That this anticipates aspects of Augustine's doctrine is clear enough, but Jean-Louis Maier suggests that we can even draw linguistic parallels between a number of passages in Hilary and Augustine's *De*

---

[29] *trin*. 4. 21.32 (CCSL 50. 205).   [30] Hilary, *trin*. 6. 29 (SC 448. 228).
[31] Hilary, *trin*. 6. 28. With this passage, compare Hilary, *trin*. 9. 30 (SC 462. 74): 'A patre enim in hunc mundum venerat, quia a Deo exierat'. Cf. *trin*. 12. 45.
[32] Hilary, *trin*. 6. 30.

trinitate 4.³³ None of Maier's parallels is conclusive, but all witness to a real coincidence of both doctrine and, in some respects, language.

Further aspects of Augustine's account are anticipated by Ambrose. In *De fide* 5, for example, Ambrose confronts the same question as Augustine: is the one who sends greater than the one who is sent? In the course of refuting this implication Ambrose interprets the Son's 'sending' as the Son making himself manifest for human minds, rather than a literal descent, for God is omnipresent. Both Old Testament 'sending' and the Incarnation serve the same purpose.³⁴ Again Maier argues that linguistic parallels suggest Augustine's direct dependence on this passage – and again his argument has merit but is not conclusive.³⁵ Ambrose also sees the Incarnation as a revealing of the Son's eternal birth from the Father, but he does not make significant use of the parallels between the two nativities in the manner that we see in Hilary.³⁶ Ambrose's argument that sending cannot mean 'descent' because God is omnipresent is found also in Jerome's translation of Didymus, and Augustine may have known both texts before he composed the early books of the *De trinitate*.³⁷

Thus, aspects of Augustine's account find significant parallels in earlier Latin theology. Nevertheless, Augustine's is distinct in its systematic character. Our bishop offers by far the most extensive and analytical discussion of the term 'sending' and when he has settled on the main features of his account he applies that account logically and across the board. At the same time, Augustine incorporates all the personal missions within a general account of the role of the visible that goes far beyond anything found in Hilary or Ambrose. Finally, we should note the sophistication with which, through the second decade of the fifth century, Augustine comes to use his account of the Son's eternal generation to show how the Son's earthly nativity reveals his eternal nativity, how the visible mission is grounded in the character of the Father's eternal act of generation. This account we will see in further detail in Chapters 9 and 10.

---

[33] Maier, *Les missions divines selon saint Augustin*, 205–6. The first parallel is between a passage drawn from the section I consider here: Hilary, *trin.* 6. 29's 'ab eo ergo qui misit, est ille qui missus est' and Augustine, *trin.* 4. 20.28's 'Mittit qui genuit, mittitur quod genitum est'. Maier, *Les missions divines*, 79–81, also points to the broader anticipations of Augustine in Filastrius and Gaudentius of Brescia.
[34] Ambrose, *fid.* 5. 7.98–9.   [35] Maier, *Les missions divines*, 209–10.
[36] For example, Ambrose, *fid.* 1. 14.89–94.
[37] Didymus, *spir.* 111–12 (and with this cf. 21).

CREATOR, CREATION AND THE ANGELS

Throughout the initial books of the *De trinitate* Augustine assumes, insinuates and at times directly asserts that to understand the character of divine sending we must understand the relationship between Creator and creation. It is the existence of all in the Father's Word and Wisdom that undergirds this relationship.[38] In the second half of this chapter I will focus on this theme – first as it appears in the initial books of the *De trinitate* and then in the first three of Augustine's tractates on John, which date from 406 or 407.

That good interpretation of texts describing the divine existence depends upon a grasp of the relationship between Creator and creation has been central to Augustine's argument since the initial discussions of *De trinitate* 1. There Augustine links the necessity of the Son being *eiusdem substantiae* with the Father to the Son's place in the relationship between created and uncreated existence through exegesis of John 1.3. The Son cannot be one of the things 'made through him' described in John 1.3, and is of the same substance as the Father because all that is not created is God.[39] Augustine thus insinuates into the argument a clear principle that makes the ultimate distinction not between material and immaterial, or between sensible and intelligible, but between created and uncreated. Immediately Augustine presents as a logical consequence that 1 Timothy 6.16 must refer to the Son and Spirit as well as the Father. Because (following 1 John 5.20) the Son is 'eternal life', the Son must not be subject to any change, and hence must also possess the immortality of which 1 Timothy 6.16 speaks. Augustine here also assumes that to speak of the Creator and of eternal life is to speak of that in which Christians are made sharers. To understand that Christ is uncreated rather than created is, for Augustine, to understand that Christ's life is the source of our continuing to live and of our eternal life. The uncreated must be life itself (and divinity does not come in degrees).[40]

It is, however, in *De trinitate* 3 that Augustine explores directly the distinction between Creator and creation. The discussion of the angelic mediation Augustine thinks to be operative in the Old Testament 'theophanies' that occupies much of this book – and much of this book's

---

[38] There is much useful discussion of these themes in Scott A. Dunham, *The Trinity and Creation in Augustine: An Ecological Analysis* (New York: SUNY Press, 2008).
[39] *trin*. 1. 6.9. See below, pp. 193f.
[40] A denser account of Augustine's understanding of the divine as life itself is offered in the first section of Chapter 8.

earliest stratum – is easily overlooked by the modern reader. To do so is a mistake. Leaving aside the later prologue to the book, around two-thirds of the text offers what amounts to a short treatise on the character of divine presence.[41] Augustine summarizes thus:

> the will of God, who makes his angels, spirits and his ministers a blazing fire, resides [in that higher and heavenly country] among spirits who are bound together in perfect peace and friendship, and melted together into one will by a kind of spiritual fire ... From there he diffuses himself through all things by certain most orderly movements of the creature [*ordinatissimis creaturae motibus*]. But as grosser and lower bodies are directed in a certain order by subtler and stronger bodies, so all bodies are directed by the spirit of life: the irrational spirit of life by the rational spirit of life, the truant and sinful rational spirit of life by the rational, pious and just spirit of life, and the latter by its Creator, from whom, through whom, and in whom [cf. Rom. 11.36] it has also been created and established.[42]

Augustine goes on to present miracles as revealing the divine power at work in *all* of creation:

> While man plants and waters, who draws up the moisture through the root of the vine to the cluster of grapes and makes the wine except God who gives the growth? But when water was changed into wine with unaccustomed swiftness at the Lord's command the divine power was revealed, as even fools acknowledge.[43]

Thus in the Eucharist also, the invisible and omnipotent God works through created realities to reveal himself and to work for our spiritual health.[44]

All things grow and change according to invisible seeds (*semina invisibilia*) or powers (*vis*) implanted from the beginning by the Creator.[45] Even the exercise of seemingly miraculous power by evil spirits or magicians occurs because God permits the co-option of the powers with which he has invested the creation. Thus the magician – just like the evil man who successfully grows corn – cannot be said to be the creator of what he might seem to effect. Rather such things occur because of 'reasons of fittingness' (*congruae rationes*) that exist in the Wisdom of God himself:[46]

> For every cause of a changeable and sensible substance and all its measure, number and weight [cf. Wisd. 11.21], from which it is brought about that it has being of such and such a nature, exists by reason of the unchangeable and

---

[41] *trin.* 3. 1.4–10.22.   [42] *trin.* 3. 4.9 (CCSL 50. 135–6).   [43] *trin.* 3. 5.11 (CCSL 50. 137).
[44] *trin.* 3. 4.10.   [45] *trin.* 3. 8.13.   [46] *trin.* 3. 8.15.

intelligible life, which is above all things and reaches even to the most remote and earthly things.[47]

The account of Creator and creation that Augustine outlines in these paragraphs is focused around an account of the existence of all in the Word, the 'intelligible and unchangeable life' referred to here. In the first quotation from Book 3 given above, the glossing of 'Creator' by allusion to Romans 11.36 ('from whom, through whom, and in whom …') shows Augustine still using the theology of creation (and of the maintenance of creation) that we saw developed in his anti-Manichaean works (and which is continued through into his mature *De Genesi ad litteram*).[48] In the first passage, the 'will of God' who binds the angels into one will 'through something like a blazing fire' and that which is responsible for the ordering of things is probably the Spirit. This language occurs a number of times in *De trinitate* 3, but Augustine shows little interest in careful delineation of roles here and primarily seeks to emphasize the joint working of the divine Will and Wisdom.[49] He is, however, very clear about the role of the divine Wisdom. Wisdom is that which 'reaches from end to end … and orders all things well' (Wisd. 8.1), which governs all things and in whom the 'seeds' of all are contained.[50] The first cause of all is that unchangeable Wisdom which governs the wise man, and the angels.[51]

It is a great mistake to think that because Augustine refuses an account of the theophanies as necessarily appearances of the Word and focuses instead on the divine use of created realities, this means that he does not envisage the relationship between Creator and creation in Trinitarian terms. Augustine is clear in these texts that the working of these appearances occurs because God speaks all things in his Word, and governs

---

[47] *trin.* 3. 8.15 (CCSL 50. 142–3).   [48] See esp. Chapter 2, p. 54f.
[49] With this passage one should compare the triadic reference to *deus, sapientia* and *voluntas* at *trin.* 3. 2.8 (CCSL 50. 133): 'Ita enim canitur: Hierusalem quae aedificatur ut ciuitas, cuius participatio eius in idipsum. Idipsum quippe hoc loco illud summum et incommutabile bonum intellegitur quod deus est atque sapientia uoluntasque ipsius, cui cantatur alio loco: Mutabis ea et mutabuntur; tu autem idem ipse es'. Cf. also the similar language in *trin.* 3. 1.6 and 3. 3.8. In 3. 3.8 it is the unchangeable Wisdom who is the first cause, in 3. 4.9 the Will of God is similarly described: this need not mean Augustine treats the two terms as synonymous, only that with the Father, Son and Spirit constitute one cause. The Spirit is first likened to the 'will of a craftsman' at *Gn. adv. Man.* 1. 5.8 and 1. 7.12. The same language appears at *Gn. litt. imp.* 16–18. The initial books of *Gn. litt.* are either contemporary with or possibly predate the initial books of *trin.* At *Gn. litt.* 1. 5.11, Augustine presents the Spirit as God's love (as love and benevolence – '*benivolentia dilectioque*' – in 1. 7.13, cf. 2. 6.14) and seems to equate this with the divine will (CSEL 28. 10): 'superferebatur utique spiritus dei, quia subiacebat scilicet bonae uoluntati creatoris quidquid illud erat quod formandum perficiendumque inchoauerat, ut dicente deo in uerbo suo: fiat lux, in bona uoluntate, hoc est bono placito eius pro modo sui generis maneret, quod factum est'.
[50] *trin.* 3. 1.6.   [51] *trin.* 3. 3.8 and 3. 4.9.

all through his omnipresent Wisdom and Spirit. This brief investigation also demonstrates that key features of Augustine's Christological epistemology are founded in his understanding of the manner in which God uses the created order as a vehicle of self-manifestation. As we grow in understanding of the Creator's presence in the creation (as far as we may), Augustine sees us as growing in recognition that the creation is immediately governed by an eternal source that does not live but is Life itself, and who thus transcends all the changeable existences and lives of the created order (and this even though we can also trace a natural hierarchy from lower to higher orders of life). The account given in *De trinitate* 3 directly mirrors Augustine's account, in *De doctrina* 2, of the manner in which the wise worshippers of the divine are able to think beyond the corporeal towards a transcendent God. Just as Christ uses his flesh – and fleshly words – to draw us towards the mystery of God, the triune God constructs and governs the intelligible created order such that it may draw the mind towards knowledge and love of, and humility before, its Creator.

Augustine does not here offer this vision as an alternative to the life of faith: this much we see in the fact that he intersperses this account of the creation with Trinitarian allusions known only in faith. We can, however, say that, for Augustine, learning to imagine the created order thus, learning to recognize that it is so, is an important part of the restoration of sight that faith effects and which will be fulfilled when faith becomes sight. At the same time, Augustine seems to see our reimagining of the created order as an essential part of our learning to think through the Trinitarian communion. Growing in understanding that the divine transcends the creation and operates through, in and with a *sui generis* power and by an immediate and mysterious presence helps us in the imagining of the divine three and their relations beyond corporeal imagery. Even in the case of those not gifted in such flights of the intellectual life, appropriate awe at the created order and humility at God's power in it perform an important function for Augustine.[52] To draw out more fully the importance Augustine places on envisaging the created order and its relationship to the Trinity I want to end by turning to the first three of his tractates on John.

---

[52] I offer an extended discussion of this point in my 'Christology as Contemplative Practice: Understanding the Union of Natures in Augustine's *Ep.* 137', in Peter Martens (ed.), *In the Shadow of the Incarnation: Essays in Honor of Brian Daley* (Notre Dame, IN: Notre Dame University Press, 2008), 190–211.

'YOU HAVE MADE ALL THINGS IN WISDOM' (PS. 103.24)

These three sermons were most likely written in 406 or 407, and thus predate the bulk of *De trinitate* 3 by a few years.[53] Augustine focuses the first sermon on exploring the nature of the Word, but he does so by suggesting also an account of the relations between Creator and creation. Our preacher announces one of the fundamental principles of his discussion: God is more present to the congregation than is Augustine himself.[54] Augustine then turns to the term 'Word', drawing out a variety of distinctions between the Word and our spoken words. Offering no philosophical term for the phenomenon, Augustine then speaks of the 'word' present in the heart when we think of God.[55] Augustine is concerned, however, that we inappropriately liken the Word to our spoken words. Because of this concern Augustine supplements his account of 'Word' with attention to a variety of other terms and analogies. This conceptual 'word' is paralleled with 'a certain plan/intention [*consilium*] born in the mind'.[56] Before the visible building which follows a design is finished, the design is perfect, invisible and unchanging. The Word may thus be called the *consilium Dei*, the plan or intention of God. Augustine immediately turns to a series of rhetorical questions designed to heighten our awareness of the *fabrica mundi*, 'the craftsmanship of the world'. By perceiving this *fabrica*, the abundance of the earth and the splendour of the sky (and 'who can adequately praise the power of seeds?'), we may be drawn to recognize something of what that Word must be who is the *consilium* for this *fabrica*:[57]

> There is no shape, no structure, no union of parts, no substance whatsoever which can have weight, number, measure unless it is through that Word, and by that creator Word to whom it was said: 'You have ordered all things by measure, number and weight' [Wisd. 11.21].[58]

Augustine's reading of the title Word is further defined when he turns to 'life'. Building on the ambiguities of John 1.3 – which Augustine reads

---

[53] For the dating of these sermons, see La Bonnardière, *Recherches de chronologie augustinienne*, 19–62. Her arguments build on and modify those of M. La Landais, 'Deux années de prédication de saint Augustin: introduction à la lecture de l'*In Iohannem*', in *Études Augustiniennes* (Paris: Aubier, 1953), 5–95.

[54] *Io. ev. tr.* 1. 7 (CCSL 36. 4): 'sed forte hoc dicetis, quia ego uobis sum praesentior quam deus. absit. multo est ille praesentior: nam ego oculis uestris appareo, ille conscientiis uestris praesidet'.

[55] *Io. ev. tr.* 1. 8 (CCSL 36. 5). On the origins of Augustine's 'interior word' terminology, see pp. 194f.

[56] *Io. ev. tr.* 1. 9 (CCSL 36. 5).   [57] *Io. ev. tr.* 1. 9.

[58] *Io. ev. tr.* 1. 13 (CCSL 36. 8).

as 'all things were made through him, and without him nothing was made, and that which was made in him was life' – Augustine uses Psalm 103.24 ('you have made all things in Wisdom') to assert that for things to be made 'through' the Word is for them to be made 'in' the Word, and that the Word is also Wisdom:

> There is, however, in Wisdom itself, in a spiritual way, a certain reason by which the earth was made: this is life.[59]

Augustine now expands on the earlier analogy of a building in design and in reality. A craftsman makes a chest, first having the chest in his *ars*, in his skill or creative knowledge.[60] When the visible chest is created, the invisible chest remains unchanging, always ready to be the basis for another chest. It is this chest in the *ars* that is life: similarly all things in the created order are life in the Wisdom of God. This life is, Augustine says at the end of the sermon, also the light who enlightens all; thus Wisdom = *ars* = reason = Life = Light. The *De trinitate* and the first few tractates on John show us that while Augustine does have a developed theology of Word, the theme of Wisdom remains foundational, as in the *De fide*. The relationship between these titles is now well integrated: the divine Wisdom is God's eternal speaking and revealing of all that he is and will create, the divine Word is the revealing of the eternal Wisdom who is life and rationality.

This tractate is the first text where Augustine likens the Word of God to the 'inner' word of human beings. The origins of this language have been the subject of much debate. One significant philosophical source for Augustine seems to be the Stoic notion of the *lekton* or the 'sayable', an incorporeal impression, thought or proposition in the mind which can be spoken. This tradition is represented in the *De dialectica* which may be Augustine's: 'whatever is perceived of a word, not by the ears, but by the mind, and is held fast within the mind itself, is called a *dicibile*, a "speakable" or "meaning"'.[61] It is likely that Augustine is also influenced by Plotinus's account of epistemology and the imagination

---

[59] *Io. ev. tr.* 1. 16 (CCSL 36. 10): 'est autem in ipsa sapientia spiritaliter ratio quaedam qua terra facta est; haec uita est'. On the theme of participation in life cf. *Gn. litt.* 2. 6.10.

[60] 'Creative knowledge' is the translation of Rettig in FoC 78. The term *ars* refers to the learnt and active knowledge or knowing of an artist who creates. As Augustine applies the term to God it also has the connotation of the principle from which all the *artes* stem. For an earlier use of this imagery see *div. qu.* 78.

[61] *dial.* 5. 50–2. The two most extensive discussions of the concept and its history are to be found in Schindler, *Wort und Analogie*, 75–118, and then (published in the same year but already offering a response to Schindler) Ulrich Duchrow, *Sprachverständnis und Biblisches Hören bei Augustin* (Tübingen: Mohr, 1965), 122–48.

in such texts as *Ennead* 4.3 and 4.4. At 4. 3.30, for example, Plotinus speaks of an account or expression (*logos*) which accompanies every thought (*noema*). The thought remains hidden, while the expression brings to light the thought in a way that enables us to apprehend our intellectual activity.[62] In the first tractate on John, Augustine describes the inner word as that which enables understanding.[63] Similarly, in a number of the works from the late 380s and 390s, we see Augustine speaking about the 'word' which is conceived internally as the basis for speech or action.[64] Thus the notion of the inner word is fairly well developed in Augustine's thought before its Trinitarian application in the early years of the fifth century.

Augustine's use of the concept to describe the Word, however, also occurs against an anti-Photinian theological background in which any description of the Word as an expressed thought might be taken to indicate the Word's temporality.[65] However little Augustine knew of the specifics of this earlier debate he is careful not to offer any hostage to fortune. In *De doctrina* 1, for the first time, we see him liken the appearance of the Word in flesh to our uttering of the word or thought in our minds: the inner thought remains without diminution.[66] In the first tractate on John, Augustine uses the concept analogically in a way which follows his earlier discussions of human inner speech, identifying that which is drawn from the memory to constitute active thought. But immediately he fits this conception into his understanding not of speech *per se*, but of the mental plan on the basis of which something is constructed. Augustine's goal here, then, is to use a concept that he thinks will make sense to his congregation as reinforcement for his well-established account of the Word as also Wisdom, as that in which the Father's plan for creation is eternally 'spoken'. It is this analogy that also enables him, in a somewhat heavy-handed manner, to name the inner Word 'as it were a son of your heart' (*quasi filius cordis tui*).[67] In earlier texts, the languages of Word and Wisdom sit in easy conjunction but without Augustine tying the two together in the way we see here.[68] We should note, however, that what we will meet in *De trinitate* 9 and 10 adds a significant extra dimension as

---

[62] Cf. *Enn.* 5. 1.3.   [63] *Io. ev. tr.* 1. 8 (CCSL 36. 5).
[64] Thus, for example, the Word conceived in the heart reveals one's basic ethical commitments, *ep. Rm. inch.* 23 (*c*.394–5). At *mag.* 1. 2 (*c*.389), inner speech is an essential part of recalling from the memory, and is that used in prayer.
[65] Hilary, *trin.* 2. 15. See also Williams, 'Monarchianism and Plotinus as the Persistent Heretical Face of the Fourth Century'.
[66] *doctr. chr.* 1. 11.12.30.   [67] *Io. ev. tr.* 1. 9 (CCSL 36. 5).
[68] For example *Gn. litt.* 1. 5.10.

Augustine reflects on the interplay of knowledge and love in the production of the inner Word.

In the second tractate on John, Augustine turns again to the language of light, this time emphasizing its omnipresence. He does so in order to cast the character of our ignorance as that of the blind person in the presence of the sun and, hence, in order to cast the shape of our return, of faith as a 'lamp' by which we see the light.[69] Coming to John 1.10's 'he was in the world, and the world was made through him, yet the world knew him not', Augustine makes further use of the craftsman analogy:

> Do not imagine that he was in the world in such a way as the earth is in the world, the sky is in the world ... But how was he? As the master builder who governs what he has made. For he did not make it in the way a craftsman makes a chest. The chest which he makes is external to him; and when it is constructed, it has been situated in another place ... Suffusing the world, God creates; being everywhere, God creates [*deus autem mundo infusus fabricat, ubique positus fabricat*]; he does not direct the structure which he constructs as someone on the outside. By the presence of his majesty he makes what he makes; by his own presence he governs what he has made [*praesentia sua gubernat quod fecit*].[70]

As in *De trinitate* 3, God governs by his immediate presence to all. This account expands that picture by emphasizing that God must thus create without making 'space' for it. Augustine also adds to the picture painted in the first tractate when, in the initial paragraphs, he emphasizes again that the Word does not change as do our words:

> This Word is the self-same, the identical, about which we spoke at great length yesterday ... He is the self-same, the identical; he is in the same manner. As he is, so he always is [*idipsum est, eodem modo est; sicut est semper sic est*]. He cannot be changed; that is, he is. And he said this, his name, to his servant Moses: 'I am who am' and 'He who is, sent me' [Ex. 3.14].[71]

In the next chapter we will discuss the description of the Word as *idipsum* – which I translate here as 'the self-same, the identical' – in more detail. Here we need only note its congruence with the first tractate's insistence on the Word as the reason and life containing without change all that is *in arte*.[72]

---

[69] *Io. ev. tr.* 2. 6.   [70] *Io. ev. tr.* 2. 10 (CCSL 36. 16).

[71] *Io. ev. tr.* 2. 2 (CCSL 36. 12). The homily delivered 'yesterday' is known to us as *en. Ps.* 121 and is considered in Chapter 8. For the complex relationship between the first few tractates on John and *en Ps.* 119–33, see La Bonnardière, *Recherches*, 46–53. Cf. *Io. ev. tr.* 1. 8 and *trin*. 15. 5.7.

[72] The absence from these first three tractates on John of Augustine's earlier account of creation as an act of converting and forming towards God seems to stem from his particular concerns here. That theology is clearly stated in contemporary texts, see for example, at *Gen. litt.* 1. 4.9, 8.14 and 9.17, a work begun at some point between 399 and 405.

Against Homoian triadologies, and against Manichaean accounts of the hierarchies of divine and created being, Augustine sets out an account of the distinction between creation and Creator in which all exists in the Wisdom of God and is governed by this Wisdom. But this is also the Wisdom eternally spoken by the Father, inseparable from and omnipresent with the Father, and the Wisdom complemented by the Spirit who completes the creation, maintains it in form and moves it towards its Creator – which is also to move the creation towards permanence in the Spirit itself who is one with Father and Son. That there is a hierarchy within the created order is clear – we have already seen Augustine speak of God governing through the rational spiritual realities of soul and angels and thus on into the material world. But the existence of *this* hierarchy must always be held in tension with the order without hierarchy that characterizes God's governing through Word and in Spirit, and which characterizes God's immediate presence to all.

Rather than saying only that growing in understanding of the created order plays a significant role in our growth in understanding of the Trinity, it is better to say that our understanding of both grows together. To understand the created order as receiving its life by participation in the Word entails us coming to understand that the Word must be unchangeable life itself; the more we understand that the Word is this, the better we can see how it is that the Word may govern all immediately and how all exists in the Word. But, as we have seen through *De trinitate* 2–4, to understand the creation's existence in the Word is only completed in confession of the Trinity, of the Father's eternal speaking of that Word and in recognition of the Spirit drawing the creation towards the Father. At this point, we see very clearly how much Augustine envisages the language of faith as a guide towards the comprehension of that which lies before us, but from which we are so easily hidden. We should also note that although the argumentation here is aimed at a variety of targets – Homoians and Platonists most prominently – the dynamics of that argument are a mature iteration of the anti-Manichaean syntheses we saw developing in the early texts considered in Chapter 2.

Two things have, I hope, been accomplished in this chapter. In the first place, the dogmatic foundations of Augustine's Christological epistemology have become clear. In the second place, this chapter has also begun to sketch Augustine's mature account of the Trinity as an ordered communion of equals established by the Father. His very clarity about the sending of Son and Spirit in order to reveal the Father suggests to us, not merely the error of a reading of Augustine's Trinitarian theology that sees him as not preserving the Father's place in the Trinitarian order, but also a number of substantive questions about *how* he envisions the divine communion and about how we conceive of the Father's status as source, as *principium*. It is time to turn (slowly) to those questions.

CHAPTER 8

Essence from essence

This chapter and the next have the character of a 'taking away' and a 'giving back'. In this chapter I argue that the tradition of reading *De trinitate* 5–7 as an account of 'subsistent relations' (albeit an inchoate one that awaits Thomas for its full actualization) misses Augustine's focus on questions of predication, and overly concretizes Augustine's inchoate hints about the substantial and immutable quality of relations between the divine three. In this respect these books of the *De trinitate* offer far less of a developed Trinitarian ontology than is frequently assumed. At the same time, however, I argue that these same books do describe some important and developed features of such an ontology that are usually missed. In particular, Augustine offers an account of the Father eternally giving rise to Son and Spirit from the Father's own substance under the conditions of divine simplicity, that rejects person and nature language as a knot of ideas that can found logically coherent discussion of the divine communion. And thus, Augustine's interpretation of the Nicene 'God from God' marks his theology as one of the most intriguing explorations of the creed's phrasing.

In Chapter 9, I continue this exercise in 'giving back', by suggesting that *outside*, but around and just after the time of writing *De trinitate* 5–7, Augustine does offer more positive and direct suggestions about the eternal relationships and intra-divine acts that constitute Father, Son and Spirit. These suggestions are articulated with increasing clarity with respect to each of the divine three in the years during which Augustine was finishing the *De trinitate* (although questions of dating remain complex here). Ultimately, however, I end these two chapters with a last exercise in 'taking away', as the texts I consider in Chapter 9 offer themes that are emergent, that are never drawn together into a summative statement. It is possible, I will suggest, to outline the lines of Augustine's mature vision of the divine communion, but in doing so we have to step further out along the path than Augustine himself does in his surviving corpus.

THE SELF-SAME, THE IDENTICAL

Before moving directly into *De trinitate* 5–7 some ground-clearing is necessary. In the first two sections of this chapter I suggest ways of approaching a number of basic questions concerning Augustine's most fundamental assumptions about the divine being. I have little new to say here, but the discussion remains an important preliminary.

It is undoubtedly the case that Augustine spends more time commenting on what it means to call God 'substance' or 'essence' than he does defining what 'person' means when applied to Father, Son or Spirit. But those readers who have been waiting for a point at which to exclaim 'ah ha, Augustine *does* "begin" from the unity of God!' should continue to hold their breath: a number of investigations must be undertaken before we can judge the meaning of this focus and before we can judge whether Augustine's discussions of divine 'essence' inappropriately pre-determine his account of the divine three.

Given Augustine's use of the Aristotelian categories in *De trinitate* 5–7 it might be supposed that the best point of departure for investigating Augustine's use of substance language in talking about God would be to look for Aristotelian definitions of his terminology. Augustine, however, offers no such clear definitions. His brief glosses – they can hardly be called 'discussions' – of the meaning of *substantia* indicate that he was familiar with something like the distinction between Aristotelian primary and secondary substance.[1] At one point he writes to Jerome, 'if every substance, or essence or whatever that which exists somehow in itself is better called, is a body, then the soul is a body'.[2] At another point Aristotelian secondary substance seems to be hinted at when he writes that,

> We speak of man or animal, the earth, the sky, the sun, the moon, stone, the sea, the air: all these things are substances, simply in virtue of the fact that they exist. Their natures are called substances. God too is a certain sort of substance [*quaedam substantia*], for anything that is not a substance is not anything at all. A substance is something that is.[3]

In fact, Augustine uses both senses of *substantia* in the same texts without clearly indicating that he wants his audience to be aware of the

---

[1] My discussion here is greatly indebted to Roland Teske, 'Augustine's Use of "Substantia" in Speaking about God', *The Modern Schoolman* 62 (1985), 147–63. Cf. Matthias Smalbrugge, 'Sur l'emploi et l'origine du terme *essentia* chez Augustin', *Aug(L)* 39 (1989), 436–46.
[2] *ep.* 166. 2.4 (CSEL 44. 550–1).   [3] *en. Ps.* 68. 5 (CCSL 39. 905).

Essence from essence

distinction.[4] We should, however, be cautious about supposing that the two Aristotelian senses of *substantia* are the sole context for Augustine's understanding of the term, especially considering his clear preference for the term 'essentia' to 'substantia' when speaking of God.

In a famous passage of *De trinitate* 7, Augustine distinguishes between *substantia* and *essentia* on the basis that the former is derived from *subsistere* and the latter from *esse*:

> [subsistence] is rightly applied to things which provide subjects for those things that are said to be in a subject, as the colour or form of a body ... But if God subsists, so that he may be properly called a substance, then there is something in Him as it were in a subject, and he is no longer simple ... But it is wrong to assert that God subsists and is the subject of his own goodness, and that goodness is not a substance, or rather not an essence, that God himself is not his own goodness, and that it inheres in him as in its subject. It is, therefore, obvious that God is improperly called a substance [*abusive substantiam vocari*]. The more usual [*nomine usitatiore*] name is essence, which he is truly and properly called, so that perhaps God alone should be called essence [*ut nomine usitatiore intellegatur essentia, quod uere ac proprie dicitur ita ut fortasse solum deum dici oporteat essentam*]. For he alone truly is, because he is unchangeable. And, therefore, he revealed his name to Moses when he said: 'I am who am: and He that is, has sent me to you' [Ex. 3.14].[5]

Thus substance is inappropriate because of the connotations that attend on *subsistere*, the verb from which it stems. *Essentia*, however, is appropriate and not merely acceptable, because of God's unchangeability. For this reason perhaps God *alone* should be called *essentia*.

In his mature work, Augustine often repeats the link between *essentia*, the verb *esse* and God's act of self-naming before Moses. For example:

> he says 'I am who am' and 'Thus shall you say to the children of Israel, he who is sent me to you' [Ex. 3.14]. He did not say, 'I am the Lord, the omnipresent, the merciful, the just one', though, if he had said that, he would have spoken truly. Instead he set aside all those names that could be applied to God and answered that he was called 'to be' itself [*ipsum esse*], as though that were his name. 'Say this to them', he said, 'He who is sent me'. For thus he is, so that, in comparison with him, those things which have been made, are not [*ita enim ille est, ut in eius comparatione ea quae facta sunt, non sint*]. They are, only if not compared with him; since they are from him; but compared with him, they are not, because

---

[4] Thus, for example, at *ep.* 166. 2.4, only a few sentences after the text quoted in n. 3, Augustine writes (CSEL 44. 552–3): 'unde intellegitur, anima siue corpus siue incorporea dicenda sit, propriam quandam habere naturam omnibus his mundanae molis elementis excellentiore substantia creatam'.
[5] *trin.* 7. 5.10 (CCSL 50. 260–1).

he is true existing, unchangeable existing, and this he is alone [*quia uerum esse incommutabile esse est, quod ille solus est*].⁶

This text parallels a number in which *est* is also treated as a or the name of God.⁷

While Augustine would certainly have found in some of his pro-Nicene predecessors assertions that only God truly is and that eternity defines he who *est*, Augustine gives the theme a detailed treatment unparalleled in previous Latin writing, and one found *in nuce* in his earliest texts.⁸ Augustine's use of the noun *essentia* is a clear sign of the extent to which Augustine has developed a dynamic mostly latent in his predecessors. The term is only rarely used before him, often where it seems to be directly translating the Greek *ousia*.⁹ Although the term probably appears in Christian Latin for the first time in Tertullian, it is Augustine who first gives it extended definition.¹⁰

The distinctiveness of Augustine's approach is also seen when we consider one other key term that he uses to speak of the divine existence. In Augustine's version Psalm 121.4 read *Ierusalem quae aedificatur ut ciuitas. cuius participatio eius in idipsum*, 'The Jerusalem that is being built as a city, it is a sharing in *the selfsame, the identical*'.¹¹ I use this double expression to translate the term where I have not left it untranslated. In his exposition of this psalm Augustine writes:

What is *idipsum*? *idipsum*. What can I say other than *idipsum*? ... What is *idipsum*? That which always is in the same way, which is not now one thing, now another. What, therefore is *idipsum*, unless that which is? What is that which

---

⁶ *en. Ps.* 134. 4 (CCSL 39. 1940).   ⁷ See for example, *conf*. 13. 31.46, *Io. ev. tr.* 2. 2.
⁸ See particularly clearly Ambrose, *fid.* 5. 26; Hilary, *trin.* 1. 5, 12.24–5; Victorinus, *adv. Ar.* 1. 31.
⁹ See Victorinus, *adv. Ar.* 3. 7 (there are numerous other uses in Victorinus's corpus), *In Eph.* 4; Ambrosiaster, *quaest. test.* 97. 3 and 8, 81. 2; Jerome, *ad Eph.* 1 (472), 2 (519) (the term also appears in Jerome's translation of Didymus, *spir.* 4, 8, 36); Hilary, *in Ps.* 63. 9, *in const.* 12 and 23; Gregory of Elvira, *fid.* 11 (CCSL 69. 223): 'tria nomina et tres personas unius esse essentiae' (and at *fid.* 56). Note that among the main pro-Nicene anti-'Arian' treatises the term appears only in Victorinus and Gregory of Elvira.
¹⁰ See the disputed texts at Tertullian, *adv. Val.* 29, *Carn.* 2. Both readings are disputed. See R. Braun, *'Deus Christianorum'. Recherches sur le Vocabulaire Doctrinal de Tertullian* (Paris: Presses Universitaires de France, 1962), 167–70, 579–85. It should be noted that these are the only third-century occurrences revealed by an LLT search.
¹¹ In what follows I have learnt much through engagement with Jean Luc Marion's *'Idipsum*: The Name of God According to Augustine', in George Demacopoulos and Aristotle Papanikolaou (eds.), *Orthodox Readings of Augustine* (Crestwood, NY: St Vladimirs Seminary Press, 2008), 167–89. It is beyond my scope here to offer extensive refutation of the claim that Augustine is an example of Heidegger's 'onto-theology' but, were there space, I would want to explore how Marion's account of the *idipsum* is not as incompatible as he might fear with the picture offered by Dominique Dubarle in his *Dieu avec L'Être* (Paris: Beauchesne, 1986), esp. 205–32. Dubarle is notoriously verbose and often inattentive to Augustine's preferred terminologies, but his central insight deserves much further examination and appreciation.

is? That which is eternal. For that which is always one thing and then another is not, because it does not abide.[12]

Augustine's development of the language of *idipsum* incorporates a theme present from his earliest texts. Immutability is the true mark of divine existence and that which marks God as the source and end of all that exists mutably. Already in the *De beata vita* to exist is to remain, and that which remains eternally is God; similar language can be found in a number of other places in the earliest works.[13] In *De moribus* I, Augustine argues that the Spirit sanctifies because the Spirit 'remains whole and immutable'. A few sentences later his description of God as Father, Son and Spirit, and as a *trinam unitatem* is immediately followed by '... *nihil aliud dicam esse nisi idipsum esse*', 'and, I shall say, nothing other than "to be" identically'.[14] Similarly, in 390, in the *De vera religione*, Augustine speaks of humanity falling away from attention to 'the *idipsum*, the unique unchanging nature'.[15] It is from this point also that we begin to find Augustine drawing in Exodus 3.14 as we saw above.[16] Augustine's immutability — as the language of 'remaining' might indicate — should not be taken as a simple projection of stasis as we see it in the created order. In his commentary on Psalm 138, Augustine remarks with reference to Wisdom's 'abiding' at Wisdom 7.27 that 'Wisdom stands firm, if we can properly say that she stands; the expression connotes immutability, not immobility [*dicitur autem propter incommutabilitatem, non propter immobilitatem*]. Nowhere is she other than she is here or there, never is she different from what she is now or was formerly. This is what God's utterance is.'[17] The Father's eternal speaking of the Word thus does not mean that the Word is static, but eternally spoken and eternally remaining.

---

[12] *en. Ps.* 121. 5 (CSEL 95/3. 90–1): 'Quid est idipsum? Idipsum. Quomodo dicam, nisi idipsum? ... Quid est idipsum? Quod semper eodem modo est, quod non modo aliud et modo aliud est. Quid ergo est idipsum, nisi, quod est? Quid est quod est? Quod aeternum est. Nam quod semper aliter atque aliter est, non est, quia non manet'.

[13] *b. vita* 2. 8, 11. Cf. *imm. an.* 7. 12 (CSEL 89. 113): 'si enim magis est ad rationem conuersus eique inhaerens, ideo quod inhaeret inconmutabili rei, quae est ueritas, quae et maxime et primitus est, cum ab ea est auersus, id ipsum esse minus habet, quod est deficere'.

[14] *mor.* 1. 14.24. For text, see p. 53. Cf. the extended discussion at *lib. arb.* 3.20–1.

[15] *vera rel.* 21. 41 (CCSL 32. 213): 'ut non inueniat idipsum, id est naturam incommutabilem et singularem'.

[16] For a chronological list of Augustine's uses of this verse, see Emilie Zum Brunn, *St Augustine: Being and Nothingness* (New York: Paragon, 1988), 119. An appendix to the book, 'The Augustinian Exegesis of "*Ego sum qui sum*" and the "Metaphysics of Exodus"' (pp. 97–118), offers a very useful discussion of Augustine's reading of Ex. 3.14.

[17] *en Ps.* 138. 8 (CSEL 95/4. 135).

Augustine's *Sermon* 7, a text which leaves few clues to its date but probably postdates *De trinitate* 2–4, concerns God's appearance in the burning bush. Having explained that the inseparable Trinity of irreducible persons appears and speaks through created realities, Augustine treats the message conveyed by the angel who speaks in the bush – the angel through whom the Lord speaks:

> So now the angel, and in the angel the Lord, was saying to Moses when he asked his name, 'I am who I am; this is what you shall say to the children of Israel: He who is has sent me to you' [Ex. 3.14]. 'Is' is a name for the unchanging [*incommutabilitatis*]. Everything that changes ceases to be what it was and begins to be what it was not. 'Is' is. True 'is', perfect 'is', real 'is', belongs only to one who does not change [*esse est. uerum esse, sincerum esse, germanum esse non habet nisi qui non mutatur*]. He alone has true 'is' to whom it is said, You will change them and they shall be changed, but you are the selfsame [*tu autem idem ipse es*] [Ps. 101.27]. What is 'I am who I am' if not 'I am eternal'? What is 'I am who I am' if not 'who cannot change'? This is no creature – not sky, not earth, not angel, not power, not thrones, not dominions, not authorities. Since then this is eternity's name, what is much more interesting is that he was prepared to have a name of mercy: 'I am the God of Abraham, the God of Isaac, and the God of Jacob' [Ex. 3.15]. That name in himself, this one for us.[18]

The links made here represent Augustine's mature synthesis – which itself differs only little from his earliest discussions. The treatment of eternity as the 'name' of God, and as synonymous with *esse* and with Exodus 3.14, reveals with particular clarity the significance of immutability. It should be paired with his comment on Psalm 101 (at around the same time as he was writing *De trinitate* 2–4) that 'eternity is the very substance of God'.[19] This portrayal of *idipsum* as a name of God for himself finds no parallel in his predecessors.

Augustine would have found some who linked God's nature as *esse* and God's eternity among his Christian predecessors (we have already seen him draw the title *aeternitas* for the Father from Hilary) but its appearance in his earliest appropriations of some Plotinian themes suggests the primacy of non-Christian sources. One of the most likely is Plotinus's *Ennead* 3.7, which has frequently been suggested as a source for Augustine's discussion of time in *Confessiones* 11. Such a link has been the matter of strong debate, in part because Augustine makes nothing in *Confessiones* 11 of Plotinus's account of time as an image of eternity (although he does elsewhere). But, a link between Augustine's *idipsum*

---

[18] *serm.* 7. 7 (CCSL 41. 75).
[19] *en. Ps.* 101/2. 2.10 (CCSL 38. 1445): 'Aeternitas, ipsa Dei substantia'.

and Plotinus's view of the eternal life and being of Intellect is perhaps more strongly founded. Plotinus identifies the life of intellect as unchanging, as simply 'is', because of its constant living identity.[20] This connection of themes closely parallels Augustine's own account.

It is, however, important to note how Augustine's use of *est* and *idipsum* is governed by his Trinitarian theology. A few examples will make this clear. In the first case, we can return to Augustine's commentary on Psalm 121. Augustine treats verse 4 not only as an occasion for reflection on divine identity and immutability, but also as a verse which speaks of the Incarnation and of salvation itself. The city, Jerusalem, that shares in the stability of the *idipsum* is the city being built on the foundation of Christ and in Christ (1Cor. 3.11). It is the city built from the 'living stones' of 1 Peter 2.5.[21] Following this glossing of Jerusalem Augustine launches into the discussion of *idipsum* considered above. After his attempt to sketch the unspeakability of the *idipsum*, Augustine exhorts us – in familiar fashion – to cling to the flesh of Christ in order that we might be taken to the inn and healed (Luke 10.30–4); this flesh will take us to the city that shares in the *idipsum*:

> Onto what should you grasp? Grasp that which Christ became for you, because that is Christ himself, and Christ himself is rightly understood by this name 'I am who I am' [Ex. 3.14], inasmuch as he is in the form of God. In that nature wherein he deemed it no robbery to be equal to God, there he is *idipsum*. But that you might participate in *idipsum*, he first of all became a participant in what you are [*ut autem efficiaris tu particeps in idipsum, factus est ipse prior particeps tui*].[22]

The passage is a fascinating blend of that which is traditional and that which is distinctively Augustine. Throughout, 'God' refers to the Father who speaks through his Word. And yet because the Word or Son is equal to God he also has the name *idipsum*.

---

[20] Plotinus, *Enn.* 3. 7.3: καὶ τῆς ἐνεργείας τὸ ἄπαυστον καὶ τὸ ταὐτὸν καὶ οὐδέποτε ἄλλο καὶ οὐκ ἐξ ἄλλου εἰς ἄλλο νόησιν ἢ ζωήν, ἀλλὰ τὸ ὡσαύτως καὶ ἀεὶ ἀδιαστάτως ... Λείπεται δὴ ἐν τῷ εἶναι τοῦτο ὅπερ ἐστὶν εἶναι. Ὁ οὖν μήτε ἦν, μήτε ἔσται, ἀλλ' ἔστι μόνον, τοῦτο ἑστὼς ἔχον τὸ εἶναι τῷ μὴ μεταβάλλειν εἰς τὸ ἔσται μηδ'αὖ μεταβεβληκέναι ἐστὶν ὁ αἰών.

[21] *en. Ps.* 121. 4.

[22] *en. Ps.* 121. 5 (CSEL 95/3. 91). The passage from Augustine's commentary on Psalm 121 that we have been considering directly mirrors (or is mirrored by) *trin.* 3. 2.8, a passage whose presentation of the Spirit as the divine will we considered in Chapter 7. Augustine links Psalm 121. 4 and Psalm 101. 27–8 as he does in his psalm commentary and suggests, '*Idipsum* is to be understood in this place as the highest and immutable good, which is God, and of his Wisdom and his Will'.

In Augustine's second exposition of Psalm 101, Christ is the *idipsum* made flesh, but Augustine emphasizes that the recognition of the immutability of the divine enables us not only to grasp the instability of this world, it shapes our desire such that we know our rest can only come through sharing in the 'years that will not fail', the eternity which is the very substance of God.[23] Augustine then emphasizes – and here we see threads followed also in the previous chapter – that to understand God as the immutable source is to see that he creates by his own Word and Power in an incomprehensible manner. To identify God as the *idipsum* thus permits and begins a movement of humble approach towards that which necessarily transcends our grasp even as we are given a language to speak towards its presence. To identify God's Word as also *idipsum* draws our attention to the incomprehensible unity between Father and Son, transcending all categories of differentiation internal to the created order.

In *Confessiones* 12 Augustine puzzles over the mutability of created being, particularly over the ability of the mutable to receive form (*species*):

Where could this come from except from you, from whom everything is insofar as it is? But the further away from you things are, the more unlike you they become – though this distance is not spatial. And so you, Lord, are not one thing here, another thing there, but the selfsame and the selfsame and the selfsame, 'holy, holy, holy, Lord God Almighty' [Rev. 4.8] [*itaque tu, domine, qui non es alias aliud et alias aliter, sed idipsum et idipsum et idipsum, sanctus, sanctus, sanctus, dominus deus omnipotens*]. In the beginning, that is from yourself, in your Wisdom which is begotten of your substance, you made something and made it out of nothing [*in principio, quod est de te, in sapientia tua, quae nata est de substantia tua, fecisti aliquid et de nihilo*]. For you made heaven and earth not out of yourself, or it would be equal to your only-begotten Son and therefore to yourself ... God, one Trinity and Trinitarian One.[24]

Augustine here presents the Father's generation of Son and Spirit as the production of others who are also *idipsum* and yet one with the Father as *idipsum*. The poetry of the language should not hide us from its distinctiveness: again Augustine relies on the very same traditional aspect of Nicaea's language that we saw in the previous chapter, the birth of the

---

[23] *en Ps.* 101(2). 10, 12–14.
[24] *conf.* 12. 7.7 (CCSL 27. 219). Luc Verheijen in his CCSL edition here returns to the reading of the Benedictine edition at PL 32. 828, rejecting the consensus of Knoll in CSEL 33 and Skutella in his Teubner edition that Augustine repeated *idipsum* only twice. While the manuscript tradition is uncertain, the theological logic of the paragraph suggests a threefold repetition. For my purposes, however, even the twofold repetition suffices to demonstrate that Father and Son may individually receive the appellation.

Son from the essence of the Father. Because the Son is born from the Father's *substantia*, the Son shares the Father's status as *idipsum*. Through this chapter and the next we will explore in more detail how Augustine develops such a theology; but even at this stage it should be clear that while his understanding of the divine as eternity and *esse* serves to distinguish (and thus relate) Creator and creation, our understanding of that theme is incomplete unless we see it as interwoven with his Trinitarian theology.

What, then, does Augustine mean when he calls God a substance? He first asserts that substance is better understood as essence, and that essence is appropriate because of God's immutable existence as *idipsum*. This notion of divine immutability is central to Augustine's earliest works when he describes God as the creator of all. Augustine sees in the changeability of things – which is not purely a matter of defect, but also of their ability to receive form – a revealing of the presence and ordering of one who is the unchangeable source of all.[25] While Augustine's use of this language provides us with fundamental noetic content about the divine, I do not think it delivers to us a fixed view of the divine unity that prevents Augustine remaining true to the Nicene principles of his predecessors. This is a statement to be tested through the remainder of this chapter and the next as we learn how Augustine *uses* his understanding of divine simplicity.

Although this discussion is for the most part beyond my purview, I suggest it is also not that helpful to try to draw out of the material we have considered a systematic presentation of the relationship of beings and God as Being (even bearing in mind that this term must stand in for Augustine's complex and consciously dynamic vocabulary for God as *est*, *ipsum esse* and *idipsum*). Whatever may or may not be the errors of a 'metaphysics' drawn from Augustine, this is not what Augustine himself most importantly does with his insight.[26] In the first place, Augustine constantly uses the articulation of the distinction between those things that 'exist' changeably and that which is *idipsum* to articulate the intelligibility of that which always remains also mysterious and ungraspable (and this is, at the same time, to paint the created order as – this side of the *eschaton* – itself finally ungraspable in its relation to the Word in

---

[25] On this point Etienne Gilson is surely at his most perceptive, and almost right, *The Christian Philosophy of Saint Augustine*, trans. L. E. M. Lynch (New York: Random House, 1960), 21–2.
[26] And it is perhaps at this point that Gilson most misses the character of Augustine's work in his search for a perennial 'Christian philosophy' whose necessary principles may be found in Augustine even if they are fully elucidated only within high Scholasticism.

208   *Into the mystery*

whom it exists). In the second place, we should not think we have understood very much about Augustine's 'metaphysics' unless we have seen that the accompaniment to his balance between the intelligibility and mysteriousness of the divine is a detailed account of the balance between longing and humility through which our *intentio* is expressed and shaped. In the third place, Augustine's exposition of the relationship between Creator and creation involves, from the beginning, a meditation on what it means to speak of the Word as that through which God creates and in which all exists. As his theology grows in sophistication, Augustine's attention to these issues only increases: to grow in understanding of the relationship between our changeability and the divine changelessness is always also to grow in understanding of what it means for the Father to generate another who is distinct and not separated from him in whom all finds its cause and existence. For these reasons, one must be cautious of all attempts to extract from Augustine a metaphysics that is not also a theology.

THE SIMPLICITY OF GOD

The ground-clearing of the previous section must now be complemented by a brief discussion of how Augustine understands the concept of simplicity. There are, I suggest, two distinct strands in Augustine's account. These two strands are complementary and aspects of the first are sometimes drawn into the second in Augustine's mature discussions, but it is helpful to understand them as distinct.

The first strand of thought links simplicity and number, specifically the simplicity of the monad that forms the basis of all multiplicity and harmony. Thus, in *De ordine* 2, when Augustine summarizes the value of the Liberal Arts, the one who has studied them usefully is the one who knows how to reduce images to the simple and intelligible numbers that order and structure them.[27] Similarly, in *De libero arbitrio* 2, Augustine argues that all sensible realities lack true unity because they are divisible or spatially extended. We can only know this because we have an innate understanding (*cognitio*) of true and simple unity. Indeed, all number consists of a multiplication of this unity. This unity, which is the core of all number, is then loosely equated with the 'interior light' and with Wisdom.[28] The language of simplicity is thus part of Augustine's attempt to articulate the intelligible structure of reality and the possibility of our progress towards contemplation of its source.

[27] *ord.* 2. 16.44.   [28] *lib. arb.* 2. 8.22

The origins of Augustine's knowledge of ancient theories concerning number and harmonics are obscure. It is clear from the *De musica* that Augustine was familiar with a number of ancient texts on harmony, and Aimé Solignac's work has plausibly suggested that Augustine knew a version of Nichomachus of Gerasa's *Introduction to Arithmetic*.[29] Not surprisingly Augustine's use of number and simplicity seems also to betray Neoplatonic influence. It has been suggested that Augustine's concern with the simple monad as the prime unit of intelligible number and the ordering principle of all may stem from some of his readings in Plotinus, and the short summary of the latter's teaching on numbers found in *Ennead* 5. 5 may well have helped Augustine organize his other reading.[30] At the same time we should not rule out a knowledge of some Iamblichean material: while Plotinus suggests the possibility that being (εἶναι) is derived from one (ἕν), it is in texts such as the Ps. Iamblichean *Theology of Arithmetic* that we find more clearly than in Plotinus the presence of the monad in all numbers because all numbers multiply the primal unity.[31]

The *De moribus* also shows us further ways in which this understanding of simplicity helps Augustine articulate the creation as an order stemming from an originating simple unity:

> Order, after all, brings what it orders to a certain fittingness. But to be is nothing else than to be one [*nihil est autem esse, quam unum esse*]. And so anything is to the extent that it attains oneness [*itaque in quantum quidque unitatem adipiscitur, in tantum est*]. For the effect of oneness is the fittingness and harmony by which those things that are composite are insofar as they are. For simple things are by themselves because they are one. But those things that are not simple imitate oneness by the harmony of their parts, and they are to the extent that they attain it. Hence the imposition of order forces them to be; a lack of order, then, forces them not to be.[32]

This passage was probably written after Augustine had returned to North Africa in 389 and shows some of the key ways in which Augustine opposed Manichaean dualist cosmology through a particular adaptation of Platonic themes. Although we have seen him speak about *simplicia* ('simple things'), it is clear that this was always a problematic concept for Augustine, in the sense that his cosmos presupposes the monad as

---

[29] Solignac, 'Doxographies et manuels', 129–37.
[30] Plotinus, *Enn.* 5. 5.4–5, cf. 5. 5.13ff. *Enn.* 6. 6 ('On Numbers') might also be a possible source. However, the link between infinity and the One that drives much of the discussion there is not a feature of Augustine's account.
[31] For example, Ps. Iamblichus, *theol. arith.* 1.   [32] *mor.* 2. 6.8 (CSEL 90. 94–5).

necessarily unique; all else only approaches simplicity. By the time of the *Confessiones* this principle is articulated clearly and Augustine stops speaking of simple things in the plural:

> You alone simply are. To you it is not one thing to live, another to live in blessed happiness, because you are your own blessedness.[33]

These passages demonstrate some of the deep connections between Augustine's understanding of God, the structure of the created order and contemplation, but in the early works Augustine only rarely uses these links between simplicity and number to explore or elucidate Trinitarian problems.

In Chapter 3, however, we briefly examined a text that is the first witness to the second strain of simplicity language in Augustine's thought – one that is far more central to his mature Trinitarian discussions. At *De fide et symbolo* 9. 20 Augustine comments on the idea that the Spirit might be understood as the communion of Father and Son. There are those, he tells us, who are unhappy with this idea because the union between two bodies does not seem to be a reality alongside those that it joins. If the two bodies are separated, there is no 'union' remaining. Such a perspective stems from an imagination overly informed by material imagery. In the divine substance there is nothing accidental. This can be seen, he repeats three times, only by those who are 'pure in heart' (Matt. 5.8). Augustine does not use either *simplicitas* or *simplex* here, but he does make two closely related points that henceforth always occur in extended discussion of the Trinity and divine simplicity: there is nothing accidental in the immaterial divine substance and whatever is there is necessarily God's substance:

> Let those who hold this opinion cleanse their hearts as best they can, in order to perceive that where the divine substance is concerned there cannot be anything of this kind, as if in this regard one thing could be the substance and something else could be accidental to the substance but not being the substance ... The fact is that whatever can be understood to be there necessarily is the substance.[34]

While these comments are compatible with the discussions of simplicity and unity that we have seen so far, the language used is distinct and appears here for the first time in his corpus.

---

[33] *conf.* 13. 3.4 (CCSL 27. 244).
[34] *f. et symb.* 9. 20 (CSEL 41. 26): 'sed hi tales cor mundum faciant, quantum possunt, ut uidere ualeant in dei substantia non esse aliquid tale, quasi aliud ibi sit substantia, aliud quod accidat substantiae, et non sit substantia; sed quidquid ibi intellegi potest, substantia est. uerum haec dici possunt facile et credi; uideri autem nisi corde puro quomodo se habeant, omnino non possunt'.

These arguments might be extrapolations from his earlier discussions of simplicity, but it is more likely that Augustine's focus on God's lack of accidents is the result of the *theological* reading that was his research for the *De fide*. Whereas Augustine's presentation of the links between simplicity and number finds only rare parallels in his immediate pro-Nicene Latin predecessors, his accounts of God's lack of accidents do find occasional precedent in those writers. Thus, for example, Ambrose writes:

> How can there be any created thing in God? For God is of a simple nature, not of one that is compounded or composite: *to him nothing can be added*, and he has in his nature only that which is divine [*cui nihil accedat, sed solum, quod divinum est in natura habeat sua*].[35]

The closest parallel to Augustine's usual phrasing is, however, to be found in Victorinus. In the first book of the *Adversus Arrium*, arguing that Father and Son represent potentiality and action, Victorinus remarks:

> The Son is therefore born, having to be actually and potentially just as the one who is to be potentially has action itself in that very self which is to be potentially. But take 'he has it himself' in this sense: *he does not have, but he is himself*; indeed, there all are simple [*non enim habet, sed ipsum est. Simplicia enim ibi omnia*]; but I spoke according to the Gospel: 'All that the Father has, the Son has likewise' [cf. John 16.15].[36]

Thus, the idea that Augustine drew his notion of simplicity from non-Christian Platonist sources and then uses it to articulate his developing Trinitarian theology may be too simple a story. Augustine certainly does develop a notion of simplicity in the context of his non-Christian readings, but the manner in which he uses that doctrine in Trinitarian contexts may be dependent on later reading in Christian authors. Let us now turn to *De trinitate* 5–7 and the *use* of simplicity.

PREDICATING RELATION (*TRIN.* 5. 3.4–8.9)

The overall aim of my treatment of *De trinitate* 5–7 will be to show that Augustine's presentation of the divine three as each being the fullness of the Godhead and as together being one God does not invalidate but rather depends upon the picture we have already seen in which the Father

---

[35] Ambrose, *fid.* 1. 16.106 (CSEL 78/8. 46).
[36] Victorinus, *adv. Ar.* 1. 19 (CSEL 83/1. 84–5). Similarly, note that Augustine's use of the language of substance and accidents in Trinitarian discussions finds only very occasional parallels in Latin tradition. See Tertullian, *adv. Prax.* 26; Victorinus, *adv. Ar.* 1. 22, 1. 30, 4. 2; Ambrose, *fid.* 1. 16.106, 5. 16.195, *Isaac* 5. 46. Victorinus's usages are by far the most pertinent, and the terminology is not surprisingly used extensively in his non-theological works.

eternally gives rise to Son and Spirit out of his own substance. Showing that and how this is so will require a number of steps: the first is for us to understand Augustine's use of terminology relating to relational predication in *De trinitate* 5.[37]

Augustine begins Book 5 by relating an anti-Nicene argument that whatever is said of God concerns God's substance.[38] Augustine's response is formulated via an examination of the Aristotelian categories. His first move is to deny that anything accidental may be predicated of God: 'in God there is nothing accidental, because there is nothing changeable or which can be lost'. This statement occurs only a few sentences after he has distinguished between two types of accident – *accidentia inseparabilia* (which, he tells us, are called in Greek ἀχώριστα) and *separabilia* – neither of which is true of God.[39] The former kind of accidents includes the blackness of a raven's feather which is lost only when there is no longer a feather, while the latter kind includes the blackness of a person's hair which may be lost even as the hair remains.

Although this distinction is founded in some Aristotelian texts outside the *Categories* – texts it is very unlikely Augustine knew – it is in the later commentary tradition that we find extensive discussion of these two types. Porphyry's *Isagoge* is the most likely source for Augustine's knowledge: Boethius reports that Victorinus translated the text, although that translation is lost to us.[40] Berthold Altaner's discussions of Augustine's

---

[37] *trin.* 5. 3.4. The literature on Books 5–7 is extensive. Of the recent discussions, I have found most helpful that of Brachtendorf, *Die Struktur des menschlichen Geistes nach Augustinus: Selbsreflexion und Erkenntnis Gottes in 'De Trinitate'* (Hamburg: Felix Meiner, 2000), 56–78.

[38] Even though I offer no discussions in this chapter about Augustine's possible opponents, it is helpful to remind ourselves that Augustine's arguments here are most likely aimed against the challenge of Latin Homoianism. Barnes, 'The Arians of Book V', has argued strongly that Augustine is concerned with Homoians rather than Eunomius or Aetius (which was the fairly consistent older scholarly judgement). Although Augustine knows a little of Eunomius – perhaps only moving beyond a one-word characterization of Eunomius as *dialecticus* by *trin.* 15. 20.38 – Barnes argues that there is nothing in *trin.* 5 that need be explained by exclusive reference to Eunomian doctrine. Even, for example, Augustine's interest in the title *ingenitus* in this book could easily stem from Homoian interest in the same term. See also the literature in n. 64 below. In critique of Barnes's argument Roland Kany (*Augustins Trinitätsdenken*, 168) suggests that Augustine may have known of Eunomius and anti-Eunomian arguments through such passages as Ambrose's *incar.* 9. 89ff. and *fid.* 5. 9.116, which are dependent on Basil. This is a helpful addition to the debate, but it is difficult to prove that Augustine knew they were anti-Eunomian arguments: from his reading of Ambrose he would have assumed they were fit for an anti-Homoian purpose, and Barnes shows that Homoian emphases mirrored some Eunomian emphases sufficiently for this to be so. There clearly is a point at which Augustine became aware of Heterousian theology and that knowledge may well have influenced the direction of his arguments in *trin.* 5, but we do not need to explain the book thus.

[39] *trin.* 5. 4.5 (CCSL 50. 209).

[40] See Boethius, *In Isagog.* 1. 1. With Augustine's distinction cf. Porphyry, *isag.* 5 (Busse, 12): διαιρεῖ ται δὲ εἰς δύο· τὸ μὲν γὰρ αὐτοῦ χωριστόν ἐστιν, τὸ δὲ ἀχώριστον. Jonathan Barnes,

Greek sources established the lack of any textual evidence in favour of the case that Augustine's understanding of relative predication is dependent on Gregory Nazianzen (against Chevalier's earlier argument that this was so), and there has been no scholarly defence of that possibility since.[41] Noting Augustine's probable use of Porphyry may add a little to Altaner's case: Nazianzen makes no use of this distinction between types of accidents. Augustine's argument appears to have proceeded independently of Greek sources at this point.

Augustine continues by asserting that in changeable things everything that is not predicated of substance must be predicated accidentally, even those things predicated according to relation. The names Father and Son in God, however, are said according to relation but 'there is no question here of an accident, because the one is always the Father and the other is always Son':

the terms [Father and Son] are not said according to substance, because each of them is not said with reference to himself, but both of these are used reciprocally, each with reference to the other. Nor are they used according to accident, because that which is called Father and that which is called Son is eternal and unchangeable in them. Consequently, although it is different to be the Father and to be the Son, still there is no divided substance, because this is not said according to substance, but according to relation. And this relation is not an accident, because it is unchangeable.[42]

---

[40] *Porphyry: Introduction* (Oxford: Clarendon Press, 2003), 220ff., offers an excellent discussion of this distinction. At *adv. Ar.* 1. 30 Victorinus refuses the idea that God and God's image relate as substance and accident and then appears to make use of Porphyrian terminology in speaking of substance as a *subiectum* with inseparable accidents. See Pierre Hadot, *Porphyre et Victorinus* (Paris: Études Augustiniennes, 1968), 2: 21.

[41] See Berthold Altaner, 'Augustinus und Gregor von Nazianz, Gregor von Nyssa', in *Kleine Patristische Schriften*, TU 83 (Berlin: Akademie-Verlag, 1967), 277–85, arguing against Irénée Chevalier's *Saint Augustin et la pensée grecque. Les relations trinitaires* (Fribourg: Collectanea Friburgensia, 1940). Altaner sees the only presence of Nazianzen in *trin* at 15. 20.38, where *or.* 29. 6 seems to be echoed (the same argument appears at *c. s. Arian.* 1. 2; Altaner argues against the possibility that Augustine is dependent on Ps. Rufinus, *fid.* 53). Other than this, Augustine knows Nazianzen only in Rufinus's surviving translations as a believer in original sin. For some up-to-date reflections in English on Augustine's knowledge of 'the Cappadocians' see Joseph Lienhard, 'Augustine of Hippo, Basil of Caesarea, and Gregory Nazianzen', in George Demacopoulos and Aristotle Papanikolaou (eds.), *Orthodox Readings of Augustine* (Crestwood, NY: St Vladimirs Seminary Press, 2008), 81–99.

[42] *trin.* 5. 5.6 (CCSL 50. 210–11): 'non secundum substantiam haec dicuntur quia non quisque eorum ad se ipsum sed ad inuicem atque ad alterutrum ista dicuntur; neque secundum accidens quia et quod dicitur pater et quod dicitur filius aeternum atque incommutabile est eis. Quamobrem quamuis diuersum sit patrem esse et filium esse, non est tamen diuersa substantia quia hoc non secundum substantiam dicuntur sed secundum relatiuum quod tamen relatiuum non est accidens quia non est mutabile'.

This, then, is the core of Augustine's argument about predication in *De trinitate* 5: in God titles may be predicated of the 'persons' according to relation, but such titles predicate nothing accidental. To understand this passage better we should note that Roland Teske has argued for the importance of a string of passages in *De trinitate* 5–7 in which Augustine distinguishes between speaking of God, thinking of God and the being of God. No speech about God is able to express God's being. Thought may do better than speech, however, if we can imagine God as far as possible as 'great without quantity, good without quality … whoever thinks of God in this way, even though he does not discover what God is, nevertheless, avoids as far as possible thinking of him what he is not'.[43] Thus, as Teske writes:

> at the level of speech about God (*dicere*), many statements about God may seem to designate an accident in God, but at the level of thought about God (*cogitare*) they must not be so understood, because in the being of God (*esse*) there is no accident.[44]

In the light of this distinction we should note that in *De trinitate* 5–7 Augustine speaks with most ease and clarity about patterns of predication. Hence he frequently speaks of a term or phrase being 'spoken' (*dicitur*) according to substance or relation. The unique pattern of predication that he thinks should obtain in the case of the Trinity is certainly founded on what he thinks must be true about God's being, but he is very cautious about laying out the structure of that being as if it could be easily thought. Thus we must be precise about the subject of discussions about relation before we attribute too easily to the *De trinitate* a clear and fully formed account of the divine three existing in relation.

The passage from Book 5 that we are considering here offers one of the most useful illustrations of the care we must show. The focus of the passage is what is 'said' about Father and Son, but Augustine also speaks tersely of the ontological conditions which make those particular patterns of predication necessary. That which we call Father and Son is eternal and unchangeable 'in them'. The reserve of this first statement is notable: the text offers a further illustration of Teske's principle in its distinction between the scriptural term 'Father' and 'that which is called Father' about whom we can say so little. But we are, nevertheless, now

---

[43] *trin.* 5. 1.2.
[44] Roland Teske, 'Properties of God and the Predicaments in *De Trinitate* V', *The Modern Schoolman* 59 (1981), 9, see also 3–5. For his distinction, Teske refers to *trin.* 5. 3.4, 6. 6.8, 7. 4.7 and 15. 5.8.

speaking directly about that reality. Augustine continues with the convoluted phrase 'it is different to be the Father and to be the Son'. His choice of vocabulary here is careful: he speaks of the *esse* of Father and Son, thus reserving the ability to say that the difference involved does not mean a divided *substantia*. Why? Because the relation of which we speak when we name 'Father' and 'Son' is immutable and not accidental. The statement must be read with care. Augustine certainly says that the relationship between Father and Son is intrinsic to what it is to be either of the two, but he does not (yet) speak directly of either existing *as* relation: his claims remain cautious and tentative. We will have to wait a number of years before he says anything more precise in this regard.[45]

After an extended refutation of the anti-Nicene argument that 'begotten' and 'unbegotten' might be predicated according to substance even if Father and Son are not, Augustine again speaks a little more directly about the characteristics of the divine being that render possible this pattern of predication:

> Thus, let us above all hold to this: whatever is said in reference to itself concerning that divine and exalted sublimity is said according to substance [*substantialiter*]; but what is said in reference to something [*ad aliquid*] is not said according to substance but relation [*non substantialiter, sed relative*]. The power of the 'of one substance' in the Father and the Son and the Holy Spirit is so great that everything which is said concerning individuals with reference to themselves is understood as adding up not to a plural number but to the singular [*tantamque vim esse eiusdem substantiae in patre et filio et spiritu sancto ut quidquid de singulis ad se ipsos dicitur non pluraliter in summa sed singulariter accipiatur*].[46]

The foundation of the argument in this quotation is Augustine's assertion that the unity of nature is of such a force that anything which can be substantively predicated of a divine 'person' is said in the singular of the three. Each is 'God' but there is only one 'God'. The manner in which he asserts this is noteworthy. Augustine does not argue from the characteristics of a shared nature *per se* – as for example Gregory of Nyssa might argue that to say three human beings is technically inaccurate because 'human being' should properly be predicated in the

---

[45] The statement that their 'substance' is undivided is highly traditional. Augustine's insistence that this is so because the relationship between Father and Son is eternal should not be taken as indicating that he sees that relationship as intrinsic to a prior unitary substance. Indeed, we should note his willingness to speak so directly about the fact that *Patrem esse* and *Filium esse* are distinct, and we should recognize that here he actually says very little about how the eternal relationship between them does not divide the substance. For further clarity we will have to look elsewhere.

[46] *trin.* 5. 8.9 (CCSL 50. 215).

singular of a group of people[47] – but by pointing to the peculiar quality of the unity to which the *homoousion* points. It is the 'force' of the *homoousion* which demands the peculiar patterns of predication that pertain in this unique case. We come to the heart of Augustine's argument when we ask *why* the *homoousion* demands this unique pattern of predication.

Augustine moves towards his answer by discussing the possible attribution to God of the nine categories subsequent to substance: quantity, quality, relation, position, habit, time, place, action, passion.[48] All can be used – and are used by Scripture – only metaphorically, other than that of action. Indeed, God alone may be described as acting or making in the truest sense and there is in him no potency. It is because of this that each of the divine three is, for example, omnipotent, but there is only one omnipotent. And because of this also:

> For God, to be is not one thing, and to be great another; on the contrary, for him to be is the same as for him to be great. Therefore, just as we do not speak of three essences, so we do not speak of three greatnesses.[49]

Lacking any accidents, God must be any qualities we predicate of God. But if so, Augustine implies, there cannot be three divine beings each of whom possesses the quality greatness, there can only be one greatness itself. Thus, under the conditions of divine, simple existence, even though faith demands that we speak of the Father generating one who is 'of the same substance', that act of generation must result in two who are one in substance, one in the indivisible unity of greatness itself (and this follows also for the breathing of the Spirit). As we shall see, Augustine offers this so far rather gnomic argument at greater length in Book 7. But before we can turn to those texts we must see how Augustine rejects the usefulness of genus and species terminologies in our attempts to grasp the divine communion.

Before turning to this task, let us return for a moment to Augustine's vocabulary. As we will see in a number of cases, the language of the *De trinitate* should not be taken as paradigmatic of even Augustine's mature corpus. The adverb *relative* and its adjectival cognates are not only rare in Augustine's theological contemporaries, they are also used only in very particular contexts in Augustine's corpus. Of the eighty-one uses that an LLT search identifies, only three do not come from Books 5–7 of the

---

[47] For example, Gregory of Nyssa, *Ablab.* GNO 3/1. 42. My comment is not intended as a judgement about relative usefulness, merely to indicate the different uses of nature language in play.
[48] *trin.* 5. 7.8.   [49] *trin.* 5. 8.9 (CCSL 50. 216).

De trinitate.⁵⁰ The language for speaking of relational predication that Augustine develops here stays here. It finds no use, for example, in his sermons. This observation becomes more interesting when we compare his use of *relative* with that of *ad aliquid*. This latter term is a synonym for the former and is a fairly obvious translation for the Greek πρός τι used in this sense (Aristotle's own term for the category). Augustine uses *ad aliquid* in this sense a number of times in these books of the *De trinitate*, and also in Books 10 and 15, but in Trinitarian discussions only twice outside this work.⁵¹ Thus when Augustine comments to Evodius that only a few (*pauci*) will understand the argument of the *De trinitate*, he likely refers not only to the complexity of the argument, but also to the fact that he has developed his argument in conversation with resources unknown to most of those to whom he preaches.⁵²

PERSON AND NATURE (*TRIN.* 5. 8.9–9.10 AND 7. 4.7–6.11)

So, then, on to Augustine's rejection of person and substance/nature language as a set of ideas with which we can fashion an account of the divine communion and unity. I will be concerned here with a section in the middle of Book 5 and the parallel discussion in the second half of Book 7. Immediately after the last passage I quoted above, Augustine offers this famous statement:

I give the name essence to what the Greeks call *ousia*, but which we more generally designate as substance. They indeed also call it *hypostasis*, but I do not know what different meaning they wish to give to *ousia* and *hypostasis*. Certain of our writers, who discuss these questions in the Greek language are wont to say *mian ousian*, *treis hypostaseis* which in Latin means one essence, and three substances … But because the usage of our language has already decided that the same thing is to be understood when we say essence, as when we say substance, we do not venture to use the formula one essence and three substances, but rather one essence or substance and three persons. Such is the way in which it is expressed by many Latin commentators, whose opinion carries great weight and who have discussed this subject, since they were unable to find a more suitable terminology for putting into words that which they understood without words.⁵³

---

⁵⁰ See *trin.* 15. 3.5, *civ.* 11. 10, *ep.* 170. 6. It is interesting also to note that the adjective *relative* appears only in Augustine and Martianus Capella (at *nupt. phil.* 4. 372, 378, 379; after consulting LLT, BTL and AL). Perhaps Augustine and Martianus knew a translation of the Categories that does not survive.
⁵¹ See *Io. ev. tr.* 39. 4 and *ep.* 238. 2.14. Both of these texts are discussed in Chapter 9.
⁵² *ep.* 169. 13. ⁵³ *trin.* 5. 8.9–9.10 (CCSL 50. 216–17).

Augustine sees the terminologies of person, substance and essence as necessary only to indicate the irreducibility of both unity and 'persons' in the face of heresy. As usual Augustine favours those anti-Monarchian traditions that rely on non-technical terminology. He continues,

> For, in truth, since the Father is not the Son and the Son is not the Father, and the Holy Spirit is neither the Father nor the Son, then certainly there are three … But when it is asked 'three what?' then the great poverty from which our language suffers becomes apparent. But the formula three persons has been coined, not in order to give a complete explanation by means of it, but in order that we might not be obliged to remain silent.[54]

This brief comment from Book 5 needs to be placed in the broader context of the extensive discussion of genus, species and individual terminologies in Book 7. In a close study of Augustine's argument, Richard Cross has argued that Augustine understands the structure and implications of such language well, but consciously rejects its usefulness. Augustine first rejects the idea that God subsists relationally because, by definition, to say that something subsists is to say that it exists in itself and not in relation to anything else. But this must also be true of 'person', so why do we not say 'one person'?[55] We cannot say 'one person' because the term carries with it connotations of non-relationality that are not apparent in truly relational terms such as 'Father.'

The overall task remains, however, to find a generic or specific term with which to answer the question 'three what?', but no such term is to be found.[56] The core of Cross's argument is that Augustine's extensive discussion of this question draws on a principle articulated clearly in Porphyry's *Isagoge*:

> Substance is itself a genus. Under it is body, and under body, animate body, under which is animal; under animal is rational animal, under which is man, and under man are Socrates and Plato and particular men. Of these items, substance is the most general and is only a genus, while man is the most special and is only a species. Body is a species of substance and genus of animate body. Animate body is a species of body, and a genus of rational animal … man is a species of rational animal, but not a genus of particular men – only a species. Everything which is proximate before the individuals will be only a species and not also a genus.[57]

---

[54] *trin.* 5. 9.10 (CCSL 50. 217).
[55] *trin.* 7. 4.9 and 7. 6.11. See Richard Cross, '*Quid tres*? On What Precisely Augustine Professes Not to Understand in *De Trinitate* V and VII', *HTR* 100 (2007), 215–32, here 218.
[56] *trin.* 7. 4.7.   [57] Porphyry, *isag.* 2 (Busse, 4–5).

This set of relationships has frequently been represented in a diagrammatic form known as Porphyry's 'Tree'. For our purposes we need only note that anything identified by a term which specifies a species can necessarily also be identified by a corresponding genus term and vice versa. The existence of a species predication implies a corresponding genus predication, and vice versa. For example, if one can say 'Socrates is a human being', one can also say that 'Socrates is an animal', and for any subject, if one can say it is an animal, one can also assign it to a subordinate species. Moreover, if it is true that Socrates and Augustine are two humans, it is true that they are two animals. Cross notes that a number of writers articulate this principle in late antiquity, but alongside the earlier evidence we found in discussing types of accident, this parallel strengthens the possibility that much of the logical argumentation in these books is drawn from Victorinus's translation of the *Isagoge*.

In *De trinitate* 7 Augustine asserts that 'person' must name either species or genus. Initially trying out 'person' as a genus term (because, despite the obvious distinctions, the term may be used of both God and humanity), Augustine goes on to add that because the three 'persons' lack 'diversity of nature' they must be of the same species and genus, but there is no term to describe the species into which the divine persons fall.[58] A little later Augustine argues that neither is essence the genus of which the persons are a species, nor is essence a genus and persons individuals. In the first case, the Porphyrian principle does not hold because we cannot infer many instances of the genus from many instances of the species (we cannot say that the phrase 'three persons' permits our speaking of three essences). In the second case, not only does the same problem obtain (we cannot reason from many individuals to many members of a species to many members of a genus), but we would also have a genus (essence) and individuals, but no species term.[59] At the same time, we cannot argue that the divine essence is a species of which the 'persons' are individuals. This, Augustine argues, is problematic because a species is always divisible into individuals and the divine essence should not be understood to be divisible in this way.[60] In all of these cases, the inherited principles of Trinitarian faith demand patterns of speech that defeat any attempt to interpret these terms according to Porphyry's logic.

Augustine suggests only one possibility remains: 'Therefore, we do not use these terms according to genus and species, but as it were according

---

[58] *trin.* 7. 4.7.   [59] *trin.* 7. 6.11.   [60] *trin.* 7. 6.11.

to matter that is common and the same [*quasi secundum communeum eamdemque materiam*]'.⁶¹ In the case of this more general analogy, Augustine argues, the problems attendant on genus and species language evaporate. Of course, to talk in this way we must attend closely to the deep failings of such language. Not only must we avoid thinking of God materially, but

> nor do we, therefore, call the Trinity three persons or substances, one essence and one God, as though three somethings subsist from one matter which [*tamquam ex una materia tria quaedam subsistant*], whatever it is, is unfolded in these three. For there is nothing else of this essence besides the Trinity [*non enim aliquid aliud eius essentiae est praeter istam trinitatem*] … [In material things] one man is not as much as three men together; and two men are something more than one man … but in God it is not so; for the Father, the Son and the Holy Spirit together is not a greater essence than the Father alone.⁶²

In the first place, then, Cross provides further evidence for why the mature Augustine would continue to prefer anti-Monarchian traditions of summary. In the second place, Cross's argument emphasizes the importance of our looking elsewhere if we are to understand how Augustine attempts to understand the unity and diversity of the persons.⁶³ In reality the loose material analogy Augustine offers at the culmination of this argument against genus and species language is not intended as a dense resource from which we might draw any extended reflection on the terminology of substance/essence/nature and person. While, when its material and temporal associations are abstracted, this analogy is largely consonant with the account of the Father's giving rise to Son and Spirit from his own essence that Augustine develops, it is not one that plays any significant role in his Trinitarian discussions here or elsewhere. Its function seems to be primarily rhetorical, emphasizing how far we must depart from genus and species concepts if we are to see the traditional terminology as logically coherent. We have already seen some hints towards a conception of the divine three existing eternally in non-accidental relation; these hints will not, however, be developed by extensive discussion of genus/species terminologies, but by further reflection on what it means for the Son to be 'God from God' and 'Wisdom from Wisdom'.

---

⁶¹ *trin.* 7. 6.11 (CCSL 50. 264).   ⁶² *trin.* 7. 6.11 (CCSL 50. 264–5).
⁶³ Cross refers to Chevalier's *Saint Augustin et la pensée grecque* without referencing Altaner's discussion (see above, n. 41). Nevertheless, Cross's main point still stands: Augustine understands such language and rejects it. Whether any of the Cappadocians endorses such language without reservation is a distinct question.

WISDOM FROM WISDOM (*TRIN*. 6. 1.1–7. 2.3)

In a discussion which runs through Book 6 and the first half of 7, Augustine explores the divine unity through articulating the Nicene language of Light from Light and God from God against the background of the divine simplicity. The shape of this argument is also governed by the need to offer convincing exegesis of texts long the subject of polemic and of pro-Nicene exploration. 1 Corinthians 1.24 takes centre stage, but we should also note the significance of John 17.3 and some possible allusions to John 14.10.

Augustine's point of departure in Book 6 is what he describes as earlier Nicene exegesis of 1 Corinthians 1.24 in which Father and Son are said to be co-eternal because the Father must always have his Wisdom present to him.[64] For Augustine such an exegesis fails because the Father is not then God in himself but only God together with the Son. The Father would only be the begetter of Wisdom, not Wisdom itself. Moreover, one could not call the Son 'Wisdom from Wisdom' and 'Light from Light' if the Father is not himself Light and Wisdom.[65] Augustine leaves this Nicene language aside for now and turns to a parallel problem with describing the Father and Son as only God together. Suggestively he twice parallels using God of Father only insofar as he is with his Son with saying that they are 'in' each other.[66] In Chapter 3 I noted that Augustine never makes significant use of the 'in' language of John 14.10: it is then interesting here that Augustine, while not attacking such language head on (it is after all language that is both biblical and strongly present in his predecessors), clearly finds it inadequate as a primary theological terminology.

The fundamental problem with the exegesis of 1 Corinthians 1.24 he has criticized, and with this use of 'in' language, is now stated clearly. Neither accords well with what Augustine takes to be the significance of the Nicene language of 'God from God':

Hence when phrases like God from God, Light from Light and others of a similar meaning are used, it is just as though one were to say, 'this, which is not the Son without the Father, comes from this which is not the Father without the

---

[64] Essential background reading to my discussion here is Michel Barnes, 'De Trinitate VI and VII: Augustine and the Limits of Nicene Orthodoxy', *AugStud* 38 (2007), 189–202. See also the discussion of sources in A.-M. La Bonnardière, 'Recherche sur les antécédents, les sources et la rédaction du livre VI du De trinitate de Saint Augustin', *AÉPHÉ* 83 (1974–5), 202–11.
[65] *trin.* 6. 1.1–1.2.
[66] *trin.* 6. 2.3 (CCSL 50. 229–30): 'quidquid autem aliud dicitur, cum Filio dicitur, vel potius in Filio ... et quod dictum est in principio erat Verbum; in Patre erat Verbum, intelligtur'.

Son, that is, this light which is not light without the Father, comes from this light, namely the Father, which is not light without the Son'.[67]

In this complex language – on which, luckily, he soon advances! – Augustine tries to present Father and Son as irreducible, as both truly 'Light' (and hence capable of being described as 'Light from Light') even as they also exist in the eternal relationship of Father and Son.

How, then, are we to understand the unity of God? Augustine first argues that Father and Son must be equal in all 'qualities' predicated of them or they will be unequal in all. In the human soul the virtues are identical:

> How much more so, then, is this true of that unchangeable and eternal substance, incomparably more simple than the human soul. For in the human soul to be is not the same as to be strong or prudent or just or temperate. But for God to be is the same as to be strong or to be just or to be wise, and to be whatever else you may say of that simple multiplicity or that multiple simplicity, whereby his substance is signified [*de illa simplici multiplicitate uel multiplici simplicitate dixeris quo substantia eius significetur*]. When we say God from God how are we to understand it?[68]

Thus the Father cannot have any 'qualities' in a greater degree than the Son. Once again, it is the same basic statement of divine simplicity that grounds Augustine's discussion, and once again the pivotal question concerns the nature of the Son's generation as 'God from God'.

Augustine turns now to a discussion of the Spirit's unity with Father and Son that I will consider in Chapter 10. To follow our argument we must leap forward to the end of Book 6. For Augustine, the perfection of divinity must govern our understanding of the divine generation:

> Since, therefore, the Father alone, or the Son alone, or the Holy Spirit alone is just as great as the Father, the Son and the Holy Spirit together he is not to be called threefold in any sense [*triplex*]. Bodies, on the contrary, increase by a union of themselves … In God himself, therefore, when the equal Son adheres to the equal Father, or the equal Holy Spirit to the Father and the Son, God does not thereby become greater than each one separately, for there is nothing whereby that perfection can increase. But he is perfect whether the Father, or the Son, or the Holy Spirit; and God the Father, the Son and the Holy Spirit is perfect, and, therefore, he is a Trinity rather than tripartite [*et ideo trinitas potius quam triplex*].[69]

---

[67] *trin.* 6. 2.3 (CCSL 50. 231).   [68] *trin.* 6. 4.6 (CCSL 50. 234).
[69] *trin.* 6. 7.9–8.9 (CCSL 50. 237–8). Cf. *trin.* 15. 17.28.

This text needs to be read as a further gloss on the meaning of 'God from God'. Augustine differentiates divine generation from a generation that results in any increase – as is the case with material bodies. The three together are thus identical to any one if the term 'God' can be used of them all. Augustine here also considers the unity of the three not by envisaging a substance in which the three share, but by speaking of their mutual activity of adhering to one another.

At the end of this passage Augustine distinguishes between *trinitas* and *triplex*:

> Nor since he is a Trinity [*trinitas*] is he, therefore, tripartite [*triplex*]; otherwise the Father alone or the Son alone would be less than the Father and the Son together. Although, to tell the truth, it is difficult to see how one can speak of the Father alone or the Son alone, since the Father is with the Son and the Son with the Father always and inseparably, not that both are the Father or both the Son, but because they are always mutually in one another and neither is alone.[70]

Augustine here takes the term *triplex* as implying a being divided into three parts: *trinitas* thus uniquely refers to the unity of Father, Son and Spirit. Two other aspects of this passage deserve comment. Augustine confesses that his discussion of what must be true of the Father alone (rather than of the Father understood with the Son) has an abstract quality because Father and Son are inseparable. It is fruitful for our reflection on the Trinity to ask whether we can call the Father God by himself, but Augustine is clear that it is also an abstraction from reality. It is also interesting that Augustine is willing to gloss the existence of the divine three with one another as an existence 'in' one another. Despite his (at the very least) expressed uncertainty about this language, it now returns, carefully qualified by its new context.

De trinitate 6 is thus an odd book. Augustine circles the issues that stimulate its production: he isolates the basic principles that must guide our attempts to think the generation of God from God, but these principles do not yet crystallize into a summary description.[71] Before we move

---

[70] *trin.* 6. 7.9 (CCSL 50. 237–8).
[71] The discussion of John 17.3 ('Now this is eternal life, that they may know you, the one true God and him whom you have sent, Jesus Christ') at *trin.* 6. 9.10, which concludes the main section of Book 6, stands as a symbol of these unresolved questions. Perhaps we should say, Augustine suggests, that the Father is the one true God, but this is also a title that may be used of each person as well as of the Trinity itself. Although this exegesis is the one Augustine adopts, he offers it only as a suggestion, going on to try out the possibility of reordering the whole verse as 'that they may know you, and him whom you have sent, Jesus Christ, the one true God'. This still begs the question of why the Spirit is not mentioned, and we should surely presuppose the presence of all where one is mentioned? These questions Augustine identifies as being reserved for a fuller

on to see that crystallization at the beginning of Book 7, however, we should note the famous coda to Book 6. The passage is usually commented on because of its explicit reference to Hilary's summative phrase 'eternity in the Father, the form in the Image, and the use in the Gift' (*aeternitas in Patre, species in imagine, usus in munere*).[72]

Reflecting on Hilary's language for the Son, Augustine tells us that this image is called form because of the perfect harmony, primal beauty, equality and similarity between Father and Son. The image is also the supreme intellect in which living and knowing and being are one. In this intellect – this 'art' – God knows all things. The Spirit or Gift is the love stemming from the embrace (*complexus*) of Father and Son which pours out onto all creatures. This summary incorporates a variety of themes from his work in the 386–93 period. The Son is *intellectus* and *forma* – intellect as the highest life identical with its existence; the unity of Father and Son is one of perfect harmony, equality and beauty; the Spirit is the love and embrace of these two. It is interesting that Augustine is able, on occasion, to turn to this language even in his mature work. There is, then, a clear continuity between Augustine's early and his later Trinitarian discussions (even given the change in language we traced in 393), especially with regard to his views of each divine person's particular characteristics, their *propria*. The change that we have seen involves a recasting of his initial Trinitarian themes (themselves drawn in part from earlier Latin pro-Nicene theology) in the light of a far greater appreciation of the central thrusts of Latin and Nicene tradition. Augustine has also developed a far more sophisticated account of how the divine economy reveals and is founded in the eternal Trinitarian ordering. But as we see in this chapter and the next two, Augustine is still in the midst of development, still thinking through the character of the divine life itself.

Augustine returns to the heart of his argument at the beginning of *De trinitate* 7 and refocuses his investigation of 1 Corinthians 1.24. He begins with a further long and convoluted account of the problems which follow from arguing that the Father is God only with or in relation to the Son. This culminates in the following assertions:

---

treatment at a future time. In a sign of Augustine's patchy final redaction of the treatise as a whole although the theological questions are faced again in Books 7 and 15, these specific verses receive no further extended discussion in the work.

[72] *trin.* 6. 10.11 (CCSL 50. 240–1). Augustine's text of Hilary does not quite correspond to the critical edition's *infinitas in aeterno, species …*, Hilary, *fid*. 2. 1 (SC 443. 276). On the expression, see Jean Doignon, '"Spiritus Sanctus … usus in munere" (Hilaire de Poitiers, *De Trinitate* 2,1)', *RThL* 12 (1981), 235–40; Studer, *Augustins De Trinitate*, 189–95.

every essence which is spoken of relatively is also something even if the relationship is excluded [*aliquid excepto relatiuo*] ... if the Father also is not something in respect to himself, then he can by no means be spoken of in relation to something else.[73]

Once again, what Augustine has to say about the category of relation is primarily about a category of predication. But this does not mean that he is not making an ontological point about the character of the relationship between Father and Son. Finding his point difficult to articulate, Augustine now summarizes and he does so by attempting once more to spell out the consequences of divine simplicity. Wisdom, he begins, is wise in itself. Those who become wise share in Wisdom, but it in no way changes as they do so. Thus the Father cannot be wise by the Wisdom he begot, and he is Wisdom itself, the cause of his own being and of his being wise. In the Father Wisdom is the same as essence:

(1.2) Therefore, the Father himself is also Wisdom, and the Son is called the Wisdom of the Father in the same sense as he is called the Light of the Father. That is to say, just as he is Light of Light, and both are one Light, so he is understood be Wisdom of Wisdom, and both are one Wisdom; therefore they are also one essence, for to be and to be wise is one and the same [*quia hoc est ibi esse quod sapere*] ... and because in that simplicity to be wise is not something other than to be, there wisdom is the same as essence ...

(2.3) since Wisdom is spoken of in reference to itself [*ad se dicitur*] – for Wisdom is wise by itself – then essence is also pointed out, and that 'to be' of his which is 'to be wise'. Thus, the Father and the Son together are one wisdom, because they are one essence, and taken singly wisdom is from wisdom as essence is from essence [*sicut essentia de essentia*]. Therefore, although the Father is not the Son and the Son is not the Father, or although the former is unbegotten, but the latter is begotten, they do not on that account cease to be one essence, since only the relationship between them is made known by these names [*quia his nominibus relatiua eorum ostenduntur*]. But both together are one wisdom and one essence, since there, to be is the same as to be wise.[74]

Augustine's argument is simple, but its consequences profound. At its heart is an application of his basic understanding of divine simplicity to the question of how the Son's generation from the Father also involves the Father and Son being of one substance. Both Father and Son are wisdom, because wisdom is a term parallel to light in the phrase 'Light from Light'. When Father or Son is said to be 'Wisdom' this means 'Wisdom itself'. Neither participates in wisdom because, if both are divine, then to be and

---

[73] *trin.* 7. 1.2 (CCSL 50. 247–8). [74] *trin.* 7. 1.2–2.3 (CCSL 50. 249–50).

to be wise are the same for both. This is so, as he points out a number of times in these books, because of wider principles from the theology of creation and salvation: God is the source of all wisdom and is the wisdom itself in whom we seek to participate. But consequently, although the language of faith demands that we say that Father and Son are distinct, we are also driven to assert that they must be one in the necessarily indivisible one wisdom itself. Because to be and to be wise are identical, the Son as Wisdom must be Wisdom itself, as is the Father.[75] In the context of the divine simplicity, therefore, it becomes possible to imagine the generation of another without division, a generation which results in two who are non-identical even as they must also be one. Thus the Father is not wise because his Wisdom is with him: he is wise because he is Wisdom itself. Augustine has shaped an account of the divine generation by means of considering what it means to speak of God from God given the simple principle that God is what God is said to possess and from his fundamental assumption that there must be one source of all. We must, however, be careful here: Augustine does not imagine that we can grasp the dynamics of such a divine generation at other than a very formal level – we have no created parallel that offers anything other than a distant likeness. And yet, if we do thus grasp the paradox of distinction and unity that lies at the heart of this exposition, Augustine thinks that we have grown in understanding and begun to see a little more clearly the plausibility and rationality of the divine.

Almost seven centuries after the *De trinitate*, Anselm of Canterbury speaks of the Father giving rise to Son and Spirit as a 'repetition of eternity in eternity'.[76] One and the same simple eternity is repeated: the Father gives rise to two who are everything that the Father is and thus each is the fullness of the Godhead. At the same time, this repetition occurs 'in' eternity and does not give rise to other 'eternities' separated in time or space, eternities *extra* to the simple eternity that is God. The Father's repetition of himself involves no division in time or space and can involve no division in the one eternity. The language is Anselm's own (with perhaps some debt to Boethius),[77] but nicely parallels key aspects

---

[75] See, for example, *trin.* 5. 10.11. In Chapter 9 I take up in more detail Augustine's consequent portrayal of each divine person as possessing the fullness of the divine rational life that is hinted at in these arguments.

[76] Anselm, *incar.* 15 (Schmitt, 2: 33): 'Deus non est aliud quam ipsa simplex aeternitas. Aeternitates autem plures intelligi nequeunt. Nam si plures sunt, aut sunt extra se inuicem aut sunt in se inuicem. Sed nihil est extra aeternitatem … Si uero in se inuicem plures esse dicuntur, sciendum est quia quotienscumque repetatur aeternitas in aeternitate, non est nisi una et eadem aeternitas'.

[77] Cf. Boethius, *trin.* 3.

of Augustine's picture. Anslem, however, does not directly aver here to Nicaea's language or to the Father generating from his own substance, thus pointing us back to the very traditional foundations of Augustine's distinctive and novel argument.

Augustine's relationship to the earlier Nicene reading of 1 Corinthians 1.24 that he rejects in *De trinitate* 6 and 7 is thus fascinatingly complex. It is tempting to describe that relationship in terms of a distinction between accounts in which the Son is eternally with the Father as his power and wisdom, and those in which there is one divine power and wisdom 'shared' by the persons. It is true that Augustine has rejected those earlier exegeses because he sees them as implying that the Father can be called God only with Son and Spirit. But it is also true that Augustine's account may be seen as strengthening rather than moving beyond the originally Athanasian exegesis which sees Word and Spirit as the Father's own, as necessarily sharing an *ousia* with the one who is their source. Nevertheless, Augustine strengthens the heart of this tradition insofar as he presents the Father as fully God, as Wisdom itself and as the eternal source of Son and Spirit. The Son shares the Father's *substantia* because he is Wisdom from Wisdom, essence from essence. But under the conditions of divine existence this means that Father and Son must be one in the one reality that is Wisdom itself.

At the same time, a question looms. What is the relationship between this account of the Father's giving rise to Son and Spirit and Augustine's hints towards an account of the divine three as essentially and eternally being in relation? In previous scholarship Augustine's tentative suggestions about the immutable relations of the Godhead in *De trinitate* 5 have been treated as far more clearly developed than is warranted, while the main thrust of *De trinitate* 6–7, culminating in the argument I have examined in this section of the chapter, has been oddly neglected. The two arguments are complementary, but I suggest the *De trinitate* gives us few clues as to how. The goal of the next two chapters is to show how Augustine does provide just the clues we need, but only elsewhere.

APPROPRIATION (*TRIN*. 7. 3.4)

Before ending this chapter, however, one further topic calls our attention. Augustine presents his conclusion that 'wisdom' is a term which refers to essence as a logical deduction from scriptural language, but in the very next section of Book 7, Augustine asks why Scripture uses the term to refer to something begotten or created.⁷⁸ Augustine thus finds himself negotiating the technique later centuries will come to know as 'appropriation', the technique that Du Roy, for one, identifies as one of the true marks of Augustine's failure.⁷⁹ Against the background of Books 5–7 read as I have suggested, we see a very different picture of the doctrine: it is one I shall briefly introduce here and then return to in Chapter 10.

Augustine sees appropriation not as an exegetical technique, but as a mode of teaching employed by Scripture.⁸⁰ In particular, it is mode of teaching by which Scripture slowly reveals to us what it means for the Son and Spirit to be 'of God'. Here, for example, Augustine argues that, in the vast majority of cases, Scripture speaks of Wisdom as begotten or made by God. Why, when Father and Spirit as well as Son must be Wisdom? Wisdom is eternally spoken by God as the Word, as his own Word, in order that the Father who speaks may reveal himself and his Wisdom. The distinct Word and Wisdom reveals the Father truly only because the Father has shared all that he is with his consequently consubstantial Son and Image.

We should remember that, throughout this passage, Augustine assumes that we are asking why Wisdom is predicated of one whom we know also to be Son and Christ. Thus when he asks about the scriptural tactic of appropriation, he is asking what do the terms Wisdom, Power and Light, which he mentions here, add to that reality we already know by its unique titles and mission? The answer seems to be that each appropriated title emphasizes the ontological equality and unity of Father and Son, and each may reveal how aspects of the Son's saving work depend upon the Son's equality to the Father, the manner in which he is from or of the Father. Thus Scripture's practice of appropriation is, for Augustine, intimately connected with Scripture's deployment of his second exegetical rule, the rule (explored in Chapter 7) that certain texts pertain only to the Son being 'of God'. Scripture attributes certain titles true of each of the divine three primarily to one, in order to reveal the character of the divine

---

[78] *trin.* 7. 3.4.
[79] The verb *appropriare* is not used for this feature of Trinitarian discourse until the twelfth century.
[80] It is important to note that Augustine here is not discussing appropriation understood as the attribution of acts (such as creation or salvation or becoming incarnate) to a particular person, but only the attribution of titles. Augustine almost always approaches questions concerning why Father, Son or Spirit is said to act in a particular case by reflecting on the appropriateness of such predication given Scripture's general pattern of identifying each, and also by reflecting on the inseparable operation of the Trinity.

communion and the dependence of Son and Spirit upon (and their equality with) the Father.

Thus, the character of the example the Son offers to us in his mission depends, for Augustine here, on our accepting that the same Son is consubstantial with the Father and that he is Mediator because following the road laid out by his humanity will lead us to his divinity, lead us to contemplation of his divinity and thus of the Father. Only as truly God can the Image and Mediator direct us towards God alone, rather than to the following of one inferior. Although Augustine's main concern here is with the Son – as Wisdom is the focus of his discussion – he offers parallel brief comments about the Spirit. First, Augustine exhorts us to follow the one mediator who can lead us to his divinity, but he does so by exhorting us to rely on the grace of the Spirit 'shed abroad in our hearts'. Then, second, he notes that the Spirit does not dwell in us, his temple (alluding to Rom. 8.9; 1Cor. 3.16) as a servant, but with the result that we are not our own but God's (1Cor. 6.19). Thus, Augustine is arguing, if somewhat gnomically, that Scripture's naming of the Spirit as the highest Love joining Father and Son (and by implication as Light and Wisdom) enables us to understand the Spirit's mission as the immediate transforming presence of God. We will return to the question of the Spirit in Chapter 10, but this brief discussion has shown that there is a close parallel between the modes of Scripture's speech about the divine three and the character of the divine missions (as explored in Chapter 7). Son and Spirit reveal their dependence on and unity with the Father – and only thus can the nature of salvation and the relationship between Creator and creation be grasped; Scripture names Son and Spirit by terms that must be true of each of the divine three in order that the true character of their status as from or of God is known and thus the character of salvation grasped and true faith, hope and love inculcated.

CHAPTER 9

Showing and seeing

From the argument so far we can draw out three key principles of Augustine's Trinitarian ontology. First, in God there is nothing accidental. Second, each of the divine three is irreducible and the fullness of God, even as the divine three are together the fullness of God. Third, the Father eternally gives rise to the Son and the Spirit from his own substance or essence such that there is a communion of co-equals. Throughout his articulation of these principles Augustine is radical in rejecting the metaphysical usefulness of genus and species terminologies, and largely reliant on a small set of principles concerning the divine simplicity. Augustine is also, I suggested, highly tentative and austere in what he says about a fourth principle which will be the focus of discussion in this chapter and the next: the principle that each of the divine three may be understood as identical with the intra-divine acts that Scripture attributes to them. In order to draw out this fourth principle, I will look mostly outside the *De trinitate*, to the two main contexts in which Augustine does gradually come to express himself far more clearly on this aspect of his Trinitarian ontology. Questions of relative dating here are complex. While the texts considered in Chapter 8 probably date from *c.*411–15, the texts that will be our main focus in these two chapters stem from the years between 412 and 427. Thus while a strong case can be made that Augustine comes to state the themes I explore here with increasing clarity after 418, it is also true that we cannot be certain how far these fuller comments about the nature of the divine three and their relationships were already clear to Augustine as he wrote *De Trinitate* 5–7. I will begin the chapter by turning to a number of texts from around the year 420 that clarify some of Augustine's earlier statements about what it means for each of the divine three to be the fullness of God.

SUBSISTENTIA PERSONARUM
('THE EXISTENCE OF THE PERSONS')

In a number of mature texts Augustine introduces a distinction between the Father and Son being *alium* and *alius*, the latter term meaning another 'thing' or 'nature', the former usually translated as 'another person'. Now, at one level this distinction is a simple way for Augustine to highlight the difference between thinking that the divine nature is divided such that the Father and Son are in every sense two separate things (*alius ... alius*), and thinking of Father and Son as two 'persons' even as they are undivided in essence.[1] But, at the same time, Augustine's choice suggests we should ask whether, in these mature texts, Augustine offers a denser account of what it is to be a divine 'person' than he has done in the texts we have already examined.

In *De civitate Dei* 11, composed *c*.418, Augustine writes:

But the Holy Spirit is another person [*alium*] than the Father and the Son, for he is neither the Father nor the Son. But I say 'another person' [*alium*] and not 'another thing' [*alius*], because he, like them, is simple, and, like them, he is the immutable and co-eternal Good ... For we do not say that the nature of the Good is simple because it is in the Father only, or in the Son only, or in the Holy Spirit only. Nor, as the heretics who follow Sabellius have supposed, is it a Trinity in name only without the real existence of persons [*subsistentia personarum*].[2]

---

[1] The distinction appears at *Io. ev. tr.* 36. 9, 37. 6, 45. 5; *civ.* 11. 10; *serm.* 140. 2 (a very late sermon against Maximinus). The translation of *alium* in this opposition as 'another person' is warranted by *an. et or.* 2. 9 (CSEL 60. 343): 'sed quia eum genuit de se ipso, non aliud genuit quam id quod est ipse. Excepto enim quod hominem assumpsit et uerbum caro factum est, alius est quidem uerbum dei filius, sed non est aliud; hoc est alia persona est, sed non diuersa natura.' The distinction appears to have no precedent in Latin Trinitarian discussion.

[2] *civ.* 11. 10 (CCSL 47. 330). Augustine's use of *subsistentia* here is a *hapax* in his corpus. The term is one which probably appears in Latin with Victorinus, who uses the term in a contrast with *substantia* (e.g. *adv. Ar.* 1. 30) and as a term for the divine three (*adv. Ar.* 2. 4, with extensive discussion of the meaning of *subsistentia*. Cf. *adv. Ar.* 3. 4, 3. 9) of which no traces are apparent in Augustine. In his discussions Victorinus sees *subsistentia* as implying concrete existence, existence with a form. In discussing the 362 Council of Alexandria in his continuation of Eusebius, Rufinus uses the term as a translation of *hypostasis* and speaks of the council fathers as thus emphasizing the importance of confessing 'tres subsistentes personas' (*hist.* 10. 30. Cf. Rufinus's translation of Nazianzen, *or.* 2. 36). In translating Origen's *De principiis*, Rufinus also uses the term mostly to mean 'existence', for example, *princip.* 1. 3.1. The Latin Irenaeus, if it be taken to date from the late fourth century, is another contemporary witness to similar usage, *adv. haer.* 2. 7.3, 4. 20.5. Augustine used Rufinus's translation of Eusebius in *civ.*, and either he or Victorinus may be Augustine's source. See also Ambrosiaster's nicely Augustinian comment, 'omne enim malum opere probatur, ut non subsistentia in crimine sit, sed uoluntas concepta ex causis' (*quaest. test.* 98. 1).

In this passage while *alius/alium* certainly implies a distinction between 'person' and essence against anti-Nicene readings, Augustine also speaks of the Spirit as himself 'the immutable and co-eternal Good' and *thus* necessarily one with Father and Son. This argument emphasizes the Spirit's possession of the fullness of the Godhead as divine 'person'/individual, and should be placed alongside a slightly later parallel from *De trinitate* 15:

> (4.6) [after asserting the superiority of life to the inanimate and intellectual life to all other forms] since we prefer the Creator to created things, we must confess that he lives in the highest sense [*summe vivere*], that he perceives all things, and understands all things [*cuncta sentire atque intellegere*] ...
>
> (5.7) But all these things ... are appropriate to the whole Trinity which is the one God, and to each person in the same Trinity. For who would venture to say either that the one God, which is the Trinity itself, or that the Father, or the Son, or the Holy Spirit is not living, or is lacking in perception [*sentientem*] or understanding [*intellegentem*] ...
>
> For what is called life in God is itself his essence and nature. God then does not live, except by the life which he himself is to himself [*nisi vita quod ipse sibi est*] ...[3]

These brief excerpts do not offer any striking new insight over the material we saw in Books 5–7, but they do offer a clarity of emphasis on what it is to be a divine 'person'. Augustine emphasizes that each of the divine three is the highest active rational life that we identify with God.[4]

The same emphasis can be seen in a persistent refrain through which Augustine partially structures *De trinitate* 15. At three points Augustine insists that each of the persons must be thought to be their own memory, intelligence and will: immediately after his summary of previous books; as he begins the argument of Book 15 itself (in the passage quoted above); then before his individual discussions of what we may learn about Word and Spirit from the likenesses he has explored.[5] This repeated insistence further emphasizes the extent to which Augustine wishes to draw attention to the existence of each of the divine three as the fullness of divine life. Augustine does so in large part so that we do not mistake his attempts to explore likenesses between Son and Spirit, on the one hand, and Knowledge or Word and Love on the other, for a theology in which the divine three only constitute one divine rational life together. This concern eventually leads him to the following clear statement:

---

[3] *trin.* 15. 4.6–5.7 (CCSL 50. 467–8).
[4] As he already does at *trin* 6. 10.11 with reference to the Word.
[5] *trin.* 15. 5.7, 15. 7.12, 15. 17.27.

(28) ... we should so conceive these three [memory, understanding, will] as some one thing [*unum aliquid*] which all have, as in the case of wisdom itself, and which is so retained in the nature of each one, as that he who has it, is that which he has ... (29) ... in that simple and highest nature, substance is not one thing, and love another, but that substance itself is love, and that love itself is substance, whether in the Father, or the Son, or the Holy Spirit, and yet the Holy Spirit is properly called love.[6]

I will return to this passage in Chapter 10; here I cite it only as a particularly clear piece of evidence for Augustine's clarity, by the time he completed the *De trinitate*, that each of the irreducible divine three exists as the fullness of the divine life, as an unchanging life that is both presence (rather than a temporal rational life of lack and discovery)[7] and action (the Aristotelian category that Augustine sees as most immediately and without question applicable to God). This clarity of emphasis helps to reinforce the account of the Father's generation of Son and Spirit as truly other (and yet without division) explored in Chapter 8, and it will provide an important backdrop to our exploration of two key contexts in which Augustine pushes further in his description of the divine three as mutually interrelated.

FATHER AND SON: SHOWING AND SEEING

Jesus said to them, 'truly truly, I say to you, the Son can do nothing of his own accord, but only what he sees the Father doing: for whatever he does, that the Son does likewise' [John 5.19].

While commentary on John 5.19 has a long history in Christian writing, only for a few decades after 360 was it the subject of extended discussion.[8] Different phrases within the verse suggested themselves to Nicene and to anti-Nicene polemicists. Augustine's own striking reading of the text is our ultimate concern, but placing that reading against a wider history will provide a narrative parallel to the more analytical treatment of Augustine's lack of interest in person and nature terminologies as complex philosophical resources in Chapter 8. My focus in this narrative is the question of how the Son can be understood as 'seeing' the Father

---

[6] *trin.* 15. 17.28–9 (CCSL 50. 503–4).
[7] See *trin.* 14. 12.16, 15. 5.7.
[8] A complementary account is offered by Basil Studer, 'Johannes 5, 19f. in der Trinitätslehre der Kirchenväter', in Jeremy Driscoll (ed.), *Imaginer la théologie catholique. Permanence et transformations de la foi en attendant Jésus-Christ. Mélanges offerts à Ghislain Lafont* (Rome: Centro Studi S. Anselmo, 2000), 515–41.

without being then thought to act subsequently to the Father or as one subordinate in power.

John 5.19 first appears in theological discussion as an anti-Monarchian text: that the Son depends on the Father and looks to him implies the existence of two irreducible realities.[9] But while this distinction is clearly asserted, the character of the Son's dependence on the Father remains far less clear. It should not surprise us, then, that in the early decades of the fourth century, even before the Trinitarian controversies had taken polemical centre-stage, we see the lineaments of two contrasting readings. On the one hand, in his *Preparation for the Gospel*, Eusebius tells us that John 5.19 expresses the same insight as a fragment of Numenius in which the latter speaks of the Creator being seated above and directing the material world, guided by sight of the ideas.[10] In his *Ecclesiastical Theology*, written against Marcellus of Ancyra in the mid- to late 330s, Eusebius offers a parallel explanation: the Son sees the ideas of all in the Father's mind (they are shown to the Son through the Father's love) and then gives all things specific form in creation. Thus the Son does the 'same things' as the Father in the sense that he copies the ideas already existing in the Father.[11] The Son's seeing is here presented as evidence for his dependence on the Father. On the other hand, Athanasius glosses the verse on a number of occasions, beginning in the *Contra Gentes*, making Christ say 'all the things that I see the Father doing, these I do likewise'.[12] This partial use of the verse is one we find in a number of (mostly) Nicene authors, emphasizing only the Son's power to do the same things as the Father.[13]

Although there is some evidence that this use of the verse pre-dates him, Eunomius offers the first surviving example of it being turned directly

---

[9] See Origen, *comm. John.* 10. 246–7, *princ.* 1. 2.6 and 1. 2.12; Tertullian, *adv. Prax.* 15.

[10] Eusebius, *prep.* 11. 18. This more consciously subordinationist usage finds a precedent in Methodius, see Epiphanius, *pan.* 64. 28.8.

[11] Eusebius, *eccl. theol.* 3. 3.54. A few years later, Cyril of Jerusalem, at *cat. lect.* 11. 23, uses the text to argue that the Son makes all things at the Father's command, providing a design which is then copied by the Son. Cyril's use of this verse partially mirrors that of Eusebius, but must be read against the wider background of his theology.

[12] Athanasius, *c. gen.* 46. His later uses can be found at *synod.* 49, *ad Afros* 7 and *Serap.* 2. 5.

[13] I say 'mostly' Nicene authors, because the letter from the Ancyran synod of 358, probably composed by Basil of Ancyra, follows this pattern. See, for example, Epiphanius, *pan.* 73. 9.3, 11.2. The first use, at *pan.* 73. 8.4, is enigmatic: Basil quotes the whole of the verse and argues it is a supplement to Prov. 8.30's 'I was by him in accord with him' presenting the Son's status more clearly. It is to be presumed he means that John 5.19 emphasizes the Son's doing of all things that the Father does and in like manner, but he does not elucidate. The letter which follows, perhaps by George of Laodicea, uses the text once, *pan.* 73. 18.2, in the same manner as Tertullian and Origen.

against Homoousians and Homoiousians.[14] Eunomius argues that 'he who creates by his own power is entirely different from him who does so at the Father's command and acknowledges that he can do nothing of his own accord, just as the one who is worshipped is different from the one who worships'.[15] One of the main responses to Eunomius's exegesis was to ignore it. Thus, only once in his *Against Eunomius* does Basil of Caesarea mention the verse, and then only to emphasize that the Son does the same things as the Father 'likewise'.[16] In his own *Against Eunomius*, Gregory of Nyssa similarly does not confront Eunomius's reading head-on, although he alludes to the verse to emphasize that Father and Son work in the same manner and that the Son imitates the Father's care for the universe (because he does what he sees the Father doing).[17]

Gregory Nazianzen does, however, offer an extensive treatment in his *Oration* 30, delivered in 380. Gregory first argues that 'cannot' has many meanings; in this case to say that the Son 'cannot' do anything means that it is 'inconceivable that' the Son would act of his own accord. This is so because the Son shares a nature with the Father, a nature that has come from the Father: 'all that the Father has is the Son's and vice versa … all things belong to both'. When the Son says 'I live because of the Father' (John 6.57), he indicates not that the Father constrains him or holds him in existence, but that the Son exists under identical conditions, timelessly and without cause (ἀναίτιως). Thus we may rule out the possibility that Father and Son sequentially undertake the same actions (e.g. creating subsequent and distinct worlds) and suggest that 'the Father indicates the outline, while the Word makes a finished product', seeing and acting not as a subordinate but in a manner we might even call 'Fatherly' (πατρικῶς)![18] Gregory thus treats the Son's seeing as a consequence of his unity of nature with the Father, but still speaks of the Son as imitating.

Didymus's *De spiritu sancto* was almost certainly written before the *Theological Orations*, and probably pre-dates them by around fifteen years.

---

[14] See below, n. 28.
[15] Eunomius, *Apol.* 20 (Vaggione 60). See also at *Apol.* 26. Eunomius may be the source of this anti-Nicene reading, but see also the discussion of Hilary below.
[16] Basil, *Eunom.* 1. 23. His lack of response to Eunomius's use continues through to *spir.* 8. 19 to show the unity of works between Father and Son and the dependence of the Son on the Father's divine power. The exception is *reg. brev.* q. 1. 48ff. (PG 31. 1081), where Basil treats the text as representing Christ's commitment to doing the will of the Father (John 6.38 and other texts), not Christ's incapacity.
[17] Gregory of Nyssa, *Eunom.* 1. 395, 441. A further allusion, showing that the Son does the same things as the Father, is to be found at *ref.* 221.
[18] Gregory Nazianzen, *or.* 30. 10–11.

236   *Into the mystery*

Also responding to Eunomius, Didymus introduces John 5.19 after stating that 'nor does the Father announce his will to the Son, who is wisdom and truth, without him already knowing it, since the Son who subsists as wise and true has in wisdom and in substance everything that the Father speaks'.[19] Thus when the Father works, the Son is already also seeing and working because the Father has shared his nature with the Son: there is no question of imitation or of a subsequent or secondary working.[20] Didymus also rules out any reception by Son and Spirit of that which they did not already have: 'the Son is said to receive the same things from the Father in which he himself subsists. For the Son is nothing other than those things which are given to him by the Father' (*Neque enim quid aliud est Filius exceptis his quae ei dantur a Patre*).[21] He 'cannot' do anything other because he cannot be separated from the Father. Didymus pursues the same general argument as Nazianzen – and indeed almost all other Greek and Latin Nicenes – in presenting the Son's seeing as a consequence of his generation from the Father and his sharing of an essence or nature, but he pursues a slightly a different line of enquiry in his account of the Son necessarily seeing and working in a unified action with the Father, without any hint of imitation on the Son's part. Of course, one might say that his emphasis on the unity of nature here is so strong that the individuality of the Son is insufficiently preserved (although it is clearly stated in other sections of the work).[22]

One of the most complex Greek pro-Nicene accounts is to be found in Cyril of Alexandria's *Commentary on John*, written around forty-five years after Gregory's *Theological Orations*. Cyril argues, first and predictably, that Christ's assertion of equality with the Father in the final clauses of the verse prevents an anti-Nicene reading of the first half. After a detailed rehearsal of the Son's unity of nature and power with the Father which follows much Greek Nicene precedent, Cyril locates the main error of his opponents in the idea that the Son imitates and learns from the Father. Dissecting the various senses of 'cannot' Cyril offers an analogy: as a human being I know the continuity of essence I have with my parents, and on this basis I know they could or could not do X because of their nature and therefore I know I cannot do X. Thus when the Son says that

---

[19] Didymus, *spir.* 158.   [20] Didymus, *spir.* 161–2.   [21] Didymus, *spir.* 165.
[22] We should note also his assertion that the unity of operation revealed in the last clause of the verse demonstrates unity of nature (an argument which responds directly to Eunomius's argument, but of which Nazianzen appears to be generally wary): this will become a standard in other Greek readings.

he cannot do anything except what he sees the Father doing, the Son means that he sees in the essence of the one who generated him and with whom he shares an essence, what such a nature does, and he acts accordingly. This seeing or knowing occurs as part of 'the conceptions proper to him as Son or the mental impressions natural to him' (ἰδίας ἐννοιας ἤτοι φυσικοῖς κινήμασιν).[23] The Son thus sees by awareness of the nature that is his by generation. Cyril complements this reading with an insistence that the Son is both co-eternal and the 'active power' (δυναμιν ... ἐνεργητικὴν) of the Father who manifests the Father's will and action.[24]

There is an Athanasian quality to this addition: where language about the relations between Father and Son seems to imply the subordination of the Son, it is supplemented by presentations of the Son as the Father's own Word, Wisdom or Power. The two terminologies mutually illuminate, but seem to sit side by side.[25] Gregory, Didymus and Cyril, then, all treat the Son's seeing as an intrinsic part of what it means for him to possess the divine nature. If one can establish that he shares the divine nature (which one does in part by arguing that Father and Son carry out the same actions) then the character of his seeing can be presented as consonant with pro-Nicene theology. All three also suggest that the Son intrinsically sees and works because of his unique mode of generation from the Father possessing all that the Father is but possessing it as gift from the Father. But 'suggest' here is an important word, this theme is still inchoate, if far more fully present in Didymus and Cyril than in Gregory.[26]

---

[23] Cyril of Alexandria, *in Io.* 2. 6 (Pusey, I. 326). Cf. on John 5.20 (Pusey I. 328): ὀθεάσαιτο ποιητὴν, ὡς ἐν ἐννοίαις ... ἢ ὡς ἀγνοοῦντα διδάσκων πάντα γὰρ οἶδεν ὡς Θεός ἀλλ' ὅλον ἑαυτὸν ἐν τῇ τοῦ γεννήματος φύσει ζωγραφῶν, καὶ τὰ ἰδίως αὐτῷ προσπεφυκότα δεικνύων ἐν ἑαυτῷ.

[24] Cyril of Alexandria, *in Io.* 2. 6 (Pusey, I. 327).

[25] Cyril's account here seems to be a development of the discussion at *dial trin.* 6. 615ff., see note SC 246, pp. 251ff.

[26] Other Greek pro-Nicene readings add little discussion of the Son's seeing. At *in Io.* 38, Chrysostom denies that the Son imitates the Father, arguing that the Son has an 'ineffable power' (PG 59. 216–17) and hence that the Son's unity of nature and power means that he cannot act except in union with the Father. A similar but more extended reading is to be found in a homily devoted to this text, which may owe something to Nazianzen (PG 56. 247–56, *CPG* 4441. 12). Chrysostom's discussion of the Son's seeing is cursory: that the Son sees the Father's substance indicates his unity with the Father because nothing else, even the angels, sees God. The reconstructed *or.* 9 of Amphilochius (CCSG 3. 175–9; cf. frags. 6–7) shows many links with Chrysostom and follows much the same argument. In the second of the Ps. Athanasian *dial. trin.* only the final clause of the text occurs and only in citation by the 'orthodox' speaker, who on one occasion argues that if the Son copies all the Father's works literally then his opponent must confess that the Son should have made another Son (see *dial. trin.* 2. 9 (PG 28. 1172), 2. 13, 2. 25). The *De trinitate* frequently attributed to Didymus offers an exactly parallel reading (*trin.* 1. 9–10 (PG 39. 284)) and another example of the standard Nicene reading (*trin.* 1. 40). Ps. Basil, *Eunom.* 4. 1 (PG 29. 676) and

238   *Into the mystery*

In fourth-century Latin texts the verse begins to appear with Phoebadius, writing *c*.358, who quotes the Son's seeming statement of inability as a statement of unity which follows from his unique sight of the Father and existence in the Father.[27] In the first book of his *De trinitate*, *c*.355–8, Hilary professes to know anti-Nicene use of John 5.19.[28] But it is only in Book 7, probably finished *c*.358–60, that Hilary deals with the text in depth. Not surprisingly Hilary transposes 'sight' into 'knowledge', arguing that the power to act found in the Son's nature comes not from successive gifts of strength, but from the Son's knowledge. But the Son, he continues, does not receive knowledge by imitating the Father's bodily performance of actions:

but by the action of the nature of God, he had come to subsist in the nature of God [*sed cum natura Dei in naturam Dei substitisset*] or, in other words, had been born as Son from the Father, [and thus] because He was aware of the Father's power and strength that was in him [*virtutis ac naturae in se paternae conscientiam*], the Son asserted that he could do nothing by himself except what he saw the Father doing.[29]

The Son is born from the Father and shares the Father's nature: he thus has 'by nature' an awareness of the Father's own power. It is this 'awareness' that constitutes his 'seeing'. Hilary adds that God's 'seeing' is never corporeal, but always a function of the power of his nature.[30] A little

---

4. 3 (PG 29. 696) make use of the final clause of the text only to demonstrate the unity of ἐνέργεια and δύναμις between Father and Son. Theodore of Mopsuestia, *in Jo*. 27, presents the Son's ability to do the 'same things' as proof of his unity of will and power with the Father. Evagrius in Basil, *ep*. 8 also reads the Son's lack of self-determination as a reflection of his unity of nature with the Father. In an odd and unique move, Evagrius also sees the Son's lack of self-determination as revealing his uncreated status because all created things endowed with reason do possess this ability!

[27] Phoebadius, *c. Ar*. 12. 4. There is some evidence of Latin Homoian usage, if from the 380s. At the Council of Aquileia Palladius condemns Nicene use of the last part of the verse because, taken alone, it fails to indicate the necessary dissimilarities between Father and Son, *scol. Aquil*. 54 (336v) (CCSL 87A. 172). For a direct Homoian usage of the whole verse see *frag. theol*. 8 (CCSL 87A. 240).

[28] We do not know his source. The verse does appear in fifth-century Latin Homoian texts, *serm. Ar*. 20 and *frag. theol*. 7 (CCSL 87A. 240). Palladius also brought up the final clauses of the verse at the Council of Aquileia (see *scol. Aquil*. 82 (SC 267. 264)), but it is unclear what significance they hold for him.

[29] Hilary, *trin*. 7. 17 (SC 448. 312). A more basic Nicene reading is offered at *c. Const*. 17: Hilary argues that if one reads the first half of the verse as denying the equality of Father and Son, the second clearly indicates equality of power. At *Psalm*. 91. 6 Hilary offers a simpler reading in which the Son's seeming statement of inability should be read as a statement of submission to the Father's will. At *Psalm*. 138. 17 and 28, although the Son shares a nature with the Father he wishes to demonstrate the Father's authority by his deference.

[30] Hilary, *trin*. 7. 17 (SC 448. 312): 'non enim corporalibus modis Deus vident, sed visus ei omnis in virtute naturae est'. Cf. *trin*. 9. 44–8. See esp. *trin*. 9. 45 (SC 462. 110): 'conscientia igitur in se

later Hilary suggests that the Father's showing of his works to the Son is the very content of the Son's being born in the divine nature.[31] On this basis Hilary can be clear that we should not speak of distinct yet parallel works of Father and Son, but of Father and Son working together in each act.[32]

Latin theology may have considerably anticipated much of the later Greek pro-Nicene reading in the person of Hilary, but Ambrose offers no deepening of clarity, and seems heavily dependent on his Greek contemporaries (especially Gregory Nazianzen). In the first two books of his *De fide*, written *c*.378, Ambrose twice uses the verse as a proof of the Son's equality with the Father and yet his submission to the Father.[33] When Ambrose wrote the later books of the work *c*.380 he turned again to the verse, this time far more fully aware of its anti-Nicene potential. In Book 4 Ambrose points out that the Son here does the *same* works as the Father; he indicates the impossibility of the Son seeing bodily or being truly unable to act; he argues that a literal reading would imply that the Father first made a world and then the Son likewise. A detailed examination of three unacceptable senses in which 'cannot' might be understood is followed by discussion of a fourth and acceptable sense: because in love and in their common nature the Son is obedient to his Father he 'cannot' do anything except what he sees the Father doing.[34]

Because the Son is of the same nature and power as the Father, he sees and acts invisibly, carrying out the Father's wishes by means of the fullness of divinity. Moreover, the Son's seeing of the Father, for Ambrose, parallels the Father's seeing of the Son: just as the Father praises his own creation but certainly foreknew its goodness, the Son sees and praises the Father not in order to know for the first time, but recognizing the Father's work as also his own.[35] The love of Son for Father, Ambrose emphasizes, rests on the inseparable activity that flows from the common nature they share. Because, and here Ambrose seems dependent on Hilary, the Father

---

naturae paternae quae in se operatur operante'. Interwoven with Hilary's argument is the pro-Nicene standard that actions reveal the power inherent in a give nature. This may be seen overtly at *synod*. 18–19. There Hilary comments on the 11th anathema of the 358 Ancyran synod. Hilary tells us that the 'heretics' read John 5.19 as indicating only likeness in power, not likeness in substance. Against this position Hilary argues that power is consequent upon nature and hints at his theology of the Son's birth in quoting John 5.26 to show that the Father gives the Son 'life in himself', which implies similarity and identity of nature and power. Cf. Michel Barnes, ' "One Nature, One Power" '.

[31] Hilary, *trin*. 7. 19 (SC 448. 316): 'ut demonstratio ipsa nativitatis esse substantia doceretur'.
[32] Hilary, *trin*. 7. 18. [33] Ambrose, *fid*. 1. 2.13 and 2. 8.69.
[34] Ambrose, *fid*. 4. 6.63 (CSEL 78/8. 179). [35] Ambrose, *fid*. 4. 6.66.

is in the Son working when the Son works, the works are inseparable.³⁶ In the Latin authors I have considered, as in the Greek, the Son's seeing of the Father is consistently approached through reflection on what it means for the Son to possess the divine nature and, in the most complex, by also utilizing arguments about the powers consequent on possession of that nature. This common approach offers an excellent example of the way in which the complex of philosophical ideas linking nature/substance, power and activity had come to be used as a resource across Nicene theologies of facing a host of theological and exegetical problems.

Augustine came to recognize the significance of John 5.19 late, the text first being mentioned either in *De trinitate* 1 or in the *De consensu evangelistarum*, which was written c.404–5. Here, in a reading that we find repeated for the rest of his career, Augustine offers the old Nicene exegesis of John 5.19, using the last clause of the verse – 'whatever [the Father] does, that the Son does likewise' – as a proof text for the Son's doing the same things as the Father.³⁷ We find a more developed reading of John 5.19 in a number of Augustine's mature texts, in two sets of the tractates on John (18, 19 and 23; 20–2), in *sermon* 126 and in *De trinitate* 2. There are a few differences between these accounts, and I will follow that of tractates 18, 19 and 23 in the belief that it is the most articulate and perhaps the latest.³⁸

---

³⁶ Ambrose, *fid*. 4. 6.68. We know that Ambrose read Didymus around this time, but precise parallels are, in this case, impossible to trace. Discussion of John 5.19 is found in a number of other Latin pro-Nicenes in the 380–400 period but without discussion of the Son's seeing. The verse does not appear in Gregory of Elvira. Faustinus refers the two parts of the verse to different *personae*: it is as the incarnate Son that Christ says he can do nothing of his own accord (*trin*. 34); as Word and Image he tells us that he does the same things as the Father (*trin*. 36). The same reading is to be found in Eusebius of Vercelli, *trin*. 3. 17. The texts which Bulhart prints as possibly Books 10 and 11 of the same work (for bibliographical details see *CPL* 105) contain examples only of the standard Nicene reading of the final clauses, see 10. 5; 11. 29, 37.

³⁷ See *trin*. 1. 6.11; *cons. ev.* 1. 4.7. For an example of him later continuing to offer this reading see *symb. cat.* (= *serm*. 398) 5. Augustine himself does not seem to have faced much pressure from Homoians over the text: it is noticeable that Maximinus does not refer to the text in their debate. The text is alluded to at *serm. Ar.* 20 and Augustine replies at *c. s. Arrian*. 14 and 23. 20, as we see at *c. s. Arrian*. 22. 18, 28. 26, he sees his answer as enabling him to continue deploying the old Nicene reading. For a complementary reading of Augustine's usage see Studer, 'Johannes 5, 19f. in der Trinitätslehre', 535–42.

³⁸ See *trin*. 2. 1.13. Detailed exposition of Augustine's mature reading occurs only in *Io. ev. tr.* 18–23, and *serm*. 126. The sequence of sermons from 18 to 23 begs many questions. Although La Bonnardière argued that 18–23 was a continuous sequence, David Wright and M.-F. Berrouard demonstrated that in all likelihood Tractates 20–2 constitute a distinct group: see David Wright, 'Tractatus 20–22 of Augustine's *In Iohannem*', *JThS* ns. 15 (1964), 317–30; M.-F. Berrouard, 'La date des Tractatus I–LIV de saint Augustin', *REAug* 7 (1971), 105–68; idem in BA 72. 9–46. While La Bonnardière places 18–23 after 418, Berrouard places 18–19 and 23 earlier, between 413 and 416, possibly in 414, while the later sequence dates from c.419, after *c. s. Arrian*. The character of the evidence allows no certainty here. For my purposes it need only be the case that all of

Augustine sets up his reading by distinguishing between faith and understanding, emphasizing the difficulty of a mortal, material human being discussing the immortal, spiritual divine.[39] He then invokes the first of the exegetical rules we discussed in Chapter 4: the Father is greater than Christ according to the flesh, equal according to the divinity. This rule is used both to make the congregation aware of the task that will await them (reading this verse without imposing material qualities on God) and to present John 5.19 as an opportunity for us to hear 'the inner dweller sound through his dwelling place' against the Jews who had just heard him claim equality with God in John 5.18.[40] Augustine tells us that the 'Arians' see Christ as then, in verse 19, admitting his own inferiority to the Father as a concession to the Jews' anger.

Augustine's offensive against these 'Arians' begins by invoking John 1.1's claim that the Word was God. The Arian can only reply that there are two Gods, one greater and one lesser; the Catholic admits the equality of Father and Son as God but also as undivided love (*indiuiduam caritatem*).[41] In this love – the Spirit – Father and Son are one not two Gods. Augustine now asks his audience and putative opponents to bear in mind not only John 1.1 but also John 1.3, 'all things were made through him'. The 'Arian' reading 'the Son cannot do anything of himself', Augustine tells us, imagines two craftsmen, the Father as the master training his apprentice, the Son, the latter observing and copying the former. But, if one thinks thus, then John 1.3 is being ignored, for the Father makes *all* things *through* the Word: there can be no primary making without the Word which then serves as a model for imitation.[42]

Augustine now focuses our attention on the Son's seeing: it is this that precedes doing in John 5.19. We see, but cannot see God. Because we forget this distinction, we use that which we can see to explain that which

---

tractates 18–23 are either contemporary with or later than *trin.* 5–7. I find intriguing the suggestion of Clemens Weidmann at CSEL 93/1A. 12, n.14, that the 'three sermons against the Arians' Augustine describes himself as having sent to Carthage in *ep.* 23*. 3 are three of the tractates on John. Weidmann assumes *Io. ev. tr.* 20–2 constitute this set, but 18, 19 and 23 are equally plausible. *serm.* 126 seems to me dependent on the argument of *c. serm. Ar.*, while one could argue that the discussion of *trin.* 2 dates from the earliest stratum of the book, it seems to have a summary quality that follows from it being added when its content had already been formulated.

[39] *Io. ev. tr.* 18. 1. The tactic is developed at greater length in *serm.* 126 where he seems to be trying out his mature reading of the Son's seeing on an audience he fears will fail to understand.
[40] *Io. ev. tr.* 18. 2 (CCSL 36. 181).
[41] *Io. ev. tr.* 18. 4. I leave this pneumatology without comment here: in the next section of the chapter I discuss it at length.
[42] *Io. ev. tr.* 18. 5. The invocation of John 1.3 alongside John 5.19 is found in a number of previous Latin Nicenes.

we cannot.[43] It cannot be that the Son sees some works done by the Father and then does others, because the verse insists that the Son does the same things as the Father 'in like manner'.[44] To explain the force of 'in like manner' Augustine offers the analogy of thinking and writing: the hand writes the same letters as the heart thinks, but not 'in like manner'. But how does the Father 'show' to the Son and how does the Son 'see'? We cannot deny that the Word or Son sees and hears because of Scripture (Ps. 93.9's 'He who planted the ear, does he not hear? Or he who formed the eye, does he not perceive?'). But,

> Both to see and to hear are together in the Word; and to see is not one thing, to hear another, but hearing is sight and sight is hearing.[45]

For proof that this is so, Augustine makes a move that should be no surprise to readers of the book so far: he suggests that we turn inward and realize that in the 'heart' the eyes and the ears are the same.

Right at the end of this section of the sermon Augustine suddenly takes us to the heart of his solution:

> In your flesh you hear in one place, you see in another; in your heart you hear there where you see. If the image [does] this, how much more powerfully [does] he [do it] whose image this is? Therefore the Son both hears and the Son sees; and the Son is the very seeing and hearing [*et ipsa visio et auditio Filius*]. And for him hearing is the same as being, and for him seeing is the same as being [*et hoc est illi audire quod esse, et hoc est illi uidere quod esse*]. But for you seeing is not the same as being, because even if you should lose your sight, you can still be, and if you should lose your hearing, you can still be.[46]

Augustine, then, directly identifies the Son and his seeing (and hearing). This move is in some ways parallel to the tactics we have seen in his predecessors, characterizing the Son's seeing as consequent upon his possession of divine nature, but Augustine makes no use of the terminology of person and nature as a resource for explaining his solution. He turns instead to his by now standard account of divine simplicity: the Son is that which we predicate of him. Because the Son is unchangeable and indivisible, the Son's being must be identical with his act of seeing. In consequence the Son's seeing is constitutive of his being and the Son's seeing must be identical to all his other acts.[47]

---

[43] *Io. ev. tr.* 18. 6. [44] *Io. ev. tr.* 18. 8. [45] *Io. ev. tr.* 18. 9 (CCSL 36. 186).
[46] *Io. ev. tr.* 18. 10 (CCSL 36. 186). Cf. *serm.* 126. 15 (PL 38. 705): 'Videre enim Verbi si videas, forte in eo quod vides videre Verbi, ipsum Verbum videbis; ut non aliud sit Verbum, aliud videre Verbi'.
[47] This last supposition is based on the identity of the Son's 'seeing' and 'hearing' that Augustine articulates here and is borne out in his mature discussion of inseparable operation at *Io. ev. tr.* 23. 11, for which see below.

Showing and seeing 243

Over the following days Augustine preached on the same passage from John twice more, in sermons that survive as *Tractates* 19 and 23 of the series. In *Tractate* 23 Augustine emphasizes, again, the failure of any bodily analogy for speaking or showing: 'simplicity is there. The Father shows the Son what he is doing and by showing begets the Son.'[48] Here Augustine pushes further through careful attention to the verbs used in John 5.19 and 20. He remarks that showing logically precedes seeing, and follows the same procedure in the case of the Father as he had followed in the case of the Son: the Father's showing, and his eternal begetting of the Son, must be identical with his being. But if so, then the showing and seeing of John 5.19 must also describe the constitutive relationship of Father and Son eternally established by the Father.

Two further aspects of the sequence of *Tractates* 18, 19 and 23 deserve comment: the account of inseparable operation that Augustine offers in *Tractate* 23; the 'relational' nature of the divine three that begins to emerge more clearly here than in the texts we have so far seen. At the end of *Tractate* 18 Augustine had commented on his exploration of the mind's 'seeing' and 'hearing' (which occur in the same place): 'when we speak about these things, when we reflect upon them, we are training ourselves ... we train ourselves in ourselves'.[49] In a fascinating passage of *Tractate* 23 Augustine again attempts to train his congregation 'in themselves' by speaking of human *memoria* and *cogitatio*. Something is seen through the eyes and committed to memory; once it is so committed one's *cogitatio* or *intentio* goes elsewhere. But – offering an example found frequently in his corpus – if someone says 'Carthage' the *intentio cogitationis* is drawn towards the memory and the memory shows something to thought and a vision appears in the *cogitatio*. We should also note, Augustine tells us, that the memory and the activity of thinking are *eiusdem substantiae*. In this process of recalling Carthage there is no material sign in the process of showing, but there was a showing:

What the Father shows the Son, he does not receive from without. The entirety is done within [*intus totum agitur*]; for there would be no creatures unless the Father had made them through the Son ... the Father showed it to be made and the Son saw it to be made, and the Father made it by showing it because he made it through the Son seeing it [*sed faciendam pater monstrauit, faciendam filius uidit, et eam pater demonstrando fecit, quia per filium uidentem fecit*]. Thus it ought not to be disturbing because it was said 'but only what he sees the Father doing'; it was not said 'showing'. For through this it was signified that for the

---

[48] *Io. ev. tr.* 23. 9 (CCSL 36. 238): 'simplicitas ibi est. pater ostendit filio quod facit, et ostendendo filium gignit'.
[49] *Io. ev. tr.* 18. 11 (CCSL 36. 187).

Father 'to do' is the same as 'to show', so that from this it may be understood that he does all things through the Son seeing [*ut ex hoc intellegatur per Filium videntem omnia facere*]. Neither that showing nor that seeing is temporal ... But the Father's showing begets the Son's seeing in the same way as the Father begets the Son. Showing, of course, generated seeing; not seeing showing. If we could look more purely and more perfectly, we would perhaps find that the Father is not one thing and his showing another, nor is the Son one thing and his seeing another [*fortasse inueniremus nec aliud esse patrem, aliud eius demonstrationem, nec aliud filium, aliud eius uisionem*].[50]

Augustine describes the creation of the World as an inseparable act of Father and Son by arguing that the Father's conjoint actions with the Son (and by implication with Spirit) are founded in the Father's eternal generation of the Son, in the Father's eternal showing to the Son and the Son's eternal seeing and doing.[51] In this way of putting the matter, Augustine moves beyond the duality of speaking first about the Father's generation and spiration of Son and Spirit and then, second, about the mode or order of their actions, about the various 'roles' that might be accorded each. Instead (and we see here a particularly clear laying out of the position present a few years earlier in *De trinitate* 2 and 4 explored in Chapter 7), the Father's eternal establishing of the divine communion is the foundation of all inseparable actions of the three, even those which happen externally in time. We can also say that the manner in which the divine three act together reflects their eternal relationships: the Father acts as the source, the Son acts as the one who is from the Father, the one in whom all things are planned and through whom all things are, and the Spirit acts as the one in whom all things find their stability and rest (although as with so many themes here Augustine never articulates this as a general principle).[52] This account is a distant cousin of Augustine's early attempts to speak of the Trinity as the triune/threefold cause of all, but far more theological density is given through attention to the mutual relationships predicated of the divine three by Scripture.

In these tractates Augustine also speaks much more directly than in *De trinitate* 5–7 of Father, Son and Spirit as existing in a unique mode that we can with some reservations describe as 'relational'. In the first place, Augustine's equation of the Son and his seeing of the Father suggests that

---

[50] *Io. ev. tr.* 23. 11 (CCSL 36. 240–1).
[51] Although Augustine does not discuss the question here, we may surmise fairly easily that Augustine does not thus consider the creation to be eternal. See *Io. ev. tr.* 1. 17.
[52] I am grateful to Keith Johnson for suggesting this point.

the Son's existence is one eternally oriented towards the Father and oriented towards revealing and imaging the Father. It is important to note, again, that while the Son is constituted by the relationships in which the Father generates him eternally, he can only be so *because* he is also life in itself, the fullness of the Godhead and, hence, necessarily simple. The divine three are relational in a manner that follows from the unique manner of their irreducible substantiality.

The same perspective is to be found later in *Tractate* 19, when Augustine considers John 5.26 ('For as the Father has life in himself, so he has granted the Son also to have life in himself'). Augustine begins, predictably enough, by emphasizing that the Father does not have life by participation in what is not his own, 'but he "has life in himself", so that life itself is, for him, he himself' (*ut ipsa vita sibi sit ipse*).[53] How, then, should we imagine the Son having life?

> The Father is Life, not by a 'being born'; the Son is Life by a 'being born' ... the Father, in that he is, is from no one; but in that he is the Father, he is on account of the Son [*Pater quod est, a nullo est; quod autem Pater est, propter Filium est*]. But the Son, both in that he is the Son, is on account of the Father, and in that he is, is from the Father [*Filius vero et quod Filius est, propter Patrem est; et quod est, a Patre est*] ... Therefore, the Father remains life, the Son also remains life; the Father, life in himself, not from the Son, the Son, life in himself, but from the Father.[54]

In this passage Augustine does not speak only about what is 'said' (*dicitur*), but about what is. With this text we should compare a passage from *Tractate* 39, on John 8.25–7. This tractate is difficult to date with any certainty, but seems most likely to have been written in the same period as the two series of tractates on John 5.19:

> For example, a man and another man, if the one should be a father, the other a son. That he is a man is in respect to himself; that he is a father is in respect to the son ... For the name Father has been *said* in respect to something [*Pater enim nomen est dictum ad aliquid*], and son in respect to something: but these are two men. But in truth, God the Father *is* Father in respect to something [*At vero Pater Deus ad aliquid est Pater*], that is to the Son; and God the Son *is* Son in respect to something, that is, to the Father. But as those are two men, not so are these two Gods.[55]

Taken together these two texts offer an excellent picture of Augustine's mature attempts to speak about the persons existing in relationship – and

---

[53] *Io. ev. tr.* 19. 11 (CCSL 36. 194). [54] *Io. ev. tr.* 19. 13 (CCSL 36. 196–7).
[55] *Io. ev. tr.* 39. 4 (CCSL 36. 346).

the tensions that persisted in those attempts. In the passage from *Tractate* 19, Augustine speaks about the Father existing both as Father, *propter Filium*, and as Life, as Life in himself. But the Son is Life in himself not without qualification; he is 'Life from the Father' and then, at the level of his Sonship, he 'is' also towards the Father. At every point the Son is the fullness of the divine 'from' and 'towards'. The Father, however, 'is' with reference to the Son only as Father: as Life he is Life in himself, and not 'in himself and towards'. Augustine does this, I presume, because of a need to preserve the Father's status as *principium*: he does not want to speak of the Father as Life in himself, not simply 'from' no one, but also always towards Son and Spirit. It is important to note that the most basic distinctions he draws here – between the divine three as they are in relation, and as they are simply as divine – are possible because of the language originally used to speak about questions of predication, and perhaps these distinctions will always be partly unsatisfying when used of an ontological context in which both 'levels' are equally substantial (in the sense of non-accidental).

In both *Tractate* 19 and 39 these distinctions sit alongside exegetical themes that speak of the divine three as identical with their intra-divine acts. But while, once again, 'person' and 'nature' language plays virtually no part in these texts, Augustine does, for once, continue to make use of this technical language developed in the *De trinitate*. The usefulness of the language for Augustine, I suspect, lies in the resources it offers for emphasizing two individually important truths of Trinitarian theology – the existence of each of the divine three as the fullness of divinity, the existence of each eternally *ad aliquid*. The fact that this language presents those two truths as a paradoxical conjunction for those of us who think within the created order may not necessarily be a mark against it; the difficulty of grasping this paradox takes us to the heart of the incomprehensible nature of what it is to be one of the divine three within the divine unity and communion.

It is, however, also worth noting that the particular distinction between the manner in which Father and Son are Life itself (or any other appropriated title) that we find in *Tractate* 19 never becomes standard in Augustine: in his other series of tractates on John 5.19 and roughly contemporary texts he speaks more simply of Father and Son being Life in themselves and Father and Son relatively.[56] Augustine thus still seems to be experimenting, searching for ways of using this language alongside his other emerging modes of speech. The passage from *Tractate* 39 offers an important parallel. It is, first, the one text where Augustine explicitly

---

[56] For example, *Io. ev. tr* 22. 9–10; 39. 4.

contrasts questions of predication and ontology in order to assert that Father, Son and Spirit exist *ad aliquid* (and thus we must beware, throughout this chapter and the next, of assembling too easily a complete doctrinal jigsaw from pieces that perhaps do not entirely fit together). But, second, note that the form of expression used here offers us another slight variation on that used in *Tractate* 19. Here Augustine speaks of *Pater Deus* being *Pater* in relationship to the Son. This phrasing relies on the same distinction between being God and being Father, carries with it the same tensions, and is once again subject to a certain experimental modification. In the next chapter, discussion of the necessity of *redoublement* – speaking of the same reality from different angles in Trinitarian theology – perhaps sheds a little further light on the usefulness of this language to Augustine.

One further topic for discussion is suggested by Augustine's account of the Father existing *propter Filium*, 'on account of / because of / with reference to the Son'. The Father establishes an order from eternity in which he eternally exists as Father, eternally is one who shows to the one who sees; may we, then, say that the Father, from eternity, establishes that his existence is determined by the expression and imaging of himself that is the Son? There is nothing in Augustine that might allow us to conceive of a retroactive action of Son on Father (the divine life being conceived of dialectically), but can we say that the Father defines who he is, defines the being of God by this generation (and spiration)? Augustine (like all Nicenes of this period) offers little in this direction. He does, of course, speak of the Father speaking all that will be in the Son – all operations *ad extra* are founded in the ordering of the divine life. But the difficulty of finding a text which offers a clear parallel, a text in which the Father determines who he is, what it is to be God, by his act of generation is striking. Other than the difficulty of scriptural warrant for such a discussion (and we have seen how much Augustine attempts to keep his account close to Scripture), I suspect Augustine only very rarely ventures towards such statements because of his absolute insistence on the divine being as necessarily and eternally fullness. In this regard, the final sentences of *Tractate* 39 should attract our attention:

The Father is truthful [*verax*], he is truthful from himself [*de suo*], because he generated Truth [*quia genuit veritatem*] ... See how God is truthful, not by participating in, but by generating Truth [*non participando, sed generando veritatem*].[57]

---

[57] *Io. ev. tr.* 39. 8 (CCSL 36. 349).

The language of this rhetorical flourish – the contrast of participating in truth or generating truth (as opposed to the more obvious contrast between participating in or simply being truth itself) – is never repeated and has no direct precedent in Latin theology. The Father is truthful out of himself – and here *de suo* seems equivalent to *in se* in being in opposition to 'by participation' – because, or in the fact that, the Father is the one who generates Truth itself. What is the force of the *quia*, 'because'? We can know that the Father is Truth itself, Augustine seems to be saying, because we know that from eternity the Father generates the perfect image who is also Truth itself. It seems likely that the phrasing depends upon an account of the inexhaustible and generative nature of the one source of all, as opposed to any created reality that must participate in any of the virtues. Because the Truth itself, the Word, is such a reality and is generated as God from God we can say that the Father is true not by participating in his Truth (as if the Father were truthful because he shared in the Truth who was with him) but because he is the fullness who generates from eternity another who is fullness.

Augustine, then, presents the form of God's eternal generativity and perfection as the eternal generation of Truth from himself. In such a picture the sheer mystery of the Father's eternally giving rise to Son and Spirit is not interpreted (or even perhaps 'restricted') by any language of the Father's eternal self-expression through Word and Spirit: the depth of the Father's love remains mystery and fullness. One constant strand of argument through this book has been that the Father's *monarchia*, his status as *principium* and *fons*, is central to Augustine's Trinitarian theology. The discussions of these central chapters of the book should, however, have also made clear that many things come under the umbrella of asserting the importance of the Father's status as *principium*. For Augustine, the Father's status as *principium* is eternally exercised through his giving the fullness of divinity to Son and Spirit such that the unity of God will be eternally found in the mysterious unity of the *homoousion*. It is too blunt a reading, I think, to say that Augustine sees the Father's giving – especially, as we shall see in Chapter 10, his giving to the Son that the Spirit will proceed also from the Son – as a handing over of priority in any way (to do so would, I suspect, be to think too easily of the Father exercising an autonomous 'free' choice with reference to Son and Spirit). While we should resist too clear or extensive a synthesis in the face of Augustine's experimental and emergent thought, it should be clear that his account of the Trinitarian communion suggests to us an account of the Father's status as *principium* that holds in fruitful tension the Father's role with the importance of seeing both Son and Spirit as fully sharing in the one divine fullness and the interrelated persons as the matrix through which divine activity, the Father's activity from eternity always occurs.

I focused this chapter around one set of his homilies on John 5.19, not at random but because this text seems to have been a fundamental stimulus in the evolution of Augustine's vision. I will end the chapter by considering the sources for Augustine's exegesis of this text. We should begin by examining the possibility that Augustine's reading of John 5.19 is simply an adaptation of Plotinus's understanding of intellect as constituted by its gaze on the One. The idea is present at *Ennead* 5. 1.7, a text it seems likely Augustine had read first back in 386/7.[58] While the parallel between Plotinus's reflections and Augustine's account of the Son as seeing is close, we need to note features of Augustine's account that prevent us from saying with any certainty that Plotinus is his one or main source. It is clear, in the first place, that Augustine's account is shaped by his commitment to Nicene principles, and that he knew well the texts in which his Latin predecessors reflected on this text. Thus he prioritizes the Father's 'showing' over the Son's 'seeing' because of scriptural and Nicene pressures, and articulates his account in aid of showing the co-eternity of Father and Son. In the second place Augustine structures his argument by means of his standard account of the divine being what it is said to 'have': and these principles are sufficient to account for his solution. The parallel between Augustine and Plotinus here may, then, not indicate source.

At the same time, however, there are few clear indications of which previous Nicene accounts have influenced Augustine. Of Ambrose's reading there are no traces. Hilary's statement that the Son's power to act stems from his knowledge of the Father and that the Father's showing to the Son is the content of his birth offers something of a parallel. The question becomes even more complex when we note Augustine's account of the verse in the *contra sermonem Arrianorum* of 418 or 419. This work, written in response to a Homoian pamphlet that had been forwarded to Augustine, seems to have stimulated a close reading of his Latin predecessors in the search for appropriate anti-'Arian' material. New themes drawn from Ambrose appear, and we find this reading of John 5.19 offered as the one extensive reading of the text:

Scripture said that the Son does nothing on his own, because he does not have his origin from himself. Hence, he sees the Father doing whatever he does,

---
[58] See Chapter 1.

because he sees that he has the power of doing it from him from whom he sees that he has the nature by which he exists.[59]

This reading of the verse closely parallels that of Hilary, but what are we to make of its appearance? Questions of dating in this period are not all resolvable with clarity, but it is at least possible that all Augustine's mature readings of John 5.19 postdate the *contra sermonem Arrianorum*. If so, then we could envisage Augustine's close engagement with Hilary prompting the series of reflections represented by the two series of tractates on John (18, 19, 23 and 20, 21, 22), *sermon* 126 and later additions to the *De trinitate*. There is, however, no need to assume this position. While Augustine's copying from Hilary here may certainly show that he did know and resort to the exegeses of his Latin predecessors when exploring this text, it may simply be that Augustine felt a summary of Hilary's reading was the most appropriate option for this particular text. It is noticeable that Augustine's mature expositions of John 5.19 all develop slowly over considerable sections of text (or are included in the *De trinitate*, a work intended for an intellectual elite). Augustine may thus have felt that clarity and rhetorical power of the *Contra sermonem Arrianorum* would be most enhanced by offering a brief exposition already well attested in anti-Arian tradition. Thus, the influence of Plotinus and Hilary may both be fairly read into Augustine's mature treatments of John 5.19, and the force of his idiosyncratic genius is surely apparent, but exact source relationships will likely remain obscure. We need now to move on from John 5.19 and ask whether this account of Father and Son was complemented by a parallel account of the Spirit.

---

[59] *c. s. Arrian.* 9. 14.

CHAPTER 10

Loving and being

THE SPIRIT AS AGENT OF UNITY

In earlier chapters I traced the emergence of Augustine's account of the Spirit's 'role' in the Trinity. We followed his early accounts of the Spirit's status as that which draws us to God, as the love through which we are drawn, as the will and goodness of God in creation, and as the love between Father and Son. In the summary of Trinitarian faith at the beginning of *De trinitate* 1 we first see Augustine making reference to texts that identify the Spirit as the Spirit of Father and the Spirit of Son, such as Galatians 4.6 ('God has sent the Spirit of his Son into our hearts') and Romans. 8.9–11 ('the Spirit of Christ ... the Spirit of Him who raised Christ from the dead'). This language is again mentioned in the 9th of his tractates on John and in summary statements in *Sermon* 52 and *De trinitate* 4, and then is first subject to extensive discussion in *De trinitate* 5 and 6. Further extensive discussion is offered around a decade later in *De trinitate* 15, and the language is also present in many summary contexts.[1] Augustine's reflections on this language constitute a key plank of his increasingly subtle mature treatments of the Spirit.

In Book 5 Augustine tells us that the Spirit is spoken of relatively (*relative dicitur*) when he is said to be of the Father and of the Son; but the relation that is spoken of is only revealed by the title Gift. The Spirit is the Gift of Father (John 15.26) and of Son (Rom. 8.9) and that which they give is 'some sort of ineffable communion' (*ineffabilis est quaedam ... communio*). Thus the Spirit is named something common to both – 'Spirit' – that we might know that it is their communion that we receive.[2]

---

[1] See *Io. ev. tr.* 9. 7 and *Trin.* 1. 4.7, 1. 8.18, 4. 20.29. The relevant texts from Books 5–6 and 15 are discussed below. For the use of this language in summary statements and short discussions see, for example, *Io. ev. tr.* 9. 7 (probably its first appearance after *trin.* 1).

[2] *trin.* 5. 11.12 (CCSL 50. 219). While Augustine commonly speaks of the Spirit as Love, it should be noted that he also frequently supplements this with other possible titles and with important qualifiers – the Spirit as 'something common'. In large part, I suspect he does so because Scripture

Augustine exhorts us to remember that even though Spirit is a relative title here, we are speaking of a relation that goes only one way: the Gift is of the Father and of the Son – we should not speak of 'the Father of the Spirit' in case we think of the Spirit as another Son.[3] Later in Book 5, Augustine also argues that the Spirit is eternally and unchangeably Gift (*sempiterne donum*) even if he is given in time.[4]

These various themes are drawn out a little further in Book 6:

> Whether [the Holy Spirit] is the unity between [Father and Son], or their holiness, or their love, or whether the unity, therefore, because he is the love, it is obvious that he is not one of the two. Through him both are joined together; through him the begotten is loved by the begetter, and in turn loves him who begot him; in him they preserve the unity of spirit through the bond of peace, not by a participation, but by their own essence [*non participatione sed essentia sua*], not by the gift of anyone superior to themselves but by their own gift [*neque dono superioris alicuius sed suo proprio*] ... Whatever the Holy Spirit is, therefore, it is something common [*commune aliquid*] between the Father and the Son. But this communion is consubstantial and co-eternal ... and this again is a substance, because God is a substance, and 'God is Love' [1 John 4.16].[5]

The passage suggests as many questions as it answers, but those questions reveal important developments under way in Augustine's thought. In the *De fide et symbolo* Augustine's concern was to argue that the Spirit could be conceived of as irreducible even as he was also a relation between Father and Son. Here we find a far more complex set of concerns related to the task of conceiving the Spirit as 'something common'. In *De trinitate* 5 Augustine has already inferred the Spirit's irreducibility from a standard grammatical argument: if we speak of giver and gift and of the Spirit 'of' Father and Son as the Gift, we find the Spirit's distinctiveness insinuated in Scripture's linguistic patterns. But, in the last sentence of the passage from Book 6 quoted above, Augustine hints at a far more complex argument in his statement that because God is substantial so must love be. In the paragraphs immediately preceding this quotation Augustine

---

predicates of the Spirit a number of common titles which must be identical in God – each one thus escaping the analogies that present themselves in the created order. The complexity of the Spirit's existence as fully 'person' and yet as that which is given by Father to Son, as the essence of Father and Son – a theme explored later in this chapter – only enhances the mystery of the Spirit's existence and the difficulty of naming. But, for Augustine, this difficulty stems not from a failure of naming on Scripture's part, but from the fact that to understand the Spirit is to understand one of the deepest mysteries of the divine life.

[3] *trin.* 5. 12.13.

[4] *trin.* 5. 15.16–16.17. In the penultimate section of this chapter, I discuss Augustine's description of Father and Son as the one *principium* of the Spirit.

[5] *trin.* 6. 5.7 (CCSL 50. 235).

has argued that if we say of Father and Son 'God of God' we necessarily signify two realities, each of which has the unique mode of existence in which the virtues are identical and identical with the being of those realities: both 'God' and 'God' must be fully God.[6] If then, the Spirit is the love or communion of Father and Son, and 'God is Love' (1John 4.16), then the Spirit as love *must* be substantial, fully identical to all that we might name as the 'qualities' of divinity, or the Spirit could not be termed 'God'.[7] Augustine here offers an early version of his insistence that each of the divine three is fully the rational life of wisdom itself that defines divinity. This may help us to see why Augustine sees the Spirit as necessarily an irreducible divine 'person', but it forces upon us some hard questions about the relation between the Spirit as irreducible 'person' and as the essence of Father and Son.

In the passage from Book 6 we are examining, Augustine speaks of the Spirit as distinct from Father and Son *and as also* a gift from and of *the essence* of Father and Son. To be precise he states that Father and Son give their own gift, not that which they are given by another, and they are one in that gift not by participation but by their own essence (*essentia*). We have seen enough to rule out the possibility that Augustine understands Father and Son to be one because they participate in a divine substance prior to their individuality, and so his meaning here seems to be that 'their own gift' which is also that 'in which' they are one without participation is their own essence. In this context we should also note Augustine's invocation of 1 Corithians 6.17 ('he who cleaves to the Lord is one spirit'). Someone cleaving to the Lord does not increase the Lord, and thus Father and Son cleaving to each other, or the Spirit doing likewise to Father and Son does not increase the divinity.[8] This argument further reinforces the sense that Books 5 and 6 present the Spirit as irreducible person *and* as the essence of Father and Son. Even if this reading is correct, however, Augustine offers only a few clues as to the manner in which he links the Spirit's existence as the essence of Father and Son and as distinct individual. Following through some of the ways in which Augustine speaks of

---

[6] *trin.* 6. 2.3–4.6.
[7] With this argument should be compared Augustine's account in *ep. Io. tr.* 7. 4–6. In passing it is worth noting how little of Augustine's argument there depends on the possibility of reversing *deus* and *dilectio* in 1John 4.8. The possibility of so doing in Latin serves mostly as icing on the cake of his argument. The same passage also offers an important instance of Augustine using his second exegetical rule (as explored in Chapter 6): because love is also 'of' God it must refer either to Son or Spirit.
[8] *trin.* 6. 8.9.

the Spirit in subsequent discussion may help us a little in understanding the direction of his thought even in *De trinitate* 5–7.

In the first place, if we look forward a few years to *De trinitate* 15, not surprisingly we see much greater clarity in Augustine's discussion of the Spirit's agency. Once again, while 'gift' itself is used by Scripture of that which is given to Christians for their salvation,[9] Augustine contends that the Spirit is *eternally* gift on the basis of further links that he suggests Scripture invites us to draw.[10] The term 'gift' is used, Augustine tells us, *because* the Spirit is also love.[11] That which the Father gives us is the Spirit of his Son (Gal. 4.6), but the gift *of* the Spirit *is* the Spirit, and the Spirit is love (Rom. 5.5). 'Love' like 'Spirit' is a term which may be predicated of all three persons, but, Augustine argues, Scripture uses it so that when we grasp that the love which the Spirit gives is the Spirit, we will understand that the love which we receive is the love with which Father and Son love each other. Augustine then emphasizes the Spirit as an active giver of himself:

> Nor because they give and he is given is he, therefore, less than they, for he is so given as the Gift of God that he also gives himself as God [*Ita enim datur sicut dei donum ut etiam se ipsum det sicut deus*]. For it is impossible to say of Him that he is not a master of his own power, of whom it was said: 'the Spirit breathes where he will' [John 3.8] ... there is no subordination of the Gift and no domination of the givers, but the concord between the Gift and the givers [*concordia dati et dantium*].[12]

The Spirit gives himself as the Father's gift and as the Son's gift. Father and Son are one because the Spirit gives himself in the begetting of the Son and gives himself as the Son's love for the Father.[13] This text takes us forward to around 420, but it may be complemented with an exegetical analogy that appears much earlier in Augustine's thought.

---

[9] See *trin.* 15. 19.35.

[10] See, for example, *trin.* 5. 16.17 (CCSL 50. 224): 'sempiterne Spiritus donum'.

[11] See *trin.* 15. 18.32. As we saw, the first explicit linking of the two titles occurs at *fid.* 9. 19. The association of the Gift of God with the love that is spoken of in Rom. 5.5 also begins around the same period, see, for example, *exp. prop. Rm.* 20 and 52.

[12] *trin.* 15. 19.36 (CCSL 50. 513).

[13] My language here owes something to Rowan D. Williams, '*Sapientia* and the Trinity: Reflections on the *De trinitate*', in B. Bruning *et al.* (eds.), *Collectanea Augustiniana: Mélanges T. J. Van Bavel* (Leuven: Leuven University Press, 1990) [= *Aug(L)* 40–1 (1990–1)], 1: 317–32, here 327–8: 'The Spirit is "common" to Father and Son not as a quality characterizing them equally, an impersonal attribute, but as that active divine giving, not simply identical with the person of the Father, which the Father communicates to the Son to give in his turn ... the Father, in eternally giving (divine) life to the Son, gives that life as itself a "giving" agency, for there is no pre-personal or sub-personal divinity; he gives the Son the capacity to give that same giving life'.

Before we do so, however, we must note how Augustine's reflections here reinforce the account of appropriation I offered at the end of Chapter 8. Scripture identifies the third of the divine three with a name common to each in order to suggest a reflection on the Spirit's existence being from or of God. But, unlike the case of the Son being named Wisdom, the appropriated title does not reveal further dimensions of the unique title; the Spirit is most appropriately named by a combination of appropriated titles – Holy and Spirit. Even when the unique title Gift provides the key (and Augustine does not always turn to this title), it does so because it reveals dimensions of the appropriated titles Holy, Spirit and Love. These titles must take centre stage because only meditation on them helps us to understand that all of the Spirit's actions are founded in and reveal the Spirit's status as the (co-equal) Spirit of Father and Son. Only by learning that this is so do we grasp what it means for the Spirit to be eternally gift and fully 'personal'.

We see the same perspective presented perhaps a little more clearly at *De civitate Dei* 11. 24 when Augustine asks if the Spirit may be said to be the goodness (*bonitas*) of Father and Son. Without direct scriptural warrant Augustine hesitates, but he is willing to assert that the Spirit is the holiness (*sanctitas*) of both (not as *qualitas*, but as *substantia* and *persona in trinitate*), because holiness is predicated of the Spirit *proprie*, as his own or properly. The divine *bonitas* is identical to the divine *sanctitas*, Augustine argues, and we see something of this when we ask of creation the three questions: who made it?; by what means, through what, was it made?; for what purpose was it made? We should answer that the Father effected creation through speaking his Word. But when we remember that he then 'saw that it was good', we can see that Scripture shows us the Father noting that the product accords with the blessedness that was the reason for its creation and the end to which it is aimed. But this end is the Holy Spirit, the creation finds its end in rejoicing in and adhering to the Spirit who is the divine goodness.[14] This chain of argument again locates Scripture's appropriation of common titles as part of Augustine's second rule of scriptural predication: Scripture appropriates to the Spirit terms common to each of the divine three in order to show the character of the Spirit's derivation from and consubstantiality with the Father. To

---

[14] *civ*. 11. 24 (CCSL 47. 343–4). I return to this passage of *civ*., which dates from *c*.416–18, at the beginning of Chapter 11. In this passage I assume *proprie* is used somewhat loosely. Augustine does not think that *sanctitas* is the Spirit's *proprium* in a technical sense, and thus here he must be only indicating that the combination of *sanctitas* and *spiritus* identifies *this* particular referent of *spiritus*.

see this dependence and equivalence is to see the true mystery of God's love for and immediate presence to his creation.

ACTS 4.32

In his 14th tractate on John, which has been dated to both 406–7 and *c*.413, Augustine writes that Father and Son are not be spoken of as two Gods, as Gods individually,

> For so great is the love of the Holy Spirit there [*tanta enim ibi est caritas Spiritus Sancti*], so great the peace of unity that when it is asked about each one, let your answer be 'God'; when it is asked about the Trinity, let your answer be 'God'. For if the spirit of man is one spirit when it cleaves to God, since the Apostle clearly says 'He who cleaves to the Lord is one spirit' [1Cor. 6.17], how much more is the Son as equal, cleaving to the Father, one God together with him … Hear a second testimony … 'They had one soul and one heart toward the Lord' [Acts 4.32]. If the love from so many souls made one soul and from so many hearts made one heart, how great is the love between Father and Son?[15]

The first sentence of the quotation links the power of the Holy Spirit's love and the rules of predication that govern our speech about the divine unity: the love and peace that the Spirit produces is such, not simply that God is one, but that we must confess the equality of the divine three *and* their unity. In *Tractate* 18 – discussed at length in Chapter 9 – Augustine is a little more direct about the active role of the Spirit: if the love which God sent and which makes one heart and soul out of many, how much more are Father and Son one 'in the fount of love' (*in fonte dilectionis*)?[16] It is interesting that this increasing clarity about the Spirit as the active agent of the divine unity appears in the very set of tractates where we found Augustine's mature reading of John 5.19. The parallel between these pneumatological passages and the Christological set examined in Chapter 9 continues: Augustine's mature reading of Acts 4.32 appears

---

[15] *Io. ev. tr.* 14. 9 (CCSL 36. 147–8). Acts 4.32. 'Anima una et cor unum' is the most common version of the key phrase of the verse in Augustine, but he knows more than one version. See M.-F. Berrouard, 'La première communauté de Jérusalem comme image de l'unité de la Trinité. Une des exégèses augustiniennes d'Act 4, 32', in *Homo Spiritalis. Festgabe für Luc Verheijen* (Würzburg: Augustines-Verlag 1987), 207–24. In what follows I treat only Acts 4.32. A similar case could be made by following Augustine's reading of 1Cor. 6.17. See the early use at *trin.* 6. 3 and later uses at *serm.* 238. 2, *serm.* 241. 2, *conl. Max.* 14 and 15. 20, 1. 10, 2. 10.2, 2. 20.1, 2. 22.2. In this case, Augustine speaks mostly of the Son 'clinging' to the Father to produce unity of substance, but pneumatological material is also present.

[16] *Io. ev. tr.* 18. 4 (CCSL 36. 181–2).

most clearly in *Tractate* 39, the very text in which we found Augustine speaking of Father and Son existing *ad aliquid*:

> [if] many souls through love are one soul, and many hearts are one heart, what does the very fountain of love do in the Father and the Son? ... If, therefore, 'the love of God [which] has been poured forth in our hearts by the Holy Spirit who has been given to us' [Rom. 5.5] makes many souls one soul and many hearts one heart, how much more does [the Spirit] make the Father and the Son and the Holy Spirit one God, one light, one *principium*? [*si ergo caritas Dei ... multa corda facit unum cor, quanto magis pater et filius et spiritus sanctus, Deus unus, lumen unum, unumque principium?*][17]

The same analogy also appears in a number of texts addressed directly to Homoians or Homoian converts to the Catholic faith, including his debate with the Homoian bishop Maximinus in 427.[18] Thus, following a pattern we have already traced in a number of contexts, clear statement of the Spirit as active lover and active agent of unity within the Godhead appears most clearly *c*.420, even if it seems to lie just beneath the surface of texts from around a decade earlier.

The striking character of Augustine's reading of Acts 4.32, even in its earliest forms, may be seen in comparison with his sources. The passage from *Tractate* 14 quoted above probably draws directly on Ambrose, *De fide* 1. 2:

> if in all those who believed there was, as it is written, one soul and one heart [Acts 4.32], and if everyone who cleaves to the Lord is one Spirit [1Cor. 6.17], as the Apostle has also said, if a man and his wife are one flesh, if all we mortal men are, so far as regards our nature, of one substance [*quantum ad naturam pertinet, unius substantiae sumus*]: if this is what Scripture says of created persons, that, being many, they are one, who can in no way be compared to the divine persons [*quorum nulla potest esse cum divinis comparatio*], how much more are the Father and Son one in divinity, with whom there is no difference either of substance or of will?[19]

Ambrose is the only Latin pro-Nicene to use Acts 4.32 as an analogy for the Trinity and he does so only here. The fact that in this text he uses Acts 4.32 alongside 1 Corinthians 6.17 seems to mark it as Augustine's source. But note the difference. Ambrose draws the sort of parallel one finds in a number of his Greek contemporaries between the unity of human beings in a universal nature and the unity of the divine persons.

---

[17] *Io. ev. tr.* 39. 5 (CCSL 36. 348).
[18] *ep.* 238. 2 11; *ep.* 170. 5; *conl. Max.* 12; *symb. cat.* (= *serm.* 398) 4.
[19] Ambrose, *fid.* 1. 2.18 (CSEL 78. 10–11).

He gives us little clue about the sort of universal he envisages and insists anyway that 'no comparison' is possible. Augustine uses the same texts as part of a far more complex suggestion about the effect of the persons' activity towards each other. Augustine's analogy does not rely on drawing consequences from the existence of a universal and unitary nature, but on the dynamic language of agents producing unity. Augustine's very personal reading of Acts 4.32 reflects the same theology that we found in his way of contributing to the long exegetical tradition concerning John 5.19.

THE SPIRIT AND THE LIFE OF THE DIVINE THREE

This exegesis of Acts 4.32 can now draw us back to the balance Augustine seeks between speaking of the Spirit as irreducible 'person' and as the essence of Father and Son. The complementarity of Augustine's mature accounts of Son and Spirit suggests with even greater force a vision of the divine communion as constituted by the intra-divine acts of the divine three, in an order eternally established by the Father. While Augustine does not simply identify the Spirit with the act of loving or self-giving – he uses nouns such as *dilectio* or *amor* rather than verbal or participial forms – the equation is clear enough. The Spirit is the communion of Father and Son which, as we have seen, is a mutual act of adherence and love; the Spirit is the love and the fount of love between Father and Son who eternally gives himself; the Spirit, as also 'God from God', shares in the simple mode of divine existence in which he is what he might be thought to possess. Thus, in these mature texts, Augustine presents the Spirit as the agent identical to the act of communion between Father and Son.

But Augustine is not suggesting that Father and Son are somehow brought into unity by the gift of the Spirit as an act subsequent to the generation of the Son. It makes sense only to read him as saying that the Father from eternity establishes the Son as one who is all that the Father is, and as one who loves the Father in and with the love that is God from God and also all that the Father is. The Father establishes the Son as one who also has as his essence the love that is identical with the essence of God, of the Father, but that love is also the active agent of his love for the Father. It seems true to say then both that the Son loves the Father and that the Spirit is the love and communion which joins Father and Son in love – the Son both loves (being himself love itself) and the Spirit is the love with which he loves. But, again, this is to offer a summary of emergent themes that Augustine himself never does, and even this summary misses a layer of complexity.

In the case of the Son we spoke of titles and relationships that were unique to him: in the case of the Spirit the picture is much more complex because the title 'love' is appropriated. A passage from *De trinitate* 15 quoted in the first section of the chapter may now help to reveal the complexity this creates:

(28) ... we should so conceive these three [memory, understanding, will] as some one thing which all have, parallel to wisdom itself, and which is so retained in the nature of each one, as that he who has it, is that which he has ...

(29) ... in that simple and highest nature, substance is not one thing, and love another, but that substance itself is love, and that love itself is substance, whether in the Father, or the Son, or the Holy Spirit, and yet the Holy Spirit is properly called love.[20]

Once again, because there is one simple and divine nature, we must be careful not to speak only of each of the divine three as fullness, without also noting that the fullness they possess in such a way that they are identical with it, is the one fullness that is God. And thus we cannot speak simply as if the Spirit as person were the essence of Father and Son. That the Spirit is named as love should not lead us towards a picture of Father and Son having as their essence something that is not their own, not identical with them. Rather, we must say both that Father and Son are in their essence love *and that* the Spirit is the love of Father and Son and fully another beside and in them. There is no impersonal or pre-personal essence of the persons; Father, Son and Spirit have an essence that is their own, which is eternally one, and also which is the Spirit. When Augustine notes the difficulty of grasping why the Spirit is named by terms common to each of the divine three, the difficulty does not only consist in the basic problem of understanding how divine love *must* also be irreducible 'person', it also consists in the extra complexity that reveals itself once we grasp how Father and Son are also love and love itself.[21] There is no 'essence' before the divine 'persons', and yet the persons are each identically the fullness of the Godhead, and must also in some sense be the others' essence. Thus the summary that I offered in the previous paragraph based almost entirely on the agential language of the 'interpersonal' acts of the divine three certainly corresponds to a central line of thought in the mature Augustine, but more is required.

[20] *trin.* 15. 17.28–9.   [21] *trin.* 15. 17.27.

The French Benedictine theologian Ghislain Lafont has written very suggestively about the importance of 'redoublement' – reduplication or repetition – in Trinitarian theology. If we are to do any justice to the mystery revealed in scriptural language, Lafont argues, we must describe the same ground twice over, using the language of irreducible persons and the language of a unity of essence and will. It is not simply that we should have available language for both 'levels' of Trinitarian discussion, but that we need to understand how speaking about the divine three as 'persons' involves showing that those 'persons' each possess the divine essence in a particular mode, and how speaking about the divine essence involves showing that essence to exist through and as subsisting relations.[22] The language of the last sentence should betray that for Lafont and a number of his best recent adapters, the high point of the process is reached in Thomas's peculiarly sophisticated articulation of Trinitarian terminology.[23]

I suggest that there are in fact many forms of 'redoublement' to be found in Trinitarian tradition, and that the tensions we see in the mature Augustine offer important and distinct examples from the Thomistic patterns to which those who have recently sought to appropriate Lafont have (rightly) pointed. Augustine's pattern of 'redoublement' does not proceed via an examination of the language of persons and essence, but

---

[22] Ghislain Lafont, *Peut-on Connaître Dieu en Jésus-Christ?* (Paris: Cerf, 1969), esp. 130, 160 and 234, here 130: 'Si nous reprenons l'ensemble de ces précisions sur le langage, il apparaît que l'expression trinitaire obéit à ce que l'on pourrait appeler une *loi de redoublement*: pour dire un aspect quelconque du Mystère, il faut toujours employer en succession continue deux formulas qui, sans doute, se complètent, le Révélation nous en est garante, mais dont nous ne pouvons saisir que la non-contradiction. l'aspect positif de la coexistence des aspects soulignés par ces formulas est reconnu dans la foi, sans que la raison puisse faire autre chose que le pressentir. C'est qu'en effet, ces deuz formulas nécessaires sont le plus souvent en position dialectique l'une par rapport à l'autre: d'un côte on affirme l'identité (de l'essence avec le relation, de la relation avec la procession, etc.) et de l'autre on affirme le non-identité (des même termes sous un autre rapport), et il ne s'agit pas là seulement de prises de vue logiques; le Mystère tient précisément à ce que identité et non-identité sont également réelles au moins en certains cas, quand il s'agit de l'être et de la *ratio*, bien que non sur le même plan.' At p. 234, Lafont speaks more clearly of the need for a number of different reduplications, but this point is not discussed at length. I disagree with Lafont's wider account at two key points: I do not share his narrative of the supposed separation between *theologia* and *oikonomia* after Nicaea, nor his narrative in which the mistakes of the Cappadocians are partially rectified by Augustine but only fully overcome in the synthesis of Thomas. For an excellent critique, see André D'Halleux, 'Personnalisme ou Essentialisme Trinitaire chez Les Pères Cappadociens', in *Patrologie et Oecuménisme. Recueil d'études* (Leuven: Leuven University Press, 1990), 215–68.

[23] See, for examples, Gilles Emery, 'Essentialism or Personalism in the Treatise on God in St Thomas Aquinas?', in *Trinity in Aquinas* (Ypsilanti, MI: Sapientia Press, 2003), 165–208; Matthew Levering, *Scripture and Metaphysics: Aquinas and the Renewal of Trinitarian Theology* (Oxford: Blackwell, 2004), esp. 214ff.

via the interweaving of two strands of exegesis and philosophical reflection. The first strand focuses on the divine three as active agents, and here Augustine seems to have moved cautiously towards an account of the three as existing dynamically *ad aliquid*. Such discussions culminate a line of argument emergent since Augustine's earliest attempts to state that there is nothing 'in' the Trinity other than the three persons. We can perhaps speak of a certain 'analogical personalism' here. The term 'personalism' is used in many senses: I mean by the term Augustine's insistence that the divine irreducible rational life and self-presence is essential to being God, such that there can be no pre-personal divine.[24] In this sense divine personhood is the fundamental unit of Augustine's Trinitarian ontology. Interestingly, Augustine's rejection of person and nature language is *in favour of* this 'personalism' in which, from the Father as *principium*, the divine three (each of whom is and all of whom together are the divine rational life) eternally constitute the 'one substance' of the Trinity. 'Analogical' is, however, the necessary qualifier of 'personalism' because Augustine is clear about the ways in which divine 'persons' transcend human persons and the categories that we use to speak of them.[25]

The second strand of discourse focuses on the divine three as each being the one fullness of the Godhead and as also the fullness of the indivisible Godhead inseparably with the others. The relationship of irreducible

---

[24] In using the term I am not arguing that Augustine makes any extensive equation between the 'personal' nature of God and the ultimately or foundationally 'personal' nature of the created order as an ontological principle. He does, of course, treat the 'highest' form of created existence as the inherently personal rational life of those made *in imagine Dei*.

[25] Andrew Louth in 'Love and the Trinity: Saint Augustine and the Greek Fathers', *AugStud* 33 (2002), 1–16, is one of the few recent authors to speak of Augustine's 'personalism', but he does so as a form of critique. I disagree with Louth's article in three respects. First, Augustine describes the Spirit as the love between Father and Son well before *trin.* 5–6 and the theme appears from a wide matrix of contexts, not simply an observation of the Spirit's function among Christians. Augustine's early order pneumatology in which the Spirit perfects the creation and draws it to God is of particular importance. At the same time, Augustine's attempts to link this theology to an account of what it means for the Spirit to be common to Father and Son or a *res naturae* seem to draw on a wider pro-Nicene dynamic. Second, Louth overlooks Augustine's consistent expression of the impossibility of our understanding fully what we are able to say about the divine communion, and especially about the individual existence of each of the divine three. Augustine does not, as I hope to have shown, '[move] between human and divine love without much sense of difference' (p. 6). Third, but beyond the scope of this book, I am not as certain as Louth that Augustine's Greek contemporaries offer quite such a consistent account of which scriptural texts speak of *theologia* and which of *oikonomia*. That division is still under development (see the discussions of Andrew Radde-Gallwitz, *Divine Simplicity in Basil of Caesarea* (Oxford: Oxford University Press, 2010)). Of course, there are significant differences between Augustine and his Greek (and Latin contemporaries) here: but I do not think those differences are best identified by presenting Augustine as differing because of an epistemological hubris. For discussion of another, Catholic, personalist reading of Augustine, see my '*Sempiterne Spiritus Donum*'.

persons to each other, to the one essence that God is, is not explored by manipulation of a genus or species terminology. It is explored in part by Augustine's use of some basic principles of divine simplicity to articulate the divine processions such that no division of the divine essence is involved even as each person is the fullness of that essence; in part by carefully placed insistence that appropriated titles do shape our understanding of a divine individual, but only by also showing how that individual is necessarily so absolutely 'personal' because they are identical to the one divine fullness. Thus, the case of appropriated titles offers a particularly clear example of the way in which this second strand of discourse exists in a mutual relationship with the first. This second level of discourse thus also has an 'apophatic' function, forcing upon us one key point at which the Trinitarian mystery escapes our thought (let alone our speech): the unity of the persons despite their irreducibility. A similar 'apophatic' function is of course seen also at the first level; Augustine's discussions of the persons in that manner frequently emphasizes the difficulty of our imagining the lack of the accidental in the divine three, their existence simply as what we are always tempted to imagine them as possessing.

'Apophatic' is a dangerous term to apply at a time when its popularity frequently robs it of dense significance: here I mean it as almost synonymous with Augustine's *ineffabilis*. In Trinitarian contexts *ineffabilis* seems to indicate not merely that we cannot speak of a topic; but that the rational order enables a process of intellectual ascent towards understanding, but one that enables increasing precision about how the divine transcends any categories available either in the material or the intelligible sphere.[26] At the same time, Augustine sees the divine ineffability as part and parcel of the particular intelligible structure of the creation as revealing of its Creator, rather than as preventing us from seeing the creation as intelligible in this way. But something more of this relationship will be seen through the course of the next two chapters, in discussion of *De trinitate* 9 and 10, and I leave it until then.

---

[26] One way of tracing Augustine's understanding of *ineffabilis* is to explore how he links the term with *intellectus* or *intellegere*. For example, cf. *ord*. 2. 7.24 and *qu. XVI in Matt*. 13. At *ep*. 242. 5, written to the 'Arian' Elpidius, Augustine writes: 'there are many things which may be said about the ineffability of the Trinity, not in order that it may be expressed in words – otherwise it would not be ineffable – but in order that it may be understood from the words that are said that it cannot be understood in words'. The ineffable is thus not simply resistant to understanding or speech, but requires of us a specific mode of understanding, one that finds its completion in confession of transcendence even as it achieves. Augustine is not, however, 'apophatic' if that is taken to necessarily include a ps. Dionysian sense of God's transcending of ever Goodness and Being.

AND 'FROM' THE SON?

It is enough for the Christian to believe that the only cause of all created things, whether heavenly or earthly, whether visible or invisible, is the goodness of the Creator, the one true God; and that nothing exists but himself that does not derive its existence from Him; and that He is the Trinity – to wit, the Father, and the Son begotten of the Father, and the Holy Spirit proceeding from the same Father, but one and the same Spirit of Father and Son.[27]

In the final two sections of this chapter I want to consider two questions that follow from my discussion of the divine three and their interpersonal acts. The first concerns one of the most hotly disputed questions about Augustine's pneumatology: his account of 'double procession'. The brief discussion I offer here is intended to show, first, that this account flows from some of the principles I have just outlined and, second, how it thus not only escapes some of the criticisms frequently aimed at it, but also suggests a number of lines for investigation that could lead debate on this question in new directions.

I will begin by turning to one of his most extended mature discussions of the question. At *De trinitate* 15. 17.29 Augustine famously writes:

> only he from whom the Son was begotten and from whom the Spirit principally [*principaliter*] proceeds, is God the Father. I have added principally therefore because the Holy Spirit is also found to proceed from the Son. But the Father also gave this to him, not as though he already existed and did not yet have it [*non iam exsistenti et nondum habenti*], but whatever he gave to the only-begotten Word, he gave by/in begetting him [*sed quidquid unigenito verbo dedit gignendo dedit*]. He so begot him, therefore, that the common gift should also proceed from him, and that the Holy Spirit should be the Spirit of both.[28]

This passage is frequently used to demonstrate that Augustine envisages the Father as *principium* within the Trinity. But I think it equally important that we see the extent to which Augustine is here simply filling out a picture we have already seen him sketch. Note that Augustine equates the Father's giving to the Son that the Spirit proceed from him with the Father's establishing the Spirit as the Spirit *of* Father and Son. Thus the Father's begetting of the Son is identical with the establishment

---

[27] *ench.* 3. 9.
[28] *trin* 15. 17.29 (CCSL 50. 503). Fundamental for interpreting Augustine's discussion of pneumatology in *trin.* 15 is Basil Studer, 'Zur Pneumatologie des Augustinus von Hippo (De Trinitate 15.17.27–27.50)', in *Mysterium Caritatis: Studien zur Exegese und zur Trinitätslehre in der Alten Kirche*, Studia Anselmiana 127 (Rome: Pontifico Ateneo S. Anselmo, 1999), 311–27. Studer shows clearly how this discussion should not be interpreted solely in terms of the mental 'analogy' developed in *trin.* 8–15.

of the communion of Father, Son and Spirit because *in* the begetting of the Son the Father gives his love (or substance), thus eternally establishing the Son as lover of the Father and the Spirit as the personal giving love of Father and Son.

Augustine further refines his argument a little later in Book 15:

> And he who can understand in that which the Son says: 'as the Father has life in himself, so he has given to the Son to have life in himself' [John 5.26], that the Father did not give life to the Son already existing without life, but so begot him apart from time that the life which the Father gave to the Son by/in begetting is co-eternal with the life of the Father who gave [*sed ita eum sine tempore genuisse ut uita quam pater filio gignendo dedit coaeterna sit uitae patris qui dedit*]; let him understand that, just as the Father has in himself that the Holy Spirit should proceed from the Father, it is so to be understood that his proceeding also from the Son comes to the Son from the Father [*de patre habet utique ut et de illo procedat spiritus sanctus*].[29]

Augustine also quotes at this point from *Tractate* 99:

> the Holy Spirit has it from the Father himself that he proceeds also from the Son, just as he proceeds from the Father.[30]

Augustine has refined his argument by speaking not so much of the role of the Father in relationship to the Son, but of the Father's relationship to the Spirit, and in so doing he emphasizes the importance of viewing the Father as the cause and source of the Trinitarian communion. The question of the Father's *principium* here should detain us a little further.

In the *De fide et symbolo* of 393 Augustine tells us that the Spirit is said to come from the Father so that we know there to be only one *principium*. The derivation of Son and Spirit from the Father prevents Christians from proposing a plurality of divine principles who would necessarily require a further principle common to them all.[31] In *De trinitate* 5, however, Augustine asks whether the Son can be said to be the Spirit's *principium*. If the Spirit does proceed also from the Son Augustine sees this predication as possible, but he immediately adds that only as the Father and Son are one Lord in relation to the creation are they one *principium* in relation to the Spirit.[32]

To understand this comment we must look to the paragraphs that precede it. Augustine has just argued that Father and Son are both named Creator, but are one *principium* in relation to the created order. They

---

[29] *trin* 15. 26.47 (CCSL 50. 528).   [30] *trin.* 15. 27.48 and *Io. ev. tr.* 99. 8.
[31] *fid.* 9. 19.   [32] *trin.* 5. 14.15.

are one *principium* because they are one God.³³ I suggest that this comment, in turn, needs to be interpreted in the light of Augustine's mature account of inseparable operation. As we have seen, in that account, the Father elects from eternity to work always through the Son. And thus, we can perhaps take Augustine to be arguing that just as creation is worked by the Father through the Son, so too the Spirit proceeds from the Father, but proceeds as the Father's eternal gift to the Son and eternally as the Son's love given (and giving itself) to the Father. In which case, Augustine tries to suggest, because the Father eternally works through the Son he eternally establishes it in generating the Son that both Father and Son are the *principium* of the Spirit.

But Augustine here is pressing on into territory for which no maps were (or are) available, and it is significant that apart from this one text in *De trinitate* 5 Augustine never again speaks in this manner of Father and Son as the one *principium* of the Spirit. Instead, we see him develop the formulae I quoted above, stating that the Father gives it to the Son and to the Spirit that the Spirit proceeds also from the Son. Such formulae allow him to avoid the unwanted connotations that might follow from describing the Son as also *principium*. In 427, against the 'Arian' bishop Maximinus, Augustine writes: 'when the Son spoke of the Spirit he said "He proceeds from the Father", because the Father is the author [*auctor*] of his procession. The Father begot a Son and, by begetting him, gave it to him that the Holy Spirit proceeds from him'.³⁴ Gerald Bonner correctly comments that this passage demonstrates Augustine's continuing concern to find a way of distinguishing the roles of Father and the Son in the Spirit's procession, even as the Spirit is the Spirit of both.³⁵ Augustine's account of the Father's *principium* does not, thus, involve him so much in compromising the Father's status as *principium*, but in suggesting to us that for the Father to act eternally as *principium* is for the Father eternally to give rise to two who share the divine fullness and through whom the Father eternally works. The Father's status as *principium* is thus not that of an autonomous agent who stands 'above' Son and Spirit, but one who works eternally through the Son and Spirit he generates and spirates.

Augustine never discusses directly the extent to which we can speak of the Spirit having a role in the Son's generation. But because Augustine envisages the Father eternally constituting the Son through giving him his own personal and active Spirit who is love, we do seem to be able

---

³³ *trin.* 5. 13.14.   ³⁴ *c. Max.* 2. 5.
³⁵ Gerald Bonner, 'St Augustine's Doctrine of the Holy Spirit', *Sobornost* 4/1 (1960), 51–66.

to conclude that the Son is generated *in* the Spirit. But this supposition remains just that. I suspect Augustine never discusses this question because of the lack of significant scriptural warrant, and because of his commitment to the standard *taxis* of Father–Son–Spirit. We find ourselves in the presence of ideas that certainly seem to follow from more well-established principles, but which demand of us a great deal of reserve when Scripture provides us with so little. Noting, however, that this might seem to be an implication of Augustine's presentation helps us to see even more clearly that Augustine does not see the Son as possessing any secondary mediatorial role in the eternal procession of the Spirit. This is so because our question about the possible role of the Spirit in the generation of the Son only arises because Augustine is clear that the Spirit comes from the Father to the Son as the fullness of divinity, as the personal loving that constitutes the Son as fully God in the Trinitarian life. The Son's seeing of and love for the Father occurs *because* the Son is the fullness of the divinity and in some sense has the Spirit as his essence: if the Spirit 'proceeds' from the Son it is because this is the manner in which the Father is eternally the sole Trinitarian 'cause'.

Noting that Augustine pushes tentatively in this direction is of relevance for modern debate over the *filioque*. Fundamental to recent discussions between Catholic and Orthodox theologians has been the 1995 'clarification' on the meaning of the *filioque* produced under the auspices of the Pontifical Council for Promoting Christian Unity.[36] Much of the text focuses on identifying what it takes to be persistent confusions in terminology between Latin and Greek traditions, and on establishing an outline history of the controversy. The concluding paragraphs of the text, however, suggest that Western understandings of *filioque* do not contravene assertion of the Father's priority in the Trinitarian life. One of the most interesting tactics pursued in these paragraphs is the dual argument that, first, it is 'in' the Spirit that the relationship between Father and Son achieves 'Trinitarian perfection' and that, second, the Father generates the Son 'by breathing through Him the Holy Spirit'.

---

[36] 'The Greek and Latin Traditions Regarding the Procession of the Holy Spirit', issued by the Pontifical Council for Promoting Christian Unity, *L'Osservatore Romano* (weekly English-language edition) n. 38 (1408), 20 Sept. 1995 (originally in French in *L'Osservatore Romano* n. 211 (41.050) 13 Sept. 1995). For a particularly helful outline of the history involved here, see Brian E. Daley, 'Revisiting the "Filioque": Roots and Branches of an Old Debate. Part One', *Pro Ecclesia* 10 (2001), 31–62; Daley, 'Revisiting the "*Filioque*". Part Two: Contemporary Catholic Approaches", *Pro Ecclesia* 10 (2001), 195–212.

This second point is phrased thus, I suspect, to serve the wider goal of suggesting the ecumenical possibilities of our speaking of the Spirit processing *through* the Son. Whether or not 'through the Son' as understood in current Catholic/Orthodox discussion adequately captures Augustine's intent, the terse sentences in this document do parallel some key themes in Augustine's presentation. The Father's giving of the Spirit to the Son is intrinsic to his generation of the Son as the one who loves the Father with the fullness of divine love. This line of thought has not, however, been much pursued subsequently. As an indication it may be noted that the otherwise very helpful document produced by the North American Orthodox-Catholic Theological Consultation in 2003 sees itself as following down a path opened by the earlier Vatican document, but offers no discussion of this theme.[37] This latter text builds on the first by suggesting further clarification of the range of meaning inherent in the Latin *procedere*, and by arguing that Latins use the term in a sense which accords the Father the status of 'primordial source' and 'ultimate cause' in the Trinity. But it shies away from pursuing the hints I identified in the final paragraphs of the 1995 'clarification'.[38]

The documents I have mentioned here tend to focus their energies on (what some Orthodox theologians present as the traditional Catholic tactic of) arguing historically that distinctions between Greek and Latin pneumatologies are mainly matters of terminological confusion. At the same time they struggle to suggest formulae that may point an ecumenical way forward. My sense, however, is that much work remains to be done looking in some detail at the variety of different accounts of double procession and at the wider contexts within which they occur.[39] It may well be that the Latin *procedere* covers distinctions between a number of Greek verbs, and that it is ecumenically helpful to note the confusions that have resulted, but Augustine's texts suggest to us that we need also to pay close attention to the ways in which the very flexibility of the verb means that it can be used to raise questions about how the Father

---

[37] 'The Filioque: A Church Dividing Issue?', 25 Oct. 2003. Available at http://www.usccb.org/seia/filioque.shtml.

[38] See the useful parallel discussion and critique of David Coffey, 'The Roman "Clarification" of the Doctrine of the *Filioque*', *International Journal of Systematic Theology* 5 (2003), 3–21.

[39] One of the strongest and most eloquent critiques of the Vatican 'Clarification' comes from Jean-Claude Larchet, 'La Question du "Filioque"', *Le Messager Orthodoxe* 129 (1998), 3–58. My reading of Augustine differs in almost every particular, but one parallel between Larchet and the 'clarification' is the tendency to offer a narrative distinction between positions within the tradition that divides those traditions far too easily into clear units. Further progress may perhaps be achieved by questioning further this tactic.

268   *Into the mystery*

to be *principium* within the Trinitarian life. The wide semantic range of the verb means that we must examine with some care its actual use and, when we do so, note the broader theological questions about the character of the divine life that are raised.[40]

SUBSISTING RELATIONS?

For many of those modern writers on Trinitarian theology who are strongly critical of 'Western' approaches, the idea of the divine persons as 'subsistent relations' has been read as not only intertwined with, but also dependent on, Trinitarian theologies that (often implicitly) rely on models of 'internal' self-relatedness.[41] It is moreover seen as a doctrine that either begins with Augustine or at least is the outworking of principles he establishes. This brief discussion is intended to show the complexities inherent in exploring the relationship between Thomas and Augustine on this question.

As *both* Augustine's and Thomas's texts are often misinterpreted in broad narratives of Western theology's failure, I will first spend a few moments with one key text from Thomas's *Summa Theologiae*. The notion of *relatio subsistens* – 'subsisting relation' – arises against the background of a debate concerning whether 'person' in God signifies the divine substance (or essence) or whether it signifies the *relatio*, the distinctive character of the divine person.[42] Thomas distinguishes his position from a number of alternatives. Person cannot signify the divine essence as does the word 'God', because then any use of person in the plural is an accommodation to which little sense can be attached. Perhaps, then, person directly refers to the divine essence and indirectly 'co-signifies' a relation: this opinion actually takes us little further as the problems with the term 'person' remain. Perhaps we can reverse this opinion and suggest

---

[40] We should note that Augustine understands 'procession' to be incomprehensible every bit as clearly as does Gregory Nazianzen.

[41] For example, William Hill, *The Three-Personed God: The Trinity as a Mystery of Salvation* (Washington DC: Catholic University of America Press, 1982), 61: 'the fullest implications of Augustine's thought are that God is *one* "person", within whose divine consciousness there is a threefold self-relatedness'. It may be that some Neo-Thomists offer ammunition to those seeking to make such charges in offering a narrative of Thomas's 'completing' Augustine precisely by giving a more focused alignment of Son and Spirit with mental faculties, but it is vital to avoid projecting onto Thomas Neo-Thomist positions without careful examination. For example, see Reginald Garrigou-LaGrange, *The Trinity and God the Creator: A Commentary on St Thomas's Theological Summa Ia, q. 27–119*, trans. F. C. Eckhoff (St Louis: Herder, 1952), 68.

[42] My account here owes much to that found in Emery's *The Trinitarian Theology of St Thomas Aquinas*, 114ff.

that person refers primarily to the relation and secondarily to the divine essence. This appears to have been the position of William of Auxerre.

Thomas finds this last opinion fruitful, but insufficient insofar as it does not seem to do justice to the full individuality, the being for itself, of a person. Accordingly, he develops William's solution, emphasizing that in God relations cannot exist as accidental to the divine essence: they must subsist just as does the divine essence. But, at the same time, for the word 'person' to be used appropriately, it must signify that which most truly distinguishes one person from another. The solution, then, is this: 'a divine person signifies a relation as subsisting. And this is to signify relation by way of a substance, and such a relation is a *hypostasis* subsisting in the divine nature.'[43] Continuing, Thomas writes that 'person' thus can be said to signify relation directly, but only insofar as it signifies the relation expressed in the *hypostasis* that Father, Son or Spirit is. This move then permits Thomas to say that 'person' can also be said to signify essence directly, as long as we understand that this is because essence and *hypostasis* are the same, the essence expressed by means of the *hypostasis*/relation (a point to be noted by any who would argue that a 'relation' of necessity indicates a lesser degree of irreducibility than the category of 'person' or 'hypotasis'!). Thomas's move is sophisticated and yet dependent on the application of fairly simple principles, the lack of anything accidental in God and the impropriety of understanding the divine essence to be distinct from the persons.

Thomas's understanding of a divine person as a subsisting relation needs also to be read in the context of his account of the unique character of relations of origin. Among the various kinds of relation that Thomas identifies is that of a relation which is 'real' – that is, a relation which exists 'in the nature of things' and not purely logically, existing only by way of conceptual abstraction – in both of two things related. Thomas argues that such relations in God must be founded on activity, and thus on the Father's generating of the Son and spirating of the Spirit.[44] Remembering this account of real relations in God helps because it reinforces the extent to which Thomas sees the persons, as subsisting

---

[43] *ST.* 1. q. 29. a. 4. resp.: 'Distinctio autem in divinis non fit nisi per relationes originis, ut dictum est supra. Relatio autem in divinis non est sicut accidens inhaerens subiecto, sed est ipsa divina essentia, unde est subsistens, sicut essentia divina subsistit. Sicut ergo deitas est Deus, ita paternitas divina est Deus pater, qui est persona divina. Persona igitur divina significat relationem ut subsistentem. Et hoc est significare relationem per modum substantiae quae est hypostasis subsistens in natura divina'.

[44] *ST.* 1. q. 28 a. 4, resp.

relations, existing because of the Father's eternal and ordered activity of generating and spirating.[45]

Some of the differences between Thomas and Augustine may now be apparent. As we have seen, Augustine simply does not offer (and may strategically wish to avoid) the sort of logical and philosophical precision so central to Thomas's exposition. We have seen many examples of this distinction through the course of the book: it may also be worth nothing that Augustine does not even offer clear definitions of the four traditional scholastic relations (*paternitas, filiatio, spiratio* and *processio*).[46] Nor do we see anything like Thomas's speculative attempt to demonstrate that the existence of real relations between the persons would divide the Godhead.[47] Thomas inhabits a scholastic culture and tradition that enables a very different style of work from that we see in Augustine. Thomas's preference for the use of person and nature terminology found in such Latins as Hilary and Ambrose reflects the fact that he stands in a tradition stretching from Boethius and through Alcuin and Anselm which was far more willing than Augustine to invest with deep significance for describing the structure of the Trinity a complex metaphysical terminology. This is so even as we should note that Thomas himself both takes with full seriousness the analogical character of all our talk about God and is willing to state directly that the divine cannot be comprehended by genus and species terminologies.[48]

This observation can perhaps be raised to the level of a general principle. Scholastic Trinitarian theologies draw frequently on Augustine, but often under misapprehensions: Augustine becomes a source for discussions and terminological distinctions in ways that he would not have envisaged. We can perhaps distinguish two ways in which scholastics draw on Augustine's Trinitarian theology. In the case of his discussions of love and knowledge, scholastics use Augustine in ways that allow us to see his texts as a central foundation for such discussion, even if his approach is far more tentative. As we shall see through the next

---

[45] I make no comment here on the complexities of Thomas's views on the *filioque*.
[46] *ST.* 1 q. 28 a. 4.
[47] For discussion of these in Thomas, see Emery, *The Trinitarian Theology of St Thomas Aquinas*, 89ff.
[48] For example, *in sent.* 1. 19.4.2. Richard Cross has suggested that such denials are a standard part of Western tradition after Augustine. This is an interesting claim, and I hope he will eventually offer a more extensive discussion of it. Even were it so, I do not think it would alter my account of the distinctive manner in which Augustine not only states the principle but also seeks ways to speak of the Trinity without reference to such language. See Richard Cross, 'Duns Scotus on Divine Substance and the Trinity', *Medieval Philosophy and Theology* 11 (2003), 181–201.

two chapters, Augustine's discussions of memory, intellect and will similarly have a tentative quality that is somewhat different from the immediate explanatory force that Thomas (for example) assumes they possess. But when scholastics consider person, nature and relation (as well as later use of arguments about the ways in which activity reveals power and nature), a different situation obtains. Here scholastic Trinitarian theologies are deeply imbued with the traditions of discussing such concepts mentioned at the end of the last paragraph. Augustine, and especially some key passages of the *De trinitate*, are quoted as *auctoritates* in their accounts. And yet, as we have seen, Augustine actually stands out because of the thoroughness with which he struggles not to define but to avoid such terminology.

Nevertheless, despite these differences, there is a deep consonance between Augustine's account of persons as constituted by their eternal intra-divine acts, which are in turn identical with their eternally being generated and spirated, and Thomas's account of subsisting relations. We should, however, continue to recognize that we deal here with two conceptions which emerge in very different theological-rhetorical contexts. The differences between the theological cultures and concerns of Thomas and Augustine are well illustrated by noting how, in his *Lectures on John*, Thomas's John 5.19 exegesis differs from that of Augustine. For Thomas, John 5.19 shows that Christ possesses divine power through his eternal generation and, hence, is constituted perfect in his knowledge and ability to act. Thomas begins his reading by accepting Augustine's second exegetical rule: John 5.19 reveals something about the Son's being from the Father, but should not be taken as implying inferiority.[49] A little later he comments directly on the readings of Hilary and Chrysostom: the former he takes to argue that the Word's eternal seeing of the Father indicates that the Word is eternally a perfect entity. The latter he takes to argue that a correct reading of the Son's 'cannot' shows that the Son's action conforms to the Father's. Augustine, Thomas tells us, offers both of these in different contexts.[50] A little before, however, Thomas has offered his own preferred reading. Seeing is a mode of receiving knowledge or of the derivation of knowledge, and the Son's receiving of knowledge is identical with his being generated from the Father's Wisdom. Thus the Son's 'seeing' is identical to his proceeding

---

[49] *Ioan.* 5, lect. 3, n. 747–8. [50] *Ioan.* 5, lect. 3, n. 751–3.

from the Father by an 'intellectual procession' (*procedere intelligibili processione a patre operante*).[51]

Thomas's solution parallels Augustine's: both think of the Son's seeing as identical to the Son's eternal generation. And yet there are differences. Thomas shows a clear preference for an explanation that interprets the Son's 'seeing' in terms of an already established metaphysical terminology. As part of this solution Thomas also presents the Son's 'seeing' as a cipher for the Son's intellectual procession. Augustine's solution invests the Son's 'seeing' with more significance, perhaps because he easily and naturally interprets seeing within a Plotinian context, perhaps also because he assumes a very particular style of correspondence between biblical terminology and divine reality itself. But despite these differences we are examining two options within a complex tradition. Augustine's influence here is vast, and yet not only does his work offer us a number of possible roads not taken by later tradition, but that tradition itself eventually marked out tracks that he could not have foreseen. While we can certainly speak of a 'Latin tradition' between Augustine and Thomas, good negotiation of and existence within that tradition now requires of us much sensitivity to its own internal modulations, disputes and conversations.

[51] *Ioan.* 5, lect. 3, n. 750.

PART IV

Memory, intellect and will

CHAPTER II

'But it's not fur eatin' ...'[1]

Our greatest protection is self-knowledge, and to avoid the delusion that we are seeing ourselves when we are in reality looking at something else. This is what happens to those who do not scrutinize themselves. What they see is strength, beauty, reputation, political power, abundant wealth, pomp, self-importance, bodily stature, a certain grace of form or the like, and they think this is what they are. Such persons make very poor guardians of themselves: because of their absorption in what is foreign to them, they overlook what is proper to them and leave it unguarded.[2]

INTRODUCTION

In this chapter and the next I turn to what is frequently taken to be the central and distinctive contribution of Augustine to Trinitarian theology, the attempt in the latter books of the *De trinitate* to illustrate some of the key principles of Trinitarian doctrine through analysis of triadic structures in the human *mens*. I do not aim here to offer a comprehensive interpretation of *De trinitate* 8–15 as a whole, nor even a reading that gives a full picture of Books 8–10 alone. I wish only to draw out the central lines of argument pursued through Books 9 and 10, adumbrated in Book 8 and reprised in Book 14. At the end of this investigation I will suggest the reasons behind his deployment of *memoria*, *intellegentia* and *voluntas* in Book 10. At the same time, I will be able to show why his use of these mental analogies in the *De trinitate* should not be taken as providing any warrant for the view that Augustine's Trinitarian theology treats the

---

[1] The title of this chapter and the next are a homage to Chief Dan George, who co-stars in 'The Outlaw Josey Wales'; Lone Wadi (played by George) is asked by Wales (played by Clint Eastwood) if he has any food. Producing a piece of hard candy, George holds it to his eye and utters the immortal line quoted in the titles of this and the next chapter, little knowing how well they encapsulate Augustine's approach to Trinitarian analogies in *trin.* 9–10.
[2] Gregory of Nyssa, *Cant.* 2 (GNO 6. 63–4; Mursurillo 159–60).

275

Trinity as most like a unitary self-thinking mind.³ More positively, the arguments considered in these two chapters offer us one of Augustine's most sophisticated explorations of how we may think the Trinity and thus they complete the account of Augustine's vision of analogical thinking that we began to trace in Chapters 4–6.

Augustine's argument in *De trinitate* 9–10 initially revolves around a distinction between a self-knowing necessary to the mind but constantly distorted by our attachment to the material world, and an eschatological, perfected self-knowing that would most fully image the Trinity. In our attempts to use the mind as a site for thinking the Trinity we find ourselves straining from the former towards the latter. In Book 10 Augustine develops a subtly different account of the mind: at one level the mind exhibits a distorted and constant searching for knowledge, a constant attempt to come into that which it tragically lacks and cannot find; at another level the mind is necessarily and constantly self-knowing, whatever the conscious object of our attention. Here Augustine builds on his earlier distinction by continuing to show how the perfected self-knowing intrinsic to the mind is constantly forgotten or distorted by the fallen thinker who generates a mistaken knowledge of the soul. Indeed, Augustine's argument here is structured not only by the move from one analogy for the Trinity to another but by an increasingly sophisticated analysis of the ways in which the generation of *verba interiora* is at the core of all acts of self-knowing. Thus accounts which treat these books only as an exploration of the analogical adequacy of different accounts of the mind's structure miss something vital: one of Augustine's central concerns here is to analyse the dynamics of fallen self-knowing and hence of analogical practice itself. In many ways it is this analysis that gives fundamental structure to the argument he offers.

Before turning to the *De trinitate* itself, however, I want to examine a roughly contemporary text from *De civitate Dei* 11 which provides important context for the discussions of *De trinitate* 9 and 10, especially insofar as it reveals continuities in Augustine's analogical practice

---

³ A classic account of the supposed links between a 'mental' analogy that necessarily gives primacy to the divine unity and Augustine's failures in Trinitarian theology is to be found in Du Roy, *L'Intelligence*, 447ff. It is worth noting that Michael Schmaus – even though he treats the argument of these books as paradigmatic in Augustine, as that which distinguishes him from 'the Greeks' and as a direct mental analogy – goes out of his way to reject those who think either that Augustine's use of this analogy results in a semi-modalist Trinity or that Augustine intends us, on the basis of this analogy, to imagine the persons as moments in the movement of divine self-consciousness. See his *Die psychologische Trinitätslehre*, 407–8. Brachtendorf, *Die Struktur*, similarly rejects the idea that Augustine's use of the mind implies any modalism, e.g. at 255.

between this period of his career and the earlier stages that we have already discussed.[4]

DE CIVITATE DEI 11[5]

Book 11 of the *De civitate Dei* begins an exposition and defence of the Christian faith which runs through to the end of the work. It is no surprise, then, that Augustine devotes much space at the beginning of that exposition to the Trinity. Following an outline of the relationships between the divine three that we considered briefly in Chapter 10, Augustine turns to the manner in which the creation may aid our understanding of the Trinity.[6] Commenting on the refrain from Genesis 1 'and God saw that it was good', Augustine sees in these words an intimation that we should read the text as revealing to us the Trinitarian character of the divine creative act:

> it is a careful use of reason ... to understand the Trinity insinuated [*nobis insinuata intellegatur trinitas*] in the works of God as if by a veiled mode of speech [*secreto quodam loquendi modo*]: a mode intended to exercise our mind's attention [*quo nostra exerceatur intentio*] when we ask, of anything whatsoever that God has created, Who made it? By what means did he make it? and, Why did he make it? For it is the Father of the Word who said, Let it be. And that which was made when he spoke was beyond doubt made by means of the Word. Again, when it is said 'God saw that it was good', it is thereby sufficiently signified that God made what he made not from any necessity, not because he had any need of benefit, but simply from his own goodness: that is so that it might be good. And this was said after the created thing had been made, so that there might be no doubt that its existence was in harmony with the goodness for the sake of which it was made. And if this goodness is rightly understood to be the Holy Spirit, then the whole Trinity is revealed to us in the works of God.[7]

The picture that we find here is a mature articulation of principles we explored in Chapters 2 and 5. Augustine suggests that, as a response to the 'veiled speech of God' in the created order, those trained to look may exercise their mind on the problems that face us when we attempt to conceive of the Trinity as a formed life. Augustine does not simply see here an intimation of threeness and oneness – or even of the bare fact that the

---

[4] See Chapter 2, pp. 66–8, Chapter 5, *passim*.
[5] On the relationship between this text and *trin.* see A.-M. La Bonnardière, 'Le *De trinitate* de saint Augustin, confronté au livre XI de la Cité de Dieu', *AÉPHÉ* 85 (1976–7), 343–6. A complementary discussion of the dating of *civ.* without reference to *trin.* is found in Gerald O'Daly's *AugLex* article 'civitate dei (De)'. I assume a date of 416–18 for *civ.* 11.
[6] See above, pp. 189f.   [7] *civ.* 11. 24 (CCSL 47. 343–4).

persons create together or operate inseparably – he sees a reflection in each aspect of creation of the manner in which the Father creates through Word and in Spirit.

In so doing Augustine offers a mature account of the interest in threefold causality that we saw in connection with his earliest analogical explorations of the Trinity. Augustine's account is, however, integrated with the mature account of inseparable operation discussed in Chapters 7 and 10. This is hinted at here when Augustine writes that the unity and distinction of the three questions reflect the Father's speaking of all things in the Word, and when he speaks of the Spirit as the goodness for the sake of which all was made. All that is created eternally 'exists' in the Word in whom it is spoken, and in the Word all is eternally good in the Spirit who is the Spirit of Father and of Son.

After the passage quoted above, Augustine immediately adds that the Trinity similarly orders the City of God itself, founded by God, enlightened by God and finding its happiness in God. Other phenomena reflect the same ordering of reality, and the phenomena Augustine identifies reveal much. First he turns to the three divisions of philosophy (*physica, logica, ethica*), which Augustine takes to originate with Plato even though Plato saw only that God was nature's author, the giver of intelligence and the inspirer of love. At the same time there are three things that everyone who seeks to practice an art must have: natural aptitude, education and practice (*natura, doctrina, usus*), three judged by assessing natural skill, knowledge and its fruit (*ingenium, scientia, fructus*). Turning the argument back towards its beginning Augustine now argues that it is from these three that philosophy – 'the discipline by which a blessed life is achieved' – takes its threefold division of natural, rational and moral. In philosophy (as in the act of observing the created order in general) we should discover that we are not our own author, that we need God as our teacher and that we need God to bestow upon us an inner joy (*suavitas intima*).[8] Through this list of triads, Augustine demonstrates further fundamental continuity with his earlier reflections on 'analogical' practice. All are constituted by orderings of our thought and education which enable a human life aimed towards the creator and our true end; all reflect the character of the divine life as the Father's acting through Word and in Spirit; all reveal the created order to be intelligible and the appropriate context for our return towards the Father because of the character of its creation by and existence in the Trinitarian life. Reflecting back on the discussion of Chapter 7,

---

[8] *civ.* 11. 25 (CCSL 47. 345).

when we see that such triadic reflections remain central to Augustine's mature practice, it perhaps becomes even clearer why Augustine places so much emphasis on the right understanding of creation's existence in the Word as fundamental to the reorientation of the mind towards which the Christian life leads. To understand the creation as created in the Word *is* to understand it as created for return towards the Father.

Only now does Augustine come to the *imago Dei* in humanity. The image is not equal to God and does not share his substance, he tells us. We exist, we know our existence and we love our existence and knowledge of it.[9] Following his now well-developed anti-Sceptical arguments, Augustine adds that because this knowledge and love does not depend on the mediation of the senses it is certain and provides an anti-sceptical bulwark. Meditation on our knowledge and love continues in two directions. First, we find these acts mirrored even in realities below us: Augustine here hinting that although the triad of being–life–mind serves primarily to describe a hierarchical ordering of reality, even the existence of that without life or mind still mirrors those higher forms. Second, we must admit that we love the love with which we love truth. This discussion possibly echoes one we shall see in *De trinitate* 8: but there Augustine is clear that the love with which we love *is* the Spirit within us. All this, Augustine avers, is in the image of the Creator who is eternity, eternal truth and eternal and true love. The very form of this last triad shows how this mature account of the creation's triadic and teleological structure has been shaped by his mature Trinitarian theology. The multiplication of adjectives here plays out for us another tactic in his on-going struggle to articulate a vision of the divine three as each being that which marks divinity as such.[10] Augustine now speaks once more of God's presence in the creation, using the famous image of God as the one who leaves his 'tracks' (*vestigia*) through the creation: 'Contemplating his image in ourselves, therefore, let us, like that younger son of the Gospel, come to ourselves, and arise and return to him whom we had forsaken by our sin'.[11] I offer 'tracks' for *vestigia* because of the emphasis Augustine places on those tracks leading towards the one who left them and on our following towards their author.

Augustine's mature clarity about the existence of the *imago* even in fallen humanity enables him to present the image in the soul as the clear

---

[9] *civ.* 11. 26 (CCSL 47. 345): 'Nam et sumus et nos esse novimus et id esse ac nosse diligimus'.
[10] civ. 11. 28 (CCSL 47. 348): 'est aeternitas, aeterna veritas, aeterna et vera caritas'.
[11] *civ.* 11. 28 (CCSL 47. 348).

highpoint of the creation's reflection of its triune creator.[12] The *imago* here is the mind's existence, knowledge and love, but we should note that Augustine's identification of this as the *imago* follows directly on from and seems to be commentary on his description of *natura, doctrina* and *usus* as a threefold division which highlights the structure of the life one must live towards the truly blessed life. The division is somewhat artificial because Augustine sees the created order itself as existing always towards the Creator: the temporal process by which one moves towards the Creator mirrors and plays out over time the process of conversion towards the Creator that constitutes the creation itself.

In Chapter 2 I suggested that at the core of Augustine's analogical practice are two basic foci: the created order as a reflection of its threefold Creator; the threefold structure of the process by which the mind is reformed towards God. Already implicit in this earliest material, but only drawn out more fully in the *Confessiones*, as we saw in Chapter 5, is a third site, the human mind as such. Although Augustine begins then to use threefold *cogito*-type accounts of the mind's self-certainty as reflecting the Trinity, it is only really in the second half of the *De trinitate* that he articulates with any density an account of the mind's self-knowing in the Word as a site for analogical exploration of the Trinity as that which constitutes us as in the image of God. What we see in *De civitate Dei* 11 is a mature sketch of the relationships between these various analogical sites. The sheer size and complexity of *De trinitate* 8–15 makes it all too easy for us to assume that Augustine now *only* sees the mind as analogical site. It seems to me far more plausible that we think of *De civitate Dei* 11 as offering a mature vision of the broader context within which the extended *exercitatio* of *De trinitate* 9–10 takes place.

If I have construed the significance of *De civitate Dei* 11 correctly, then we can distinguish between these three interrelated analogical sites and the other analogies for aspects of Trinitarian faith Augustine deploys. The majority of those, such as light and word metaphors, were both highly traditional and yet also developed by Augustine. Augustine's central strand of metaphorical reflection is something very much his own, and while his talk of *vestigia* might be taken as a category that must include all analogies, the core context within which he developed that notion stems from his long anti-Manichaean and anti-sceptical reflection on the creation's intelligibility.

---

[12] I comment on Augustine's developing notion of the *imago* in Chapter 5, pp. 137–8.

Of course, recognizing this distinction forces upon us another question: how does this peculiarly Augustinian strand of analogical reflection shape or even govern his understanding of the Trinity itself? I have, I hope, already begun to indicate the complex nature of any satisfying answer to this question. Because Augustine consistently uses his Trinitarian faith to guide what he finds in a given analogical site, and because he makes use of a number of different Trinitarian images and languages, judgements about how any given analogy shapes his Trinitarian theology demands the most careful attention. It is time then to turn to one of the most important texts in his corpus for anyone seeking to answer this question: *De trinitate* 8–10.

DE TRINITATE 8: THE *EXORDIUM*

The editorial history of *De trinitate* 8–10 is unclear. The three books appear to have been written as a unit but, as we shall see, there are good reasons for supposing that the hurried manner in which the work was finally brought before the public meant that Augustine never fully integrated what may be two versions of an argument, one in Book 9, the other in Book 10. At the very end of Book 8 Augustine likens his achievement in that book to the sketching of an *exordium* in a speech. The *exordium*, the introductory section of a speech, lays the foundation for the main argument.[13] It is worth noting, however, that an *exordium* was not intended to sum up a case, nor even to begin a case by setting out its initial points. The *exordium*'s purpose was to gain the attention and sympathy of the court for the case which was to follow. As Quintilian tells us, 'at this stage we are not yet accepted, the attention of the audience is fresh and watchful'.[14] If Augustine intended to describe Book 8 as an *exordium* in this sense then we may see him as drawing the attention of his audience by offering a number of discussions that reflect common themes of his theology but each of which raises paradoxes that beset the one seeking to 'see' better the character of the Trinitarian relationships. This combination of familiarity and strangeness sets the scene for the more careful argument of Books 9 and 10.

---

[13] *trin.* 8. 10.14 (CCSL 50. 291): 'Ita hoc dixisse suffecerit, ut tamquam ab articulo alicuius exordii cetera contexamus'. It is worth noting for readers following my argument only in modern English translations of *trin.* that those translations assume that both *exordium* and the verb *contexto* are intended in their senses of the warp on the loom and the weaving of cloth. But both terms also have a technical rhetorical sense, and it is thus that I have taken them.

[14] Quintilian, *inst.* 4. 1.59.

Augustine begins *De trinitate* 8 by exploring the difficulty of our seeing the Trinity. He exhorts his readers to see the Truth itself, the God who informs all goodness and truth in the world. But we find ourselves unable to maintain our gaze on this truth. How then can we see God? Augustine uses the language of sight and of our failure to see in order to dramatize a problem with all attempts to see, know and understand God – as is clear from the ease with which he changes vocabulary in these opening paragraphs. Augustine eventually focuses the problem by posing a contrast between our ability to imagine Paul or Christ and our inability to imagine God. In the former cases we possess numerous examples of people that provide us with a basis on which to imagine Paul and Christ; in the case of God we possess no general categories that can offer us such help.[15]

Augustine turns to a related question: *why* do we love the apostle Paul? First, Augustine insists that we love Paul's just soul (*animus*). We are able to love his soul because we ourselves have a soul. How then can we love the justice of his mind if we ourselves are not just, if we cannot see it in ourselves? The answer is that justice is present to the soul: to speak of it we do not need to go through a process of recalling images of what is absent (as when we imagine Carthage) or constructing images of something that we imagine (such as the Alexandria we have not visited).[16] This presence is not, Augustine continues, the presence of another just mind in the mind of the one who is not yet just. It is, in fact, the 'interior truth', the *veritas interior* that is a *forma* present to the mind. This, says Augustine, is the unique instance in which we may love something while it is still unknown to us:

> For we find nothing similar to it other than itself [*praeter ipsam*], so that by believing we might love it when it is unknown, by reason of something similar that we already know. For whatever thing of this kind one may have seen is itself [*quidquid enim tale aspexeris, ipsa est*].[17]

Augustine's analogical exploration of the Trinity is poised between an insistence that we possess no general categories within which to place the God who is one and three and his equally strong insistence we can progress in understanding of God because Truth itself is present to our minds.

Augustine now focuses on the character of our love for this form and truth. If the question of how we may love that for which we have no

---

[15] *trin.* 8. 5.8. [16] *trin.* 8. 6.9. [17] *trin.* 8. 6.9 (CCSL 50. 283).

categories (the Trinity) is solved by reference to the presence of truth to the mind, then in the character of our love for that truth and in our ability to develop knowledge of that truth lies the solution to the question of how we may grow in understanding of the Trinity. 'True love', which simply is the only love deserving of the name, is 'that we should live justly by cleaving to the truth' (*ut inhaerentes veritati iuste vivamus*). The moral/spiritual character of the one who seeks is thus integral to any search to understand the Trinity. A few paragraphs later Augustine notes that the true love with which we love the form or truth present to us *is* God: 'and with what is the one who is filled with love filled except with God?' (*Et quo nisi Deo plenus est, qui plenus est dilectione?*).[18] It is love itself, *ipsa dilectio*, which unites the whole creation to God. We may, then, come to know God even though we have no categories within which to 'place' God because we love that form and truth with God's own love. This discussion is of particular importance because it shows the extent to which Augustine's account of growth in understanding of the Trinity is framed in an explicitly Trinitarian manner: we grow in knowledge because of and through the informing and inflaming work of Son and Spirit.

These arguments also condition what may seem to some to be Augustine's first 'analogy' for the Trinity. Augustine imagines answering someone who attempts to love, and gradually comes to believe the scriptural description of God as love active within the soul, but cannot yet see that love as Trinitarian. Augustine's answer is ultimately that the failure to see the Trinitarian structure of love stems from the weakness of our sight and that the language of faith enables us to analyse more truly the love which we might be tempted to claim to know:

> But one may object, 'I see love and I conceive it in my mind as best I can, and I believe the Scripture when it says: "God is love, and he who abides in love abides in God" [1John 4.16], but when I see it I do not see the Trinity in it'. But you most certainly do see the Trinity if you see love [*Immo vero vides Trinitatem, si caritatem vides*][19]

The description of a triad in the act of love that follows is based on the assumption that love is necessarily triune *because* love is God. The description is part analogy, part invitation to use the language of faith to explore that which one *thinks* one understands. Having already shown that when we love truly we love from God, Augustine now insists that to love is to love something in the act of loving.[20] Further, when we love, we love our

---

[18] *trin.* 8. 8.12 (CCSL 50. 287).   [19] *trin.* 8. 8.12.
[20] Here see Rowan D. Williams, '*Sapientia* and the Trinity', esp. 322–3.

love itself and when we love we always love that which we love through or in love – the ablative here seems to be both instrumental and causal. When we love our brother, then, our loving is always for another in the act of love and is always founded on the presence in us of an active loving enabling us to love. So far, Augustine's account is not an analogy between a structure of loving in the created order and the loving that constitutes the Trinitarian life, but a description of the manner in which we love in and because of the Spirit's presence. It is the description of a structure of loving in the created order, founded in the divine love that will also illustrate the nature of the Trinitarian love *per se*.

Augustine draws out these dense sentences by emphasizing that, for John (quoting 1John 2.10), the perfection of justice (*iustitia*) is found in the love of a brother (*fratris dilectio*), but that this is so because such love *is* the love that is God (quoting and interpreting 1John 4.7–8).[21] This passage mirrors Augustine's discussion of the Christian's love for Paul's just soul. We love the Apostle's soul because we see justice in our own soul, because we exist in the Truth and because 'our' love is the Spirit uniting lover and beloved. Augustine does not here parse out the divine three individually in the structure of loving he has suggested, but he does emphasize towards the end of this passage that our love for the Apostle is a love for the form (*forma*) of justice that Paul exemplifies (love for this form is encouraged by faith in those who have lived according to the form).[22] There is here a hint that our love, which is the love that is God, is a love which loves Justice itself, the Word. In other words, there is a hint that our loving is already caught up in the love of Spirit for Son. To state matters thus, is also to beg key questions: how far can the constantly mediated life of growing in love and knowledge mirror the eternal fullness of the divine love? Is there within us a triad which better illustrates that eternal fullness?

At the end of this discussion Augustine comes directly to that which is frequently read as his initial 'analogy'. Love is, he concludes, love of the Good (*amor boni*), a statement which must be about both our acts of love and love itself, God. Thus, 'love is of someone who loves, and something is loved with love. So, then, there are three: the lover, the beloved, and the love. What else is love, therefore, except a kind of life which binds or seeks to bind some two together?' This is an analogy of sorts: the act of love (and it seems that he continues to intend the act of our love for the just person or our appropriate love for our brother or sister) in which

---

[21] *trin.* 8. 8.12.   [22] *trin.* 8. 9.13, taking up again themes from 8. 6.9.

the lover's love attempts to bring lover together with beloved mirrors the Trinitarian life. And yet, again, it is an analogy of a very special sort, one founded in the life of divine loving within which our loving is taken up. Thus, at another level it is not analogy but description, description of the manner in which the eternal and unchanging life of love acts within creation.

The *exordium* that constitutes Book 8 thus offers arguments that build on some of the fundamental themes of Augustine's writing: the presence of the love of God within Christians; the presence of God to the created order; parallels between the temporal process of return to God and the divine eternal life. And yet these themes have been used to shape a discussion of how we may grow in understanding of the Trinity that is considerably more advanced than anything we have so far seen in Augustine's corpus. Throughout this passage Augustine makes use of the language of faith to interpret that which he analyses and thus his analogical procedure here is founded on and shaped by two principles. We may grow in understanding of God, despite our lack of categories for the divine, because God is present to us; we may grow in understanding because the language of faith provides us tools to analyse that which is before us and within us, but not grasped.

DE TRINITATE 9. 1.1–5.8: THE PARADOX OF SELF-KNOWING[23]

At the very beginning of Book 9 Augustine suggests that we turn from exploring the triadic shape of loving in general to the particular case of self-love.[24] Reminding his readers that he and they are seeking

---

[23] Throughout Chapters 9 and 10, I have spoken of 'self-knowing' rather than 'self-knowledge' in order to emphasize that Augustine's concern is with the 'life' of knowledge in the mind, not merely with knowledge as content. The literature on these books is extensive. Of recent accounts that of Brachtendorf, *Die Struktur*, is particularly helpful. His account of the distinction between Neoplatonic ascent (e.g. 124–5), as something which reaches beyond to the source of all, and Augustine's, in which there is only 'ascent' to the knowledge given by analysis of created analogues, is helpful. At the same time, I present the situation as more fluid because of Augustine's dialectical moves beyond the image to speak of the conditions of the divine existence itself. While this may not result in knowledge (where that is seen as a putting aside of faith), it certainly involves a growth in understanding, an enlarging of faith towards knowing. Because of the same fluidity I am also not entirely convinced by his 'A Natural Understanding of "Trinity" in St Augustine?', *AugStud* 29 (1998), 199–209. In one sense he is certainly right: implicit knowledge of the Trinity precedes our search for understanding. At the same time I think Brachtendorf underplays Augustine's presentation of the difference between the image (and our capacity even to understand that) and that of which it is the image.

[24] *trin.* 9. 2.2 (CCSL 50A. 294).

to understand the Trinity of persons related to one another (*trinitatem relatarum ad invicem personarum*), Augustine suggests that we are now faced with the particular question of whether love is proper only to the Spirit or whether to Father and Son as well. In an initial investigation of this topic he recognizes that talk of the mind and its love of itself seems to involve only two terms. Calling us to concentrate further, Augustine suggests we must work harder to see the image of God in ourselves. As a first step he argues that the mind can only love itself if it knows itself, and we have returned to a triadic structure.[25] I have already discussed in Chapter 5 Augustine's use of a triad of being, knowing and willing in the *Confessiones*. Augustine's use of that triad there owes as much to the needs of his developing Trinitarian theology as to any particular secular precedent. The triad of *mens*, *notitia* and *amor* seems to be a variation of that earlier triad, and scholars writing on the *De trinitate* have rightly seen it here as emerging from and formalizing the relationship between love and knowledge sketched in Book 8, once again shaped by the demands of Nicene Trinitarian faith.[26] Once again, Augustine's 'analogical' investigation involves in its very origins the use of that which it seeks to illustrate to shape an account of the analogy.

The introduction of the mind's self-knowing refocuses a key question from Book 8; seeking presumes knowledge of that which is sought, but from where do we know the mind?[27] Augustine's brief discussion of the seemingly paradoxical truth that we search for that which must in part be already known introduces a strand of reflection on the mind's incorporeal and intelligible life that is vital to the argument of both these books. The mind knows corporeal things through the senses, but knows incorporeal things through itself. Because it is incorporeal, the mind must know itself through itself.[28] At this point Augustine's account of

---

[25] *trin.* 9. 3.3. Although Augustine speaks, through the latter half of the *De trinitate*, about both *animus* and *anima*, he locates the *imago Dei* and both of the triads he considers in Books 9 and 10 in the *mens*, the highest 'part' of the soul. Augustine distinguishes fairly consistently between the 'higher' and 'lower' soul and identifies the higher reasoning functions of the *mens* as the governing 'part' of the soul. Augustine does not offer any dense account of the nature of the difference between 'higher' and 'lower' parts of the soul, but he sees the *mens* as a better image of the divine simplicity because it is here that the human ability to know and love God finds its seat (*trin.* 14. 12.15. Cf. *lib. arb.* 3. 25.75). For the varying and sometimes inconsistent ways in which Augustine divides the soul, see the useful summary in Gerard O'Daly, *Augustine's Philosophy of Mind* (London: Duckworth, 1987), 11–15.

[26] Thus, for example, Schindler, *Wort und Analogie*, ch. 6. See my discussion of Theiler, p. 136.

[27] *trin.* 9. 3.3 (CCSL 50A. 295–6): 'mens enim amare se ipsam non potest nisi etiam nouerit se. nam quomodo amat quod nescit?'

[28] *trin.* 9. 3.3 (CCSL 50A. 296): 'ergo et semetipsam per se ipsam novit, quoniam est incorporea'. This discussion takes up the latter half of *trin* 8. 6.9.

the mind's intellectual self-presence serves mostly to heighten the paradox that the searching mind must already know itself; eventually this account will take on a central role both enabling the mind to serve as an important analogical site for exploring the Trinity, and enabling Augustine to explain why our attempts to think beyond the categories of the corporeal world so easily fail.

Having come to the view that the mind knows and loves itself, Augustine launches into an excellent example of the way in which he reads the mind partly through the use of Trinitarian logic in order to render more comprehensible that logic itself. Augustine begins by telling us that the three are 'equal' when they are 'perfected' or 'completed.'

> The mind therefore and its love and knowledge are three [*tria*], and these three are one, and when they are perfected they are equal [*aequalia*]. If the mind loves itself less than it is … then it sins and its love is not complete. Again if it loves itself more than it is, for example, if it loves itself as much as God is to be loved, though it is incomparably less than God, here too it sins by excess, and does not have a complete love of itself. It sins of course with even greater perversity and wickedness when it loves the body as much as God is to be loved.[29]

Thus, while the three necessarily exhibit part of the Trinitarian logic in being three and one – because they exist in the incorporeal mind and are nevertheless distinct – they most fully exhibit that logic only when the three are 'completed' through achieving relative equality and rest. The conditions under which the three lack perfection are those of distorted and inappropriate desire – conditions that for Augustine mark even the existence of those within the body of Christ. Their perfection will involve, he explains, the mind not loving itself as something greater or less than it is (either as only body or as God).[30] Whereas the discussion of love as Trinitarian in Book 8 assumes that the love with which the Christian loves is necessarily Trinitarian, the discussion of the mind's self-knowing here interposes a central reality: perfected and equal self-knowing is only possible in the purified mind. *Mens*, *notitia* and *amor* thus function as analogical site both by drawing us to recognize that this would be an important likeness when perfected, and by stimulating us to reflect on how our knowing now fails to image the divine rest.

---

[29] *trin.* 9. 4.4 (CCSL 50A. 296–7). Scholarship on these books has sustained a long discussion about the sort of thing Augustine envisages when he speaks of *notitia* here, for an outline see the note at BA 16. 591–3. Augustine's vagueness in this book is overcome in Book 10 and for my purposes I need not pursue the question.

[30] *trin.* 9. 4.4.

Augustine now tells us that *mens*, *notitia* and *amor* are 'rolled up' or 'enfolded' (*tamquam involuta*) in the soul and must be 'unrolled' so that they may be seen and numbered.[31] Augustine 'sees' and 'numbers' the three as substantial realities by identifying a number of false ways in which we might envisage them. Although he does not say so directly, each false path is a path already rejected as inappropriate for envisioning the Trinity earlier in the work. Once again the *exercitatio* of reading the mind as an image depends as much on a knowledge of that which we seek to understand, as it does on a knowledge of the analogical site within which our minds are exercised. Thus, the mind's knowledge and love cannot be accidental to the mind. The immateriality of the three and the mind's immediate and total self-knowledge means that we cannot conceive of *mens*, *notitia* and *amor* as parts within a whole. The same principles prevent us understanding the three according to any language of mixture; the three are in each other and yet are each whole by themselves and all in all; the three are spoken of relative to each other and yet are inseparable. Of course, throughout, Augustine is also using a series of assumptions concerning the mind's incorporeal existence (many of which have Platonic origins) as the context within which his dialectical *exercitatio* occurs. This exercising of the mind also interweaves arguments about the nature of the relationship developed in Books 5–7. Thus, most importantly, Augustine suggests the relationship between love and knowledge is more like that between two friends (because both have substantial existence) than that between a coloured body and its accidental colour.[32]

This passage offers us a perfect example of what we might call the discursive analogical practice demonstrated throughout Books 9–10. Although I use the term 'analogy' here Augustine appears to avoid the term *analogia* in favour of a number of terms that indicate a much looser set of likenesses (*similitudines*).[33] *Analogia* implies to Augustine the possibility of our grasping the proportion between the terms involved, and we can grasp no such relation between the Creator and any part of the creation. In this discursive practice, Augustine models the mind's exercising of itself through showing us his own process of reflecting on the different conditions of intelligible and sensible reality. In this process Augustine

---

[31] *trin.* 9. 4.5 (CCSL 50A. 297–8). [32] *trin.* 9. 4.6.
[33] See my '"Remember that you are Catholic" (*serm.* 52, 2)', 59–63. To the literature cited there should be added Marsh H. McCall, *Ancient Rhetorical Theories of Simile and Comparison* (Cambridge, MA: Harvard University Press, 1969). Marsh's account of the use of *similitudo* as the primary and widest category of comparison in both Cicero and Quintilian is particularly useful.

does not move consistently from corporeal likenesses that are easier to grasp but less revealing to likenesses more difficult to grasp but that better reveal relationships or modes of existence possible within the intelligible realm. Instead Augustine performs for us a discursive interplay between these levels as he tries to draw the mind into recognizing both its abilities to reason about the intelligible and the constant threat that it will be seduced into importing inappropriate material conditions. This discursive quality is only enhanced by the use of the Trinitarian logic as a tool for investigation and as that which we seek to understand.

At one level the discussion we are considering in Book 9 focuses on the mind's love and knowledge under any circumstances. Augustine's argument that knowledge and love are irreducible *substantiae*, named relatively and existing in an incorporeal quasi-simple mode of existence, is not a comment about the perfected mind, but about the mind as such. At the very end of this discussion, however, Augustine turns again to the possibility of the mind's perfection:

How they are all in all [*tota … in totis*] we have already shown above; it is when the mind loves all itself and knows all its love and loves all its knowledge, when these three are complete with reference to themselves [*quando tria ista ad se ipsa perfecta sunt*].[34]

Thus at both the beginning (as we saw above) and end of this discussion, Augustine opens up a space between the self-knowing and self-loving mind on the path to purification and the self-knowing and self-loving of the perfected mind. Only in the latter is there a fully Trinitarian image in the equality of love and knowledge.

Thus Augustine does not simply discover the perfected mind's self-knowing structure in the mind, he partly constructs this structure from the logic of Trinitarian faith, and partly constructs it by abstraction, imagining the mind's activity without the marks of fallen existence as he envisages them. Thus we see the twofold problem with an assertion that in Book 9 Augustine begins to use the *mens* as analogy for the Trinity: in the first place, he partly uses the language of Trinitarian faith to construct that analogical site: in the second place, we must imagine, beyond our fallenness, the perfected mind if we are to see how the *mens* might function as analogy. We might already say, then, that the *mens* functions as analogy not merely because the *imago Dei* is there located, but because in the *mens* we find the site at which human failure to know and

[34] *trin*. 9. 5.8 (CCSL 50A. 301).

love God finds its source, and the site whose restoration will enable that knowledge and love.

My brief mention of human fallenness in the previous paragraph enables us also to note a theme here heard only *sotto voce*, but which becomes central through the rest of Book 9. In his initial account of the character of self-knowing in the mind not yet perfected Augustine speaks of knowledge as 'a kind of life in the reason of the knower', greater than body 'not by mass, but by power'.[35] Self-knowing goes astray when the mind is perceived along with other things; the mind that can separate itself from what it is not and know itself as the power that it is may know itself perfectly and rest in that knowledge. These sentences hint that Augustine locates the failure of unpurified self-knowing in the mind's strange inability to separate itself from images of what it is not. The presence of this theme should not surprise us – it is already a familiar one in Augustine's corpus before this date. But we should note how its gradual emergence as the two versions of self-knowing are delineated enables Augustine to place discussion of our search for better self-knowing centre stage. The emphasis on knowledge as continually active 'life' will enable Augustine to give this frequent theme in his work a new subtlety – and poignancy.[36]

DE TRINITATE 9. 6.9–12.18: VERBUM INTERIOR

At the beginning of *trin.* 9. 6.9, Augustine steps back from his account of the perfected self-loving mind resting in its own knowledge, to ask about the character of the knowledge in which one might rest and the manner of our progress towards such knowledge. He suggests that we know in two ways, either in ourselves (and these things may then be communicated via signs to one who believes) or in the truth itself which is present to us (such things can be spoken of and may be seen identically by others

---

[35] *trin.* 9. 4.4 (CCSL 50A. 297): 'illa [notitia] enim vita quaedam est in ratione cognoscentis; corpus autem non est vita. Et vita quaelibet quolibet corpore maior est, non mole, sed vi'.

[36] Brachtendorf, *Die Struktur*, 119, divides Book 9 into two main sections, also ending the first at *trin.* 9. 5.8. He reads the first section of the book as focusing on attempts to illustrate the Trinitarian relations in the human *mens*, but makes little of the manner in which Augustine uses the logic of Trinitarian faith to guide his analysis and little of Augustine's division between the *mens* as it knows and loves now, and the knowing and loving of the purified *mens*. Brachtendorf reads the second half of Book 9 as concerned with the origins of *notitia* and *notitia sui*, thus focusing on the relationships between the elements of the *mens* considered in the first section. I read the second half as indeed focusing on the theme of knowledge's production, but because I see Augustine focusing on this theme in order to highlight his epistemological reflections on the human ability to grow in knowledge given the character of fallen human knowing.

who know them in the Truth).[37] The Truth that is spoken of here is the divine Wisdom and Word who informs all things. When we speak of the mind well, and judge rightly how the mind ought to function, we make judgements in the light of the Truth itself. These judgements are not made through the sensory organs but with what Augustine names here as the mind's own *visus* or *intuitus*.[38]

The true knowledge that results from our judging in this Truth involves generating or 'uttering' something analogous to a 'word' in the mind.[39] Such 'words' born in the mind are at the root of all human action for good or ill. Augustine offers a basic division between types of 'word': they occur as a result of a fundamental love either for the Creator or for creatures.[40] In the case of 'words' founded in an inappropriate love for the created order we can distinguish between the *verbum* as *conceptum* and *natum*: the word is conceived when we desire its fulfilment but born only when that desire is actually fulfilled. Only words conceived in the true love of spiritual realities are simultaneously born: one who loves justice has a will or love that rests in the knowledge that is conceived because that which is desired is immediately present.[41] Augustine then asks whether all *notitia* can be considered a word. His answer is that while it can in a loose sense, the words with which he is concerned are those that are joined with love.[42]

We should remember at this point that when Augustine introduces the concept of the *verbum interior* he is careful to define it as *tamquam verbum*: *verbum* is not by itself fully adequate to grasp the reality he attempts to describe. That is particularly clear here, for now he turns to the notion of image (*similitudo* and *imago*) to describe the same reality – once again using a range of terms drawn from Trinitarian contexts to illustrate his investigation of the mind. All positive knowledge of form (*species*) is like that which is known. Our knowledge of God is in some manner like God and we become like God when we know God. Knowledge of bodies

---

[37] *trin.* 9. 6.9.
[38] *trin.* 9. 7.12 (CCSL 50A. 303–4): 'In illa igitur aeterna ueritate ex qua temporalia facta sunt omnia formam secundum quam sumus et secundum quam uel in nobis uel in corporibus uera et recta ratione aliquid operamur uisu mentis aspicimus'.
[39] *trin.* 9. 7. 12 (CCSL 50A. 304): (immediately following the text quoted in the previous note) 'atque inde conceptam rerum ueracem notitiam tamquam uerbum apud nos habemus et dicendo intus gignimus, nec a nobis nascendo discedit'. I discussed the development of Augustine's notion of the interior word on pp. 194–6.
[40] *trin.* 9. 7–8.13 (CCSL 50A. 304): 'Quod uerbum amore concipitur siue creaturae siue creatoris, id est aut naturae mutabilis aut incommutabilis ueritatis. Ergo aut cupiditate aut caritate.'
[41] *trin.* 9. 9.14. [42] *trin.* 9. 10.15.

misleads when we judge ourselves to be in the same class as that of which we have a likeness within us. Thus when the mind knows and loves itself appropriately an image is born within the mind that perfectly matches the mind: the knowledge or image is expressed from the mind and known as perfectly equal.[43] At this point we have circled back to the account of the perfect equality of mind, love and knowledge sketched at the end of *De trinitate* 9. 5.8, except that now we have a clearer understanding of the conditions under which such equality is possible.

In these sentences we also see one aspect of Augustine's earlier comment that knowledge is 'like a life in the mind of the knower' being a little more filled out. Augustine adapts from his non-Christian Platonic sources (discussed below) a conception of knowledge as an activity and as a desire in order to aid his account of the moral shape of the mind's activity. The production of the 'word' or 'image' in the mind creates a dynamic to our desiring: an economy of lack when we desire inappropriately and seek those things that cannot satisfy and an economy of fullness when we desire spiritual goods and may rest in our knowledge. Thus Augustine's account of the life of knowing emphasizes the reflexive function of recollection. The movement of knowledge and love involved in the bringing forth of 'words' necessarily shapes one's desire and self-understanding (especially when we see that *notitia* is image as well as word). To find ourselves between the perfect self-knowing of the purified mind and the necessary but hidden self-knowing of the mind as such is to find ourselves living the life of the fallen mind, constantly drawn by the mind's habitual gaze, even as we struggle to see the reality of the Truth in which our true judgements are made.

Thus the discussion of the *verbum interior* relates to the initial section of Book 9 by offering *both* an account of the life of knowledge in the perfected *mens* as the continual production of a revealing image in love, *and* an account of how our searching and desiring is currently distorted. Indeed, it is the latter concern that appears to be at the forefront. While consideration of these books has tended to focus on the viability of the analogy offered by Augustine and on the details of his account of the *mens*, Augustine focuses his reflection on the foundations of analogical

---

[43] *trin.* 9. 11.16 (CCSL 50A. 307–8): 'Ex quo colligitur, quia cum se mens ipsa nouit atque approbat sic est eadem notitia uerbum eius ut ei sit par omnino et aequale atque identidem quia neque inferioris essentiae notitia est sicut corporis neque superioris sicut dei. Et cum habeat notitia similitudinem ad eam rem quam nouit, hoc est cuius notitia est, haec habet perfectam et aequalem qua mens ipsa quae nouit est nota. Ideoque et imago et uerbum est quia de illa exprimitur cum cognoscendo eidem coaequatur, et est gignenti aequale quod genitum est.'

practice in the structure of even the fallen mind's life in the Truth itself, and on the character of the moral progress and the life of faith that must accompany growth in reflection on the *imago* even in those able to think the mind as incorporeal.

Book 9 does not end here. As soon as he has returned to the unity and equality of mind, knowledge and love in true contemplation of self, Augustine asks why knowledge or image or word is said to be born (*gignit*), but love is not. This is a question, he tells us, that many ask of the Trinity itself: why is the Son begotten and the Spirit not?[44] Once again, the language of Trinitarian faith is a guide for the exploration of the mind. In an attempt to answer the question by exploring the *imago*, Augustine offers a distinction between knowledge as a type of 'coming into' what is known (*inventum est*) while love is an *appetitus* that must precede and focus the act of knowing. This appetite may not be the love with which the known is loved, but the two are related and may both be called will.[45] The argument ends abruptly, but this question will be taken up at the very beginning of the next book.

What should we take from Book 9? In the first place, Augustine's rather seamless turn to the question of *interiora verba* nicely illustrates the point that his concern is to illustrate not so much the Trinity, but the inseparable operation of the Trinity as the Father's acting always through Word and Spirit. Once again we see that for Augustine the Trinity is always a formed life, a life formed by the Father. In the second place, Augustine's focus on the conceived Word also demonstrates that an intrinsic part of his argument concerns the difficulty of thinking the divine when the mind as life is constantly drawn towards inappropriate materialistic judgement. In the character of the mind's life as image is found both the source of our failure and the potential source of our success. Because our knowing is a life inseparable from the mind as such (understood as activity), its habits give a cast to all the mind's activity; but because the life of knowing is a life that is always in the informing Word, we *may* (through grace) be drawn towards rest in a true image. But much remains to be developed.

CONCLUSION: THE GHOST AT THE BANQUET?

It is because Augustine seems to make so little of the triad being–life–mind that scholars have been wary of suggesting Augustine engaged the

---

[44] *trin.* 9.12.17. [45] *trin.* 9.12.18 (CCSL 50A. 309–10).

one Christian text in which such triads are the basis for a Trinitarian ontology: Victorinus's *Adversus Arrium*. For Pierre Hadot, while Victorinus offers a highly complex ontology of divine being based on applying Porphyry's triad of being–life–mind, Augustine has no developed ontology of divine being, choosing instead to follow a highly personal and more 'psychological' path.[46] In Chapter 1, I followed Cipriani in suggesting that good evidence exists for the presence of Victorinus in Augustine's earliest texts. In later chapters I have also suggested that while Augustine does not use the being–life–mind triad as a Trinitarian terminology in the manner of Victorinus, Augustine does consistently use it to describe both the hierarchy of existence and the character of the divine life as a perfect intellectual life. It seems also to have been the inspiration behind Augustine's gradual development of the triad mind–knowledge–love.

The uniqueness of Victorinus, especially in relation to his sources, has become increasingly apparent since the seminal account of Hadot in the 1960s and 1970s. Hadot's account rests on an account of the centrality to Porphyry of the being–life–mind triad. Hadot places much weight on this triad's presence in one fragment of an anonymous commentary on the Parmenides that he attributed to Porphyry. The question of whether one can use this commentary as a key to the rest of what remains of the Porphyrian corpus has, however, only been compounded by some significant subsequent scholarship that has questioned Hadot's attribution.[47] This recent scholarship has emphasized Victorinus's original contribution to these traditions: his extensive development and application of the being, life, mind triad is without clear parallel in either Plotinus or Porphyry – although it represents an engagement with both. Against this background it only seems more likely that Augustine's use of the triad stems from a knowledge of Victorinus, and his restriction of its role is a possible reaction to Victorinus.

A number of other general and specific parallels present themselves. Most generally, the *Adversus Arium* offers the *only* extensive Latin

---

[46] An argument most clearly developed in Pierre Hadot, 'L'image de la Trinité dans l'âme chez Victorinus et chez saint Augustin', *SP* 6 (1962), 409–42. There is no doubt that this argument advances, in scholarly terms, on the attempt of Paul Henry to argue in rather vague terms for Victorinus's influence on Augustine, 'The *Adversus Arium* of Marius Victorinus, the First Systematic Exposition of the Trinity', *JThS* ns. 1 (1950), 42–55.

[47] See Hadot, *Porphyre et Victorinus*. For more recent critique see, for example, Mark Edwards, 'Porphyry and the Intelligible Triad'; Matthias Baltes, *Marius Victorinus. Zur Philosophie in seinen theologischen Schriften* (Munich: K. G. Saur, 2002); and Gerald Bechtle, *The Anonymous Commentary on Plato's 'Parmenides'* (Bern: Paul Haupt, 1999). Whereas Baltes wishes to date the commentary after Porphyry (and Iamblichus), Bechtle argues for a pre-Plotinian date.

predecessor to Augustine's attempt to explore triadic structures in (some part of) the human soul understood as possessing by nature an image of the Trinitarian persons as mutually indwelling and operating inseparably within the divine simplicity. In *De trinitate* 12 Augustine famously condemns any presentation of the generation of Son and Spirit via the language of male and female principles.[48] While commentators usually assume Augustine is condemning some form of Gnostic theology, once again the one surviving parallel for such ideas within the Latin Trinitarian theology known to Augustine is Victorinus. These few examples give a good sense of the character of the evidence that can be adduced: no one piece offers a certain textual or exegetical parallel, but there is a great deal that suggests Augustine writes with Victorinus in mind.[49]

At *De trinitate* 9. 4.5, Augustine argues that knowledge and love have substantial existence in the mind while also being one. This assertion may echo Plotinus's assertion in *Ennead* 5. 3 that in the necessary multiplicity of self-thinking *Nous* there are a number of activities all of which are *ousiai*.[50] Plotinus offers his opinion as a critique of peripatetic accounts of the simplicity of intellect, and we may see in Augustine's endorsement a similar implied critique of Aristotle's presentation in *Categories* of knowledge as accidental to the *Nous*.[51] Nevertheless, we should also note in Victorinus a parallel mode of argumentation based on theological need. At *Adversus Arium* 1. 63, for example, Victorinus insists that as the soul is the image of the Trinity the soul is at once 'to be', 'to live' and 'to understand':

these three are individuated as in their own substances, without being separated by sectioning, by division, by overflow, by extension or reproduction, but they are always three, each one really existing in the other which really exists also, and this, substantially ... And just as the Father is 'to be', while the Son is twofold in movement and act, likewise the soul as soul is as the paternal power, while vivification and understanding are in movement.[52]

---

[48] *trin.* 12. 5.5. The relevant Victorinus passages are *adv. Ar.* 1. 51, 58, 64. These passages may well demonstrate engagement with the *Chaldean Oracles*.

[49] In his 'La presenza di Mario Victorino nella riflessione trinitaria di Agostino', *Aug(R)* 42 (2002),', 300–4, Cipriani argues that Augustine's account of the *verbum interior* in *trin.* 9 is an attempted refutation of Victorinus's account of the Son's procession. His argument here appears weak and I have not considered it in the text.

[50] *Enn.* 5. 3.12. One might also draw parallels with Plotinus's account of the substantive existence of some 'qualities' in the One at *Enn.* 2. 6.1.

[51] See Aristotle, *Cat.* 8b. 25ff. Brachtendorf, *Die Struktur*, 130ff.; offers the most extensive and best reading of these sections of Book 9 as a possible refutation of Aristotle.

[52] *adv. Ar.* 1. 63 (CSEL 83/1. 163): 'et sicuti pater esse est, filius autem duo, sed in motu et in actu, sic anima in eo quod anima ut potentia patrica, vivificatio autem et intelligentia in motu'. With

Victorinus here argues that each of his three has substantial existence, but as we have seen Augustine do many times, he argues that the soul must possess such a diversity in unity *because* the divine being which it images is likewise structured. And so, while we might seek to explain Augustine's argument about the substantial existence of knowledge and love on the basis of his engagement with Plotinus (or Aristotle) alone, it may be that Victorinus provided Augustine with an important precedent for manipulating mental triads on the basis of Trinitarian theology. Thus, it is true that Augustine does not share the well-developed ontology of divine being that Victorinus offers; and it is true that Augustine offers an account of 'analogy' that intentionally avoids Victorinus's claim that the soul and God demonstrate shared ontological dynamics. But it is also true that there are a number of important structural parallels between the two treatises, and even where the two authors disagree strongly, we should not forget that disagreement is an important form of engagement, if one sometimes more difficult to trace.

The *De trinitate* follows a pattern we have seen in a number of texts throughout Augustine's career. While there is no doubt that Augustine's thought is deeply imbued with some Platonic *doctrines*, the deepest influence of those doctrines on his arguments in Book 9 is to be found in his use of a series of cannibalized themes from Neoplatonic accounts of the life of *Nous*, not in detailed engagement with Neoplatonic triadic structures as such. This should not, however, be taken as an argument for interpreting the particular triads that Augustine discusses as the product of his own genius for psychological observation (as some older scholarship tended to do). As we shall see, the second and fuller version of his argument that constitutes Book 10 is a remarkable blending of Ciceronian and Neoplatonic themes.

---

this we should compare *adv. Ar.* 1. 19: 'λόγος autem in manifesto, actio enim. Quae actio, habens omnia quae sunt in potentia, vita et cognoscentia, secundum motum producit, et manifesta omnia'. With these texts one can also compare 1. 58, 4. 16, 3. 7 and especially 3. 9 (CSEL 83/1. 206): 'Hoc igitur satis clarum faciet esse quod pater est et vitam quod est filius et cognoscentiam quod est spiritus sanctus unum esse et unam substantiam, subsistentias tres'. Augustine shows no awareness of the distinction between *substantia* and *subsistentia*.

CHAPTER 12

'... It's just fur lookin' through'

in the *De trinitate* as in the *Contra Academicos*, the slowness and the detours in the argumentation are intentional: it is a dialectical exercise which has the aim of training, of exercising the intelligence to raise itself towards that which is highest, to make us ascend, as Augustine loves to repeat, *ab inferioribus ad superiora*, to make us enter *ab exterioribus ad interiora*.[1]

SETTING UP *DE TRINITATE* 10: *SE NOSSE – SE COGITARE*

In the first sentence of Book 10, Augustine describes his task as one of approaching that which he seeks to explain with a more thorough or precise attention.[2] Treatments of the relationship between the two books have frequently focused on the relative adequacy of the two triads of *mens, notitia, amor* and *memoria, intellegentia, voluntas*. I suspect, however, that the things Augustine seeks to explain more thoroughly are not primarily the terms of these triads, but the complexities of arguing that the mind knows itself in all acts of knowing and seeking, even in those that constitute an on-going process of increasing forgetfulness of self amid the created order. Only if we can understand this dynamic more clearly, Augustine is arguing, will we be able to understand how the mind knows in the presence of, informed by the Word and how it is that the mind forgets this presence and may return to it. Only by such a return can we grow into our status as both image and likeness and thus most clearly be the analogical site that we should be.

---

[1] Henri-Irénée Marrou, *Saint Augustin et la fin de la culture antique*, 323. This judgement is intertwined with Marrou's repeated insistence that Augustine composed badly and in disconnected fashion, a judgement that he later to some extent recanted, see section XIII of the 'retractatio' published in this edition at pp. 665–72.
[2] *trin.* 10. 1.1 (CCSL 50A. 310): 'Nunc ad ea ipsa consequenter enodatius explicanda limatior accedat intentio'.

297

Augustine begins the book with the very theme that was the focus of the final paragraphs of Book 9: the relationship between love and knowledge in the mind's self-knowing. Desire for knowledge of something must, Augustine argues, be preceded by some sort of knowledge about that which is desired.[3] What then is the knowledge that precedes the mind's search for its own nature? For Augustine, the mind that seeks to know itself must already know itself in some sense. Augustine's answer is that the mind knows itself in the act of knowing, it knows itself as knowing. Self-knowing of some sort is implicit in the movement of intellectual life. The mind, then, which seeks to know itself, at least knows itself as seeking (*deinde cum se quaerit ut noverit, quaerentem se iam novit*).[4] Further, given the mind's existence as incorporeal intelligence, the mind's knowledge of itself is knowledge, by the whole of itself, of its whole self.[5] Augustine's initial discussion of the mind's necessary self-knowing offered in Book 9 is here clarified by an account of the mind's self-knowing as present in every act of seeking and knowing.

These doctrines find close parallels in Plotinus's *Ennead* 5. 3 and the passages of Porphyry's *Sententiae* that interpret and summarize *Ennead* 5. 3:

Does he then see himself with another part of himself? But in this was one would be the seer and another the seen; but this is not self-knowledge. What, then, if everything of this kind is, in a way, composed of exactly similar parts, so that the seer does not differ in any way from the seen?[6]

Intelligence, therefore, is simultaneously thinker and thought, all that thinks and all that is thought ... It does not contain one part that thinks, while another would not think.[7]

It is not clear which version of these arguments Augustine encountered, although the closeness of Augustine's account to both these texts renders direct borrowing on one highly likely.[8] Augustine's assumption

---

[3] *trin.* 10. 1.2–2.4.   [4] *trin.* 10. 3.5 (CCSL 50A. 318).
[5] *trin.* 10. 3.6–4.6.   [6] Plotinus, *Enn.* 5. 3.5.
[7] Porphyry, *sent.* 44. See the tabulation by Cristina D'Ancona in Luc Brisson (ed.), *Porphyre: Sentences*, 2 vols. (Paris: Vrin, 2005), 248–50.
[8] Jean Pépin, 'Le tout et les parties dans la connaissance de la *mens* par elle-même (*De Trin.* X 3, 4 – 4, 6)', in Johannes Brachtendorf (ed.), *Gott und sein Bild. Augustins* De Trinitate *im Spiegel gegenwärtiger Forschung* (Paderborn: Schöningh, 2000), 105–26, offers the most extensive consideration of this theme. Not surprisingly he opts for Porphyrian influence, but the evidence is extremely uncertain. In his 'Une nouvelle source de saint Augustin: le ζήτημα de Porphyre "Sur l'union de l'âme et du corps"', *Revue des Études anciennes* 66 (1964), 53–107, Pépin offers a highly suggestive argument that Augustine's typology of mixture offered in discussion of the relationship between love and knowledge at *trin.* 9. 4.7–5.8 owes to Porphyry (pp. 94–100), and a series of further (but less convincing) Porphyrian parallels in *trin.* 9 (pp. 101–7).

that incorporeal reality does not occupy place also finds direct parallels in Plotinus and Porphyry.[9] Similarly, his account of knowledge as a 'life' finds echoes at Plotinus's *Ennead* 5. 1.6, 5. 3.6 and 6. 2.8.[10] It is unclear whether Augustine knew Plotinus's *Ennead* 6. 4–5 ('On the Presence of Being, One and the Same, Everywhere as a whole'), although Robert O'Connell argued fairly persuasively that he did.[11] If Augustine knew this text, it also may have shaped his account of mind. Throughout Books 9 and 10, then, we see Augustine deploying a range of Neoplatonic themes that had not previously made their way into his Trinitarian reflection. The character of intellectual life within a Platonic context is, however, a topic that has interested Augustine since his earliest works.[12] As well as influencing Augustine's account of the mind, one might also argue that these ideas have influenced his mature presentations of the interpenetration of the divine three and their individual possession of the entirety of the divine intellectual life. Such influence is, however, impossible to demonstrate with certainty, and one might explain the same development as a logical outworking of his earlier Trinitarian discussions.

When Augustine argues that the mind necessarily knows itself *qua* mind, he not only returns us to and develops a paradox that has been present since Book 8 (we can only seek for that which is in some sense already known), he also maps out the ground on which he can move forward. As we shall see, Augustine will use this account of the mind necessarily knowing itself in its own mental life to emphasize again that our search for the *imago* within us is inseparable from our search to understand what prevents that knowledge and how the impediment may be removed. In a deft stroke Augustine asks why the Delphic oracle commands 'know thyself' if we cannot but know ourselves.[13] As we will discuss at more length

---

[9] For example, Plotinus, *Enn*. 6. 4.1 and 8–11; Porphyry, *sent*. 42.
[10] For example, Plotinus, *Enn*. 5. 1.6: οἷον καὶ ἡ ψυχὴ λόγος νοῦ καὶ ἐνέργειά τις, ὥσπερ αὐτὸς ἐκείνου. We should note, however, especially in the light of my comments about Victorinus as a possible alternate source, that if Augustine knew *Enn*. 6. 2.8, his adaptation of the language of life and movement to describe both knowledge in the *mens* and the Word itself involved either ignoring or not understanding the complexities of Plotinus's argument.
[11] See Robert J. O'Connell '*Ennead* VI, 4 and 5 in the Works of Saint Augustine', *REAug* 9 (1963), 1–39.
[12] In addition to the evidence from Chapter 6 that Neoplatonic texts influenced Augustine's early epistemology, we should note also the gnomic *div. qu*. 18. The discussion of the character of intellect at *Gn. litt*. 12. 10.21 further demonstrates on-going reflection on these questions prior to *trin*. 9–10. On this last text, see Jean Pépin, 'Une curieuse declaration idéaliste de "De genesi ad litteram" [XII, 10, 21] de saint Augustin, et ses origins plotiniennes ["Ennéade" 5, 3, 1–9 et 5, 5, 1–2]', in *Revue d'Histoire et de Philosophie religieuses* 34 (1954), 373–400.
[13] Augustine's place in late antique use of the Delphic oracle is discussed in great detail by Pierre Courcelle in his *Connais-Toi Toi-Même de Socrate à Saint Bernard* (Paris: Études Augustiniennes,

later in the chapter, much ancient commentary interpreted the famous apothegm as a call to knowledge of one's soul, and Augustine offers a Christianized reading combining Stoic and Platonic themes: the oracle commands us to know ourselves so that we may live according to our nature, in awareness of our place in the ontological order, and living with rightly ordered desire.[14] The ignorance of God that is the consequence of wrongly ordered desire has as its corollary an ignorance of the true nature of the human being. Even as we recognize the beauty of things through the presence of the divine beauty, we do not desire divine beauty for itself or seek to mirror it with the Spirit's aid: we seek to possess beauty itself for our own. In such desire we love more intently that which is only increasingly distant from God, and we become more and more uncertain of our ability to retain the objects of our desire. The love of material things is thus a glue that makes it harder and harder for us not to think of ourselves as like those things that we most love.[15]

In the midst of this account of the link between fallen desire and fallen self-knowing Augustine distinguishes between knowing oneself as *se nosse* and as *se cogitare*:

> Thus, although it is one thing not to know oneself [*se nosse*], and another thing not to think of oneself [*se cogitare*] (for we do not say that a man, skilled in many branches of knowledge, is ignorant of grammar when he is not thinking of it, because he is then thinking of the art of medicine) … yet the force of love is so great that the mind draws in with itself those things upon which it has long reflected with love and to which it has become attached by its devoted care, even when it returns in some way to itself [*cum ad se cogitandam quodam modo redit*].[16]

The former (*se nosse*) is the mind's innate self-knowing, the self-knowing that Augustine has already suggested is necessarily present if we were to seek but which is oddly hidden from us because the mind's gaze has

---

1974–5), 1: 125–63. The discussion of *trin.* 9 and 10 begins at p. 151. Courcelle assumes Augustine's Platonism to be fundamentally Porphyrian, flavoured throughout his career by an account of the soul's inward turn and ascent that he takes to be dependent on Porphyry's *sent.* and lost treatise on the Delphic oracle (even though the Plotinian themes are also present). As I indicated in the first two chapters and here, while *trin.* 9 and 10 demonstrate a number of arguments that may well derive from Porphyry, the evidence for such dependence in the early works seems far weaker. Courcelle's discussion of God's presence, pp. 137–40, deserves note.

[14] *trin.* 10. 5.7 (CCSL 50A. 320): 'Utquid ergo ei praeceptum est ut se ipsa cognoscat? Credo ut se cogitet et secundum naturam suam uiuat, id est ut secundum suam naturam ordinari appetat, sub eo scilicet cui subdenda est, supra ea quibus praeponenda est; sub illo a quo regi debet, supra ea quae regere debet.'

[15] *trin.* 10. 5.7. [16] *trin.* 10. 5.7 (CCSL 50A. 321).

'*... It's just fur lookin' through*' 301

become obsessed with the material.[17] Having made this observation, Augustine returns to ancient speculation on the nature of the soul: the more the soul is understood as a physical reality, the more we see the effects of desire as it falls away from God.[18] But even as it falls further into ignorance the mind knows itself as someone may be said to know a subject even when they are thinking of something very different.

Thinking of oneself truly (*se cogitare*) receives little definition in the passage quoted above, but over the next few paragraphs Augustine begins to sketch its basic principles.[19] Most importantly, thinking of oneself truly involves distinguishing oneself from what one is not, as we see in the refrain heard throughout this passage:

Therefore the mind does not have to look for itself as if it were not available to itself.[20]

Let [the mind] then recognize itself and not go looking for itself as if it were absent, but rather turn on to itself the attention of its will, which had it straying through other things.[21]

Let the mind then not go looking for a look at itself as if it were absent, but rather take pains to tell itself apart as present.[22]

The latter two of these quotations occur after Augustine characterizes active self-knowing as an *inventio* (a heavily freighted term whose significance we will discuss shortly). Augustine plays with the idea that one 'comes into' (*in-venire*) knowledge: how can the mind 'come into' knowledge about itself? Being told to know oneself is not like being told to know an object. But, he continues,

when it is said to the mind: 'know thyself', in that instant in which the mind understands what is meant by "yourself", it knows itself [*eo ictu quo intellegit*

---

[17] Cf. *trin*. 10. 6.8 (CCSL 50A. 321): 'Errat autem mens cum se istis imaginibus tanto amore coniungit ut etiam se esse aliquid huiusmodi existimet. Ita enim conformatur eis quodam modo non id exsistendo sed putando.'

[18] *trin*. 10. 7.9–7.10. The passage may well reflect Cicero, *Tusc*.1. 9.18–11.22. Cf. 1.16.38 and 1. 27.66.

[19] The term 'cogitare' has attracted a good deal of scholarly discussion. The best introduction to that material is Gerard Watson, 'Cogitatio', in *AugLex*. G. Verberke, 'Pensée et discernment chez s. Augustin: Quelques réflexions sur le sens du termes "cogitare"', *RecAug* 2 (1962), 59–80, is still helpful.

[20] *trin*. 10. 7.10 (CCSL 50A. 323): 'ideoque non se tamquam sibi desit mens requirat'.

[21] *trin*. 10. 8.11 (CCSL 50A. 325): 'Cognoscat ergo semetipsam, nec quasi absentem se quaerat, sed intentionem uoluntatis qua per alla uagabatur statuat in se ipsa et se cogitet'. Cf. Cicero, *Tusc*. 1. 22.59, *fin. 3*. 22.73, 5. 16.44, *leg*. 1.

[22] *trin*. 10. 9.12 (CCSL 50A. 325): 'Non itaque uelut absentem se quaerat cernere, sed praesentem se cures discernere'.

quod dictum est te ipsam cognoscit se ipsam], and it knows itself for no other reason than that it is present to itself [*quod sibi praesens est*].[23]

Simply by the fact of the mind's necessary presence to itself, self-knowing follows in an instant of self-recognition. And yet, as we have seen, the character of this knowing is dependent on the desire that is its inescapable context. The self-knowing and self-presence intrinsic to mental life are obscured by the mind's joining to itself images of those things external to the mind that have become the focus of our desire. What is necessarily known in that instant of self-recognition can only be the subject of appropriate and true attention when the mind has been educated towards appropriate objects of desire, and into a concomitant practice of distinguishing the intelligible from the material. Thus, although Augustine has begun to sketch an account of the mind as necessarily self-knowing, it remains the case (as it was in Book 9) that Augustine sees our ability to grasp that intrinsic self-knowing as dependent on the reformation of the human mind. Once again a true grasp of self is eschatological, for the moment we may only strain towards a vision of true self-knowledge and towards a vision of that in us which is *imago*.

It is important to note the extent to which the account of the *verbum interior* developed in the latter half of Book 9 underlies Book 10. Given the complex redaction history of the *De trinitate*, it is unclear whether we should read Books 9 and 10 as successive stages in an argument which is following a well-planned course, or as successive attempts at the same argument, drawn together under pressure when Augustine came back to them when writing the final books after the theft of the first twelve. In either case, it is his account of the mind's life as the production of *verba interiora* that drives both accounts. This account enables an extended meditation on and diagnosis of our failure to think that which should be at the heart of our thinking, and it shapes a series of reflections on the difference between the mind's constantly unfulfilled fallen desiring and the self-presence that constitutes the mind's self-knowing existence. In turn, drawing the mind towards recognizing the self-presence of intellectual existence will also enable Augustine to propel the gaze of those who follow his argument out (or in) towards the eternal active presence of the divine Word and Truth in whom all our knowing occurs. But this is to step far beyond where we have reached.

[23] *trin.* 10. 9.12 (CCSL 50A. 326).

DE TRINITATE 10. 10.13–12.19: MEMORIA, INTELLEGENTIA AND VOLUNTAS

At *De trinitate* 10. 10.13, Augustine suggests that we try to distinguish those acts of the mind that we can be certain are intrinsic to the mind. We are certain that we are, that we live and that we understand. Augustine treats these three as indicating levels of existence, and thus the mind should know that it lives as intelligence, the highest activity of the mind.[24] Augustine discerns within the life of intelligence a range of activities. First he identifies willing (*velle*), remembering (*meminisse*) and understanding (*intellegere*), and then offers a list of the mind's powers (*vis*): living, remembering, understanding, willing, thinking, knowing, judging.[25]

Augustine once again reads ancient disputes about the nature of the soul as resulting from varying degrees of desire for corporeal objects. He rejects again any account of the mind's activities as accidental to the mind as a body or as accidental to the body itself, insisting that the mind must know itself as a whole when it searches for itself and must thus know its own *substantia* in knowing itself. Were the mind's activities to be understood as accidental, knowledge of the mind would be knowledge through images of a distinct reality. The Delphic oracle is now given a further twist:

And thus it belongs to that whole which is commanded to know itself, to be certain that it is none of those things of which it is uncertain, and to be certain that it alone is that only, which it is certain that it is [*idque solum esse se certa sit quod solum esse se certa est*].[26]

This certainty is achieved by distinguishing between things that are known as absent through the imagination and those activities – like living, remembering, understanding and willing – that it thinks 'with some inner, non-simulated but true presence' (*quadam interiore non simulate, sed vera praesentia*).[27]

As Augustine returns to the notion of the mind's self-knowing as a form of presence – a concept he keeps, I suspect, intentionally vague – the notion of the *verbum interior* that he has been using to explore the mind's self-knowing is increasingly revealed as only analogous to the reality he is seeking to describe. There is no temporal sequence involved in the mind's

---

[24] *trin.* 10. 9.13.   [25] The former in *trin* 9. 10.13–10. 10.13 and 9. 10.14–10. 10.14.
[26] *trin.* 9. 10.16–10. 10.16 (CCSL 50A. 328–9).   [27] *trin.* 9. 10.16 (CCSL 50A. 329).

self-thinking: the mind does not reach into the memory for an image of itself and then form a 'word'.

At *De trinitate* 10. 11.17, Augustine takes forward the discussion by asking us to focus on just three of the things about which the mind can be certain: *memoria, intellegentia, voluntas*. Augustine is clear that there are other activities about which the mind is certain: this triad represents a choice from a range of possibilities and thus should not be understood as an identification of 'faculties' constitutive of the soul.[28] We consider these three, he tells us, when we assess the aptitude of a child for education, and we consider the formed relationship of these three when we consider a mature person's learning and the use they make of their learning.[29]

In the final paragraphs of Book 10 Augustine sums up how these three exhibit the Trinitarian logic. Taking up again the triad of being–life–mind, Augustine asserts that our three terms are one life, mind and substance (*vita ... mens ... substantia*): they are the one life of intelligence discussed above. Each one is also itself fully itself life, mind and being. At the same time the three are named relative to each other. Each contains each of the others, and each contains all of them. The three are also equal (*aequalia*).[30] In this passage we see with a new clarity a key distinction between the triads of *mens, notitia* and *amor*, and *memoria, intellegentia* and *voluntas*. In the case of the earlier triad, Augustine was clear that the three would be equal only when the mind's knowledge of itself is 'equal' to itself, a situation obtaining only in the purified mind. In these final paragraphs of Book 10, Augustine asserts, however, that memory, intellect and will are co-equal and inseparable in the mind without offering any comment that limits this equality and unity to the mind in any particular state. In one sense, then, this new triad better captures the manner in which the life of intellect as such may be understood to image the Trinitarian life. But Augustine continues to speak of the mind as known appropriately (and hence known as *imago*) only when the mind knows itself in a form of active self-presence, not by searching for itself and claiming to know itself as an object. Augustine also seems to be clear that this active self-presence, free from the distortions that follow from the

---

[28] Cf. David Manchester, 'The Noetic Triad in Plotinus, Marius Victorinus, and Augustine', in Richard T. Wallis (ed.), *Neoplatonism and Gnosticism* (Albany, NY: SUNY Press, 1992), 219: 'the phenomenology of *memoria, intellegentia*, and *voluntas* which he drives to ever greater interiority, transparency and self-sufficiency is a noetic analysis and not, as so often expressed, a "psychology." The three moments ... are the self-constituted life of the *mens animi*, the mind of the soul. They are not, in the medieval or modern sense, "faculties" of the soul, but instead the internal structure of spiritual self-disclosedness'. See also Brachtendorf, *Die Struktur*, 192.

[29] *trin.* 10. 11.17. [30] *trin.* 10. 11.18 (CCSL 50. 331).

attachment to the mind of inappropriate imagery, will only be a *known* reality when mind has been purified from its fallen life.

In the final paragraph of the book Augustine asserts again that the mind always knows, remembers and understands itself, but does not always think (*cogitare*) of itself as distinct from things which are not itself. Memory and understanding easily seem to be one rather than two in the mind's self-knowing, and unless we speak in terms of an active desire for what is not known, the reality of love/will may be doubted. Hence Augustine feels it important to embark on another *exercitatio* in Book 11. Thus, right at the end of the book Augustine provides yet further evidence that the mind's intellectual life and self-presence may be the premier analogical site for understanding the Trinity only because the language of faith guides our investigation and only through a long process of *exercitatio* and purification – both intellectual and moral. The investigations of Books 9 and 10 thus do not circumvent either the language of faith or the reformation of existence that Christ initiates and guides – they depend upon both these things. But before we consider Augustine's sources here, and then leave the latter half of the *De trinitate*, we should consider briefly aspects of Book 14, which offer a reprise of Book 10's argument.

REPRISE: *DE TRINITATE* 14

Maybe five years or a little more after Augustine had originally written *De trinitate* 9–10, he returned to the same subject in Book 14, offering what amounts to a gloss on the argument of Book 10.[31] In particular we find him returning to the distinction between *se nosse* and *se cogitare*. After an initial statement of the inescapability of self-knowledge Augustine states,

> such, however, is the power of thinking that the mind cannot even set itself in some fashion in its own view except when it thinks about itself [*Tanta est tamen cogitationis uis ut nec ipsa mens quodam modo se in conspectu suo ponat nisi quando se cogitate*]. Nothing is in the mind's view except what is being thought about, and this means that not even the mind itself ... can be in its own view except by thinking about itself. Though, as a matter of fact, how can it not be in its own view when it is not thinking about itself, seeing that it can never be without itself ... I cannot really fathom.[32]

---

[31] He has little to say about Book 9, leading us to think that he considered Book 10 the more successful argument.

[32] *trin.* 14. 6.8 (CCSL 50A. 430–1).

Again, Augustine circles familiar ground. We should not think we can explain the mind's forgetting of itself by means of a corporeal division of the mind, rather we should think that the mind's gaze (*conspectus*) belongs to its nature and that that gaze brings things into its own 'sight' by acts of cognition – by an act of 'incorporeal conversion' (*incorporeal conversione*) – that are otherwise hidden in a 'secret knowledge' (*arcana quadam notitia*) called the memory.[33] But even this is a paradox: the mind can examine itself only by an active cognition of itself, but how could it have escaped its own gaze?

The division – in self-knowing – between the act of cognitive gazing and the secret knowledge of the memory prompts Augustine to ask whether we can say that understanding (*intellectus*) pertains to acts of cognition while knowledge (*notitia*) pertains to the memory.[34] It might seem that Augustine has promoted just such a distinction both here and in Book 10, but no. If it were so then the mind's self-knowing would not be permanent, and there would be no constant trinity of memory, understanding and will in the mind's self-knowing. Augustine argues that one who knows a discipline necessarily understands that discipline even if he is actively thinking about something else.[35] The hidden depths of the mind thus contain *notitiae* that are brought into the open, but these *notitiae* may in some sense be said to be already understood.[36] There is then a permanent image in the mind's deepest self-knowing even when that knowing is hidden from our direct gaze. This must be so if the mind's self-presence and knowing is to be an *imago* of the divine life, but the more clearly we articulate the presence of this constant the greater the paradox of our ignorance of self becomes: 'I do not know in what marvellous way, if one can say this, we do not know that we know.'[37] This argument pushes Book 10 a little further, reworking the analogy of one who knows many things offered in Book 9 to describe a real self-knowing and understanding that is a constant self-presence.

But we should be wary of stopping here, a few further steps in Augustine's argument must be followed. A little later Augustine states:

> The truth of course is that from the moment it began to be it never stopped remembering itself, never stopped understanding itself, never stopped loving itself, as we have already shown. And therefore, when it turns to itself in thought, a trinity is formed in which a word too can be perceived. It is formed of course out of the very act of thought [*ex ipsa cogitatione*], with the will joining the two

---

[33] *trin.* 14. 6.8 (CCSL 50A. 431–2).   [34] *trin.* 14. 6.9 (CCSL 50A. 432–3).
[35] *trin.* 14. 7.7.   [36] *trin.* 14. 7.9 (CCSL 50A. 433–4).   [37] *trin.* 14. 7.10–14. 7.9–10.

together. It is here more than anywhere that we should recognize the image we are seeking.³⁸

The importance of this passage lies in its clear statement that the image of God is not simply to be found by uncovering the mind's continuous self-knowing structure. The image is found in the trained and purified mind's active cognition of itself as remembering, understanding and willing.

Second, Augustine adds in the next paragraph:

> This trinity of the mind is not really the image of God because the mind remembers, understands and loves itself, but because it is able also to remember and understand and love him by whom it was made. And when it does this it becomes wise. If it does not do it, even though it remembers, understands and loves itself, it is foolish.³⁹

It becomes clear in the following paragraphs that the last sentence refers to the one who undoubtedly remembers, understands and loves her- or himself simply because it cannot be taken away from the human mind, and yet is consumed by love of created things and ignorant of God – ignorant, in fact, of the one in whom he or she exists. The mind exhibits best its nature as image when it remembers, understands and loves itself appropriately – without being consumed by desire for created objects – and both towards and in its Creator. Augustine's language here is strong: the mind that 'cleaves' to God shares in the divine nature and sees all that it sees in that unchangeable nature.⁴⁰ The mind is perfected as *imago Dei* not merely when the object of desire is God, but when its act as mind is towards, from and in the divine.

Yet, as ever, running through these paragraphs is a strong sense that we are not yet there: the mind now cries out in repentance to God, aware that it cannot master its own loves.⁴¹ 'For the time being', Augustine tells us, 'when [the mind] sees itself it does not see anything unchangeable'. This paragraph may well begin in conscious imitation of *De trinitate* 9. 6.9, which introduces Augustine's discussion of the very same topic, the *verbum interior*.⁴² Our unhappiness is a result of the strange forgetting that characterizes the fallen life that is still in some sense necessarily 'in' God. The mind begins to recall God when it accepts his Spirit and knows that it needs God's grace to rise. Such a mind does not remember

---

³⁸ *trin.* 14. 10.13 (CCSL 50A. 441). ³⁹ *trin.* 14. 12.15.
⁴⁰ *trin.* 14. 14.20 (CCSL 50A. 448–9): 'In illa itaque natura cum feliciter adhaeserit immutabile uidebit omne quod uiderit'.
⁴¹ *trin.* 14. 14.18. ⁴² *trin.* 14. 15.20–1 (CCSL 50A. 449).

its former happiness, but must be reminded of it by the Scriptures. Such a mind can, however, remember God because it is admonished by grace to turn and recognize the presence of the one in whom the mind exists.[43] The renewal of the Spirit of the mind (Eph. 4.23) is the process within which the mind is gradually turned to the love of spiritual things.[44] The Christian life is thus here cast as a gradual education in the production of 'words' about things in awareness of the truth itself, in awareness of the presence of the Word. Our skill at using the mind as an analogical site for contemplating the Trinity grows both as we nurture the Christian life – allowing grace to draw us into the transference of the affections that Christ initiates and guides – and as we thus gradually come to share more fully in the Trinitarian life .

A CICERONIAN TRIAD

Why, then, does Augustine turn to the language of *memoria*, *intellegentia* and *voluntas*? We should begin by noting where this triad does and does not occur in his corpus. Including some variations on the third term found in Book 15 of the *De trinitate*, Augustine uses the triads *memoria*, *intellegentia*, *voluntas* and *memoria*, *intellectus*, *voluntas* around thirty-five times in his corpus. This rather vague figure stems from the difficulty of assessing passages where its constituent terms are discussed over a number of complex sentences. Even with such imprecise figures it is striking that over twenty of these uses occur in the *De trinitate*. Indeed, the triad is used in directly Trinitarian contexts outside this work in just three texts.[45] And so, from all the homilies on John and 1 John where Trinitarian topics frequently occur, from the *Confessiones*, from his extensive expositions of the Psalms, as well as from the vast majority of his sermons and letters, this triad is absent from discussions of Trinitarian doctrine. Equally importantly, the triad is not a standard feature of Augustine's psychology. Reflection on the will, on memory and on the act of cognition is of course a central thread in Augustine's corpus, but this particular triad is not.[46]

That the triad of *memoria*, *intellegentia* and *voluntas* finds its origin in Cicero has long been noted, but rarely commented on in any depth.[47] The triad first appears fairly early in Augustine's writing career. At *De*

---

[43] *trin.* 14. 15.21.   [44] *trin.* 14. 16.22–17.23.
[45] *serm.* 52. 19–21 (3); *ep.* 169, 2 and 6 (3); *c. s. Arrian.* 9. 16 (3–4).
[46] For an example see my discussion of *Io. ev. tr.* 23, pp. 243–4.
[47] For example Schindler, *Wort und Analogie*, 58–60, notes but makes little of the triad's Ciceronian origins.

diversis quaestionibus 31, Augustine quotes *verbatim* a passage of Cicero's *De inventione* in answer to a question about how Cicero defined the virtues.[48] The *inventio* of Cicero's title was the practice by which orators chose the appropriate style and content for a speech. An extended tradition of reflection on the practice of *inventio* resulted in a large body of literature that categorized varieties of speech, varieties of legal case, causality, morality and appropriate styles of reasoning. The passage with which we are concerned comes from a section of the work in which Cicero offers an account of virtue as part of his initial division of those things to which the orator should appeal in deliberative speeches. Invoking a traditional discussion, Cicero speaks of the relationship between what is 'useful' (*utilis*) and what is 'honourable' (*honestum*). In common with Stoic ethics, Cicero insists that even though it might seem that an orator must choose whatever is useful to make a case, whether or not that accords with what seems to be good or honourable, the two are never truly in conflict. One learns what constitutes appropriate behaviour only by learning to attend to the Good itself. Thus Cicero moves on to describe the *honestum*, the honourable.[49]

That which is simply honourable is virtue, and virtue is a habit of mind by which the mind may live in harmony with nature and reason. The very first thing to be considered under the heading of virtue is *prudentia*, wisdom, and this, Cicero tells us, is constituted by the appropriate interplay of three mental activities: memory (*memoria*), understanding (*intelligentia*) and foresight (*providentia*).[50] The reasons for the subtle difference between Cicero's triad and Augustine's are laid out by Augustine himself. At *De trinitate* 14. 11.14, Augustine again tells us that Cicero divided *prudentia* into three parts, *memoria*, *intellegentia* and *providentia*. But, he continues, those like Cicero who offered this account were mistaken, for human beings have no ability to foresee the providentially ordained future. Thus, it is now *voluntas* that joins together memory and understanding so that the human being may be attentive to the Good.

---

[48] *div. qu.* 31 (the purpose of the question is given at *retr.* 1. 26); Cicero, *inv.* 2. 53.160.

[49] Cicero's brief account of the *honestum*, the honourable, can be supplemented from Seneca's *ep.* 120 (which Augustine probably did not know). Seneca here describes two approaches to ethics. For some the good and the honourable are defined by reference to what is useful and what constitutes appropriate duty. Seneca's account of the one who possesses true virtue will probably be familiar to all readers of Augustine; such a one, writes Seneca, will have the hope of eternity set before her eyes, she will know that nothing except God is superior to the soul and will never lose sight of the true nature of virtue and vice. The one who possesses virtue in this way will live a life of harmony with nature and with the order of things.

[50] There are other definitions clearly in the same orbit, although none use exactly Cicero's form. See, for example, *rhet. Her.* 3. 2.3.

In passing it should be said that we cannot be certain when Augustine first conceived of an extended exploration of these three for Trinitarian purposes. Augustine uses the triad thus both in *Sermon* 52 and at *De trinitate* 4. 21.30. The first of these is usually dated without much certainty to *c.*410, while the latter was most likely *c.* 411. In both cases Augustine not surprisingly treats the triad as illustrating the unity of the Father acting always through Son and in Spirit, but little more is done. If we are reasonably secure in dating *De trinitate* 9–10 to 417–18 then it was not until this point that Augustine made use of this new triad to develop in any extensive way his earlier inchoate reflections on human mental life as an analogical site.

Within the rhetorical tradition, observation of the three activities to which Augustine draws our attention is frequently mentioned as fundamental to the assessment of ability and formed character. As we have seen, Augustine alludes to this traditional usage in *De trinitate* 10 and, while only Cicero brings together these three in this order, discussion of *memoria* or *intellegentia* (or *cogitatio* understood as a closely related term) in this context is commonplace. For example, Quintilian writes:

> As soon as a boy is entrusted to him, the skilled teacher will first spy out his ability [*ingenium*] and character [*natura*]. In children the principal sign of ability is memory.[51]

Quintilian then cautions a teacher to watch how well a child memorizes, how fast and accurately a child can recall things from memory, and how discerning a child is in the imitation of examples. On at least one occasion Augustine himself uses the triad in a related fashion to name the structuring activities of the moral life. In a numerological section of *Contra Faustum* 12 we read, in the midst of commentary on the fact that 27 (the day of the month on which Noah entered the ark) is 3 cubed:

> There is a trinity in the means by which we are, as it were, squared or fitted for every good work. By the memory we remember God, by the understanding we know him, by the will we love him.[52]

Augustine's adaptation of Cicero's triad in the context of a very broadly Platonic account of the mind's nature must also be read against the background of Cicero's own interweaving of rhetorical, Stoic and Platonic themes. *De trinitate* 10 demonstrates some close parallels with Cicero's discussion of the Delphic oracle in the *Tusculan Disputations*.[53] At 1. 22.52,

---

[51] *inst.* I. 3.1.   [52] *c. Faust.* 12. 19.
[53] See Schindler, *Wort und Analogie*, 247–8; Courcelle, *Connais-Toi*, 154–63.

Cicero argues that the Delphic oracle is a command to the soul to know and see itself through itself, an argument based on the doctrine that the soul is a self-moving reality that knows itself as self-moving.[54] On this basis Cicero assumes that the oracle encourages a knowledge of the soul as the immortal and divine element of the human composite.

This reading obviously enough differs from Augustine's attempt to consider the *mens* as the 'highest' part of the soul not because of its 'divinity' but because it is the site of a knowing and desiring occurring in the presence of Truth itself. Nevertheless, Cicero proceeds to describe the unique powers (*vis*) of the soul by drawing attention to *inventio*, *cogitatio* and *memoria*.[55] Cicero does not intend these three as a triadic structure, rather he names three activities that he sees as having significant overlap and interrelationship. In a way readers of Augustine's *De trinitate* 10 should find familiar, the act of *cogitatio* is interwoven with *inventio* and thus with *memoria*, but memory not understood as powerful because of its capacity to contain many things, but as powerful when considered with *inventio* to be the source of recollection and reasoned thought.[56] A very similar account is to be found in *Tusculan Disputations* 5. The person with appropriate *ingenium* ('natural intelligence') and *studium* ('devotion') will be able to study towards the truth, learning about the harmony of the cosmos, the virtue to be found within the soul, and the power of dialectic (the three divisions of Stoic philosophy: physics, ethics and dialectic). It is the Delphic oracle that calls us to the second of these tasks, towards the virtue in the soul, the discovery of which is also for the mind to know itself in union with the divine mind.[57]

Augustine has transformed Cicero's account. In particular, a Neoplatonic account of the mind as intellectual life and movement, in which the intellect knows the whole of itself, and must know itself not

---

[54] *Tusc.* 1. 22.52: 'Est illud quidem vel maximum animo ipso animum videre'. At 1. 23.53–4, Cicero quotes and endorses Plato's assertion at *Phaedrus* 245c–d that the soul is self-moving and can know itself to be so.

[55] Cicero, *Tusc.* 1. 25.61 and 26.65. Cf. Augustine, *an. et or.* 4. 9 and 14, where his own triad is used not to describe the structure of the mind as such, but to identify some of the mind's unique powers.

[56] Edward Booth, 'St Augustine's "*notitia sui*" Related to Aristotle and the Early Neo-Platonists', *Aug(L)* 28 (1978), 187, argues for 'detailed textual similarities' with Aristotle's *On Memory and Recollection*. Unfortunately those that are offered can all be accounted for by transmission through the Latin rhetorical and philosophical traditions. The parallel patterns of thought he identifies are most definitely present, however, and his discussion of Augustine's eclectic borrowings in his own doctrine of *memoria* (pp. 188ff.) is helpful.

[57] *Tusc.* 5. 24.68–25.72, here 25.70: 'ut ipsa se mens agnoscat coniunctamque cum divina mente se sentiat'.

as a distinct object, provides Augustine with the tools for exploring the self-knowing and loving that he argues must be intrinsic to the mind. And yet, each of these latter two concepts – knowing and loving – owes to multiple sources, and each has also been transformed by his theological commitments.[58] The philosophical idiosyncrasy of Augustine's account can be seen clearly in his description of the mind's necessary and complete activity of self-knowing. He does so not by adapting Neoplatonic accounts of the character of intellect in relation to that which is its source, or accounts of the necessary duality of intellect (let alone the complex relations of *Nous* and *Psuche*), but by trying to suggest notions of *memoria* and *cogitatio* – themselves adapted from Latin rhetorical and philosophical (probably Ciceronian) tradition – removed from their normal temporal connotations.

One further aspect of the complex background to *memoria*, *intellegentia* and *voluntas* should be noted. Robert Dodaro has recently published two articles concerning the relationship between the four principal virtues of prudence (*prudentia*), temperance, courage and justice, and the 'theological' virtues of faith, hope and charity (although Augustine does not call them by this traditional title). In the political or civic context *prudentia* guides the statesman in making choices about human affairs. But, at a number of points, Augustine speaks about the transformation of these traditional virtues by the theological. In *Epistula* 155 (c.413–14), for example, Augustine remarks that in the heavenly city there will be no struggle of virtue against vice, but the virtues will continue to persist in transformed forms identical to love of God or wisdom (*sapientia*). Thus, whereas prudence consisted in judging right from wrong, in heaven it will consist in adhering to God in love.[59] Our practice of the virtues in this life should consist in moving towards this heavenly state, and prudence should thus focus on choices that reflect our desire to love God above all else.[60] Indeed our search to act prudently should also be guided by the theological virtues, which on their own promote *vera pietas*, true piety, the 'knowledge and love of the true God'.[61] Thus, when he wrote *De trinitate* 9–10, Augustine already had in place a notion of *prudentia* which saw continuity between judgements about good and bad actions in this

---

[58] Many of which have already been discussed earlier in the book. But we should note also that Augustine's reference at *trin*. 10. 5.7 to the mind being commanded to know itself so that it might live 'according to nature' closely reflects Cicero at *fin*. 5. 9.24ff. and Ambrose, *exc. Sat.* 1. 45.1 (which itself may be dependent on Cicero). Cf. Cicero, *fin*. 3. 16.5.

[59] *ep.* 155. 3.12. See Robert Dodaro, 'Political and Theological Virtues in Augustine, *De Trinitate*', *Medioevo. Rivista di storia della filosofia medievale* 31 (2006), 31–46.

[60] *ep.* 155. 4.13.   [61] *ep.* 155. 1. 2. Cf. *civ.* 10. 3.

life and the eternal clinging to God in love that constitutes eternal life. Against such a background an adaptation of Cicero's three constituents of *prudentia* could easily provide the basis for discussion of an image of the Trinity at the heart of human intellectual life, a discussion which could consider not only the mind's attention to objects in the created order, but also the possible reformation of the image through increasing love of God.[62]

In *De trinitate* 12, Augustine offers a more extensive discussion of the interactions between the political/civic and theological virtues as part of his distinction between *scientia* and *sapientia*. He speaks of *ratio scientiae* ('reasoning pertaining to knowledge') as including, among other things, reflection on the temporal and changeable, and on all things necessary to learn appropriate conduct in the world – including the political virtues.[63] *Ratio sapientiae* ('reasoning pertaining to wisdom') Augustine defines as 'the love of God by which we desire to see God, and believe and hope that we shall', or, as Dodaro puts it, 'the faith, hope and charity through which the mind reflects on God and on those eternal things that pertain to God, such as true virtue and beatitude'.[64] The intersection between these two is found in the person of Christ. Because Christ is the Word made flesh, each of his human words and deeds also expresses a divine truth. In Book 13, Augustine presents Colossians 2.3 ('in whom are hid all the treasures of wisdom and knowledge') as demonstrating that the unity of knowledge and wisdom parallels the unity of two natures in Christ's one person. Christ mediates to us both knowledge – of his life and deeds, and of morality – and wisdom because the knowledge he imparts may, through grace, lead to contemplation of eternal realities. The closeness is such that there are occasions on which one may call knowledge wisdom and vice versa.[65] Faith, hope and love thus aid and shape the political virtues. At the same time, and as we saw in Chapter 6, wisdom finds its term in mystery; in wisdom we have a true understanding of eternal realities, but never a full grasp.[66]

---

[62] Dodaro does not discuss Ambrose's similar but simpler transformation of Cicero's account of *prudentia*. At *off.* 1. 25.117–18 *prudentia* consists in knowledge of truth (*in veri consistere cognitione*) and at 1. 27.126 *prudentia* begins in reverence and piety to the Creator (*deferre auctoris studium atque reverentiam*) and thus is the foundation of all virtue. For discussion of Ambrose's transformation, see Ivor Davidson, *Ambrose: De Officiis* (Oxford: Oxford University Press, 2002), 2: 549–69. Ambrose does not demonstrate an account of higher and lower virtues, but he does reorient *prudentia* as, at all levels, a choosing of the good based on Christian faith. His account may well have provided Augustine with further precedent.

[63] *trin.* 12. 14.21.   [64] *trin.* 12. 14.22; Dodaro, 'Political and Theological Virtues', 38.

[65] *trin.* 13. 19.24.

[66] See also the discussion of Dodaro's *Christ and the Just Society* in Chapter 6, pp. 161f.

In this book I have avoided offering anything like a full treatment of the *De trinitate*, but the last paragraph should indicate some ways in which the discussions of Books 12–14 follow closely the map sketched in Books 9–10. A true *se cogitate*, essential if we are to imagine the Trinity as best we can, must be fostered not only by intellectual exercise, but by growth in love for God as the transcendent and immediately present giver of grace. Diagnosis of our fallen imaginations, and exhortation to a reformation of our loving is to be found in these books, but the latter is little filled out. Only with the fuller account of the distinctions between the inner and the outer person and the role of Christ in shaping *scientia* and *sapientia* in Books 12–14 do we see these exhortations expanded into a fuller programme of purification. But Augustine's discussion of the manner in which *scientia* may lead to *sapientia* found there is best viewed as a continuation and development of principles inherent in a wide-ranging notion of *prudentia* covering a continuum from judgement about the good in this life to adherence to God in heaven. I began this section of the chapter by discussing how Cicero and ancient discussions of the Delphic 'know thyself' provide some of the key background to these books of the *De trinitate*. The account of *prudentia* Dodaro suggests supplements those ancient discussions by returning us to a fundamental Augustinian theme: the priority of love. Augustine has here taken up a language that already in his theology locates the character of our choices in this life around the character of our love, and describes the perfection of our prudential choosing though an account of a purified love of God. These connections should become even clearer when we think for a moment about some possible Neoplatonic parallels to Augustine's discussion.

Dodaro draws attention to two Neoplatonic accounts that may have influenced Augustine. Plotinus sees the four traditional political virtues as 'lower' virtues that are mirrored by a corresponding set of 'higher' virtues or 'purifications'. The higher enable the soul to transcend the evils that result from its attachment to the body; they have the same names but new modes of operation: prudence (*phronesis*) now enables thought about intellectual reality that is not influenced by inappropriate images stemming from the body, and contemplation of realities that Intellect possesses immediately.[67] In Porphyry we see the outline of a different tradition in which four higher principles or virtues are the appropriate

---

[67] Plotinus, *Enn*. I. 2.1–3. For this discussion, see Robert Dodaro, 'Political and Theological Virtues in Augustine, Letter 155 to Macedonius', *Augustiniana* 54 (2004), 445–56.

complement to the practice of the 'lower' virtues – faith, truth, love and hope.[68] This account may be an attempt to offer a Neoplatonic alternative (one which resists supposed Christian anti-intellectualism) to Paul's triad at 1 Corinthians 13.13. The parallel between Augustine's account of the role of faith, hope and love and the political virtues is, then, strong, although we must be tentative about asserting direct influence. Placing *De trinitate* 9 and 10's use of *memoria*, *intellegentia* and *voluntas* against this background further indicates that the primary set of sources on which Augustine drew were Latin rhetorical and philosophical traditions, but those traditions read in the light of Neoplatonic doctrinal commitments. One of the most important consequences for my argument of noting this background to Augustine's language is the emphasis it places on the *imago* in the *mens* as an *imago* in need of and in the process of transformation, and the concomitant manner in which it de-emphasizes the significance of ancient triadic accounts of mental structure for interpreting the *De trinitate*.

CONCLUSION

Augustine places the triad of *memoria*, *intellegentia* and *voluntas* at the culmination of Books 9–10 and 14 because it enables him to explore two interrelated sets of themes in human intellectual life. In the first place, Augustine uses this triad to describe the process of our coming into knowledge of things external to us, or of making judgements about our actions. But the better he describes our self-knowing, the more Augustine must also distinguish between the process of coming into knowledge and the immediate active self-presence that must be ours *qua* human beings. As we have seen, Augustine struggles to describe this second self-knowing. He does so in part because it is paradoxically both necessarily there and more fully there when we are able to turn to ourselves accurately in thought, and in part because all our knowing is marked by seeking and lack – the reality of constant noetic presence exceeds our grasp.

Augustine thus uses our triad to open a space for discursive dialectical reflection on the distinction between intellectual life as a searching for that which is absent, and true self-knowing. Such dialectical reflection draws the mind to recognize the difficulty of understanding what should not have been forgotten. But, in exercising our minds on ourselves in this manner, we are also training ourselves to imagine the divine life, itself

---

[68] Porphyry, *sent.* 32. Dodaro, 'Augustine, Letter 155', 456–61, discusses further evidence for this tradition in later Neoplatonic authors.

beyond seeking and lack, itself a life that is presence. This reflection on the mind becomes only more complex when we remember Augustine's insistence that the mind's knowing occurs because of the Word's informing and transcendent presence. And so the space Augustine opens between our fallen knowing and the mind's self-presence is also used to propel the mind's speculative gaze towards the divine, both narrowing more precisely what defeats the intellect (as we reflect on the difference between presence and seeking what we lack), and making clear how far the reality of the divine exceeds even what may be discovered in any created analogical site (as we reflect on the difference between uncreated fullness and the limited nature even of human noetic self-presence).

In the second place, Augustine uses our triad to analyse the mind's fallen inability to attend to itself and to God, as well as the character of the mind's possible reformation. Augustine's analysis of the interrelationship between memory and desire facilitates his account of the manner in which the mind is drawn towards its habituated objects of desire even when it attempts to think of itself. This analysis, in turn, points both to the possible role of dialectical exercises in training the mind to think beyond the material (and even towards the insufficiency of the intelligible as it known to us) and to the need for grace (as we admit our inability to retrain our noetic habits). In a fuller treatment of the latter half of the *De trinitate* we could show how Christ's grace-full provision of interwoven *scientia* and *sapientia* that leads us through faith towards divine mystery fulfils Augustine's emphasis (present since the 390s) on our need for appropriate objects of desire and the power to move towards those objects. The triad of *memoria*, *intellegentia* and *voluntas* shows itself perfectly suited for describing the mind that is most appropriately restored in this manner, a mind constantly in movement and seeking, but one in thrall to its habitual loves. Thus, even though it has not been a feature of Augustine's earlier descriptions of the mind's structure, this triad focuses central themes of his psychology with a real advance in clarity.

A complex background in Roman rhetorical and moral philosophical literature, and in Neoplatonism, sets the stage for both of these investigations. The Roman rhetorical tradition, and specifically Cicero, enables Augustine to use the three constituent activities that must be appropriately trained and co-ordinated for the formation of *prudentia*. In addition, Neoplatonic accounts of virtue possibly enable Augustine's use of this triad to name the mind's choosing of the good at all levels. The long tradition of reflection on the Delphic 'know thyself' frames Augustine's exploration of the mind as a preliminary to greater knowledge of the divine. Platonic accounts of intellectual life and self-knowing make possible Augustine's discussion of self-presence (and the paradoxes he draws from this which have a very distinctly Christian twist). The argument we have seen played out through this chapter and the last also offers us the most sophisticated example of Augustine's mature adaptation of practices learnt in the school of the Liberal Arts. A basic use of dialectical tools is here used in exploration of analogical sites long in preparation – although the turn to specific consideration of the *mens* as *imago Dei*, and the account of mental life here sketched, represent a decisive deepening of all his earlier treatments.

At the same time, these books of the *De trinitate* have demonstrated on a grand scale a principle that we saw early in Augustine's career: his analysis of the analogical site in question is conducted not only in order to discover the Trinity therein reflected, but also *with* the analytical tools of, and in the light of, a faith commitment to the language of Nicene faith. Trinitarian faith guides as much as it is explored by Augustine's dialectical reasoning. Thus I have not placed at the heart of this book discussion of the suitability of *memoria, intellegentia* and *voluntas* as a Trinitarian 'analogy' as if Augustine offered us an account of the mind and said 'this is the best I can offer as an illustration of Father, Son and Spirit'. In the first place, this is not how Augustine's analogical procedure works (as should now be clear). In the second place, appreciating how Augustine does use his analogical procedure is much enhanced when we slightly de-centre Books 8–15 of the *De trinitate* as a source for his mature Trinitarian theology. By seeing what he develops in other contexts we are better able to appreciate what Augustine is seeking to illustrate and explore in *De trinitate* 8–15, and we are better able to appreciate where these books represent innovation in Trinitarian theology and where not.[69]

In the conclusion to his *L'Intelligence de la foi*, Olivier Du Roy treats Augustine's description in *De civitate Dei* 11 of the various analogical sites within the created order that may be taken as the inviting speech of God as an unrealized sketch for a more acceptable mode of Trinitarian reflection sadly missed by Augustine in the *De trinitate*. Here, for Du Roy, the solipsism of the *De trinitate*'s gradual penetration into the depths of the individual mind as image is partially overcome. This, I suggest, is one of Du Roy's oddest judgements. We have no reason not to take the discussion of the *De civitate Dei* 11 as offering the wider context within which

---

[69] I have already offered some suggestions to this end, see pp. 277f.; in the Epilogue I offer some further reflection on how far the triad of *memoria, intellegentia* and *voluntas* is used to illustrate the character of the divine life and relationships.

that of *De trinitate* 9 and 10 occurs. The latter discussion relies on the same basic sense of the hierarchy of existence and the character of the life of intellect that we have seen since the *Confessiones*. In this context the developed investigation of the *mens* as analogical site – especially when we remember that one of the tools used in that investigation is an understanding of the triadic nature of the soul in training towards God – is only to be expected in a work aimed at only the most able of his audience. Throughout, Augustine's explorations are set within the account of ascent towards understanding, an ascent grounded in Christ's revealing and drawing that we explored in Chapters 5 and 6. Throughout also, Augustine is not exploring how the Trinity may be known independently of that revealing and drawing, but showing how that revealing leads us to read anew God's creation with the eyes and terms of faith, and showing us how that drawing pulls us into a fuller life within the intelligible order. There is more to be said about the ways in which we should read Augustine's use of *memoria*, *intellegentia* and *voluntas* as indicating, or not, as revealing to us his fundamental Trinitarian orientation, but before I offer that 'more', we should take a breath.

EPILOGUE

Catching all three

In *The Magnificent Seven* (1960), the iconic Robert Vaughn plays Lee, the dapper but penniless hired gun who has lost his nerve and is on the run. The final irony is that he chooses to follow Chris (Yul Brynner) south to defend a Mexican village – 'a deserter', as he puts it, 'hiding in a battlefield'. Late one night, woken by nightmares, he reveals his growing fear to two of his hosts; his decline is given a physical symbol as he swipes at three flies on the table where he sits. He opens his fist to reveal just one: 'One? There was a time I would have caught all three.' For many commentators, Augustine is a sadder character even than Robert Vaughn's 'Lee': there never was a time when all three Trinitarian persons were grasped. Such views usually stem from treating the language of memory, intelligence and will as his sole analogy for the Trinity and assuming that, hence, Augustine can really only comprehend God as one (mind). Those who see Augustine failing to treat the Spirit as a fully irreducible divine 'person' only confirm the judgement.

The reading of Augustine that I have offered differs because I have argued that we must take seriously his insistence that the divine three are irreducible, and that he consistently founds the unity of God in the Father's eternal act of giving rise to a communion in which the mutual love of the three constitutes their unity of substance. My account also differs because I have argued that we must read Augustine's Trinitarianism as blending and contrasting a number of different constellations of theological terminologies, metaphorical resources and patterns of speech. The interaction (and in some cases transition) between these various constellations is perhaps best grasped by thinking chronologically.

The earliest constellation we find in Augustine's Trinitarian theology is a rather uneasy combination of language from his readings in non-Christian Platonism, and from his earliest readings in Latin Nicene theology. This soon becomes incorporated into a broader field of terminology describing the Son as the Father's Wisdom and, after 393, supplemented by a sophisticated account of the Son as the Father's Word. But Augustine's development between 387 and 393 is also cast by his anti-Manichaean (and anti-Sceptical) concerns. This polemical context stimulated Augustine to develop an account of the threefold causal action of the Trinity upon the intelligible cosmos, which could thus enable human knowledge of the divine.

I argued in the first two chapters of the book that we do not see in his early Trinitarian discussions any clear evidence that Augustine articulates the Trinity via Plotinus's three primary *hypostases*. Indeed, while his initial understanding of Father and Son does owe partially to Plotinus – and, contra Du Roy, clearly involves an inchoate account of these two apart from the economy – Augustine's earliest accounts of the Spirit seem somewhat halting. Only slowly Augustine developed an account of the Spirit as the love, peace and concord between Father and Son, and as the agent who enables Christians to draw together in unity, which seems to have been indebted to diverse sources. Even as we see these themes emerging, Augustine is already clear that the divine three are irreducible, that they share one nature and power, and that they operate inseparably. Very soon Augustine begins to interpret the doctrine of inseparable operation in the context of his concern to show that the intelligible creation has one perfect source.

While Augustine's earliest work shows clear evidence of fairly extensive reading in his pro-Nicene predecessors, it is only from 393 that we find him using a constellation of phrasings that reveal knowledge of Latin anti-Monarchian theology. Nevertheless, once he has taken on board this language it remains fundamental to him. When we see the centrality of this language to previous Latin tradition it becomes less and less viable to envisage Augustine as the most egregious representative of a semi-modalist tradition, or even as the unexpected distorter of a previously orthodox Latin tradition. Augustine's own adaptations of this anti-Monarchian language seamlessly accompany his clear insistence on the inseparability of the divine three throughout his work.

Over the course of his career we also see a growing confidence and sophistication in patterns of speech and exegesis that I suggested, rather clumsily, we describe as 'analogically personalist'. Attention to and performance of Scripture's agential language – coupled with insistence on the irreducibility of Father, Son and Spirit – is intrinsic to the anti-Monarchian traditions mentioned in the previous paragraph and then to pro-Nicene theology. This language considers foundational Scripture's primary dramatic language concerning the interaction of Father, Son and Spirit. At some point *c*.410 we begin to see Augustine developing these traditions by treating the intra-divine acts Scripture predicates of the divine three as constitutive of them. This shift provides new resources for Augustine to present the mutual love of the three – and the Father's eternal act of giving rise to Son and Spirit – as constituting the unity of the Trinity.

Accompanying Augustine's use of such primary agential language – especially after the *Confessiones*, but *in nuce* from 393 – is a careful attention to the paradox that each of the three is the fullness of the divine life, and yet that the divine fullness is never anything but one and unique. Thus presentation of each of the divine three as an agent is frequently accompanied by insistence on formulae or accompanying patterns of thought that draw us to recognition of divine transcendence.

These various constellations of terminologies, ideas and patterns of speech are interwoven in complex ways over time. We do not usually see the simple abandonment of earlier patterns, but their incorporation into new forms in an overall trajectory of development that I have tried to trace. Thus, Augustine's early account of the Son as Wisdom is developed and incorporated into his account of the Son as Word; his account of the Spirit as something common between Son and Father is taken up and subject to much development as he reflects on the 'Spirit of' texts in his mature work; his early explorations of threefold causality are significantly reworked into his mature account of the inseparable operation of the three being founded in the Father's eternal acts. This process of slow transformation made possible Augustine's occasional turns back to earlier terminology (as we saw at the end of *De trinitate* 4), and perhaps also made it possible for him to incorporate the results of what seem to have been intense periods of reading in his immediate forebears – in preparation for his address to the bishops of Africa in 393, in preparation for beginning the *De trinitate*, in response to the 'Arian sermon' sent to him *c*.418, and in debate with the Homoian bishop Maximinus in 427.

I have also argued that all the constellations of themes mentioned above form the background to the discussions found in the latter half of the *De trinitate*. Consideration of *memoria*, *intellegentia* and *voluntas* occurs, for example, at the same time as Augustine is developing his clearest accounts of the irreducibility of the three as each possessing the fullness of what it is to be God. How then are we to understand the significance of this analogical resource, and specifically how far does it provide the basis for Augustine's mature understanding of the relationship between Father and Son?

My answer to this last question must *in nuce* be clear by now. Presentations of Augustine's Trinitarian theology as dependent upon and finding its highpoint in an account of the necessary relationship between love and knowledge in the mind are mistaken in according this language such an all-encompassing role. Good interpretation of the role of this language depends, in part, on assessing its relative prominence among the range of terminologies and languages I have just sketched. Reflection on the relationship between knowledge and love is apparent in some of Augustine's earliest texts, but originally his concerns are with the character of human knowing. That concern begins with a highly traditional Latin philosophical concern: what is it that enables our search for the blessed life? Augustine very soon comes to present the problem in terms of the question 'how can we search for something – or desire it – without already in some manner knowing it?' But, Augustine also comes to this question with a clear sense that the human person has an innate love for self and for the survival of self, while the human mind has a natural affinity for the intelligible and for its creator. Thus the fact of the human search for God presupposes an interplay between desire and knowledge, the former shaped by the latter. The two find their joint fulfilment in contemplation of and adherence to God.[1] At the same time, as we have seen, Augustine also seems to have drawn on a number of Neoplatonic epistemological themes, in particular the sense that the conception of an idea involves an act of recovery from the memory in the light of a unifying act of will.[2]

These philosophical dynamics do not seem to play any role in Augustine's earliest conception of the role of the Spirit as love, either in the created order or in God. It is only in the latter half of the *De trinitate* that we find Augustine using a reflection on the interrelationship of knowing and loving to explore the relationship between Son and Spirit. Even here Augustine teases. In *De trinitate* 15, Augustine discusses Son and Spirit in order, and prefaces his discussions with a statement that each of the divine three must be its own memory, intelligence and will.[3] In his discussion of the Son, Augustine identifies a number of ways in which the Son is like *intellegentia* or the *verbum interior*.[4] In so doing Augustine speaks of the *scientia Dei* and the *verbum Dei*. Whereas, in us a *verbum* is born from our *scientia*, the Father's knowledge *is* his Word and Wisdom and essence (because there to be and to be wise are identical).[5] Thus, once

---

[1] *div. qu.* 35. 2. [2] See Chapter 5, pp. 129–30. [3] See Chapter 9, pp. 232f.
[4] *trin.* 15. 9.15–16.26. [5] *trin.* 15. 13.22.

again, the notions of *intellegentia* and *verbum interior* as they are present in the human mind (and especially the fallen human mind) provide a resource for Augustine's discursive analogical practice alongside his most well-established Trinitarian terminologies, but mostly insofar as they partly help to develop awareness of where we fail to grasp the dynamics of the divine life. In the following paragraphs, Augustine makes use of the idea of the necessarily temporary *verbum interior* in us to argue that only God can eternally speak a true Word that is eternally Image.[6] But, even here, as throughout this discussion of the Word, he does not reflect on the *relationship between* knowledge and love as a resource for understanding the relationship between Son and Spirit other than through the implication that love and knowledge are inseparable.

When Augustine comes to the Spirit he first rehearses his argument that love is to be appropriated to the Spirit.[7] He then describes the functions of the Spirit within the context of identifying the Spirit as Gift. Along the way he gets a little sidetracked, most notably into a discussion of Eunomian errors. Only near the end of the discussion does Augustine state directly that whereas he had previously tried to show how the relationship between memory and understanding helps us to imagine that between Father and Son, now he is trying to show how the Spirit may be imagined by reflection on our love or will.[8] Augustine first states that the will is necessarily attracted to or repelled by that which it encounters. If so, the response of will either occurs in simple ignorance (inconceivable, one imagines, because of the implied irrationality), or there must be some kind of memory and understanding (and hence thought, *cogitatio*) intrinsic to the will. Augustine's point follows directly enough from his discussion of the necessary interplay between love and knowledge, but involves an added level of sophistication in its clarity that while it might seem as if the life of (human) intellect can be broken down into the interplay of memory and intelligence joined by will/love, no reduction to discrete parts or faculties is possible. Each must already involve the other two. The point is argued in large part to reiterate Augustine's principle that each of the divine three is necessarily their own memory, intelligence and will. One corollary, of course, is the impossibility of using the triad Augustine has deployed to illustrate each divine person *simpliciter*.[9]

---

[6] *trin.* 15. 15.25.   [7] Beginning at *trin.* 15. 17.27.   [8] *trin.* 15. 21.41.
[9] Schmaus, *Die psychologische Trinitätslehre*, 399–411, offers a good discussion of the ways in which Augustine identifies the differences between the triad in us and the Trinity itself; his subsequent discussion (pp. 411ff.) of the ways in which Augustine does liken each term of the triad to a divine person is far less convincing.

It is then, probably not surprising that, throughout this short discussion, Augustine only hints at parallels between the relationship of Son and Spirit and that between understanding and will. Thus, for example, he does not speak directly about the love that must be intrinsic in the Father's own eternal expression of the Word who is the Truth, even though we seem to see something of this theme when he insists that, in the utterance of a true word, love and understanding must already be present because such an utterance is in fact the discovery of an innate knowing.[10] While the language of the necessary interplay between knowing and loving certainly hints at the necessary relationship of Son and Spirit, it is also the case that we can only comprehend the necessity by imagining an intellectual process in which one moment presupposes the other. Even in the case of human intellectual life, as we saw above, such a picture only scratches the surface. It is, thus, the very sort of analogy that is frequently foisted onto Augustine is the very sort that he cannot offer! As in the case of Augustine's use of the *verbum interior* discussed above, it is the matrix of well-established theological terminologies in Augustine's writing that provides the context within which he interprets the potential of an analogy between Spirit and will. Thus, will throughout is identified with love, and meditation on the Spirit as Love and Gift takes centre stage. The dogmatic focus of the pneumatological exposition here, in texts that we explored in Chapter 10, remains the analogically personalist language of the Spirit as the unifier of Father and Son.

That I think Augustine uses and blends different terminological and metaphorical constellations over a long career should not, however, be taken to imply that I think his Trinitarian theology incoherent. In the first place, the attempt to negotiate different constellations in this way is common to many pro-Nicene theologians, Greek and Latin. The draw of a single underlying schema was attractive to some, of course (and to many more modern scholars who have sought to organize Patristic Trinitarian theologies by means of such models), but most Nicene writers find themselves supplementing and holding in tension multiple images and terminologies even as they make use of particular favourite themes.[11] In the

---

[10] *trin.* 15. 22.42.
[11] I see my argument here as parallel to that of de Halleux, 'Personnalisme ou essentialisme'. It is not simply that the two alternatives do not grasp the distinctions and similarities between Greek and Latin theologies, it is that the alternatives themselves are far too blunt a heuristic for analysing the texts they are used to describe. For reflections on how new readings of Augustine might shape the conversation of modern Latin theology, see my 'Into the Cloud of Witnesses: Latin Trinitarian Theology Beyond its Modern "Revivals"', in Robert Wozniak (ed.), *Rethinking Trinitarian Theology* (New York: Continuum, forthcoming 2011).

second place, it may be that theologies which undertake such a balancing act are importantly faithful to the complex dynamics of Scripture's language, even as they also attempt a particular (Nicene) articulation of them. For example, Scripture offers the language of Father and Son and does so in ways that invite us to imagine those terms as if they referred to two individual agents of the kind that we are familiar with as human beings. At the same time, Scripture itself troubles that implicit analogy when it speaks of the Son as Word and Wisdom and Image. Reflection on these very terms is one of the ways in which Augustine himself disrupts our tendency to think of Father, Son and Spirit as too easily like human persons. This simple example could easily be multiplied into a long list of complex terminological tensions, parallels and supplementations within Scripture.

The course I have taken in this Epilogue should draw us back with fresh concerns to the question with which it began. It may have seemed initially as if I were posing the question 'Did Augustine catch all three?' only to insist that he did *because* he offers a model for imagining the Trinity that we can embrace and which is different from the psychological model we are so often told is his. But my account is not of this kind. I have suggested that Augustine's mature vision of the Trinitarian life is comprehended best as a bringing into mutual illumination of a number of different Trinitarian constellations. Even though I have suggested that Augustine's Trinitarian theology follows a clear trajectory of evolution and, in its mature forms, offers an emergent and powerful account of the life of the divine three constituted by their intra-divine acts, Augustine seems to see this way of exploring the divine life as a way of bringing together a variety of scriptural (and philosophical) resources and dynamics, not as a 'model' which can simply carry the field. The foundational quality of a Scripture that points towards divine *mystery*, the complexity of that Scripture's speech, and our knowledge of human noetic fallenness and necessary humility all undergird the provisional and complex nature of Augustine's mature Trinitarian styles. Thus, while I certainly think that Augustine offers us a peculiarly deep and compelling articulation of Nicene principles, we should follow Augustine in his own recognition that the 'catching' of all three is only ever well done if the necessary failure of all such attempts this side of the final vision is confessed. Ultimately then, Robert Vaughn's 'Lee' is not to be despised because of his fear and physical decline, but perhaps celebrated as a truer type of the human condition before the mystery of God. Of course, there never was a time when we would have caught all three in this fallen life. If it is also true that it is *we* who are caught by all three so that we one day might catch them, our surest foundation is found only when we admit our weakness and follow Augustine's own injunction:

> Hold with unshakeable faith that the Father and the Son and the Holy Spirit are a Trinity and that there is, nonetheless, one God – not that the divinity is common to these as if it were a fourth – and that it is itself the ineffably inseparable Trinity.[12]

---

[12] *ep.* 120. 2.12.

Bibliography

ANCIENT SOURCES

For each text I have indicated the modern edition used and the best (or in many cases only) English translation, where one is available. I have often adapted the translations referenced; I have not noted such changes individually.

ALEXANDER OF ALEXANDRIA

ep. Alex.	*Letter to Alexander of Byzantium.* H. G. Opitz (ed.), *Athanasius Werke* 3/1 (Berlin: De Gruyter, 1934), U. 14, pp. 19–29.

AMBROSE OF MILAN

Abr.	*On Abraham.* CSEL 22/1; Theodosia Tomkinson (trans.), *Saint Ambrose of Milan. On Abraham* (Etna, CA: Center for Traditionalist Orthodox Studies, 2000).
exc. Sat.	*On the Death of his Brother Satyrus.* CSEL 73.
fid.	*On the Faith.* CSEL 78; NPNF II.10.
hex.	*Homilies on the Six Days of Creation.* CSEL 32/1; FoC 42.
Hex.	*On the Hexameron.* CSEL 22; FoC 42.
hymn	*Hymns.* Jacques Fontaine, *Ambroise de Milan. Hymns* (Paris: Cerf, 1992).
incar.	*On the Mystery of the Lord's Incarnation.* CSEL 79/8.
in Psalm	*Exposition of Twelve Psalms.* CSEL 64.
Isaac	*On Isaac, or the Soul.* PL 14; FoC 65.
Luc.	*Commentary on Luke.* CSEL 32/4; Theodosia Tomkinson (trans.) *Exposition of the Holy Gospel According to Saint Luke,* 2nd edn (Etna, CA: Center for Traditionalist Orthodox Studies, 2003).
myst.	*On the Mysteries.* CSEL 73; NPNF II.10.
off.	*On the Duties of the Clergy.* Ivor Davidson, *Ambrose: De Officiis,* 2 vols. (Oxford: Oxford University Press, 2002).
spir.	*On the Holy Spirit.* CSEL 79; FoC 44.

symb.	*An Explanation of the Creed for Catechumens.* R. H. Connolly (ed.), *The Explanatio Symboli ad Initiandos: A Work of St. Ambrose* (Cambridge: Cambridge University Press, 1952).

AMBROSIASTER

ad Rom.	*Commentary on Romans.* CSEL 81/1.
ad Eph.	*Commentary on Ephesians.* CSEL 81/3.
ad Thess.	*Commentary on Thessalonians.* CSEL 81/3.
quaest. test.	*127 Questions on the Old and New Testaments.* CSEL 50.

AMMONIUS

in cat.	*Commentary on Aristotle's Categories.* CAG IV/5. S. Marc Cohen and Gareth B. Matthews (trans.), *Ammonius on Aristotle's Categories* (London: Duckworth, 1991).

AMPHILOCHIUS OF ICONIUM

or.	*Homilies.* CCSG 3.

ANONYMOUS HOMOIAN TEXTS

A fuller bibliography of anonymous and onymous Homoian texts may be found at *CPL* 680–708

coll. Ver.	*The Arian Collection of Verona.* CCSL 87A.
frag. theol.	*Theological Fragments.* CCSL 87A.
in Job	*Anonymous Commentary on Job.* CSEL 96.
scol. Aquil.	*Scholia on the Acts of the Council of Aquileia.* CCSL 87A; SC 267.
serm. Ar.	*The Arian Sermon.* CSEL 92; WSA 1/18.

ANSELM OF CANTERBURY

incar.	*A Letter on the Incarnation of the Word.* F. S. Schmitt (ed.), *S. Anselmi Cantuariensis Archepiscopi Opera Omnia* (Stuttgart: Friedrich Frommann, 1984), 2: 3–35.

ARISTOTLE

Cat.	*Categories.* Loeb.
leg.	*On the Laws.* Loeb.

ARIUS OF ALEXANDRIA

ep. Eus.	*Letter to Eusebius of Nicomedia.* H. G. Opitz (ed.), *Athanasius Werke* 3/1 (Berlin: De Gruyter, 1934), U. 1, pp. 1–3.

ATHANASIUS OF ALEXANDRIA

ad Afros	*Letter to the African Bishops.* PG 26; NPNF II.4.
c. Ar.	*Orations Against the Arians.* Metzler/Savvidis (ed.), *Athanasius Werke* I/1 (Berlin: De Gruyter, 2000–1); NPNF II.4.
c. gen.	*Against the Nations.* Robert W. Thompson (ed. and trans.), Contra Gentes *and* De Incarnatione (Oxford: Clarendon Press, 1971).
Serap.	*Letters to Serapion Concerning the Holy Spirit.* PG 26.529–676; C. R. B. Shapland, *The Letters of Saint Athanasius Regarding the Holy Spirit* (London: Epworth Press, 1951).
synod.	*On the Councils of Ariminium and Seleucia.* H. G. Opitz (ed.), *Athanasius Werke* II/1 (Berlin: De Gruyter, 1941); NPNF II. 4.

PS. ATHANASIUS

dial. trin.	*Dialogues on the Trinity.* PG 28.

AUGUSTINE OF HIPPO

All abbreviations for works of Augustine are those of *AugLex*

an. et or.	*On the Soul and its Origin.* CSEL 60; WSA 1/23.
b. vita	*On the Blessed Life.* CCSL 29; FoC 1.
c. Acad.	*Against the Academics.* CCSL 29; ACW 12.
c. Adim.	*Answer to Adimantus.* CSEL 25/1; WSA 1/19.
cat. rud.	*On Catechising the Uninstructed.* CCSL 46; WSA 1/10.
civ.	*De civitate Dei.* CCSL 47; Augustine, *The City of God against the Pagans*, trans. and ed. R. W. Dyson, Cambridge Texts in the History of Political Thought (Cambridge: Cambridge University Press, 1998).
conf.	*Confessions.* CCSL 27; *Saint Augustine: Confessions*, trans. Henry Chadwick (Oxford: Oxford University Press, 1991).
conl. Max.	*Debate with Maximinus, Bishop of the Arians.* PL 42; WSA 1/18.
cons. ev.	*On the Harmony of the Evangelists.* CSEL 43; NPNF II.6.
Cresc.	*To Cresconius, A Donatist Grammarian.* CSEL 52; BA 31.
dial.	*On Dialectic. Augustine's De dialectica*, trans. B. D. Jackson, ed. J. Pinborg (Dordrecht: Reidel, 1975)
div. qu.	*On 83 Diverse Questions.* CCSL 44A; WSA 1/12.
doctr. chr.	*On Christian Teaching.* CCSL 32; R. P. H. Green, *Augustine: De Doctrina Christiana* (Oxford: Clarendon Press, 1995).
duab. an.	*On the Two Souls.* CSEL 25/1; WSA I/19.
en. Ps.	*Expositions of the Psalms.* CCSL 38–40; CSEL 93/1A (Ps. 1–32), 95/3 (119–33), 95/4 (134–40); WSA 3/14–17.
ep.	*Epistula.* Most of Augustine's letters are available in CSEL 34, 44, 57 and 88. *ep.* 1–150 are also available in a new edition in CCSL 31, and I have used that where possible. For details of available editions for other letters, see the table by Robert Eno in Fitzgerald, *Augustine Encyclopedia*, 299–305; WSA 2/1–4.

ep. Rm. inch.	*Unfinished Commentary on the Letter to the Romans.* CSEL 84; P. F. Landes, *Augustine on Romans* (Chico, CA: Scholars Press, 1982).
ex. prop. Rm.	*Commentary on Statements in the Letter to the Romans.* CSEL 84.
exp. Gal.	*Commentary on the Letter to the Galatians.* CSEL 84; Eric Plumer (intro. and trans.), *Augustine's Commentary on Galatians* (Oxford: Clarendon Press, 2003).
f. et symb.	*On the Faith and the Creed.* CSEL 41; WSA FoC 27.
c. Faust.	*Against Faustus.* CSEL 25/1; WSA I/20.
Gn. adv. Man.	*A Commentary on Genesis Against the Manichaeans.* CSEL 91; WSA 1/13.
Gn. litt.	*A Literal Commentary on Genesis.* CSEL 28/1; WSA 1/13; ACW 41 and 42.
Gn. litt. imp.	*A Literal Commentary on Genesis, an Unfinished Book.* CSEL 28/1; WSA 1/13.
gramm.	*On Grammar.* Keil 496–524.
imm. an.	*On the Immortality of the Soul.* CSEL 89; FoC 2.
lib. arb.	*On Free Will.* CCSL 29; ACW 22.
mag.	*On The Teacher.* CCSL 29; WSA 1/3.
c. Max.	*Against Maximinus the Arian.* PL 42; WSA 1/18.
mor.	*On the Catholic and Manichaean Ways of Life.* CSEL 90; WSA 1/19.
mus.	*On Music.* PL 32; FoC 2.
nat. b.	*On the Nature of the Good.* CSEL 25/2; WSA I/19.
ord.	*On Order.* CCSL 29; FoC 1.
quant.	*On the Greatness of the Soul.* CSEL 89; ACW 9.
qu. Mt.	*Sixteen Questions on Matthew.* CCSL 44B.
retr.	*Retractations.* CSEL 36; FoC 60.
rhet.	*The Principles of Rhetoric.* C. Halm (ed.), *Rhetores Latini Minores* (1863), 137–51; Remo Giomini, 'Aurelius Augustinus "De rhetorica"', *Studi latini e italiani* 4 (1990), 7–82.
s. dom. m.	*On the Lord's Sermon on the Mount.* CCSL 35; ACW 5.
c. s. Arrian.	*Against the Arian Sermon.* CSEL 92; WSA 1/18.
c. Sec.	*Against Secundinus, A Manichee.* CSEL 25; WSA 1/19.
serm.	*Sermon.* There is no complete edition of Augustine's sermons in Latin. For details of modern editions, see the table by Eric Rebillard in Fitzgerald, *Augustine Encyclopedia*, 774–89; WSA 3/1–11.
Simpl.	*To Simplicianus.* CCSL 44; WSA I/12.
sol.	*Soliloquies.* CSEL 89; FoC 2.
symb. cat.	*On the Creed to Catechumens.* CCSL 46; FoC 27.
trin.	*On the Trinity.* CCSL 50/50A; FoC 45.
util. cred.	*On the Usefulness of Believing.* CSEL 25/1; WSA 1/8.
vera rel.	*On True Religion.* CCSL 32; WSA 1/8.

BASIL OF CAESAREA

Eunom.	*Against Eunomius.* SC 299 and 305.

PS. BASIL

Eunom. 4	*Against Eunomius* Book 4. PG 29.
Hex.	*On the Hexameron.* SC 26; FoC 46.
Reg. brev.	*Shorter Rules.* PG 31.
spir.	*On the Holy Spirit.* SC 17; trans. Blonfield Jackson, rev. David Anderson, *St. Basil the Great On the Holy Spirit* (Crestwood, NY: St Vladimir's Seminary Press, 1980).

BOETHIUS

In Isagog.	*Smaller Commentary on Porphyry's Isagoge.* CSEL 48.
in Porph.	*Commentary on Porphyry's Isagoge.* CSEL 48.
trin.	*De trinitate.* Loeb.

CASSIODORUS

inst.	*Institutions of Divine and Secular Learning.* R. A. B. Mynors, (ed.), *Cassiodori Sentoris Institutiones* (Oxford: Clarendon Press, 1937); Cassiodorus, *Institutions of Divine and Secular Learning, On the Soul,* trans. James W. Halporn, intro. Mark Vessey (Liverpool: Liverpool University Press, 2004).

CICERO

fin.	*On the Ends of Good and Evil.* Loeb.
inv.	*On Finding.* Loeb.
leg.	*On the Laws.* Loeb.
Nat. deo.	*On the Nature of the Gods.* Loeb.
orat.	*The Orator.* Loeb.

PS. CICERO

rhet. Her.	*On Rhetoric to Herennius.* Loeb.
Tusc.	*Tusculan Disputations.* Loeb.

CYRIL OF ALEXANDRIA

dial. trin.	*Trinitarian Dialogues.* SC 231, 237, 246.

in. Io. Commentary on John. P. E. Pusey (ed.), *Sancti Patris nostril Cyrilli archepiscopi Alexandrini in D. Ioannis Evangelium*, 2 vols. (Oxford: Clarendon Press, 1872; rpt. Brussels, 1965).

CYRIL OF JERUSALEM

cat. lect. *Catechetical Lectures.* PG 33; LCC 4.

DAMASUS

ep. 1 (*confidimus quidem*) 'We indeed believe'. Ed. and trans. Field, *Communion*, 10–15.

ep. 2 (*1ˢᵗ frag: ea gratia*) '... by this grace'. Ed. and trans. Field, *Communion*, 14–17.

ep. 4 (*tomus Damasi*) *Tome of Damasus.* Turner, *EOMIA* 1. 2.1.

DIDYMUS THE BLIND

spir. *On the Holy Spirit.* SC 386; Lewis Ayres, Mark DelCogliano and Andrew Radde-Gallwitz (trans.), *Athanasius and Didymus on the Spirit* (Crestwood, NY: St Vladimir's Seminary Press, forthcoming).

EPIPHANIUS OF SALAMIS

pan. *The Medicine Chest Against All Heresies.* GCS 25, 31, 37, NF 13; Frank Williams (trans.), *The Panarion of Epiphanius of Salamis*, 2 vols. (Leiden: Brill, 1987).

EUNOMIUS OF CYZICUS

apol. *Apology.* Richard P. Vaggione (trans. and ed.), *Eunomius: The Extant Works* (Oxford: Oxford University Press, 1987).

EUSEBIUS OF CAESAREA

eccl. theol. *Ecclesiastical Theology.* GCS 14.

prep. *Preparation for the Gospel.* PG 21; trans. E. H. Gifford, *Preparation for the Gospel*, 2 vols. (Eugene, OR: Wipf and Stock (previously Oxford, 1903)).

EUSEBIUS OF VERCELLI

trin. *On the Trinity.* CCSL 9.

FAUSTINUS

trin.   *On the Trinity.* CCSL 69.

FILASTRIUS OF BRESCIA

haer.   *A Book on the Different Heresies.* CCSL 9.

GAUDENTIUS OF BRESCIA

tract.   *Tractates.* CSEL 68.

GREGORY OF ELVIRA

fid.   *On the Faith.* CCSL 69.
tract.   *Twenty Tractates (of Origen) on the Holy Scriptures.* CCSL 69.

GREGORY OF NAZIANZEN

or.   Orations. I have used texts only from the 'Theological Orations' nos. 28–31. SC 250; Frederick W. Norris (intro. and comm.), Lionel Wickham and Frederick Williams (trans.), *Faith Gives Fullness to Reasoning: The Five Theological Orations of Gregory Nazianzen* (Leiden: Brill, 1991).

GREGORY OF NYSSA

Abl.   *To Ablabius. On Not Three Gods.* GNO 3/1.
Cant.   *Commentary on the Song of Songs.* GNO 6; Gregory of Nyssa, *Commentary on the Song of Songs*, trans. Casimir McCambley OCSO (Brookline, MA: Hellenic College Press, 1987).
Eunom.   *Against Eunomius.* GNO 1 and 2; NPNF II.5.
ref.   *Refutation of Eunomius's Confession.* GNO I/2; NPNF II.5. 101–34.

HILARY OF POITIERS

c. ant. Par.   *The Parisian Anti-Arian Collection.* CSEL 65; Lionel Wickham (trans.), *Hilary of Poitiers: Conflicts of Conscience and Law in the Fourth-Century Church*, Translated Texts for Historians 25 (Liverpool: Liverpool University Press, 1997).
c. Const.   *Against Constantius.* SC 334 (CPL 461).
in Const.   *To Constantius, A Book.* SC 334 (CPL 461).
in Matt.   *Commentary on Matthew.* SC 254, 258.
in Ps.   *Tractates on the Psalms.* CSEL 22.

Psalm.	Expositions of the Psalms. CSEL 22.
synod.	On the Synods. PL 10; NPNF II.9.
trin.	On the Trinity. SC 443, 448 and 462; FoC 25.

IRENAEUS OF LYON

adv. haer.	Against Heresies. SC 263–4, 293–4, 210–11, 100, 152–3; ANF 1.

ISAAC 'THE JEW'

exp.	An Exposition of the Catholic Faith. CCSL 9.
fid.	Fides Isaatis (or De trinitate et incarnatione) / The Faith of Isaac. CCSL 9.

JEROME

ad Eph.	Commentary on Ephesians. PL 26.
ad Gal.	Commentary on Galatians. CCSL 77.

JEROME OF STRIDON

Lucif.	Disputation between the Luciferians and the Orthodox. PL 23. 155–82.

PS. IAMBLICHUS

theol. arith.	The Theology of Arithmetic.

JOHN CHRYSOSTOM

in Io.	Homilies on John. PG 59; NPNF 1/14.

JUSTIN MARTYR

Tryph.	Dialogue with Tryhpo the Jew. Ed. Miroslav Marcovich, *Iustini Martyris Dialogus cum Tryphone*, Patristische Texte und Studien 47 (Berlin: de Gruyter, 1997); trans. Thomas B. Falls, rev. Thomas P. Halton, ed. Michael Slusser (Washington DC: Catholic University of America Press, 2003).

LACTANTIUS

inst. div.	Divine Institutes. CSEL 19; Anthony Bowen and Peter Garnsey (trans.), *Lactantius: Divine Institutes* (Liverpool: Liverpool University Press, 2003).

MARINUS

vit. Procl.   *Proclus, Or On Happiness. Vitadi Prodo,* ed. R. Masullo (Naples: D'Auria, 1985); tr. Mark Edwards, *Neoplatonic Saints* (Liverpool: Liverpool University Press, 2000).

MARIUS VICTORINUS

ad Cand.   *To Candidus the Arian.* SC 68; CSEL 83/1; FoC 69.
Adv. Ar.   *Against the Arians.* SC 68; CSEL 83/1; FoC 69.
ep. Cand.   *Letter of Candidus to Marius Victorinus.* SC 68; CSEL 83/1. My own view is that this letter was written by Victorinus himself, though the question is controversial.
hom. rec.   *On Accepting the Homoousios.* SC 68; CSEL 83/1.
hymn.   *Hymns.* SC 68; CSEL 83/1; FoC 69.
in Cic. rhet.   *Commentary on Cicero's Rhetoric.* Ed. C. Halm, *Rhetores Latini Minores* (Leipzig: Teubner, 1863), 153–304.
in Eph.   *Commentary on Ephesians.* CSEL 83/2.

MARTIANUS CAPELLA

nupt. phil.   *On the Marriage of Mercury and Philology.* James Willis (ed.) (Teubner, 1983); William Harris Stahl and Richard Johnson with E. L. Burge (trans.), *Martianus Capella and the Seven Liberal Arts. Vol. II. The Marriage of Philology and Mercury* (New York: Columbia University Press, 1977).

NICETAS OF REMESIANA

apell.   *De diversis appellationibus.* A. E. Burn, *Niceta of Remesiana. His Life and Works* (Cambridge, 1903); FoC 7.
instr.   *Instructions to Candidates for Baptism.* Klaus Cranber (ed.), *Instructio ad Competentes: Frühchristliche Katechesen aus Dacien* (Regensburg: F. Pustet, 1964); FoC7.

NICHOMACHUS OF GERASA

intr.   *Introduction to Arithmetic.* Martin Luther D'Ooge (trans.), *Nichomachus of Gerasa: Introduction to Arithmetic* (Ann Arbor: University of Michigan Press, 1938).

NOVATIAN

trin.   *On the Trinity.* CCSL 4; FoC 67.

ORIGEN OF ALEXANDRIA

comm. John.	*Commentary on John.* SC 120, 157, 222, 290, 385; FoC 80, 89.
Princ.	*On First Principles.* SC 252, 253, 268, 269, 312; *Origen: On First Principles,* trans. Henry Butterworth (Gloucester, MA: Peter Smith, 1973).

PETER LOMBARD

sent.	*The Sentences. Magistri Petri Lombardi Parisiensis episcope Sententiae in IV libris distinctae,* 2 vols. (Grottaferrata: Editiones Collegii S. Bonaventurae ad Claras Aquas, 1971–81); Peter Lombard, *The Sentences, Book 1: The Mystery of the Trinity,* trans. Giulio Silano (Toronto: PIMS, 2007).

PHOEBADIUS

c. Ar.	*Against the Arians.* CCSL 64.

PLATO

Phaedrus	OCT; Edith Hamilton and Huntington Cairns (eds.), *Plato: The Phaedrus. Collected Dialogues* (Princeton: Princeton University Press, 1961).

PLOTINUS

Enn.	*Enneads.* Loeb.

PORPHYRY

isag.	*Introduction. CAG* IV/1; Jonathan Barnes, *Porphyry: Introduction* (Oxford: Clarendon Press, 2003).
sent.	*Pathways to the Intelligible.* Luc Brisson (ed.), *Porphyre: Sentences,* 2 vols. (Paris: Vrin, 2005), trans. John Dillon, 2: 795–835.

POSSIDIUS OF CALAMA

vita	*Life of Augustine.* A. A. R. Bastiaensen (ed.), *Vita di Cipriano, Vita di Ambrogio, Vita di Agostino* (Milan: Fondazione Lorenzo Valla, 1975), 339–451; FoC 15.

POTAMIUS OF LISBON

ad Ath.	*Letter to Athanasius.* Ed. A. Wilmart in *RevBen* 30 (1913), 280–3; PL 8. 1416.

QUINTILIAN

inst.   *The Orator's Education*. Loeb (2001 edition).

QUODVULTDEUS

Symb.   *Sermons on the Creed 1–3*. CCSL 60; ACW 60.

RUFINUS

Symb.   *Commentary on the Apostles' Creed*. CCSL 20; ACW 20.

RUFINUS OF AQUILEIA

Comm.   *Commentary on the Apostle's Creed*. CCSL 20; ACW 20.
Hist.   *Continuation of Eusebius's Church History*. *GCS* 9; Philip R. Amidon (trans.), *The Church History of Rufinus of Aquileia. Books 10 and 11* (Oxford: Oxford University Press, 1997).

RUFINUS 'THE SYRIAN'

fid.   Mary W. Miller, *Rufini presbyteri Liber de fide: a Critical Text and Translation with Introduction and Commentary* (Washington DC: Catholic University of America Press, 1964).

SENECA

ep.   *Letters*. Loeb.

TERTULLIAN

adv. Prax.   *Against Praxeas*. CCSL 2; Ernest Evans, *Tertullian's Treatise Against Praxeas* (London: SPCK, 1948).
Carn.   *On the Flesh of Christ*. SC 216 and 217.

THEODORE OF MOPSUESTIA

In Jo.   *Commentary on John*. Robert Devresse, *Essai sur Théodore de Mopsueste* (Vatican: Biblioteca Apostolica Vaticana, 1948), 288–420; Theodore of Mopsuestia, *Commentary on the Gospel of John*, trans. George Kalantzis, Early Christian Studies 7 (Strathfield: St Paul's Publications, 2004).

THEODORET

eccl. hist.   *Ecclesiastical History*. GCS 44; NPNF II.3.

THOMAS AQUINAS

in sent.   *Commentary on the Sentences of Peter Lombard.* Ed. P. Mandonnet and M. F. Moos, 4 vols. (Paris: Lethielleux, 1929–47).

Ioan.   *Commentary on John*; *Super Evangelium S. Ioannis Lectura*, ed. R. Cai (Turin: Marietti, 1951); trans. and ed. D. Keating et al. *Commentary on the Gospel of John*, 2 vols. (Washington DC: Catholic University of America Press, 2010).

ST   *Summa Theologiae.*

VICTRICIUS OF ROUEN

laud.   *In Praise of the Saints.* CCSL 64.

ZENO OF VERONA

tract.   *Tractates.* CCSL 22.

SECONDARY SOURCES

I reference here only works that I have cited in the text. For a fuller bibliographies, see Kany, *Augustins Trinitätsdenken*, and the on-line bibliography available at www.augustinus.de, the website linked with *AugLex*.

Alfaric, Prosper. *L'evolution intellectuelle de saint Augustin. i. Du manichéisme au néoplatonisme* (Paris: Émile Nourry, 1918).

Altaner, Berthold. *Kleine Patristische Schriften*, TU 83 (Berlin: Akademie-Verlag, 1967).

Anatolios, Khaled. 'Oppositional Pairs and Christological Synthesis: Rereading Augustine's *De Trinitate*', *Theological Studies* 68 (2007), 231–53.

Arnold, Johannes. 'Begriff und heilsökonomische Bedeutung der göttlichen Sendungen in Augustinus De Trinitate', *RecAug* 25 (1991), 3–69.

Athanassiadi, Polymnia and Frede, Michael (eds.). *Pagan Monotheism in Late Antiquity* (Oxford: Clarendon Press, 1999).

'The Chaldean Oracles: Theology and Theurgy', in Athanassiadi and Frede (eds.), *Pagan Monotheism*, 149–83.

Ayres, Lewis. 'Into the Cloud of Witnesses: Latin Trinitarian Theology Beyond its Modern "Revivals"', in Robert Wozniak (ed.), *Rethinking Trinitarian Theology* (New York: Continuum, forthcoming 2011).

'The Holy Spirit as the Undiminished Giver: Didymus the Blind's *De Spiritu Sancto* and the Development of Nicene Pneumatology', in Janet Rutherford and Vincent Twomey (eds.), *The Theology of the Holy Spirit in the Fathers of the Church* (Dublin: Four Courts Press, forthcoming).

'Into the Poem of the Universe: *Exempla*, Conversion and Church in Augustine's *Confessiones*', *ZAC* 13 (2009), 263–81.

'*Sempiterne Spiritus Donum*: Augustine's Pneumatology and the Metaphysics of Spirit', in George Demacopoulos and Aristotle Papanikolaou (eds.), *Orthodox Readings of Augustine* (Crestwood, NY: St Vladimir's Seminary Press, 2008), 127–52.

'Christology as Contemplative Practice: Understanding the Union of Natures in Augustine's *Ep.* 137', in Peter Martens (ed.), *In the Shadow of the Incarnation: Essays in Honor of Brian Daley* (Notre Dame, IN: Notre Dame University Press, 2008), 190–211.

'*Nicaea and its Legacy*: An Introduction' and 'A Response to the Critics of *Nicaea and its Legacy*', *HTR* 100 (2007), 141–4, 159–71.

'Augustine on the Rule of Faith: Rhetoric, Christology, and the Foundation of Christian Thinking', *AugStud* 36 (2005), 33–49.

Nicaea and its Legacy: An Approach to Fourth-Century Trinitarian Theology (Oxford: Clarendon Press, 2004).

'"Remember that you are Catholic" (serm. 52,2): Augustine on the Unity of the Triune God', *Journal of Early Christian Studies* 8 (2000), 39–82.

'The Grammar of Augustine's Trinitarian Theology', in Robert Dodaro and George Lawless (eds.), *Augustine and his Critics* (London and New York: Routledge, 1999), 56–71.

'The Christological Context of De Trinitate XIII: Towards Relocating Books VIII–XV', *AugStud* 29 (1998), 111–39.

Babcock, William. 'Christ of the Exchange: A Study in the Christology of Augustine's *Enarrationes in Psalmos*', unpublished PhD diss., Yale University, 1971.

Baltes, Matthias. *Marius Victorinus. Zur Philosophie in seinen theologischen Schriften* (Munich: K. G. Saur, 2002).

Barnes, Michel René. 'The Other Latin Nicenes of the Second Half of the Fourth Century', in Lewis Ayres and Mark Del Cogliano (ed.), *Unity and Diversity in Nicene Theology* (forthcoming).

'Latin Theology up to Augustine', in Peter Phan (ed.), *The Cambridge Companion to the Trinity* (Cambridge: Cambridge University Press, forthcoming).

'*De Trinitate* VI and VII: Augustine and the Limits of Nicene Orthodoxy', *AugStud* 38 (2007), 189–202.

'The Visible Christ and the Invisible Trinity: MT. 5:8 in Augustine's Trinitarian Theology of 400', *Modern Theology* 19 (2003), 329–55.

'Exegesis and Polemic in Augustine's *De Trinitate* I', *AugStud* 30 (1999), 43–59.

'Re-reading Augustine's Theology of the Trinity', in Stephen T. Davis, Daniel Kendall and Gerald O'Collins (eds.), *The Trinity: An Interdisciplinary Symposium on the Trinity* (Oxford: Clarendon Press, 1999), 145–76.

'"One Nature, One Power": Consensus Doctrine in Pro-Nicene Polemic', *SP* 29 (1997), 205–23.

'Augustine in Contemporary Trinitarian Theology', *TS* 56 (1995), 237–50.

'De Régnon Reconsidered', *AugStud* 26 (1995), 51–79.

'The Arians of Book V, and the Genre of *De Trinitate*', *JThS* 44 (1993), 185–95.

Barry, M. Inviolata. *St. Augustine the Orator: A Study of the Rhetorical Qualities of St. Augustine's Sermones ad populum* (Washington DC: Catholic University of America Press, 1924).

Bavel, Tarcisius J. van. *Recherches sur la Christologie de Saint Augustine. Le Humain et le Divin d'après saint Augustin* (Fribourg: Éditions Universitaires, 1954).

Beatrice, Pier Franco. 'Quosdam Platonicorum Libros: The Platonic Readings of Augustine in Milan', *Vigiliae Christianae* 43 (1989), 248–81.

Bechtle, Gerald. *The Anonymous Commentary on Plato's 'Parmenides'* (Bern: Paul Haupt, 1999).

Bell, David N. '"Essere, Vivere, Intelligere": The Noetic Triad and the Image of God', *RThAM* 52 (1985), 5–43.

'The Tripartite Soul and the Image of God in the Latin Tradition', *RThAM* 47 (1980), 16–52.

Berrouard, M.-F. 'La première communauté de Jérusalem comme image de l'unité de la Trinité. Une des exégèses augustiniennes d'Act 4, 32', in *Homo Spiritalis. Festgabe für Luc Verheijen* (Würzburg: Augustinus-Verlag, 1987), 207–24.

'La date des Tractatus I–LIV de saint Augustin', *REAug* 7 (1971), 105–68.

Blond, Jean-Marie Le. *Les Conversions de Saint Augustin* (Paris: Aubier, 1950).

Bochet, Isabelle, *'Le Firmament de L'Écriture': L'Herméneutique Augustinienne* (Paris: Études Augustiniennes, 2004).

Saint Augustine et le Désir de Dieu (Paris: Études Augustiniennes, 1982).

Bonner, Gerald. 'St. Augustine's Doctrine of the Holy Spirit', *Sobornost* 4/1 (1960), 51–66.

Booth, E. 'St. Augustine's "notitia sui" Related to Aristotle and the Early Neo-Platonists', *Aug(L)* 27 (1977), 70–132, 364–401; 28 (1978), 183–221; 29 (1979), 97–124.

Bourassa, F. 'L'Intelligence de la foi', *Gregorianum* 59 (1978), 375–432.

'Théologie trinitaire chez s. Augustin', *Gregorianum* 58 (1977), 675–725.

Bouton-Touboulic, Anne-Isabelle. *L'Ordre Caché: La notion d'ordre chez saint Augustin* (Paris: Études Augustiniennes, 2004).

Boys-Stones, G. R. *Post-Hellenistic Philosophy: A Study of its Development from the Stoics to Origen* (Oxford: Oxford University Press, 2001).

Brabant, Olivier. *Le Christ: centre et source de la vie morale chez s. Augustin* (Gembloux: J. Duculot, 1971).

Brachtendorf, Johannes. *Augustins 'Confessiones'* (Darmstadt: Wissenschaftliche Buchgesellschaft, 2005).

'The Decline of Dialectic in Augustine's Early Dialogues', *SP* 38 (2001), 25–30.

Die Struktur des menschlichen Geistes nach Augustinus: Selbsreflexion und Erkenntnis Gottes in 'De Trinitate' (Hamburg: Felix Meiner, 2000).

'A Natural Understanding of "Trinity" in St. Augustine?' *AugStud* 29 (1998) 199–209.

Brachtendorf, Johannes (ed.). *Gott und sein Bild. Augustins De Trinitate im Spiegel gegenwärtiger Forschung* (Paderborn: Schöningh, 2000).
Brown, Peter. *Augustine of Hippo*, 2nd edn (Berkeley, CA: University of California Press, 2000).
Burnell, Peter. *The Augustinian Person* (Washington DC: Catholic University of America Press, 2005).
Burton, Philip. 'The Vocabulary of the Liberal Arts in Augustine's *Confessions*', in Karla Pollman and Mark Vessey (eds.), *Augustine and the Disciplines: From Cassiciacum to* Confessions (Oxford: Oxford University Press, 2005), 151–5.
Catapano, Giovanni. 'The Development of Augustine's Metaphilosophy: Col 2:8 and the "Philosophers of this World"', *AugStud* 38 (2007), 233–54.
Cavadini, John. 'Simplifying Augustine', in John Van Engen (ed.), *Educating People of Faith: Exploring the History of Jewish and Christian Communities* (Grand Rapids, MI: Eerdmans, 2004), 63–84.
  'The Structure and Intention of Augustine's De trinitate', *AugStud* 23 (1992), 103–23.
Cavallera, F. 'Les Premières formules trinitaires de s. Augustin', *Bulletin de Littérature Ecclésiastique* 31 (1930), 97–123.
Chevalier, Irénée. *Saint Augustin et la pensée grecque. Les relations trinitaires* (Fribourg: Collectanea Friburgensia, 1940).
Chin, Catherine M. *Grammar and Christianity in the Late Roman World* (Philadelphia: University of Pennsylvania Press, 2008).
Ciprani, Nello. 'La presenza di Mario Victorino nella riflessione trinitaria di Agostino', *Aug(R)* 42 (2002), 261–313.
  'Agostino lettore dei commentari paolini di Mario Vittorino', *Aug(R)* 38 (1998), 413–28.
  'Le opere di Sant'Ambrogio negli scritti di Sant'Agostino anteriori all'episcopato', *La Scuola Cattolica* 125 (1997), 763–800.
  '*La retractatio* agostiniana sulla processione – generazione dello Spirito Santo (Trin. 5,12,13)', *Aug(R)* 37 (1997), 431–9.
  'L'influsso di Varrone sul pensiero antropologico e morale nei primi scritti di S. Agostino', in *L'etica cristiana nei secoli III e IV: eredità e confronti* (Rome: Augustinianum, 1996), 369–400.
  'Le fonti Cristiane della dottrina trinitaria nei primi Dialoghi di S. Agostino', *Aug(R)* 34 (1994), 253–312.
Coffey, David. 'The Roman "Clarification" of the Doctrine of the *Filioque*', *International Journal of Systematic Theology* 5 (2003), 3–21.
Conybeare, Catherine. 'The Duty of a Teacher: Liminality and the disciplina in Augustine's De ordine', in Mark Vessey and Karla Pollman (eds.), *Augustine and the Disciplines* (Oxford: Clarendon Press, 2005), 49–65.
Courcelle, Pierre. *Connais-Toi Toi-Même de Socrate à Saint Bernard*, 3 vols. (Paris: Études Augustiniennes, 1974–5).
  Les Confessions de Saint Augustin dans la tradition littéraire (Paris: Études Augustiniennes, 1963).
  Recherches sur les Confessions de Saint Augustin (Paris: E. De Boccard, 1950).

Coyle, Kevin. '*Concordia*: The Holy Spirit as the Bond of the Two Testaments', *Aug(R)* 22 (1982), 427–56.
  Augustine's De Moribus Ecclesiae Catholicae: A Study of the Work, its Composition and its Sources (Fribourg: The University Press, 1978).
Cross, Richard. 'Quid tres? On What Precisely Augustine Professes not to Understand in De Trinitate V and VII', *HTR* 100 (2007), 215–32.
  'Duns Scotus on Divine Substance and the Trinity', *Medieval Philosophy and Theology* 11 (2003), 181–201.
Crouse, Robert. '*Paucis mutatis verbis*: St. Augustine's Platonism', in George Lawless and Robert Dodaro (eds.), *Augustine and his Critics* (London: Routledge, 2000), 37–50.
Daley, Brian E. 'Revisiting the "*Filioque*": Roots and Branches of an Old Debate. Part One', *Pro Ecclesia* 10 (2001), 31–62.
  'Revisiting the "*Filioque*". Part Two: Contemporary Catholic Approaches', *Pro Ecclesia* 10 (2001), 195–212.
  'The Giant's Twin Substances: Ambrose and the Christology of Augustine's "Contra Sermonem Arrianorum"', in Joseph T. Lienhard *et al.* (eds.), *Augustine: Presbyter factus sum*, Collectanea Augustiniana 2 (New York: Peter Lang, 1993), 477–95.
Daniélou, Jean. *The Origins of Latin Christianity*, trans. David Smith and John Austin Baker (Philadelphia: Westminster Press, 1977).
de Halleux, André. 'Personnalisme ou Éssentialisme Trinitaire chez Les Pères Cappadociens', *Revue Théologique de Louvain* 17 (1986), 129–55, 265–92 [reprinted in *Patrologie et Oecuménisme. Recueil d'études*, Bibliotheca Ephemeridum Theologicarum Lovaniensum XCIII (Leuven: Leuven University Press, 1990), 215–68].
Dillon, John. 'Logos and Trinity: Patterns of Platonist Influence on Early Christianity', in G. Vesey (ed.), *The Philosophy in Christianity* (Cambridge: Cambridge University Press, 1989), 1–13.
Dodaro, Robert. '"Omnes haeretici negant Christum in carne venisse" (Aug., serm. 183.9.13): Augustine on the Incarnation as Criterion for Orthodoxy', *AugStud* 38 (2007), 163–74.
  'Political and Theological Virtues in Augustine, De Trinitate', *Medioevo. Rivista I storia della filosofia medievale* 31 (2006), 29–48.
  Christ and the Just Society in Augustine (Cambridge: Cambridge University Press, 2004).
  'Political and Theological Virtues in Augustine, Letter 155 to Macedonius', *Augustiniana* 54 (2004), 431–74.
Doignon, Jean. 'La Prière liminaire des *Soliloquia* dans la ligne philosophique des Dialogues de Cassiciacum', in J. den Boeft and J. van Oort (eds.), *Augustiniana Traiectana* (Paris: Études Augustiniennes, 1987), 85–105.
  'La "praxis" de l'admonitio dans les dialogues de Cassiciacum de Saint Augustin', *Vetera Christianorum* 23 (1986), 21–37.
  '"Spiritus Sanctus ... usus in munere" (Hilaire de Poitiers, *De Trinitate* 2,1)', *RThL* 12 (1981), 235–40.

Donini, Pierluigi. 'Testi e commenti, manuali e insegnamento: la forma sistematica e i metodi della filosofica in età potellenistica', *ANRW* II. 36.7 (1994), 5027–100.
Döpp, Siegmar and Geerlings, Wilhelm (eds.). *Dictionary of Early Christian Literature*, trans. Matthew O'Connell (New York: Crossroad, 2000).
Doucet, Dominique. 'L'Ars Memoriae dans les Confessions', *REAug* 33 (1987), 49–69.
Drobner, Hubertus. 'The Chronology of St. Augustine's *Sermones ad populos* II: Sermons 5–8', *AugStud* 34 (2003), 49–66.
Person-Exegese und Christologie Bei Augustinus (Leiden: Brill, 1986).
Dubarle, Dominique. *Dieu avec L'Être* (Paris: Beauchesne, 1986).
Duchrow, Ulrich. *Sprachverständnis und Biblisches Hören bei Augustin* (Tübingen: Mohr, 1965).
Dunham, Scott A. *The Trinity and Creation in Augustine: An Ecological Analysis* (New York: SUNY Press, 2008).
Du Roy, Olivier. *L'Intelligence de la Foi en la Trinité selon Saint Augustin. Genèse de sa Théologie Trinitaire jusqu'en 391* (Paris: Études Augustiniennes, 1966).
Edwards, Mark J. 'Porphyry and the Intelligible Triad', *Journal of Hellenic Studies* 110 (1990), 14–25.
Eichenseer, Caelestis. *Das Symbolum Apostolicum beim Heiligen Augustinus* (St Ottilien: Eon, 1960).
Emery, Gilles. *The Trinitarian Theology of St. Thomas Aquinas*, trans. Francesca Murphy (Oxford: Clarendon Press, 2007).
'Essentialism or Personalism in the Treatise on God in St. Thomas Aquinas?' in *Trinity in Aquinas* (Ypsilanti, MI: Sapientia Press, 2003), 165–208.
Field, Lester Jr. *On the Communion of Damasus and Meletius: Fourth-Century Synodal Formulae in the* Codex Veronensis LX (Toronto: Pontifical Institute of Medieval Studies, 2004).
Folliet, Georges. 'La Correspondance entre Augustin et Nébridius', *L'opera letteraria di Agostino tra Cassiciacum e Milano – Agostino nelle terre di Ambrogio (1–4 ottobre 1986)* (Palermo: Edizioni Augustinus, 1987), 191–215.
Garrigou-LaGrange, Reginald. *The Trinity and God the Creator: A Commentary on St. Thomas's Theological Summa Ia, q. 27–119*, trans. F. C. Eckhoff (St Louis: Herder, 1952).
Geerlings, Wilhelm. *Christus Exemplum. Studien zur Christologie und Christusverkündigung Augustins* (Tübingen: J. C. B. Mohr, 1978).
Gemeinhardt, Peter. 'Lateinischer Neunizänismus bei Augustin', *Zeitschrift für Kirchengeschichte* 110 (1999), 149–69.
Genovese, Armando. *S. Agostino e il Cantico dei Cantici* (Rome: Institutum Patristicum Augustinianum, 2002).
Gerber, Chad. *The Spirit of Augustine's Early Theology: Contextualizing His Pneumatology* (Aldershot: Ashgate, forthcoming).
Gersh, Stephen. 'Porphyry's Commentary on the "Harmonics" of Ptolemy and Neoplatonic Musical Theory', in Stephen Gersh and Charles Kannengiesser

(eds.), *Platonism in Late Antiquity* (Notre Dame, IN: University of Notre Dame Press, 1992), 141–55.
Gilson, Etienne. *The Christian Philosophy of Saint Augustine*, trans. L. E. M. Lynch (New York: Random House, 1960).
Gioia, Luigi. *The Theological Epistemology of Augustine's* De trinitate (Oxford: Oxford University Press, 2008).
Grillmeier, Alois. *Jesus der Christus im Glauben der Kirche. Band 1: von der Apostolichen Zeit bis zum Konzil von Chalcedon (451)*, 3. Aufl. (Freiburg/Basel/Wein: Herder, 1990).
Hadot, Ilsetraut. *Arts libéraux et philosophie dans la pensée antique* (Paris: Études Augustiniennes, 1984).
Hadot, Pierre. *'Porphyre et Victorinus': questions et hypothèses*, Res Orientales 9 (Bures-sur-Yvette: Groupe pour l'Étude de la Civilisation du Moyen Orient, 1996).
'Théologie, exégèse, révélation, écriture dans la philosophie grecque', in Michel Tardieu (ed.), *Les Règles de l'interprétation* (Paris: Cerf, 1987), 13–34.
Porphyre et Victorinus, 2 vols. (Paris: Études Augustiniennes, 1968).
'L'image de la Trinité dans l'âme chez Victorinus et chez saint Augustin', *SP* 6 (1962), 409–42.
'Être, vie, pensée chez Plotin, et avant Plotin', in *Les Sources de Plotin*, Entretiens sur l'Antiquité classique V (Geneva: Fondation Hardt, 1960), 107–57
'*De lectis non lecta componere* (Marius Victorinus, adversus Arrium II 7). Raisonnement théologique et raisonnement juridique', *SP* 1 (1957), 209–20.
Hagendahl, Harald. *Augustine and the Latin Classics* (Stockholm: Almqvist & Wiksell, 1967).
Hahn, August. *Bibliothek der Symbole und Glaubensregeln der Alten Kirche* (Breslau: Morgenstern, 1877).
Hankey, Wayne. 'Judaism, Islam, and Christianity in Medieval Europe, Difference and Unity: The "Religions of the Book" and their Assimilation of Hellenistic Philosophical Theology', in Susan Harris (ed.), *Multiculturalism and Religious Freedom* (Charlottetown: St Peter Publications, 2005), 81–127.
'Denys and Aquinas: Antimodern Cold and Postmodern Hot', in Lewis Ayres and Gareth Jones (eds.), *Christian Origins: Theology, Rhetoric and Community* (London: Routledge, 1998), 139–84.
Hanson, R. P. C. *The Search for the Christian Doctrine of God: The Arian Controversy 318–381 AD* (Edinburgh: T & T Clark, 1988).
Harrison, Carol. *Rethinking Augustine's Early Theology: An Argument for Continuity* (Oxford: Oxford University Press, 2006).
Heine, Ronald. 'The Christology of Callistus', *JThS* 49 (1998), 56–91.
Henry, Paul. 'The Adversus Arium of Marius Victorinus, the First Systematic Exposition of the Doctrine of the Trinity', *JThS* n.s. 1 (1950), 42–55.
Plotin et L'Occident. Firmicus Maternus, Marius Victorinus, Saint Augustin et Macrobe (Louvain: Spicilegium Sacrum Lovaniense, 1934).

Hill, William. *The Three-Personed God: The Trinity as a Mystery of Salvation* (Washington DC: Catholic University of America Press, 1982).
Hombert, Pierre-Marie. *Nouvelles recherches de chronologie augustinienne* (Paris: Études Augustiniennes, 2000).
  Gloria Gratiae. Se glorifier en Dieu, principe et fin de la théologie augustinienne de la grâce (Paris: Études Augustiniennes, 1996).
Humfress, Caroline. *Orthodoxy and the Courts in Late Antiquity* (Oxford: Clarendon Press, 2007).
Johnson, D. W. 'Verbum in the Early Augustine (386–397)', *RecAug* 8 (1972), 25–53.
Kany, Roland. *Augustins Trinitätsdenken. Bilanz, Kritik und Weiterführung der modernen Forschung zu 'De trinitate'* (Tübingen: Mohr Siebeck, 2007).
  '"Fides contemnentes initium": On Certain Positions Opposed in *De Trinitate*', *SP* 27 (1993), 322–8.
Kenney, John Peter. *The Mysticism of Saint Augustine: Rereading the Confessions* (London: Routledge, 2005).
Kloos, Kari. 'Seeing the Invisible God: Augustine's Reconfiguration of Theophany Narrative Exegesis', *Augustinian Studies* 36 (2005), 397–420.
Kursawe, Barbara. *Docere, Delectare, Movere. Die official oratoris bei Augustinus in Rhetorik und Gnadenlehre* (Paderborn: Schöningh, 2000).
La Bonnardière, A. M. 'Le verset paulinien Rom., v. 5 dans l'oeuvre de saint Augustin', *AugMag* 2. 657–65.
  'Le *De trinitate* de saint Augustin, confronté au livre XI de la Cité de Dieu', *AÉPHÉ* 85 (1976–7), 343–6.
  'Le *De trinitate* de saint Augustin éclairé par sa correspondance', *AÉPHÉ* 84 (1975–6), 317–22.
  'Recherche sur les antécédents, les sources et la rédaction du livre VI du *De trinitate* de Saint Augustin', *AÉPHÉ* 83 (1974–5), 202–11.
  'Recherche sur la structure et la rédaction des livres II à IV du *De trinitate* de Saint Augustin', *AÉPHÉ* 82 (1973–4), 171–6.
  'Recherche sur la structure du *De Trinitate* de saint Augustin', *AÉPHÉ* 80–1 (1971–2 and 1972–3), 293–7.
  Biblia Augustiniana. A. T. Le Livre de la Sagesse (Paris: Études Augustiniennes, 1970).
  Recherches de chronologie augustinienne (Paris: Études Augustiniennes, 1965).
Lafont, Ghislain. *Peut-on Connaître Dieu en Jésus-Christ?* (Paris: Cerf, 1969).
La Landais, M. 'Deux années de prédication de saint Augustin: introduction à la lecture de l'*In Iohannem*', in *Études Augustiniennes* (Paris: Aubier, 1953), 5–95.
Larchet, Jean-Claude. 'La Question du "Filioque"', *Le Messager Orthodoxe* 129 (1998), 3–58.
Lausberg, Heinrich. *Handbuch der literarischen Rhetorik*, 2 vols. (Munich: Max Hueber, 1960).
Law, Vivien. 'St. Augustine's "De Grammatica": Lost and Found?' *RecAug* 19 (1984), 155–83.

Lebreton, Jacques. 'Saint Augustin théologien de la Trinité. Son exégèse des théophanies', *AugMag* 2, 821–36.
Levering, Matthew. *Scripture and Metaphysics: Aquinas and the Renewal of Trinitarian Theology* (Oxford: Blackwell, 2004).
Lienhard, Joseph T. 'Augustine of Hippo, Basil of Caesarea, and Gregory Nazianzen', in George Demacopoulos and Aristotle Papanikolaou (eds.), *Orthodox Readings of Augustine* (Crestwood, NY: St Vladimir's Seminary Press, 2008), 81–99.
Contra Marcellum: Marcellus of Ancyra and Fourth-Century Theology (Washington DC: Catholic University of America Press, 1999).
'Augustine on Dialectic: Defender and Defensive', *SP* 33 (1997), 162–6.
Lof, L. Johan van der. 'L'exégèse exacte et objective des théophanies de l'Ancien Testament dans le "De Trinitate"', *Aug(L)* 14 (1964), 485–99.
Louth, Andrew. 'Love and the Trinity: Saint Augustine and the Greek Fathers', *AugStud* 33 (2002), 1–16.
Luhtala, Aneli. *Grammar and Philosophy in Late Antiquity: A Study of Priscian's Sources* (Amsterdam: John Benjamins, 2005)
Markschies, Christoph. 'Was ist lateinischer "Neunizanismus"?' *Zeitschift für Antikes Christentum* 1 (1997), 73–95.
Ambrosius von Mailand und die Trinitatstheologie (Tübingen: J. C. B. Mohr, 1995).
McCall, Marsh H. *Ancient Rhetorical Theories of Similie and Comparison* (Cambridge, MA: Harvard University Press, 1969).
Madec, Goulven. *La Patrie et la voie. Le Christ dans la vie et la pensée de saint Augustin* (Paris: Desclée, 1989).
Ambroise et La Philosophie (Paris: Études Augustiniennes, 1974).
'Une lecture de Confessions VII, IX,13–XXI,27. Notes critiques à propos d'une thèse de R.-J. O'Connell', *REAug* 16 (1970), 79–137.
Maier, Jean-Louis. *Les Missions divines selon saint Augustin* (Fribourg: Éditions Universitaires Fribourg Suisse, 1960).
Majercik, Ruth. 'The Existence–Life–Mind Triad in Gnosticism and Neoplatonism', *Classical Quarterly* 42 (1992), 475–88.
Manchester, David. 'The Noetic Triad in Plotinus, Marius Victorinus, and Augustine', in Richard T. Wallis (ed.), *Neoplatonism and Gnosticism* (Albany, NY: SUNY Press, 1992), 207–22.
Margerie, Bertrand de. 'La doctrine de Saint Augustin sur l'Esprit Saint comme communion et source de communion', *Aug(R)* 12 (1972) 107–19.
Marion, Jean Luc. '*Idipsum*: The Name of God According to Augustine', in George Demacopoulos and Aristotle Papanikolaou (eds.), *Orthodox Readings of Augustine* (Crestwood, NY: St Vladimir's Seminary Press, 2008), 167–89.
Marrou, Henri-Irénée. *Saint Augustin et la fin de la culture antique* (Paris: Éditions E. De Boccard, 1938).
Meijering, E. P. *Augustine: De Fide et Symbolo: Introduction, Translation, Commentary* (Amsterdam: J. C. Gieben, 1987).

Merriell, D. Juvenal. *To the Image of the Trinity: A Study in the Development of Aquinas' Teaching* (Toronto: Pontifical Institute of Medieval Studies, 1990).
Mohrmann, Christine. *Études sur le latin des chrétiens*, 3 vols. (Rome: Edizioni di Storia e Letteratura, 1961–3).
Moreschini, C. O. Tommasi. 'L'androginia di Cristo-Logos: Mario Vittorino tra platonismo e gnosi', *Cassiodorus* 4 (1998), 11–46.
Oberhelman, Steven M. *Rhetoric and Homiletics in Fourth-Century Christian Literature* (Atlanta, GA: Scholars Press, 1991).
O'Brien, William J. 'The Liturgical Form of Augustine's Conversion Narrative and its Theological Significance', *AugStud* 9 (1978), 45–58.
O'Connell, Robert. *The Origin of the Soul in St. Augustine's Later Works* (New York: Fordham University Press, 1987).
  St. Augustine's Early Theory of Man, A.D. 386–391 (Cambridge, MA: Harvard University Press, 1968).
  'Ennead VI, 4 and 5 in the Works of Saint Augustine', *REAug* 9 (1963), 1–39.
O'Daly, Gerald. *Augustine's Philosophy of Mind* (London: Duckworth, 1987).
O'Donnell, James J. *Augustine: Confessions*, 3 vols. (Oxford: Clarendon Press, 1992).
  'Augustine's Classical Readings', *RecAug* 15 (1980), 144–75.
O'Meara, Dominic J. *Pythagoras Revived: Mathematics and Philosophy in Late Antiquity* (Oxford: Clarendon Press, 1989).
O'Meara, John J. *Porphyry's Philosophy from Oracles in Augustine* (Paris: Études Augustiniennes, 1959).
Pacioni, Virgilio. *L'Unità Teoretica del* De Ordine *di S. Agostino* (Rome: Millenium Romae, 1996).
Pelikan, Jaroslav. 'Canonica regula: The Trinitarian Hermeneutics of Augustine', in Joseph C. Schnaubel and Frederick van Fleteren (eds.), *Augustine: Second Founder of the Faith. Collectanea Augustiniana I* (New York: Peter Lang, 1990), 329–43.
Pépin, Jean. 'Le tout et les parties dans la connaissance de la *mens* par elle-même (*De Trin.* X 3, 4 – 4, 6)', in Johannes Brachtendorf (ed.), *Gott und sein Bild*, 105–26.
  Saint Augustin et la dialectique (Villanova, PA: Villanova University Press, 1976).
  'Une nouvelle source de saint Augustin: le ζήτημα de Porphyre "Sur l'union de l'âme et du corps"', *Revue des Études anciennes* 66 (1964), 53–107 (reprinted in *'Ex Platonicorum Persona'*): *Études sur Les Lectures Philosophiques de Saint Augustin* (Amsterdam: Hakkert, 1977)).
  'Une curieuse declaration idéaliste de "De genesi ad litteram" [XII, 10, 21] de saint Augustin, et ses origins plotiniennes ["Ennéade" 5, 3, 1–9 et 5, 5, 1–2]', in *Revue d'Histoire et de Philosophie religieuses* 34 (1954), 373–400 (reprinted in *'Ex Platonicorum Persona'*.
Perez Paoli, Ubaldo Ramón. *Der plotinische Begriff von UPOSTASIS und die augustinische Bestimmung Gottes als Subiectum* (Würzburg: Augustinus-Verlag, 1990).

Pintaric, Drago. *Sprache und Trinität. Semantische Probleme in der Trinitätslehre des hl. Augustins* (Salzburg: Pustet, 1983).
Pizzani, Ubaldo 'L'enciclopedia agostiniana e i suoi problemi', in *Congresso Internazionale su S. Agostino nel XVI centenario della conversione, Roma, 15–20 settembre 1986* (Rome: Augustinianum, 1987), 331–61.
Pollman, Karla. *Doctrina Christiana: Untersuchungen zu den Anfägen der christlichen Hermeneutik unter besonderer Berücksichtigung von Augustinus De doctrina Christiana* (Fribourg: Universitätsverlag Freiburg Schweiz, 1996).
Prestige, G. L. *God in Patristic Thought* (London: Heinemann, 1936).
Primer, Adolf. 'The Function of the *genera dicendi* in *De doctrina christiana* 4', in Duane Arnold and Pamela Bright (eds.), *De doctrina Christiana: A Classic of Western Culture*, vol. 1 (Notre Dame, IN: University of Notre Dame Press, 1995), 68–86.
Radde-Gallwitz, Andrew. *Basil of Caesarea, Gregory of Nyssa, and the Transformation of Divine Simplicity* (Oxford: Oxford University Press, 2009).
Ratzinger, Joseph. 'The Holy Spirit as *Communio*: Concerning the Relationship of Pneumatology and Spirituality in Augustine', *Communio* 25 (1998), 324–37.
Reutter, Ursula. *Damasus Bischof von Rom (366–384): Leben und Werk* (Tübingen: Mohr Siebeck, 2009).
Rist, John. *Plotinus: The Road to Reality* (Cambridge: Cambridge University Press, 1967).
Rombs, Ronnie. *St. Augustine and the Fall of the Soul: Beyond O'Connell and his Critics* (Washington DC: Catholic University of America Press, 2006).
Schindler, Albrecht. *Wort und Analogie in Augustins Trinitätslehre* (Tübingen: J. C. B. Mohr, 1965).
Schmaus, Michael. *Die psychologische Trinitätslehre des hl. Augustinus* ([photomechanical reprint] Münster: Aschendorff, 1967).
Schwartz, Eduard. 'Über die Sammlung des Cod. Veronensis LX', *Zeitschrift für die neutestamentliche Wissenschaft und die Kunde des Urchristentums* 35 (1936), 1–23.
Sedley, David N. 'Plato's *Auctoritas* and the Rebirth of the Commentary Tradition', in Jonathan Barnes and Miriam Griffin (eds.), *Philosophia Togata II: Plato and Aristotle at Rome* (Oxford: Clarendon Press, 1997), 110–29.
Shanzer, Danuta. 'Augustine's Disciplines: *Silent diutius Musae Varronis?*' in Karla Pollman and Mark Vessey (eds.), *Augustine and the Disciplines: From Cassiciacum to Confessions* (Oxford: Oxford University Press, 2005), 69–112.
Simonetti, Manlio. 'Note su Faustino', *Sacris Eruditi* 14 (1963), 50–98.
Slusser, Michael. 'The Exegetical Roots of Trinitarian Theology', *TS* 49 (1988), 461–76.
Smallbrugge, Matthias. 'La notion de la participation chez Augustin. Quelques observations sur le rapport christianisme-platonisme', *Aug(L)* 40 (1990), 333–47.

'Sur l'emploi et l'origine du terme *essentia* chez Augustin', *Aug(L)* 39 (1989), 436–46.
La nature trinitaire de l'intelligence augustinienne de la foi (Amsterdam: Rodopi, 1988).
Solignac, Aimé. 'Doxographies et manuels dans la formation philosophique de saint Augustin', *RecAug* 1 (1958), 113–48.
'Réminiscences plotiniennes et porphyriennes dans le début du "De ordine" de saint Augustin', *Archives de Philosophie* 19 (1936), 148–56.
Sorabji, Richard. *The Philosophy of the Commentators 200–600 AD*, 3 vols. (London: Duckworth, 2005).
(ed.). *Aristotle Transformed* (London: Duckworth, 1990).
Strange, Stephen K. 'Porphyry and Plotinus' Metaphysics', in George Karamanolis and Anne Sheppard (eds.), *Studies in Porphyry*, Bulletin of the Institute of Classical Studies, Supplement 98 (London, 2007), 17–34.
'Plotnius, Porphyry, and the Neoplatonic Interpretation of the Categories', *ANRW* II.36.2 (1987), 955–74.
Studer, Basil. *Augustins De Trinitate. Eine Einführung* (Paderborn: Schöningh, 2005).
'Augustins De Trinitate in seinen theologischen Grundzügen', *Freiburger Zeitschrift für Philosophie und Theologie* 49 (2002), 49–72.
'Johannes 5, 19f. in der Trinitätslehre der Kirchenväter', in Jeremy Driscoll (ed.), *Imaginer la théologie catholique. Permanence et transformations de la foi en attendant Jésus-Christ. Mélanges offerts à Ghislain Lafont* (Rome: Centro Studi S. Anselmo, 2000), 515–41.
'Zur Pneumatologie des Augustinus von Hippo (De Trinitate 15.17.27–27.50)', in *Mysterium Caritatis: Studien zur Exegese und zur Trinitätslehre in der Alten Kirche*, Studia Anselmiana 127 (Rome: Pontifico Ateneo S. Anselmo, 1999), 311–27.
The Grace of Christ and the Grace of God in Augustine of Hippo: Christocentrism or Theocentrism? trans. Matthew J. O'Connell (Collegeville, MN: Liturgical Press, 1997).
'History and Faith in Augustine's De Trinitate', *AugStud* 28 (1997), 7–50.
'La teologia trinitaria in Agostino d'Ippona: continuità della tradizione occidentale?' in *Cristianesimo e specifità regionali nel mediterraneo Latino (sec. IV–VI)*, Studia Ephemerides Augustinianum 46 (Rome: Augustinianum, 1994), 161–77.
'"Sacramentum et exemplum" chez saint Augustin', *Recherches Augustiniennes* 10 (1975), 87–141.
Zur Theophanie-Exegese Augustins. Untersuchung zu einem Ambrosius-Zitat in der Schrift 'De videndo Deo' (ep. 147) (Rome: I. B. C. Liberia Herder, 1971).
Tardieu, M. *Recherches sur le formation de l'Apocalypse de Zostrien et les sources de Marius Victorinus*, Res Orientales 9 (Bures-sur-Yvettes: Groupe pour Étude de la Civilisation du Moyen-Orient, 1996).
TeSelle, Eugene. 'Porphyry and Augustine', *AugStud* 5 (1974), 113–47.

Augustine the Theologian (New York: Herder and Herder, 1970).

Teske, Roland J. 'The World Soul and Time in Augustine', in *To Know God and the Soul: Essays on the Thought of Saint Augustine* (Washington DC: Catholic University of America Press, 2008), 219–23.

'St. Augustine and the Vision of God', in F. van Fleteren *et al.* (eds.), *Augustine: Mystic and Mystagogue, Collectanea Augustiniana* 3 (New York: Peter Lang, 1994), 287–308.

'Augustine's Use of "Substantia" in Speaking about God', *The Modern Schoolman* 62 (1985), 147–63.

'Properties of God and the Predicaments in De Trinitate V', *The Modern Schoolman* 59 (1981), 1–19.

Testard, Maurice. *Saint Augustin et Cicéron*, 2 vols. (Paris: Études Augustiniennes, 1958).

Theiler, Willy. *Porphyrios und Augustin* (Halle: M. Niemeyer, 1933).

Trelenberg, Jörg. *Das Prinzip 'Einheit' beim frühen Augustinus* (Tübingen: Mohr Siebeck 2004).

Ulrich, Jörg. *Die Anfänge der Abendländischen Rezeption des Nizänums* (Berlin: De Gruyter, 1994).

Vannier, Marie-Anne. *'Creatio', 'Conversio', Formatio' chez S. Augustin* (Fribourg: Editions Universitaires Fribourg Suisse, 1991).

Verberke, G. ' Pensée et discernement chez s. Augustin: Quelques réflexions sur le sens du terme "cogitare"', *RecAug* 2 (1962), 59–80.

Verbraken, Pierre. 'Le Sermon CCXIV de Saint Augustin pour la Tradition du Symbole', *RevBen* 72 (1962), 7–21.

Verhees, J. 'Augustins Trinitätsverständnis in den Schriften aus Cassiciacum', *RecAug* 10 (1975), 45–75.

Verwilghen, Albert. 'Le Christ médiateur selon Ph 2,6–7 dans l'oeuvre de saint Augustin', *Aug(L)* 41 (1991) 469–82.

Christologie et Spiritualité selon Saint Augustin. L'hymne aux Philippiens (Paris: Beauchesne, 1985).

Watson, Gerard. 'St. Augustine and the Inner Word: The Philosophical Background', *ITQ* 54 (1988), 81–92.

Weinandy, Thomas. *The Father's Spirit of Sonship: Reconceiving the Trinity* (Edinburgh: T & T Clark, 1995).

Wetzel, James. *Augustine and the Limits of Virtue* (Cambridge: Cambridge University Press, 1992).

Whittaker, John. 'Platonic Philosophy in the Early Centuries of the Empire', *ANRW* II.36.1 (1987), 81–123.

Wilken, Robert. '*Spiritus sanctus secundum scripturas sanctas*: Exegetical Considerations of Augustine on the Holy Spirit', *AugStud* 31 (2000), 1–18.

Williams, Daniel H. 'Monarchianism and Plotinus of Sirmium as the Persistent Heretical Face of the Fourth Century', *HTR* 99 (2006), 187–206.

Ambrose of Milan and the End of the Arian–Nicene Conflicts (Oxford: Clarendon Press, 1995).

Williams, Rowan D. 'Augustine's Christology: Its Spirituality and Rhetoric', in Peter Martens (ed.), *In the Shadow of the Incarnation: Essays in Honor of Brian Daley* (Notre Dame: Notre Dame University Press, 2008), 176–89.
  '*Sapientia* and the Trinity: Reflections on the *De trinitate*', in B. Bruning *et al.* (eds.), *Collectanea Augustiniana: Mélanges T. J. Van Bavel* (Leuven: Leuven University Press, 1990) (= *Aug(L)* 40–1 (1990–1)), 1: 317–32).
Winkler, Klaus. 'La théorie augustinienne de le mémoire à son point de départ', in *Augustinus Magister: Congrès International Augustinien Paris, 21–24 septembre 1954*, vol. 1 (Paris: Études Augustiniennes, 1954), 511–19.
Wright, David. '*Tractatus* 20–22 of Augustine's In Iohannem', *JThS* n.s. 15 (1964), 317–30.
Zum Brunn, Emilie. *St. Augustine: Being and Nothingness* (New York: Paragon, 1988).

Scripture index

Genesis
1.2 46
1.20 46
2.22 109
18 156–9

Exodus
3.14 196, 201, 203, 204
3.15 204
33.11–23 160–3

Deuteronomy
6.13 119, 145

Psalms
5.4 147
15.11 147
17.3 139
18.15 139
27.8 163
29.6 139
62.8 139
67.10 167
93.9 242
101 206
101.27 204
103.24 193, 194
103.29–30 64
121.4 202, 205
138 203
138.7 181

Proverbs
8.27 101
8.30 234

Wisdom
1.1 83, 163
7.21 48
7.25 185

7.27 185, 203
8.1 191
11.21 61, 190, 193

Sirach
24.3 145
24.5 145

Isaiah
7.14 109
44.24 101
53.8 51

Jeremiah
23.24 181

Ezekiel
37 47
37.13 47

Daniel
7 159

Matthew
3.17 87
5.8 143, 163, 210
7.8 31, 35
10.28 168
12.18 89
12.28 89, 90
16.18 162
17.5 96

Mark
1.11 96

Luke
4.18 49, 89
19.12 157

John

1.1 79, 241
1.2–3 144
1.3 189, 193, 241
1.4 160
1.10 196
3.6 89
3.8 254
4.7 139
4.24 89
5.18 105, 241
5.19 105, 145, 178, 180, 233–50, 256, 258, 271
5.19–21 145
5.21 47
5.22 145
5.26 145, 239, 245, 264
5.29 178, 179
6.35 35, 36
6.38 35, 36, 235
6.45 35, 36
6.57 235
7.28 187
7.39 185
8.25–7 245
10.30 98, 105
10.30–4 205
12.28 96
12.44 154
14.6 31, 82, 101, 157
14.8 151
14.9 50
14.9–11 151
14.9–12 101
14.10 46, 48, 49, 50, 181, 221
14.11 50
14.16 98
14.26 186
14.28 152, 153
15.26 99, 180, 186, 251
16.13 35, 36
16.13–15 179
16.14 52, 180
16.15 211
16.18 35, 36
16.27 166
16.28 82, 153–4, 185
17.3 100–3, 147, 221, 223
17.4 82
17.5 180
17.19 182
17.21 157
20.11 152
20.17 168
20.22 185, 186

Acts

4.32 256–8
5 88, 89

Romans

1.3 89, 110
1.20 51, 89, 90
5.5 54, 57–8, 87, 254, 257
8.9 251
8.9–11 90, 251
8.11 47
8.15 88
8.25 147
8.32 86
8.39 52
11.33–6 145
11.34–6 87
11.36 48, 51, 54–6, 59, 70, 145, 191

1 Corinthians

1.24 31, 55, 82, 84, 221–7
2.12 49
2.15 140
3.2 129
3.11 205
3.17 163
6.17 253, 256, 257
6.19 119
8.6 48, 59, 144, 145, 149
13.12 147, 163, 165
14.14–15 148
15.24–8 143
15.28 80, 83, 147, 156–9
15.42–8 30
15.52 36
15.54 35

2 Corinthians

5.6 151
5.19 51
6.5–7 163

Galatians

1.6–7 154
4.4 110, 183
4.4–5 109
4.6 251, 254
4.9 35, 36
4.21–6 110

Ephesians

1.18 163
3.17–19 164–5
3.19 164

Ephesians (*cont.*)
4.22–5 168
4.23 308

Philippians
2.5–7 111
2.6–7 110, 146–7, 156–9, 166
2.7 153–4
3.3 119
3.13 145

1 Timothy
2.5 147
6.14–16 103, 144
6.16 55, 84, 102, 145, 160, 189

Hebrews
2.4 147

1 Peter
2.5 205

1 John
1.3 145
2.10 284
3.2 52, 147
4.4 35
4.7–8 284
4.8 253
4.16 252, 253
4.18 88
5.20 145, 189

Revelation
4.8 37–9

General index

Alcuin of York 270
Alfaric, Prosper 14
Altaner, Berthold 2, 58, 212
Ambrose of Milan 2, 106, 172, 270
  De Isaac vel anima 150
  inseparable operation in 47–50
  on Acts 4.32 257
  on John 5.19 239
  on missions and processions 188
  on *persona* 81
  on Phil. 2.6–7 and 1Cor. 15.28 157
  on theophanies 159
  with ref. to Augustine's works after 33, 101, 102, 145, 150, 180, 202, 211, 212, 312
  with ref. to Augustine's works to 18, 30, 31, 33, 34, 36, 38, 46, 51, 56, 63, 73, 75, 79, 80, 81, 87, 88
Ambrosiaster 56, 80, 81, 85, 202, 231
Ammonius of Alexandria 124
Amphilochius of Iconium 237
Anselm of Canterbury 226
Apuleius 2, 16
Aristotle 108, 295
  Categories 200, 212, 216
Arius 75
Arnold, Johannes 143
ascent in Neoplatonism 122–4
Athanasius of Alexandria 49, 75, 234
Athanassiadi, Polymnia 16
  ps. Athanasius, *dial. trin.* 237
Augustine
  analogy in 22, 66–7, 116
    analogical triads – *see* 'Augustine, triads in'
    different sites for in mature thought 280
    'discursive analogy' in *trin.* 9 288–9
    in *civ.* 11 279
    in *conf.* 13 133–8, 139
    in *trin.* 8 283–5
    soul as site for 137–8, 222, 243, 280
  angels in 189

anti-Homoian polemic in 55, 171–3
anti-Manichaeanism in 42, 52–71
anti-Monarchianism in 72–82, 97–100, 320
contemplation in 148–51, 166–7
creation in 54, 84, 189–97, 264
  intelligibility of 55–6, 277–9
Deus, use of 78–9, 100–3
  see also 'Augustine, Father, theology of'
dialectic in 112–15
exegesis – *see* 'exegesis, grammatical'
Eucharist 190
exemplum and *sacramentum* 168
faith in 144, 147–8, 150–2, 184–5
  corresponds to reality 163–5
  desire and 152–5
  mystery and 159–63
  understanding and 104
  see also 'Augustine, understanding'
Father, theology of 83, 178–87, 263–5, 319–20
  as eternally speaking the Word 182, 278
  as 'eternity' 58, 204
  as *principium* in 386/7 24
  as *summum modum* 31
grace 166–9
grammar in 113
imago Dei 279, 307
'inner word', doctrine of 276, 290–3, 311
  origins of 194–6
Jesus Christ 3, 22
  ascension of 153
  'Christological epistemology' 57, 146–7, 151–5, 161, 165
  exegesis of in two *formae* 146, 154
  participation in grace of 166–70
  see also 'Augustine, *Missio*'
Liberal Arts in 124–33
memory in 129–30, 306
  see also 'Augustine, triads; memory; understanding'
Missio, meaning of 181–3, 184–5

355

Augustine (*cont.*)
  Nicene language in 96, 199, 206, 221
  numerology 208–10
  'person' in – *see* 'Latin pro-Nicene theology, person in'
  Platonism in 13–20, 37–9, 40–1, 84, 121–8, 173
  presence of God to soul 130, 282–3, 307
    and interior word 291–2
  relation
    ontology of 215, 227, 244
    predication of 212–15
    'subsisting relations' 268–72
  rhetoric in 65, 106–17
    structure of *trin.* 8 281
  'rule of faith' in 27
  self-knowing
    interpretation of Delphic oracle 299, 303, 310
    in *trin.* 9 286–7, 289
    in *trin.* 10 298–302
    knowing oneself as not absent 300, 303, 306
    se nosse and *se cogitare* 300–2
    two types in *trin.* 9 and 10 276
  Son, theology of 84–6
    as forma 224
    as Image 70
    as *intellectus/Nous* 24–5, 26–8, 37, 224
    as life 193, 245
    as the one who sees the Father 242–4
    as Truth 30, 284, 291
    as Wisdom in 30, 52, 83, 182, 191, 194, 208, 221
    as Word 82–6, 182, 323
      Word and creation 189–97
      see also 'Augustine, inner word'
    generation of 85–6, 179, 180, 206, 216, 258
      as essence from essence 225–6
      as wisdom from wisdom 225
      not as 'emanation' 28
      Spirit's role in 265
    perfected by turning to *summum modum* 31
  Soul in 25, 286
  Spirit, theology of 28, 179–80, 183, 185, 251–9, 320, 322, 323
    as conforming us to God 52, 54
    as *deitas* 88–92
    as Gift 22, 62, 91, 251, 253–6
    as love 22, 57–8, 88–92, 224, 253, 254, 256–9
    as *ratio*, *logos* and Soul for Du Roy 20, 23–6, 33
    as Spirit 'of' 251
    as 'something common' 252

  as will of God 64, 191
  double procession of 186, 263–8
  in *fid.* 86–92
  lack of clarity about eternal *proprium* in early works 57
  'order pneumatology' in 61–5
  triads in
    aeternitas, species, usus 224
    being, knowing, willing 134–6
    being, life, mind 135, 293, 304
    eternity, truth, love 138
    natura, disciplina, usus 136, 278
    ingenium, virtus, tranquilitas 136
    ingenium, scientia, fructus 278
    lover, loved, love 283–5
    memory, understanding, will 233, 259, 271, 303–5, 307, 308–17, 322
    mens, notitia, amor 136, 286–90, 304
    physica, logica, ethica 278
  Trinity, theology of
    critiques of 1
    knowledge of pro-Nicene in AD 386 27–9, 37–9
    new readings of 2–4
    principles of Trinitarian ontology 230, 261
    supposed unitarian tendencies of 4
    (a) divine attributes and names:
    divine substance or essence 200–2
    divine visibility in 160
    idipsum, God as 196, 202–7
    immutability 203
    power, as Trinitarian term 27, 29
    simplicity 208, 216
    (b) nature of divine communion:
    appropriation 227–9, 255, 259
    as love 283–5
    as threefold cause 62, 278
    constituted by Father 180–1
    constituted by inter-personal acts 199, 242, 245, 258–62
    divine persons as fullness of divine life 139, 232–3, 245, 261
    'in' language 221
    inseparable operation of 67–71, 182, 242, 265, 278
    irreducibility of 259
    'person' and 'nature', rejection of 217–20
    personalism, analogical 261
    principium and *intellectus* in early works 24–5, 26–8, 37
    'redoublement' in discourse about 260
    trinitas rather than *triplex* 222
    unity resulting from *homoousion* 215
    see also 'Augustine, relation'

Trinity and Redemption in 5
understanding 116–17, 121, 126–8, 130–3

Works
Acad. 23, 25, 31
c. Adim. 54, 76, 148
an. et or. 25, 231, 311
bapt. 172
beata v. 23, 27, 28, 30–7, 203
civ. 2, 14, 101, 217, 231, 277–81, 317
conf. 9, 14, 15, 39, 107, 129, 132, 133–8, 139, 158, 164, 171, 202, 206, 210
conl. Max. 85, 86, 97, 100, 149, 160, 256, 257
  divine visibility in 160
cons. ev. 70, 85, 240
c. Faust. 29, 55, 310
c. Max. 160, 265
c. Sec. 31
c. s. Arrian. 4, 86, 100, 119, 240, 249
Cresc. 114
div. qu. 31, 34, 57, 62, 79, 80, 136, 157, 178, 194, 299, 309, 322
doctr. chr. 106–7, 113, 114, 192, 195
  Liberal Arts in 131–3
duab. an. 135
ench. 101, 155, 263
en. Ps. 35, 155
  16 155
  25(2) 155
  33 155
  68 200
  101 206
  101(2) 204
  121 196, 205
  134 202
  138 203
ep. 35, 129
  11 21, 59–71, 137
  14 69
  54–5 164
  120 100, 149
  140 164
  147 149
  148 149
  166 200
  169 217
  170 171, 217, 257
  171 171
  173 171
  174 100, 118
  238 171, 217
  242 262
  *23A 171
  *24 107
  *28 107
ep. Io., tr. 178, 253

ep. Rm. inch. 195
exp. Gal. 155
f. et symb. 5, 72–82, 156, 210, 230, 251, 264
Gn. adv. Man. 61, 64, 191
Gn. litt. 63, 148–9, 182, 191, 194, 195, 197, 299
Gn. litt. imp. 191
haer. 143
imm. an. 25, 127, 150, 203
Io. ev. tr. 31, 193–6
  1 129, 244
  2 202
  6 100
  9 251
  12 155
  14 256
  17 85
  18–23 240
  18,847b–f 256
  20 105
  23,849b–f 93
  36 231
  37 231
  39 217, 245, 256
  40 171
  45 231
  98 129
  99 264
  105 97
lib. arb. 21, 34, 79, 80, 83, 127, 135, 150, 154, 203, 208
mag. 113, 195
mor. 52–9, 203
mus. 21, 25, 127, 209
nat. b. 31
ord. 23–30, 64, 113, 125–7, 150, 208, 262
praed. sanct. 101
qu. Matt. 262
quant. 54, 127, 129, 130, 150
retr. 30, 72, 100, 118, 121, 171
serm. 35, 160, 204
  23 162
  46 85, 171
  52 66, 108–17, 310
  53 163
  71 181
  92 85
  126 240
  140 231
  212 97
  214 85, 97
  215 29
  229O 171
  238 256, 257
  241 256
s. dom. m. 131, 155
Simpl. 34, 166

Augustine (*cont.*)
Works (*cont.*)
  sol. 21, 23, 28, 29, 30, 35–7, 57, 113, 135
  symb. cat. (= *serm.* 398) 29, 240, 257
  trin. 2, 4, 138
    dating of 118–20
    1 95–103, 144–55, 189, 240, 251
    2 160, 161–2, 178–83
    3 189–92, 205
    4 166–8, 184–7, 251, 310
    5 211–18, 251, 264
    6 135, 221–4, 252, 256
    7 201, 218–20, 224–6
    8 281–5
    9,934b–f 100
    10,949b–f 135
    11 295
    13 100
    14 136, 233, 305–8, 309
    15 29, 85, 101, 196, 217, 222, 232, 254, 259, 263, 322
  vera rel. 21, 55, 57, 62, 68, 82, 104, 150, 203
Ps. Augustine
  dial. 194
  rhet. 81

Balthes, Matthias 294
Bardy, Gustave 62
Barnes, Jonathan 212
Barnes, Michel René 4, 29, 45, 60, 73, 143, 173, 212, 221, 239
Barry, M. Inviolata 111
Basil of Ancyra 234
Basil of Caesarea 49, 63, 235
  Ps. Basil, *Eunom.* 4 237
Beatrice, Pier Franco 15
Bechtle, Gerald 294
Berrouard, M.-F. 240, 256
Boethius 212, 226, 270
Bonner, Gerald 265
Booth, Edward 173, 311
Bouton-Touboulic, Anne-Isabelle 64
Boys-Stones, G. R. 15
Brachtendorf, Johannes 113, 212, 276, 285, 290, 295
Burton, Philip 114

Candidus the Arian 28
Cappadocians 142
Cash, J. C. xi
Catapano, Giovanni 167
Catholic/Orthodox dialogue 266
Cavadini, John 133
Cavallera, F. 27
Chaldean Oracles 15

Chevalier, Irénée 213, 220
Chin, Catherine M. 113
Cicero 2, 16, 25, 34, 65, 106, 110, 124, 125, 136, 308–12
Cipriani, Nello 26–35, 79, 126, 295
Conybeare, Catherine 127
Councils and Creeds
  Aquileia 48
  Ariminium 43
  Milan 97
  Nicaea *see* 'Augustine, Nicene language in' and 'Latin pro-Nicene theology'
Coffey, David 267
Courcelle, Pierre 122, 150, 300, 310
Coyle, Kevin 52, 57, 58
Cross, Richard 3, 218–20
Crouse, Robert 14, 19
Cyril of Alexandria 236
Cyril of Jerusalem 234

Daley, Brian 266
Damasus, of Rome 44, 73, 78, 85
  as key source in early years 79
De Régnon, Théodore 1
de Halleux, André 260, 324
Didymus the Blind 58, 81, 188, 202, 235, 237
Dillon, John 25
Dodaro, Robert 162, 168, 172
Doignon, Jean 34, 35–6, 224
Donini, Perluigi 15
Drobner, Hubertus 80
Dubarle, Dominique 202
Duchrow, Ulrich 194
Dunham, Scott A. 189
Du Roy, Theodore 1, 17, 22–41, 54, 58, 60, 65, 88, 135, 136, 138, 228, 276, 317, 320
  thesis regarding Augustine 20–2

Edwards, Mark 135, 294
Eichenseer, Caelestius 97
Emery, Gilles 260, 268, 270
Eunomius of Cyzicus 212, 234
Eusebius of Caesarea 234
Eusebius of Vercelli 56, 76, 79, 102, 156, 240
Evagrius of Pontus 238
Evans, Ernest 73, 77, 86, 89
exegesis, 'grammatical' 40

Faustinus 50, 80, 81, 85, 98, 156, 240
Field, Lester Jr. 73
Filastrius of Brescia 80, 85

Garrigou-Lagrange, Reginald 268
Gaudentius of Brescia 79
George of Laodicea 234

General index

Gerber, Chad 21, 24, 61, 65
Gilson, Etienne 207
Gioia, Luigi 179
Giomini, Remo 125
Gregory of Elvira 51, 56, 75, 80, 81, 85, 156, 202, 240
Gregory of Nazianzen 213, 235, 268
Gregory of Nyssa 51, 216, 235, 275
Gregory Thaumaturgus 58
Grillmeier, Alois 146
Gryson, Roger 43

Hadot, Ilestraut 18, 125
Hadot, Pierre 15, 108, 135, 213, 294
Hagendahl, Harald 16
Hankey, Wayne 19
Hanson, R. P. C. 43, 46
Harrison, Carol 14
Heine, Ronald 73
Henry, Paul 17, 294
Hilary of Poitiers
  with ref. to Augustine's works to 2, 33, 50, 51, 56, 58, 65, 74, 75, 76, 78, 80, 81, 85, 87, 89
  with ref. to Augustine's works after 33, 101, 150, 179, 180, 188, 195, 202
  Aquinas and 270, 271
  Holy Spirit in 90–1
  on John 5.19 238, 249
  on missions and processions 186
  on Phil. 2.6–7 and 1Cor. 15.28 156
  on theophanies 159
  see also 'Augustine, triads in'
Hill, William 268
Hombert, Pierre-Marie 79, 118–20, 160
Homoian texts (anonymous) 100, 160, 180, 238
Humfress, Caroline 107

Ps. Iamblichus 209
Irenaeus of Lyon 16
Isaac Judaeus 81, 99

Jackson, B. Darrell 125
Jerome, of Stridon 80, 81, 202
John Chrysostom 237, 271
Johnson, D. W. 84
Justin Martyr 13, 41

Kany, Roland 2, 118–20, 212
Kenney, John Peter 122
Kloos, Kari 143

La Bonnardière, A.-M. 57, 58, 61, 118–20, 193, 221, 240, 277

Lafont, Ghislain 260
La Landais, M. 193
Larchet, Jean-Claude 267
Latin pro-Nicene theology 43–51
  inseparable operation in 46–51
  natura in Latin Theology 81–2
  Nicene language in 78
  'person' in 77, 79–82
  proprium in 86–7
  spiritus, as synonym for divinity in 89
  substantia in 79–81
  theology of Father in 43, 44
  use of 'in' language 91
  see also 'Augustine, Trinity, theology of'
Lausberg, Heinrich 65, 108–11
Law, Vivien 125
Le Blond, Jean Marie 169
Lebreton, Jules 172
Levering, Matthew 260
Liberal Arts 124
  see also 'Augustine, Liberal Arts in'
Lienhard, Joseph 46, 114, 213
Lof, Johann van der 172
Louth, Andrew 261
Lucifer of Cagliari 98

McCall, Marsh 288
Madec, Goulven 17, 18, 23, 29
Maier, Jean-Louis 172, 187
Manchester, David 304
Manichaeism 17, 26, 30
Marion, Jean Luc 202
Marius Victorinus
  with ref. to Augustine's works to 15, 16, 17, 27–30, 32–3, 34, 36, 38, 48, 50, 56, 74, 76, 80, 81, 82, 85, 87
  with ref. to Augustine's works after 33, 102, 135, 150, 156, 202, 213, 231
  as possible source for *trin.* 9 294–6
  Spirit as *copula* in 91
  simplicity in 211
Markschies, Christof 44, 74
Marrou, Henri-Irénée 113, 114, 124, 297
Martianus Capella 65, 217
Maximinus, Homoian Bishop 4, 97, 100, 160–1
Meijering, E. P. 72
Methodius of Olympus 234
Mohrmann, Christine 112

Neo-Pythagoreanism 18
Nicetas of Remesiana 44
Nichomachus of Gerasa 209
Novatian 50, 74, 80, 81, 86, 98
  on theophanies 159

Oberhelman, Steven 112
O'Connell, Robert 14, 17, 20, 24, 65, 299
O'Daly, Gerard 25, 286
O'Donnell, James 16, 17, 42, 129, 139
O'Meara, John J. 14, 18
Optatus of Milevis 46–7
Origen of Alexandria 234
Ossius of Cordoba 82

Pacioni, Virglio 125
Pelikan, Jaoslav 147
Pépin, Jean 113, 114, 125, 298, 299
person *see* 'Latin pro-Nicene theology' *and* 'Augustine, Trinity'
Phoebadius of Agen 51, 56, 78, 80, 85, 98, 156, 238
Pizzani, Ubaldo 125
Plotinus 13, 15, 16, 27, 31–2, 39, 63, 64, 135, 194, 204, 209, 299, 320
  ascent in 122–4
  as source for Augustine on John 5.19 249
  dialectic in 123
  logos in 20, 23–6
  Nous 23–5
    as life 299
    as self-knowing 295, 298
  psuche, in 33
  The One in 31
  world-soul in 24, 25, 39
Pollman, Karla 131
Porphyry 13, 15, 17, 25, 125, 136, 294, 299, 300
  Augustine's knowledge of 17, 212
  Porphyry's 'tree' 218
  self-knowing in 298
Potamius of Lisbon 80, 82
Prestige, G. L. 77
Primmer, Adolf 106
pro-Nicene theology – *see* Latin pro-Nicene theology

Quintilian 34, 65, 81, 110, 111, 281, 310
Quodvultdeus of Carthage 46

Radde-Gallwitz, Andrew 261
Rist, John 24
Rombs, Ronnie 14
Rufinus of Aquileia 46, 150, 231

Sabellianism 30

Scepticism 17, 30
Schindler, Albrecht 137, 194, 286, 308, 310
Schmaus, Michael 276, 323
Sedley, David 15
Seneca 34, 136, 309
Serdica, council of 44–5, 76, 77
Shanzer, Danuta 125
Simonetti, Manlio 99
Sirmium, 'Blasphemy' of 43
Slusser, Michael 146
Smallbrugge, Matthias 200
Solignac, Aimé 18, 31, 129, 209
Sorabji, Richard 15
Strange, Stephen 13
Studer, Basil 4, 23, 105, 115, 122, 172, 183, 224, 233, 240, 263
Synesius of Cyrene 16

Tertullian 50, 66, 74, 76, 78, 81, 85, 86, 89, 97, 202, 211, 234
  on *persona* 79
  on theophanies 159
Teselle, Eugene 17
Teske, Roland 25, 200, 214
Testard, Maurice 16, 17
Theiler, Willy 136
Theodore of Mopsuestia 238
Thomas Aquinas 268, 271–2

Ulrich, Jörg 44

Vannier, Marie-Anne 64
Varro, Marcus Terentius 16, 125
Verberke, G. 301
Verbraken, Pierre 97
Verhees, J. 27
Verhwilghen, Albert 146
Victricius of Rouen 76

Wales, Josey 275
Watson, Gerard 301
Wilkinson, Kate 20
William of Auxerre 269
Williams, Daniel H. 43, 73, 172, 195
Williams, Rowan D. 254, 283
Wright, David 240

Zeno of Verona 80
Zum Brunn, Emilie 203

Lightning Source UK Ltd.
Milton Keynes UK
UKOW02n0810101214

242907UK00002B/58/P

9 780521 838863